MUSIC

for
Elementary
Classroom Teachers

Charles R. Hoffer

University of Florida

WAVELAND
PRESS, INC.

Long Grove, Illinois

For information about this book, contact:
Waveland Press, Inc.
4180 IL Route 83, Suite 101
Long Grove, IL 60047-9580
(847) 634-0081
info@waveland.com
www.waveland.com

To

C. Allan Hoffer and family
and
Martha (Hoffer) Teater and family

Contents

PART III
HELPING TO TEACH MUSIC   65

PART IV
ENRICHING ELEMENTARY SCHOOL
CLASSROOMS WITH MUSIC   167

Preface

What? Another book on elementary school music methods? Well, yes and no. Yes, *Music for Elementary Classroom Teachers* does deal with teaching and using music in elementary school classrooms. But, no, there are two major differences between it and other methods books.

First, *Music for Elementary Classroom Teachers* recognizes the fact that the vast majority of classroom teachers have taken only one or occasionally two courses in music during their undergraduate years. Although valuable and helpful, these courses amount to only about one-twentieth the amount of preparation in music required of music specialists. Furthermore, students who major in music have also had much more experience and a greater interest in music upon entering college than elementary education majors, or else they wouldn't be music majors. Therefore, it is simply not reasonable or logical to expect elementary education majors to have anywhere near the interest or level of skill that music majors possess.

Second, *Music for Elementary Classroom Teachers* recognizes that fact that classroom teachers can enrich the teaching of other subjects with music and make classroom routines more pleasant by using it. Music can be a valuable aid for classroom teachers. And they are the ones, not music specialists, who can utilize music whenever the time seems right for it. Therefore, several chapters are devoted to suggestions for using music in elementary school classrooms.

The Goals of This Book

Music for Elementary Classroom Teachers seeks to prepare future classroom teachers to be competent in two ways. One is to contribute to their students' learning of music. In most cases, this means complementing and supplementing the instruction in music provided by music specialists. Classroom teachers can assist and follow up to a limited degree what music specialists have taught. Music specialists are delighted to have classroom teachers make such efforts, and the students will learn more in the process. In some situations, however, classroom teachers are expected to provide all the music instruction for their students. Whether they are totally responsible for music instruction or not, future classroom teachers can benefit from an introduction to some of the ways in which elementary school students learn music.

This book also seeks to help classroom teachers to take advantage of the enrichment that music can provide in their teaching of other subjects. A classroom becomes a more lively and interesting place when music is incorporated in the instructional process. Not only are topics enriched through the use of music, the students' attitudes toward school can also become more positive. The musical contributions of classroom teachers create a win/win situation for teachers and students.

Music for Elementary Classroom Teachers limits the number of topics and the depth of coverage to what most future classroom teachers will be able to use. These topics include rudimentary aspects of music and taking advantage of the elementary music series textbooks. Instead of the approximately 150 songs and 450 large pages found in some elementary music methods textbooks, readers are provided with fewer songs and activities that serve as exemplars. Future classroom teachers are then encouraged to make use of the songs and other materials in the music series books.

Music for Elementary Classroom Teachers is divided into four parts. Part I discusses the reasons for including music in elementary school classrooms and the planning and arrangements for providing music instruction. Part II seeks to develop rudimentary musical skills on the part of future classroom teachers in making music and understanding music notation. The more competent a person is in music, the more likely he or she is going to use it in elementary school classrooms. Part III provides information about teaching the subject of music to elementary school students. Part IV contains suggestions for enriching the teaching of language arts and reading, social studies, science, mathematics, and the other arts with music, as well as helping special learners. In addition, it provides many ideas for using music to contribute to classroom routines and develop a more pleasant classroom atmosphere.

Acknowledgments

I would like to thank Jeni Ogilvie, Debbie Vasco, and Katy Murphy who handled the editorial and production work at Waveland Press. Special thanks to Tom Curtin who directed the acquisition and production of the book. My thanks go to Russell McCutcheon for creating the music notation that appears throughout the book. I wish to recognize the work of Marjorie Malzahn as a coauthor with me of an earlier book on elementary music methods.

Also, I wish to thank my wife, Mimi, for her valuable editorial suggestions and for her patience and support.

MUSIC IN ELEMENTARY SCHOOL CLASSROOMS

Everyone seems to understand the reasons for including reading, math, and social studies in elementary school classrooms. Even the old song "School Days" contains the words ". . . reading and writing and 'rithmetic . . ."—even if it does remind us of the "hickory stick." But why music? Why learn about it? What can it do for students and teachers? And how can its benefits and values best be incorporated into classrooms?

Chapter 1 explores the need to include music in the elementary school curriculum. It describes why every child deserves at least a basic education in music. It also explains that music can contribute to the students' learning in other areas of the curriculum and to the atmosphere of classrooms, and why including music in elementary schools is truly a beneficial situation for everyone!

Chapter 2 describes the respective roles of music specialists and classroom teachers. Each category of teacher brings strengths to the setting, but each also has inherent limitations on what can be accomplished in music. For this reason, by far the best arrangement is one in which the activities of classroom teachers and music specialists complement each other for the benefit of the students. This chapter offers suggestions for how music and classroom teachers can work together. It also discusses what classroom teachers can do when they have sole responsibility for music to provide some music instruction to their students.

Chapter 3 deals with planning for music instruction from two different viewpoints. One involves lessons that seek to have the students learn music. The other discusses planning the enrichment that music can provide in the learning of other subjects in elementary school.

The Importance of Music

Music is important in human life. All over the world people spend countless hours listening to and performing music, and they spend huge amounts of money for instruments, recordings, and equipment for playing music. People dance, sing, play instruments, and create new tunes throughout the globe. In fact, more Americans attend performances of music than attend professional baseball, basketball, and football combined.*

Music has also been present in every age in every part of the world. The walls of ancient Egyptian buildings picture people playing instruments and singing, and the Bible tells how David soothed King Saul with his music. When universities were founded in Europe in the thirteenth century, music was one of the four subjects included in their basic curriculum, called the *quadrivium*. The breath and depth of humans' interest in music are indeed impressive.

* *1997 Survey of Public Participation in the Arts: Summary Report.* Washington, DC: National Endowment for the Arts, 1998. Also *The Sport Attendance Database*, http://www.kenn.com/sports/index.html

The Value of Music

Why are music and the other fine arts so vital? There are several reasons, but a very significant one is that the arts represent a fundamental difference between existing and living. Life is more than physical survival, more than having enough food and keeping warm in cold weather. Humans are not content to just get by. They want to make their lives interesting, rewarding, and satisfying. They notice sights and sounds and have feelings about them. And they find life richer because of these feelings and experiences.

Consider this: You could use a large cardboard carton as a bedside table. It would cost little or nothing, and it could hold a clock, lamp, and other objects. But you really wouldn't be satisfied with a cardboard box. Why? Because you want something that's more attractive and interesting. The desire to reach beyond immediate needs is not a luxury; it is a basic part of human nature. It's something that makes us different from animals. Without this desire for quality in life, people are lacking in an important human quality. There are good reasons why music has existed—and still exists—in every civilization.

Music has several values in addition to its contributions to the quality of life. One is the psychological value in expressing human feelings. Words are limited when it comes to saying exactly how we feel. If you were asked to describe your feelings over the death of a loved one, the birth of a baby, or the union of a man and woman in marriage, you would find it a real struggle. You would probably end up thinking that you hadn't expressed how you *really* feel. Music has the power to reach deep into our emotions, which is one reason it is often involved in events like weddings and funerals.

Music can also contribute to learning, especially in the area of language development. Children in primary grades who have trouble pronouncing words accurately also often have trouble singing accurately. Improvement in speaking or singing usually results in improvement in the other skill. Whatever is involved in the processing of sound, it is usually affects both speech and music. In fact, teachers of foreign languages often have their students sing songs in the new language, because singing the words seems to improve students' pronunciation of them. And it is a well-known fact that stutterers almost never stutter when they sing.

Music can contribute to the learning of virtually all subjects, but not in the clear way that it can in language development. Thus the positive effects of incorporating music in other areas of the curriculum have, as of this time, not been substantiated very well by research. Beyond facilitating learning directly, music strongly contributes to students' attitudes toward school, which in turns leads to improved academic achievement. A classroom that has varied and interesting activities is simply more stimulating for students. In short, they are going to learn more under such conditions.

It is no coincidence that students active in music and the arts score significantly higher on SAT examinations when they graduate from high school.*

* Educational Testing Service, Princeton, NJ, 2002.

Whether stronger students are attracted to music and the arts or whether those courses make them academically more able is probably impossible to determine. But the result is clear: something beneficial is happening with students and music.

Why Include Music in Schools?

The most important role of schools is to teach subjects and skills that enable people to function successfully in society. When mathematics, music, science, and other subjects move beyond a rudimentary level, they exceed the teaching capabilities of most families, because parents lack the time and/or expertise. Few people are able to teach their children physics or economics, and very few have the time or ability to organize and direct a children's choir!

It is no accident that every nation seeking to be a part of the modern world has established a system of schools. They seek to have schools that:

1. prepare citizens to be competent and productive;
2. encourage a sense of national cohesiveness through a common language and set of societal values;
3. build on the accomplishments of the past so that each generation does not need "to reinvent the wheel"; and
4. help people lead richer, fuller lives.

Music certainly contributes to the second and fourth goals.

In the United States these goals are manifested in the America 2000 national curriculum effort that took place in the early 1990s. This effort was begun in 1989 and resulted in the publication of educational standards in seven major areas of the curriculum, one of which was music and the arts. The statements of standards were first developed by committees of professional leaders and teachers. Drafts were then submitted for comment from all interested educators and the public in general. After all the comments had been considered, a final version was developed and submitted to the U.S. Department of Education. The document, *National Standards for Arts Education: What Every Student Should Know and Be Able to Do,* was then approved by both houses of Congress and signed by President Clinton in March 1994.

The nine content standards are:

1. Singing, alone and with others, a varied repertoire of music
2. Performing on instruments, alone and with others, a varied repertoire of music
3. Improvising melodies, variations, and accompaniments
4. Composing and arranging music within specific guidelines
5. Reading and notating music
6. Listening to, analyzing, and describing music
7. Evaluating music and music performance

8. Understanding relationships between music, the other arts, and disciplines outside the arts

9. Understanding music in relation to history and culture*

Two points are worth remembering about America 2000 and its standards. One is that music and the fine arts were included along with science, mathematics, language, and other subjects. They were considered an integral part of the curriculum for elementary and secondary schools. Laid to rest are any doubts that music and the fine arts are not "basic" in schools!

The second significant point is that the various documents developed in America 2000, the first-ever comprehensive federal curriculum effort, represent a national consensus for each subject-matter area carrying the imprimatur of the federal government. It's much more than report of one committee or a professional association's views.

Music as a Subject

Music is a field of study, an academic discipline. It involves a body of information and skills with which every child should become acquainted, at least to some degree. There are concepts related to the structure of music, as well as specialized techniques and skills in performing and creating it. A huge amount of music has been created in Western civilization; as well, an enormous amount of music comes from other cultures and parts of the world. Music is a vast and varied subject.

Like other subjects, music is learned through effort and concentration. In the school situation, the emphasis needs to be on learning the subject, because time in school is such a valuable commodity. This does not mean that music should be only hard work; music should also be fun. Rather, it means that a child's musical development is heightened as understanding increases and skills are mastered.

Like other subjects, most children will learn music in the school, or they will end up knowing very little about it. Without music instruction in school, only a small minority of children whose families have a high degree of interest in music will receive much education in it, and even then it will probably be in only one particular type of music.

Popular music is heard virtually everywhere, so the students will be familiar with it without formal instruction. What's more, popular music represents only a tiny and very transitory portion of the world of music. Almost all popular music is literally "here today, gone tomorrow." Music that is more likely to be "here today, here tomorrow" merits most of the attention in the school curriculum. The main justification for the use of some popular music is the fact that it can help make the subject seem more relevant to the students.

---

* *National Standards for Arts Education: What Every Student Should Know and Be Able to Do.* (Reston, VA: Music Educators National Conference, 1994.)

Music as an Aid in Teaching

True, music is an academic discipline that all students should become acquainted with in school. But there's more to it than that! As previously mentioned, music can do much to help in teaching other subjects and promote a more interesting and lively classroom atmosphere. Classroom teachers can enrich their classrooms with music in at least two respects.

First, music can add a valuable dimension to the learning of other subjects. For example, when studying about the pioneers settling America's plains, the children can sing or listen to some of the songs associated with that era; or when studying phrases and rhyme schemes in stories and poems, they can examine them in songs; or they can go through the multiplication times tables by chanting or singing them; and there are many other examples of using music to enhance the learning process. Suggestions for using music in these ways are offered in chapter 14.

Music can also make the elementary school classroom a more lively and interesting place. In many states the past few years have seen considerable emphasis on student accomplishment in terms of reading and math as measured by standardized tests. In turn, teachers have often felt that they should devote even more hours to these two subjects, which were already receiving large amounts of time. Such a school day can easily become tedious for many students. An opportunity to be involved with music can be a welcome change of activity. These uses of music are discussed in chapter 15.

CODA

There are three good reasons why music should be an integral part of the elementary school curriculum.

1. It is important in people's lives.
2. It requires some instruction for most students to move beyond mere acquaintance.
3. It can contribute to learning in other areas of the curriculum and to more positive attitudes toward school and learning.

PROJECTS

1. Keep a log of the times and places in which you encounter music in a three-day period. Then put them into categories such as "With TV shows," "While doing other things like studying," and so on.
2. Make a list of public occasions (sporting events, ceremonies, etc.) where music has a role.

3. Describe the three situations in your life in which you like to have music.

4. Write a short paragraph about the importance of including music in elementary schools.

REVIEW QUESTIONS

1. In what ways does music contribute to the quality of people's lives?

2. Why are the national standards in music especially significant?

3. In what ways is music an academic discipline?

4. Why shouldn't popular music be the main ingredient in the elementary school music program?

5. What are three good reasons for including music in elementary schools?

2

The Teachers
of Music

- Music Teachers
- Classroom Teachers
- Need for Cooperation
- Music Specialist Initiatives
- Classroom Teacher Initiatives
- Complementary/ Complimentary Attitudes
- Attitudes of Classroom Teachers
- Classroom Teachers as Music Teachers

Who teaches and uses music in elementary schools? That's an easy question to answer: Music teachers *and* classroom teachers. But each is going to teach and use it in a somewhat different way. Let's begin by examining why this is so.

Music Teachers

Music teachers are certified in the subject area of music. Their undergraduate training has included special instruction in teaching music in the schools. In many universities, music majors spend about half of their undergraduate program in their major area of music, including courses in music theory, music history and literature, applied study on an instrument or in voice, music methods, conducting, and ensembles. Their subject-matter knowledge and performance skills are clearly superior to almost all elementary education majors, who normally take only one or two courses in music.

This amount of preparation in music indicates that certified music teachers are strong in making musical decisions, as well as in designing and carrying out a sequence of music instruction that flows from one grade level to the next. But they face several obstacles in educating children in music:

- Most school budgets allow for hiring only enough music teachers to teach each classroom for about thirty or forty minutes a week. Music specialists would really like to have more time with the students, but that is simply not possible in most school districts.

- Usually music specialists can meet with classes only on appointed days and times. They have little flexibility in their schedules.

- Music specialists often teach more than 175 students a day, which means that it takes them weeks just to learn their students' names, to say nothing of ever knowing them well.

- Because they teach a variety of classes at different grade levels, it's not easy for them to relate what they do in music to what a particular class is studying in other subjects.

Classroom Teachers

Teachers who majored in elementary education easily surpass music teachers in their opportunities to integrate music at appropriate times in conjunction with other subjects. They also have the advantage of knowing their students much better. But they have these disadvantages:

- Classroom teachers are almost always less competent in music, both in terms of knowledge and in skills, such as singing or playing instruments. They are seldom able to make the on-the-spot judgments needed in learning a piece of music.

- Classroom teachers are responsible for many different subject-matter areas and skills, particularly reading and mathematics, on which their students may be tested with the results being widely publicized. Their attention cannot be focused on only one area.

Need for Cooperation

The easy thing to do would be to have music teachers do what they do best and have classroom teachers do what they do best, and let matters go at that. But that solution would be unfortunate for everyone, especially the students!

Why?

1. Music teachers can provide only a limited education in music. Forty minutes a week allows for only a minimal introduction to the wonderful world of music. And that instruction would probably have little relationship to the other things the students learn in school. It would, therefore, not be as meaningful for them.

2. Classroom teachers would miss out on the enrichment that music can provide in learning language arts, science, social science, and mathematics, as well as art and physical education. Music can make a real contribution toward adding variety and active classroom learning.

3. Students would not receive as much of an education in music as they deserve, and they would find their classroom life somewhat more tedious and routine. As a result, they would be less stimulated and interested in school and probably not learn as much as they could.

Music Specialist Initiatives

Music teachers need to make efforts to meet with classroom teachers early in the school year. Granted, this may take time, because music specialists may be involved with fifteen or more classroom teachers. These face-to-face, individual conferences will probably need to be scattered over several weeks before school in the morning, during lunchtime, and after school. Subsequent contacts may rely more on written notes or e-mail messages.

When they meet individually with classroom teachers, music teachers should ask three questions.

1. What in general will you be covering in social studies (science, language arts, or math) in the next month or so?

2. Are there topics in some of these areas where music could be incorporated to enrich what the students learn? In other words, what can I do in music to help you with some of the things you are teaching?

3. Are there ways in which you can contribute to your students' learning music? Because I see them for such a limited time once a week, if you could follow up and complement what I teach in music class, that would make a huge difference in what I am able to accomplish. I'll be glad to write down a few simple suggestions of ways you can provide support.

The music teacher should then provide the classroom teacher with a general outline of what is planned in music for the coming weeks or months for the particular grade level. This outline should be brief and list only general areas.

Meetings and contacts between music and classroom teachers will be more successful if a limited number of actions are suggested. The first meeting may conclude with two ideas for the classroom teacher to try in furthering music and two for using music in conjunction with other subjects. The music teacher may end up with one or two suggestions for activities in music class that will contribute to the efforts of the classroom teacher in one or two subject areas. As the year progresses, additional suggestions may be exchanged between music and classroom teachers, sometimes in written form without actually meeting together. The result will be that each accumulates ideas. In the subsequent years that music teachers work with the same classroom teachers, planning will clearly be easier

and more productive than in the first year, because both will already have a repertoire of ideas that they have tried. In short, they will have something to build on.

The tone of the meetings between music and classroom teachers should be as
positive as possible. If a classroom teacher makes statements about what he or she
will *not* be able to do, the music teacher should counter with, "I understand that,
but do you think you would be able to . . . ?" For example, many classroom teachers are reluctant to sing for their classes. In those cases, the music teacher could
suggest that the class sing a song with the ancillary CD for the music book. Hopefully, the classroom teacher will join in the singing, even if softly. Or, a work that
was played on a recording during music class can be played again on a day when
the music teacher is not available. There is no teacher who cannot play a recording!

Classroom Teacher Initiatives

Being a classroom teacher is a very demanding job. That role calls for teaching a wide variety of subjects, as well as managing a classroom. Therefore, classroom teachers cannot be expected to spend a lot of time and effort on music. On
the other hand, every classroom teacher can do *something* to contribute to their
students' learning and use of music. The fact that teaching a classroom is demanding but rewarding work does not give them a "free pass" when it comes to music!

Classroom teachers should consider what they can *reasonably* do in response
to two questions:

1. How can I help in the learning of music by my students?

2. How can music help my students learn (language arts, social studies, etc.)?

The important word in both of these questions is "help." The first question
does not ask classroom teachers to assume the lead role, only to be supportive and
helpful. The second question asks that music be incorporated in a way and to an
extent that contributes to the learning of other subjects.

Complementary/Complimentary Attitudes

The attitudes that music and classroom teachers have toward music for their
students are probably as important as their skill and knowledge in the subject. If
they lack a desire for students to enjoy the benefits and pleasures of music, their
students' learning of music is going to be significantly reduced. Figuratively
speaking, instead of a whole meal, students will receive only an appetizer. The
attitudes of classroom teachers are that important!

A positive attitude should also prevail in the interpersonal relationships
between classroom and music teachers. They should compliment each other
whenever possible. When a classroom teacher does something that contributes to
the learning of music, the music teacher should respond with genuine enthusiasm
with compliments like, "That's wonderful! Your students and I really appreciate
that!" In turn, when a music teacher does something that contributes to learning

in social studies or language arts, the classroom teacher should respond in a similar manner. Remember: No one likes to have their efforts go unrecognized.

Attitudes of Classroom Teachers

The attitudes of classroom teachers toward music are important in another way. The teachers are with their students for twenty-five or more hours a week, whereas students are with the music teacher for less than one hour a week. Therefore, classroom teachers have much more influence on how the students think and feel about something, and students are very perceptive in picking up their teachers' attitudes. They notice how their teachers talk about music and the tone of voice they use. "Well, I guess it's time for music AGAIN," said in a negative way speaks volumes to them. It tells them that music is an unimportant and unpleasant requirement, something to be endured. If this happens, the music teacher will need to work extra hard to overcome the implicit message. In the end, the children in that class will probably not get as much from their music instruction as students from classes in which their teachers' attitudes are more positive.

A few simple actions on the part of classroom teachers can go a long way toward creating a positive attitude.

1. They can accompany their students to the music room and make sure they are orderly. If there is no music room, they should make sure their class is quiet and ready to learn for the music teacher.

2. They can take a minute or two when the class returns to ask what they did in music today.

3. If they really want to show support for the music teacher, they can stay with their students for a few minutes of music class. The fact that a classroom teacher remains for a portion of a music class, even if for only a short time, tells the students a lot about the importance of music. When and if this happens, music teachers should go out of their way to thank and compliment the classroom teacher.

Classroom Teachers as Music Teachers

In a real sense, all classroom teachers are music teachers, at least to some extent. They can contribute to their students' learning of music, and they can use music to enhance their learning of the other subjects. Solid data are hard to come by, but small minorities of classroom teachers (around 10 or 15 percent) work in situations where their students receive no instruction from a music specialist. In other words, they are responsible for all the in-school instruction in music. This is certainly not a desirable situation, but it is a fact of life in some school districts. And it places an even greater obligation on classroom teachers.

What do you do in this situation? The answer is both simple and difficult. The simple answer is to do what you reasonably can, given your competencies in music, materials, and equipment available, and time constraints. The difficult part is actually finding the time and energy to do it! No matter what the circumstances are, again, every classroom teacher can do *something* to provide their students with experiences and instruction in music.

One thing that you can do in such situations, for example, is to look for ready-made materials and programs that provide instruction in music. Several states have educational radio or television shows that contain music instruction. Ever increasing numbers of CDs, DVDs, and videotapes are becoming available that provide instruction in music skills or that are on musical topics. And the music series books described in the next chapter can provide a great deal of help, especially if you have some guidance in how to use them.

Almost all classroom teachers are competent to provide a rudimentary amount of music instruction—especially after completing this course. The techniques described in instructional vignettes contained in most of the subsequent chapters in this book are tools that classroom teachers can use to help children a bit with singing, clap or tap rhythm patterns, making up new words to a song, and so on. In short, there are many techniques from which classroom teachers can choose to make a positive musical difference.

CODA

The efforts of music teachers and classroom teachers need to complement each other. That is, what one does contributes to efforts of the other. It can be—and should be—a win/win situation.

PROJECTS

1. Keep a log of "Things I can do in music." Each time you learn something in your methods course that you can probably use when you become an elementary school teacher, enter it in your log. For example, if you learn how to start a song, enter it. When you gain some ideas of playing CDs and having the students listen carefully to the music, enter that.

2. Interview a music specialist in the area where your college is located or in your hometown. Ask him or her how classroom teachers can best contribute to their students learning music. Also ask the music specialist about the extent to which classroom teachers can help in bringing music into their classrooms.

3. Conduct a similar interview with a classroom teacher. Ask the teacher about his or her efforts to help music teachers and about the ways in which music is brought into his or her classroom.

REVIEW QUESTIONS

1. What disadvantages do music specialists face in teaching music to elementary school students?
2. What disadvantages do classroom teachers face in teaching music to elementary school students?
3. Why do classroom teachers and music specialists need to cooperate and complement each other's strengths in providing the students a better education in music?
4. What are the two important questions that classroom teachers should ask themselves about teaching and using music?
5. Why is the attitude of the classroom teacher toward music so important?
6. What are some actions that classroom teachers take to indicate to their students a positive attitude toward music?

Planning Music Instruction

Planning is essential for successful teaching in all subject-matter areas. This is especially true for teachers during their first several years on the job, because they don't have a repertoire of previous experiences from which to draw. The planning by music teachers or classroom teachers for a music lesson and the planning by a classroom teacher for enriching the study of other subjects with music are two similar activities. But they also differ in several important ways.

Lesson Planning

Although there are many variations in how lessons are planned, they all cover four essential points:

1. Objectives: Short statements telling what the teacher wants the students to learn

2. Materials needed: A list of all necessary materials and equipment needed, such as books, CDs, handouts, etc.

3. Procedures for teaching objectives: Step-by-step, specific statements describing what the teacher plans to do to guide students in accomplishing the objectives

4. Assessment of what was learned: Description of how the teacher will determine how well the students met the objectives of the lesson

Planning Music Classes

Good music instruction is based on a fundamental principle: *Every music class activity should be designed to increase students' understanding of music and/or improve their musical skills.* It is not enough just to put in time singing songs or listening to CDs; furthering children's education is basic to all planning for music classes.

Although no standard format or outline exists for teaching music, certain factors need to be considered when planning is undertaken.

1. Build on what has been learned in previous music classes. Begin by recalling what the students have done in music over the last week or two. Think about what they did well and what they didn't do so well, what they liked, what did not seem clear to them, and what they know that can serve as a basis for further learning.

2. Choose two or three specific concepts or skills to teach in the lesson. The choice of what to teach may be based partly on curricular documents such as the national standards described in chapter 1, state documents, or local school district guides. Points to be learned should be stated in specific terms. The objective "To learn about the music of Mexico" is too vague. An objective like "To make appropriate choices of instruments to go with a Mexican song" is much clearer, and the children's success in learning can be assessed more accurately.

3. State objectives in terms of what the children should be able to do as a result of the instruction. Unless the students can provide evidence of how much they have learned, it is hard for teachers to determine what should be taught in subsequent music lessons. Some objectives can apply to skill. For example, "The students will learn to sing 'Los Pollitos' with accurate pitch and rhythm." Other objectives can apply to cognitive learning. For example, "Ninety percent of the class will be able to describe two features of Mexican music."

4. Select appropriate materials. A teacher who decides to emphasize Mexican music can look through the books available and select a song that represents that feature.

5. Decide how to teach the content. Suppose that the appropriate instruments to be played with a Mexican song is what the class is to learn. There are several ways to teach this. They can learn a song like "Los Pollitos" and examine its melodic features. They can try different instruments and rhythm patterns to go with the song. For example, they might decide on

A CD can be played, enabling the class to hear the sound of a Mexican song. All of these procedures are appropriate under the right circumstances. Knowing beforehand which of the several possibilities will be employed leads to more confidence and more effective teaching.

At least two types of activities should be included in a thirty- or forty-minute class period. Children, especially in the primary grades, tend to become restless and their attention wanes; consequently they do not learn as much when they stay too long on one activity.

6. Assess the success of each portion of the lesson. If the objectives have been stated in terms of what the children are able to do as a result of learning, this step will be much easier. Assessing does not mean that a formal test must be administered at the end of each period, although a quiz is certainly an option every so often. Assessment can simply be the observation of a representative sample of individuals in the class on some of the points covered. If the first few students respond appropriately to the point that was covered, it is reasonable to assume that most of the others in the class have learned that point or can do that skill.

Assessment is very important for music specialists in evaluating the amount of music learning that has taken place. Unless the classroom teacher is also responsible for teaching music, assessment of what the students learned in music class is not as important for him or her. The complementary role for classroom teachers proposed in chapter 2 means that the obligation for assessment is reduced.

7. When the preceding six suggestions have been followed, begin the next planning cycle. The results achieved in the preceding class should influence a teacher's decisions regarding subsequent topics and activities, whether to reinforce a point covered earlier or to try a different approach, or to spend more or less time on some topic. Teaching and planning are a cycle. Each music class should relate to what preceded it and to what will follow it. Adjustments should be made in this process based on the assessment of what the students have learned.

Short excerpts of music classes that reflect the teaching principles just listed appear in parts 3 and 4 of this book. These segments are set in small-sized type and indented. They offer one example of teaching an aspect of music to children. The direct quotations are not a verbatim model for teachers to follow. Instead, they are practical illustrations of various teaching procedures.

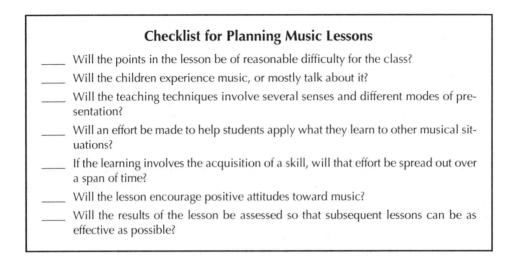

Planning for Music in the Classroom

The previous pages have described principles for classes in which learning music is the objective. But using music in the classroom to enrich the learning of other subjects is different. In this situation the objective is learning something in social science, language arts, or another subject. Music is involved as one way to make learning about the topic more effective, lasting, and interesting. Such enrichment does not just happen; it needs to be planned. To do so, classroom teachers need to consider these suggestions:

1. Examine the topics and activities related to the lesson in the nonmusic subject for places where music can contribute to the students' learning. Some topics lend themselves more easily and effectively than others for enrichment with music. Clearly, it is *not* expected that music be a part of every lesson in every subject—although that idea has some merit! The hope is that music will be used frequently and at times when it seems logical. For example, the poetry in the text of a song can be compared with a poem the students are studying.

2. Make sure the lesson and its music activity contribute to the objectives specified in state and school district curriculum documents. Many states and school districts have specified objectives under a variety of titles like "grade level expectations" that are specified for various subject-matter areas at certain grade levels. The music activity should contribute to meeting a subject-matter objective.

3. Have the necessary materials assembled prior to the lesson so that music can be integrated smoothly. The CD player and CD should be ready before they are to be used; a keyboard or mallet instrument and any books, pictures, or maps should be easily available. It's best if music is worked into a lesson without delays to find a track number on a CD or to locate a picture.

4. Use of music to enhance instruction should consume only a limited amount of time. The main purpose is to increase learning in the main subject. Attention, therefore, needs to focus on it, with music contributing to instruction.

5. Assess learning in the main subject and the effectiveness of music's contribution. The assessment of music's contribution should be in terms of how successful its contribution was, and how it might be made more effective in subsequent instruction.

Music Series Textbooks

Three publishers currently market very attractive series of graded music books for use in the elementary schools: McGraw-Hill/Macmillan, Silver Burdett/Scott Foresman, and Warner Bros. Publications; a series published by GIA Publications is currently available for grades 1, 2, and 3.* Each grade level of K–5 has one book for students and a parallel book for teachers. The teacher edition contains exactly the same material as the student book, but in addition it includes a wealth of teaching suggestions.

The books are replete with colored pictures and illustrations, and their content is planned with the help of experts in elementary music education and consultants in related areas like ethnic music. They are thoroughly indexed in a variety of classifications. Sets of CDs that include all the music presented in the books are available, plus other ancillaries such as transparencies, DVDs, and CDs.

The teacher editions contain a huge amount of material. When first examined, they can seem overwhelming in the amount music, activities, and teaching suggestions they offer. Apparently the idea is to provide teachers with a large smorgasbord of music and activities, so that they have a great number of choices.

The books contain a planned sequence of instruction in music, although in the case of McGraw-Hill/Macmillan and Silver Burdett/Scott Foresman, one must look for a small symbol that indicates that a certain lesson is part of the basic program of study. The Warner Bros. books are more specific in their instructional sequence.

Five pages of Lesson 10 from the Warner Bros. series, *Music Expressions*, Book 2, are reproduced on pages 22–26. The initial page for all the lessons in the series provides an outline of the contents and materials included in the lesson. The next page presents the instructional framework for the lesson, which includes the National Standards, thinking and life skills, curriculum connections, and assessment.

The teaching suggestions and questions are placed above and to the sides of the songs, which appear exactly as they are in the student book. The suggestions for this lesson include playing a mallet instrument and beginning to understand music notation in addition to singing and listening. The five pages from the Warner Bros. book contains practical suggestions for assessing the students' learning up to that point in the lesson.

---

* See Appendix A for more complete information on these book series.

LESSON SNAPSHOT

OBJECTIVES:
- The student will sing and identify patterns in music notation.
- The student will notate rhythm patterns.
- The student will compare visual art and music.

CONTENT	PURPOSE	ACTIVITY	STUDENT BOOK PAGE #	MEDIA CD*/DVD†	TRACK
"Skip to My Lou"	Identify patterns in music notation	Sing Read	60–61	CD 3	24, 25
"Haak Gyo Jong"	Identify repeated "sol-la-sol-mi" pattern (aurally and from notation)	Sing Read	64–65	CD 3	26 Language Instruction: 27
Listen and Write the Music	Take dictation	Listen Notate			
Recording Progress	Assess dictation	Teacher observes and records			
"Hunt the Cows"	Perform singing game Identify **AB** form	Sing Move Listen	66–67	CD 3	28
Artwork: *Nine Lives* by Jim Tweedy	Identify **AB** pattern	Observe	68		
"Hunt the Cows"	Respond to aural cues	Sing Listen Move			
Extension: Mallet Instruments	Add crossover bordun accompaniment to "Haak Gyo Jong"	Sing Play			

* Tracks shown in green indicate accompaniment tracks. Tracks shown in red indicate practice tracks. These differentiated learning tracks are recorded at a slower tempo to help at-risk and special-needs learners with singing, movement, and language. These are explained within the lessons.

† The DVD is also available in VHS format.

TEACHER REFLECTIONS

NATIONAL STANDARDS

- NS1 (Singing)
- NS6 (Listening)
- NS5 (Reading and Notating)
- NS7 (Evaluating)

CRITICAL THINKING

- Core Thinking Skills:
  Observing, Encoding, Recalling, Identifying Attributes and Components, Representing, Identifying Relationships and Patterns, Identifying Errors

- Bloom's Correlation:
  Knowledge, Comprehension, Application, Analysis

- Critical Thinking Process:
  Pattern Recognition

- Response Type:
  Verbal, Discussion

- Lesson Content Target:
  Patterns

- Thinking Direction:
  Metacognition

MUSIC FOR LIFE CATEGORIES

- Music to Remember
- Music for Fun and Imagination
- Music From Many Nations
- Music for Moving

CURRICULUM CONNECTIONS

- Language Arts
- Art

VOCABULARY

- Pattern (review)
- Verse (review)
- Refrain (review)
- Form (new)

ASSESSMENT

- Type:
  Formative, Structured Product

- Assessable Component:
  Theoretical—Notation

- Assessment Response Mode:
  Responding

- Tool:
  Observation, Scoring

- Scoring Guide:

- Criterion:
  The student correctly writes simple rhythm patterns presented by the teacher

3 = Both patterns are correctly notated with little or no errors

2 = Both patterns are correctly notated, but the errors indicate a developing understanding of notation

1 = One or both of the patterns are incorrectly notated, and the errors indicate a less than acceptable understanding of notation

0 = The notation is absent or indicative of no understanding of notation

LIFE SKILLS

- Stay on Task
- Follow Guidelines

MATERIALS

- Worksheet #2 (Assessment): Listen and Write the Music*
- PR2*

* Worksheets and the Second Grade Progress Record are found in the Teacher Support Pack.

LESSON 10

EXPRESSIONS

My music is best understood by children and animals.

—Igor Stravinsky

CONCEPTS *Patterns (visual art, movement, rhythmic, melodic)*

FOCUS THE LESSON

1 "Skip to My Lou"

STRANDS: Perform: *Sing*;
Read/Notate

Teacher Note: "Skip to My Lou" was introduced in lesson 9.

CD 3:24
CD 3:25

- **Student Book:** Invite the children to look at the music notation on pages 60–61 as they sing "Skip to My Lou."

- *What is a pattern?* (Something that repeats)

- *Look at both the music and the words. Do you see any patterns? Where?* (The opening three phrases of the song have the same words; phrase 1 and phrase 3 are the same)

DEVELOP THE LESSON

2 "Haak Gyo Jong"

STRANDS: Perform: *Sing*;
Respond/Reflect: *Listen*;
Read/Notate

- *This is a song from Korea about school bells ringing. As you hear the recording, listen for the school bells.* Play the recording (CD 3, Track 26).

CD 3:26

Language Instruction:

Teacher Note: Find Korea on a globe or world map.

CD 3:27

- **Student Book:** Look at "Haak Gyo Jong" in your book on pages 64–65 and point to any patterns in the melody.

- **Discuss the Pattern:** Measures 1–2 and 5–6 are the same ("sol-sol-la-la-sol-sol-mi").

- Teach "Haak Gyo Jong" using the pronunciation track (CD 3, Track 27). When they are ready, invite the children to sing along with the recording.

Corresponding Student Book pages 60–61

2

Haak Gyo Jong

KOREAN SCHOOL SONG
English Translation by GINA MOON

Lively!

Haak gyo jong ee heng heng heng uh suh woo ri da.

Sun - Saeng nim ee woo ri n'eul ki da ri sheen da.

English Translation:
The school bells are ringing, ring ring ring.
Let's get together.
The teacher is waiting for us.

"Haak Gyo Jong"
Continued

- **Mallet Instruments:** To add a crossover bordun accompaniment to "Haak Gyo Jong," see "Mallet Instruments" at the end of the lesson. This activity is not meant to represent the stylistic characteristics of Korean music. It is an opportunity for children to practice playing the mallet instruments in a different context.

3
Listen and Write the Music
STRAND: Read/Notate

- **Worksheet #2:** Distribute the "Listen and Write the Music" worksheets to the children.

- Clap a "ta ta ta ta" pattern (asking the children to echo the pattern) and write it on the board for the children to see.

- Clap a "ti-ti ti-ti ti-ti ti-ti" pattern (asking the children to echo the pattern) and again write it on the board for the children to see.

10

LESSON

3

Corresponding Student Book pages 64–65

CONCEPTS   Patterns (visual art, movement, rhythmic, melodic)

3 Listen and Write the Music
Continued

3 Listen and Write the Music
Continued

- Remind the children that when there is no sound in music, we call it a rest and it looks like this: Write it on the board.

- *I am going to clap a pattern. Listen very carefully to my pattern and write it on your paper.*

Teacher Note It may be necessary to repeat each pattern several times to guide the children as they write the music notation.

- Clap "ta ti-ti rest rest" and move around the room to observe the children as they write this pattern.

- *Now I am going to clap another pattern for you to write. Listen closely and write this pattern on your paper.*

- Clap "ta ti-ti ta rest" and move around the room again to observe the children as they write this pattern.

- Collect the worksheets.

Corresponding Worksheet #2

Second Grade Lesson 10
Worksheet #2

Name _____

Classroom Teacher _____

Listen and Write the Music

_____
_____
_____

_____
_____
_____
_____

Recording Progress
Notation

What:

Are the children able to write simple rhythm patterns correctly after they are aurally presented?

How:

1. Remind the children they are to do their best and most careful work on their worksheets because they will be turned in and scored.

2. Explain the scoring procedure to the children. (**Optional:** Write it on the board for the children to see.)

3. After the rhythmic dictation is completed, collect the worksheets and score them. Write the scores on the PR2.

MARKING THE PR2:
Score from 0–3

4 "Hunt the Cows"
STRANDS: Perform: *Sing, Move;* **Respond/Reflect:** *Listen*

- Invite the children to listen to "Hunt the Cows." *As you listen, decide what patterns you hear in this song*   **CD 3:28**

- *In an earlier lesson, we learned that "Skip to My Lou" is in a* **form** *called verse/refrain. Raise your hand to explain this form.*

- "Hunt the Cows" has two parts that are different and do not repeat. This type of form in music is called **AB**.

- **Student Book:** Find "Hunt the Cows" on page 66 in your books. Can you find the **A** section? Can you find the **B** section?

Teacher Note Verse/refrain was introduced through "Skip to My Lou" in Lesson 9.

- *Why do you think it is called* **AB** *form?* (The second part is different from the first)

- *Now that you understand the form of the song, it will be easier to learn it.* Teach "Hunt the Cows" by rote.

- **Play a Game:** Invite the children to form a circle and perform the traditional singing game.

- *In this singing game we are going to pretend to be the child who goes to find the cows but falls asleep in the field.*

Although the series books are not essential for teaching music, they are very helpful, especially for teachers during their initial years of teaching, for these reasons:

1. They offer a wide selection of songs and activities that have been compiled by experienced teacher/authors, so a teacher is spared the major effort of searching for songs and ideas for music instruction.

2. They provide a basic program of music learning, which is especially helpful when no music specialist or curriculum guide is available. Usually a book's content is organized around topics or units.

3. The teacher's edition for each grade level contains a detailed lesson plan for each song or activity that includes objectives, procedures, and some scripted statements and questions, and suggestions for assessment. Through the use of colored print or explanatory material in the margins, the teacher's editions provide concise information about that musical topic and how it can be taught.

4. Piano accompaniments are available for most songs in the book. The accompaniments are rather simple, so students or teachers with modest piano-playing skills can play them.

5. Teacher editions also include ideas for incorporating classroom instruments into song accompaniments.

6. Teacher editions include pronunciation guides for all foreign language songs, and translations are provided.

7. The CDs are of high quality. Most songs feature children singing; only some ethnic songs are sung by adults, who are native singers who can render the song in a valid manner. The singing of the children provides an excellent model for elementary school students. In addition, the words to foreign language songs are pronounced accurately by a native speaker. The arrangements on the CDs are tasteful, interesting, and quite authentic, with folk instruments utilized when appropriate. A helpful feature available on songs is the tracking of the accompaniment on one track and the voices on the other. The teacher can play one or the other by simply moving the balance knob on the CD player; if the knob is equidistant from its right and left positions, the voices and accompaniment are properly balanced.

8. Teacher editions offer supplementary suggestions for extending the learning activities in other arts and other subjects. These suggestions are especially valuable for use by classroom teachers.

9. For music teachers who are familiar with the methods of Carl Orff and Zoltan Kodály, recommendations are included for incorporating those teaching techniques in music classes.

10. Teacher editions include suggestions for assessing the learning of each lesson.

11. Both music and classroom teachers can make good use of the indices in the teacher's editions. They include thematic indices of topics, classified indices, and in some books, a pitch and rhythm index. Thematic correlations are sometimes included with the publishers' reading series.

CODA

The basal book series can be of much help in making plans for music instruction and use in classrooms. Teachers should think of these books as valuable sources of ideas and materials that will save them much time and effort while also fostering more learning by their students.

PROJECTS

1. Using one of the music series books mentioned in this chapter, make a plan for teaching one particular aspect of music. Cover each of suggestions 3 through 6 presented earlier in this chapter for the aspect you selected.

2. Examine one book from the three music series books cited in this chapter. After you have examined it, answer the following questions:

   a. According to the table of contents, in general how is the book organized?

   b. Does it suggest a minimum or basic curriculum that can be covered?

   c. Does it offer suggestions for relating what is learned in other subjects to music? Cite one specific example.

   d. Are suggestions provided for connecting what is learned in music to other areas of the curriculum?

   e. How is the learning of the music lesson assessed? Cite one specific example.

REVIEW QUESTIONS

1. What are the main points that all lesson plans need to cover regardless of the specifics of the format?

2. Why is it a good idea to state the objectives for a lesson in terms of what the students will be able to do as a result of instruction?

3. Why is assessment an essential component of music lessons?

4. Why is the use of the music book series a good idea?

DEVELOPING BASIC MUSICAL COMPETENCIES

W*hen you can do something competently, you are more likely to do it—and even enjoy doing it. A person who does not know how to dance, for example, avoids situations in which he or she is called upon to dance, and if ever caught in a situation that requires such a skill, that person would be extremely unhappy about it, to say the least.*

This simple fact of life has important implications for those who are preparing to be elementary classroom teachers: The chances of their doing something with music when they find themselves teaching elementary school children a year or two from now are greatly increased if they have at least a few basic musical skills and competencies. Each person has a personal perception of his or her competency level in music; no amount of cheerleading by books or professors can change that self-perception. Only successful experiences can do that.

Clearly, elementary education majors do not all start at the same point with regard to music. As is true with any subject, some of you have more musical experience and ability than others. Some have taken piano lessons, played or sung in an ensemble in high school, or have been active in church music; others have done none of these things. If you are one of those fortunate ones, you will probably be more confident and find this methods course easier than those who have not had such experiences. For those with quite limited experience, who probably constitute a majority of elementary education majors, these chapters will start a series of activities in which you can gain many of the skills that will help you feel more comfortable with music.

Chapter 4 reviews the notation of rhythm, and chapter 5 concentrates on a review of pitch. Chapter 6 focuses on learning to sing better and to use instruments that are commonly found in elementary classrooms, such as keyboards, mallet instruments, recorders, and Autoharps.

Fundamentals of Music: Rhythm

- Rhythm, Beat, and Tempo
- Note Values
- Rests
- Meters and Measures
- Sixteenth Notes, Ties, and Dotted Notes
- Compound Meters
- Borrowed Notes
- Syncopation

Almost all prospective classroom teachers have had some experience with music. Sometimes it might have been piano lessons, or singing in a choir, or playing an instrument, as well as music instruction in elementary and middle school. Sometimes a course on the rudiments of music is a prerequisite to the methods course. Whatever the amount, a brief review of the basics can be useful. This chapter and the next seek to provide such a review.

As is true of all the components of music, rhythm is impossible to describe adequately in words. One can define *rhythm* as "the organizing sense of motion that occurs as music progresses in time," but even this description is inadequate unless it's given meaning through the experiencing of rhythm. Rhythm is as basic as life itself, as fundamental as a heartbeat. To overlook this elemental nature of rhythm is to miss its essential character.

Rhythm, Beat, and Tempo

The words "rhythm" and "beat" are fundamental in music, but they are not synonymous. Rhythm is the more inclusive term and refers to the sense of movement that occurs as music progresses. The *beat* is the recurrent throb or pulse that makes a person want to tap or clap in time with the music.

The rate of speed at which the beats recur is called *tempo*. Many different tempos are possible, ranging from very slow to very fast. Whatever tempo is selected for a piece of music, it is expected to remain steady unless there's a musical reason for changing it.

Judgments about tempo depend partly on how the performer perceives the music. The most helpful fact in determining an appropriate tempo for a song is the mood or style of the music. In many songs, the most comfortable tempo approximates the rate of a normal heartbeat or a moderate walking pace.

Note Values

A note consists of an egg-shaped *head* that is usually connected to a vertical line called a *stem*. The note pictured below is called a *quarter note* and can be identified by its filled-in head and attached stem, which may point either up or down.

The duration of a sound in music is measured not by the clock but rather by the passing of consecutive beats. Although any type of note can be assigned to represent the beat, a quarter note is most commonly used. The chart below shows the relative durations of the most frequently encountered notes.

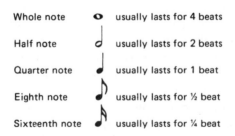

The duration of a note is called its *value*. When the basic note values are arranged in order from longest to shortest, and vice versa, a 2:1 ratio is evident between each note value and one next to it. Stated another way, each note value is twice, or half, as long as the adjacent note. This 2:1 ratio for note values is basic to the understanding of the notation of rhythm.

The relationship among the note values is shown by the following chart. The arrows represent the passing of time; they do not appear in actual music notation.

If two or more flagged notes occur consecutively, their flags are usually combined into a straight, solid *beam* connecting the ends of the stems.

Beamed notes are easier to read because they are visually grouped together to show more closely where the beats occur.

The round "Are You Sleeping?" illustrates the three most common notes values, eighth, quarter, and half notes.

ARE YOU SLEEPING?

Rests

A *rest* in music is a period of measured silence. Rests conform to the same 2:1 ratio found in note values.

Whole rest	▬	usually lasts for 4 beats
Half rest	▬	usually lasts for 2 beats
Quarter rest	𝄽	usually lasts for 1 beat
Eighth rest	𝄾	usually lasts for ½ beat
Sixteenth rest	𝄿	usually lasts for ¼ beat

To distinguish between the *whole rest* and the *half rest,* which look a lot alike, notice that the half rest sits on the third or "halfway" line of the staff, and the whole rest hangs down from the fourth (next-to-top) line. You can also think of the whole rest as being "heavier," because it lasts twice as long, and therefore it hangs down from the line because of its extra "weight." The whole rest can also indicate an entire measure of rest, regardless of the number of beats in the measure. In such cases it is called a *measure rest.*

A rest is not simply a void or a stopping place in the music. Rests are musically important, because they help set off phrases and indicate aspects of performance style. Although there may be no sound for a particular moment in the music, the listener should feel that the flow of the music is continuing.

Meters and Measures

Humans tend to perceive a succession of beats in patterns rather than as isolated, identical fragments. The ticks of a clock may be identical, but the mind tends to organize them into an orderly "tick tock" arrangement. In music, *meter* is the organizing of beats into patterns. Most of these patterns are two, three, or four beats long, although other patterns are occasionally encountered. The first beat of the pattern is performed and heard more strongly than the other beats. For example, a three-beat meter is felt as <u>beat</u> beat beat, <u>beat</u> beat beat, and so on.

A *measure* (or *bar*) is the visual representation of meter. Each measure provides the notation for one meter pattern. Adjacent measures are separated by a vertical *barline.*

The meter is usually indicated at the beginning by two numbers (or by symbols representing numbers) called a *meter signature* or *time signature.* The top number tells how many beats are in each measure, and the bottom number indicates what type of note or its equivalent lasts for one beat. A "4" on the bottom stands for a quarter note, a "2" for a half note, and so on. The exception to this rule will be mentioned later in this chapter.

Many different note values are possible within a meter. A 3/4 meter signature, for example, indicates that each measure contains three quarter notes *or their equivalent in other note and rest values.*

The first two notes of "If You're Happy" appear to form a shorter measure than is indicated by the meter signature. Such short phrases before the first barline are called "pick-up" notes (or more exactly an *anacrusis*). When pick-up notes are combined with the incomplete final measure of the song, they produce the correct number of beats for one complete measure.

IF YOU'RE HAPPY

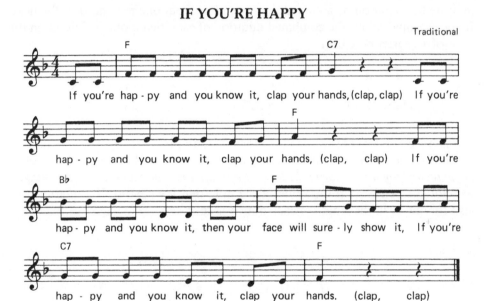

The presence of stressed and unstressed beats in a metrical pattern has implications for the way words are fitted with a melody. Each syllable of a song text needs to be placed with a sound that is similarly stressed in the music. When important words are combined with important notes, the text and the music support one another to form a more effective phrase.

Sixteenth Notes, Ties, and Dotted Notes

The following exercise may help in remembering the differences between quarter, eighth, and sixteenth notes. It may be performed several times in succession while clapping or tapping an even beat and saying rhythm syllables aloud. The pattern of four sixteenth notes can be spoken as "ti-ki-ti-ki" or "ti-ri-ti-ri"; in either case the "ti" (pronounced "tee") syllables occur with the eighth note background, which helps in learning sixteenth notes.

Sometimes the desired length of sound lies somewhere between the durations of the basic note values. To accommodate this, it's possible to combine two or more notes *of the same pitch* into one continuous sound. This is called a *tie,* and is indicated in notation by a curved line extending from one note head to the next. In the example below, the combined duration of each tied group is figured on the basis of a quarter-note beat.

A 1½-beat sound   A 3-beat sound   A 1¾-beat sound

The second note of the tie in the previous example is exactly half the duration of the first one. In the examples above, the second note can be replaced by a dot. *A dot to the right of a note extends its length by 50 percent.* The value of a dot changes, therefore, depending on the value of the note that it's next to. If a quarter note lasts for one beat, the length of each dotted note is:

$$\text{♩.} = \text{♩} + \text{♪} \qquad = 1 + \tfrac{1}{2} = 1\tfrac{1}{2} \text{ beats}$$

$$\text{♩.} = \text{♩} + \text{♩} \qquad = 2 + 1 = 3 \text{ beats}$$

$$\text{♪.} = \text{♪} + \text{♪} \qquad = \tfrac{1}{2} + \tfrac{1}{4} = \tfrac{3}{4} \text{ of a beat}$$

$$\text{○.} = \text{○} + \text{♩} \qquad = 4 + 2 = 6 \text{ beats}$$

Dotted notes are related to one another in same way that non-dotted notes are related; both reveal a 2:1 ratio. This relationship can be seen in the example below, and in the chart on page 37.

A tie should not be confused with a *slur,* which is also a curved line. In a slur, the curve forms a single arch spanning two or more notes of *different pitch.* A slur does not affect the value of the notes. It indicates that the notes are to be played smoothly; in vocal music it usually means that they are sung on the same syllable.

Compound Meters

In *simple meters* the beat subdivides into *two* background pulses. In *compound meters* the beat subdivides into *three* background pulses. Actually, compound and simple meters are about equal in terms of being difficult to perform, with the compound maybe slightly harder to read because it can have a few more combinations of rhythm values.

Although the "8" in the meter signature of many compound meters seems to indicate that the eighth note gets one beat, that is usually not the case. Remember, compound meters subdivide into threes. Half, quarter, and eighth notes divide in twos, so they won't work for compound meter. The only way to indicate the subdivision of the beat into three is a dotted note, usually a dotted quarter note. If the top number in a meter signature can be divided by 3, it is usually a compound meter. The number of beats is the top number divided by 3. For example, 9/8 meter normally is performed three beats to the measure, with the dotted quarter note or its equivalent getting the beat.

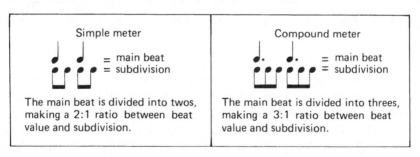

The difference between simple and compound meters can be seen in this chart:

Simple meter	Compound meter
♩ ♩ = main beat ♫ ♫ = subdivision	♩. ♩. = main beat ♫ ♫ = subdivision
The main beat is divided into twos, making a 2:1 ratio between beat value and subdivision.	The main beat is divided into threes, making a 3:1 ratio between beat value and subdivision.

In the chart the beat should be the same; it's the speed of the eighth notes that will be different.

"The Wassail Song" contains both types of meters. The meter signature for the first half is 6/8. The melody seems to skip along in a quarter-note/eighth-note pattern. The quarter equals two eighth notes and the eighth note one. Because a meter signature of 1½ above 2 isn't found in music, a 6 above an 8 is used, with the understanding the beat will be a dotted quarter or its equivalent. (Some elementary school songbooks actually indicate this with a dotted quarter note below a 2.) In any case, the bottom number indicates the value of the subdivisions, whereas the top number tells how many of those subdivisions occur in a measure.

WASSAIL SONG

The second half of the song is in simple meter—with one difference. Instead of the quarter note (or its equivalent) getting the beat, the 2/2 meter indicates that the half note receives the beat. All the proportions stay the same; it's just that a different note represents the beat. The words "love and joy" are still two notes to the beat leading to one note, whether represented by two quarters and a half note or by two eighths and a quarter note. There is no difference in how the music sounds, just in how it appears in notation.

There are several ways to count notes in compound meter. The syllables "*One*-la-lee, *two*-la-lee" are one way. Other syllables can be used such as, "*One*-tee-toe" and "*Trip*-o-let" and "One-and-a" and a fast "*One*-two-three."

Sometimes the tempo of the music in 6/8 meter is quite slow, and the eighth note actually does get the beat. This sounds (and is) confusing in some ways. In such cases the eighth receives the beat, which is divided into two sixteenth notes, as happens in simple meter.

It's probably easier—and certainly more enjoyable—to sing "The Wassail Song" with its two types of meter than it is to read about music notation and its different meters. As you sing the song, notice the different feel of the two types of meter. The song is a happy one, because the singers are rewarded for their efforts with a warm alcoholic drink from the wassail bowl.

Borrowed Notes

Once in a while music deviates from simple meter to compound for one or more beats, and sometimes a beat from simple meter can appear in songs in compound meter. These beats are called "borrowed" notes. They always appear with the appropriate number above or below that beat. Probably the most commonly borrowed pattern occurs when a three-note figure appears in a beat of a song in simple meter. The pattern is called a *triplet.* It is indicated by the number 3 above or below the triplet. "Ev'rybody Loves Saturday Night" contains two triplet beats.

EV'RYBODY LOVES SATURDAY NIGHT

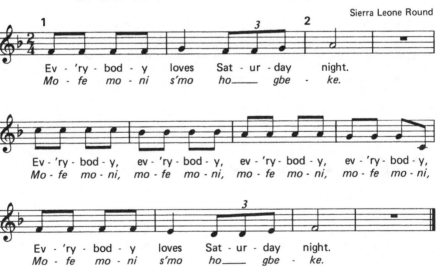

Syncopation

Syncopation is the removal of an expected accent *or* the addition of an accent where it is not expected. It is found in one form or another in many songs. For example, in the song "All God's Chillen Got Shoes" the rhythm could go like this:

1	2	3	4	1	2	3	4
"I	got	a	shoe,—		you	got	a shoe —"

Instead, the melody is made more interesting by syncopation when the "got" enters half way through the first beat and is held until halfway through the second beat.

1	2	3	4	1	2	3	4
"I	got	a shoe,——		you got		a shoe———"	

The students can easily sense the syncopation in the song, especially if they clap the beat as they sing the melody.

$\mathbf{C}$ODA

Learning the terms for the different aspects of rhythm help in understanding it, which in turn will help you in teaching it. The same is true of how rhythm is represented in music notation. Being able to follow and read notation makes you feel more confident about music.

PROJECTS

1. Practice tapping or clapping the following rhythmic patterns:

2. Sing or listen to the song "Yankee Doodle." As you do, tap the beat of the song, and notice whether it seems to be in twos (<u>beat</u> beat <u>beat</u> beat) or in threes (<u>beat</u> beat beat <u>beat</u> beat beat).

3. Sing or listen to the song "My Country 'Tis of Thee." As you do, tap the beat of the song, and notice whether it seems to be in twos (<u>beat</u> beat <u>beat</u> beat) or in threes (<u>beat</u> beat beat <u>beat</u> beat beat).

4. Practice singing "The Wassail Song" substituting rhythm syllables for the words.

REVIEW QUESTIONS

1. What is the difference between *beat* and *meter?*
2. Describe what is meant by the 2:1 ratio in terms of music notation.
3. Which beat in a four-beat measure is usually the strongest?
4. Add the *one* note or rest needed to complete the following measures:

d.

e.

5. What determines what kind of note usually gets the beat?

6. A meter signature of 6/8 usually indicates that there are _____ beats or their equivalent and the _____ equals one beat.

7. How does a dot to the right of a note head affect how long that note lasts?

8. What is the main difference between simple meters and compound meters?

9. What is a "borrowed note"?

10. What is syncopation?

5

Fundamentals of Music: Pitch

- The Keyboard
- Scales
- Key Signatures
- Intervals
- Harmony

Pitch in music refers to how high or low a note sounds. Written notes, which indicate pitch and rhythm in music, are placed on a *staff* consisting of five horizontal lines and four spaces. The staff provides fixed reference points to show the pitch exactly.

The *clef* is a symbol placed on the staff to indicate the pitches assigned to each line and space. The range of musical pitches is wide, but the range of a staff is relatively narrow, so musicians have devised a system of clefs to show what portion of the total pitch range each staff represents. Unless there is a clef, the notes on a staff have no specific pitches, only relative positions.

The *treble clef* is the curving symbol seen at the beginning of each of the songs presented in this book. The inside curl of the treble clef curves around the second line, which is the note G above middle C. The other note names on the treble clef staff can be calculated from G. Every line and space is named for one of the first seven letters of the alphabet. The first note above G is A. The seven letters proceed in normal alphabetical order as the notes get higher, and in reverse order as they get lower.

The Keyboard

Because pitch itself is intangible, a visible representation of pitches is useful. A piano keyboard and the bars on mallet instruments such as the xylophone can also provide this.

The black keys of the piano and the bars on mallet instruments are arranged in groups of twos and threes. All white keys (or the upper bars on mallet instruments) can be identified in relation to these groups of black keys. For example, every C on the piano is a white key to the left of a two-black key group; every F is a white key to the left of a three-black-key group. The white keys are named from left to right using the letters A to G. This pattern is repeated every *octave*, or every eight notes.

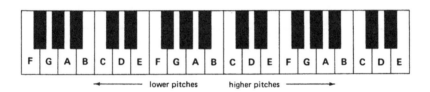

Some notes require a modifying symbol in addition to the letter name. The following three symbols are placed on the staff to the left of the notes they change. (But when spoken or written with a letter, the order is reversed so that they symbol is last. For example, C♯ is spoken "C sharp.")

Sharp   ♯   Raises the pitch one *half step,* which is the smallest pitch difference possible on keyboards.

Flat   ♭   Lowers the pitch one half step.

Natural   ♮   Cancels a sharp or flat previously applied to that note.

The sharp of any white key on the piano is the black key touching it on the *right.* The flat of any white key is the black key touching it on the *left.* If there is no black key on the given side, the nearest white key in that direction is the sharp or flat.

Every black key (or upper bar) has two names, one including the term "sharp," and the other including the term "flat." For example, the key called D sharp (because it is to the right of D) is also designated E flat (because it is to the left of E). White keys also can have two different names when there is no black key between them. For example, the white key to the left of C can be either B or Cb; C can be either C or B♯. Sharps, flats, and natural are called *accidentals.*

Middle C is the C nearest the middle of the piano keyboard. Actually, it is too low to be placed on the treble staff. Notes that are either too high or too low for the staff are indicated by *ledger lines,* which are short horizontal lines that extend the range of the staff. They are the same distance apart as the staff lines.

Scales

A *scale* is a series of pitches covering one octave that moves up or down according to a specified pattern of intervals. Eight-tone scales (or one-octave scales) are the most common, and they can be built on any note, which then becomes the *tonal center, tonic,* or *keynote.* Consecutive numbers are often assigned to the notes or steps of a scale to show the relationships that occur among them. Here is a scale built on C:

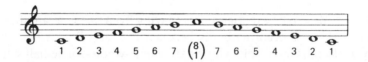

When eight-tone scales are written on the staff, there must be a note on every line and space between the low and high keynotes, so that all seven letters are represented in the scale. No letter can be left out or duplicated; there can't be a G and a G♯ in the same scale. The eight-tone scale uses only the seven letters of the musical alphabet, because the eighth step has the same name as the first.

A *major scale* has this pattern of whole and half steps:

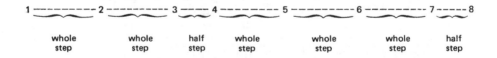

Although the scale has eight notes, it has only seven intervals, because intervals exist *between* pitches. In music the distance from one pitch to another is termed an *interval.*

A scale can also be pictured as steps on a ladder or stairs. The steps of a major scale are not of equal height, however, because the distance between 3–4 and 7–8 is only a half step.

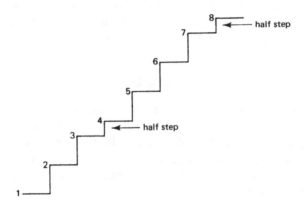

A major scale can be experienced by playing from one C to another on a keyboard. The half steps occur naturally between E–F and B–C, where there is no black key. As long as the whole-whole-half, whole-whole-whole-half step arrangement is followed through the use of the correct black keys, a major scale can be built on any note.

Complete major scales in which one note follows another for one octave are rarely encountered in song melodies. Instead, a scale is the "musical skeleton" on which melodies are based. Two familiar songs that have complete scales in their melodies are associated with Christmas, "The First Noël," and "Joy to the World." Brackets have been placed over the scale in these examples.

A *minor scale* is similar to a major scale in that all seven notes in the musical alphabet are used. The main difference lies in the first five notes, in which the third step is lowered. The pattern of the first five notes is:

Whole   Whole Half   Whole   Whole

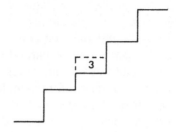

The first five notes of all minor scales are the same, but there are three different versions of the sixth and seventh steps of minor scales. Rarely do elementary music teachers need to deal with these different types. The first five notes are what is significant about minor scales.

Minor scales have a characteristic sound that is sometimes called "sad" or "dark," although no words can truly describe the quality. The darker aspect of music in minor keys may be due in part to the lowered third step, which distinguishes it from music in major keys.

A *pentatonic scale* is found in a number of folk melodies. As the name implies (*penta* means "five" in Greek), the scale has five notes. The pattern is the same as that of the black keys on a keyboard. Because it has no half steps, the harsh sound of notes a half step apart is avoided. For this reason, the pentatonic scale is often used for the initial efforts at improvising music by elementary school students.

Key Signatures

Frequently you will see some sharps or flats to the right of the clef at the beginning of each line of a piece of music. These sharps or flats are called the *key signature*. They indicate that certain notes throughout the piece, unless changed by a natural sign (♮), are to be raised or lowered, depending on the key signature. Once they are in the right key, singers tend to sing the sharp or flat notes intuitively. It's quite another matter when playing an instrument. A player must pay careful attention to accidentals, notes that are raised or lowered from their usual place.

One can usually figure out the tonal center by looking at the key signature. But this ability is not necessary for classroom teachers. The basal songbooks always provide the name of the key for each song in the teacher's edition. Also, in the case of songs, the notes to be raised or lowered tend to take care of themselves when sung. In addition, the music for classroom instruments is generally quite simple with few changed notes.

Intervals

As was pointed out earlier in this chapter, an interval is the distance from one pitch to another. To calculate an interval, a person may apply a "1" to either of the two notes and count by step to the other, including the final note. The count is by alphabetical letters, not half-step spacings. For example, the interval of G up to B is a third, counted G A B; it is not a fifth as would happen if half steps were counted.

Interval names stay the same whether the two sounds occur separately or together, and the presence of a sharp, flat, or natural does not change the basic name of the interval. Musicians add qualifying words to indicate the number of half steps encompassed by a given interval: for example, the term "minor third," which describes the "cuckoo" interval more specifically.

As mentioned previously, an octave is an interval of eight notes extending from one tone to the nearest tone of the same name. An octave is the most consonant interval in music. The two sounds blend so well together that one seems to duplicate the other. In fact, it is sometimes difficult to tell which octave a sound is in. Try whistling a note and then matching it on a keyboard, and you will discover that finding the right octave is not so easy.

Harmony

Harmony is the simultaneous sounding of pitches. Its main function is to provide accompaniment or background for melodies. A *chord* is a combination of three or more tones sounding together. A *triad* is a particular type of chord that consists of three notes, each a third apart. Traditionally, chords in music in Western civilization are built in thirds, whether they have three, four, or five notes.

The *root* of a chord is the pitch on which the chord is built. The term "root" does not mean the keynote of the scale; it refers to just one chord. The root is often the lowest note in a chord, but it doesn't need to be. The notes can be rearranged so that another note is the lowest, but the root remains the same. For example, the notes C-E-G form a C chord. It is still a C chord if G is the lowest note and its remaining two notes are C and E.

An Arabic number such as 1, 3, or 6 refers to a single note and indicates its position in a given scale. Roman numerals such as I, IV, and V refer to a complete chord and indicate the scale step on which it is built.

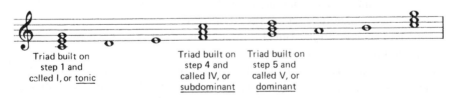

Triad built on
step 1 and
called I, or <u>tonic</u>

Triad built on
step 4 and
called IV, or
<u>subdominant</u>

Triad built on
step 5 and
called V, or
<u>dominant</u>

Certain chords appear much more often than others, especially in the relatively simple songs that elementary school students usually sing. The three most prominent are the I, IV, and V chords in a key. The I chord almost always is the final chord, and the V chord usually precedes it. Songs that fail to end on a I chord sound incomplete. The choice of chords is dictated by the important notes in the melody. If the same chord, say the I chord, is sounded throughout a song that's more than few measures long, the points where the melody and harmony don't jibe will be obvious; they will sound like amateurish mistakes.

A *seventh chord* has four pitches a third apart. The chord is so named because the interval from the root to its fourth note is the interval of a seventh. V chords often are seventh chords, and are indicated by a small 7 to the right of the V, like V7.

Chords in songbooks are usually indicated by the letter name of the root. The G chord contains the notes G-B-D and the F chord contains the notes F-A-C, for example. A seventh chord based on G is G-B-D-F. Chords can be played on a keyboard instrument or a guitar, but the simplest way is with an Autoharp, which is presented in the next chapter.

CODA

Understanding how pitches are depicted in music notation is not essential for teaching some of the aspects of music in elementary schools classrooms, but it certainly helps. The students will be seeing and learning the basics of music notation. Classroom teachers who have a fundamental understanding of music notation will be more confident and able to help their students in learning music.

PROJECTS

Select a song from this book or one of the elementary music series.

1. Read through it, naming the notes.

2. Sing the song with note names in place of the words.

3. Look for letters indicating which chords harmonize the melody.

4. Notice the final note of the song.

5. If a piano or mallet instrument is available, practice playing the song, even if you use only one or two fingers.

6. Count the number of intervals in the songs. How many seconds, thirds, etc., are there?

7. Look for names of notes that are altered because of the key signature or because of sharps and flats that appear in the song.

SKILL DEVELOPMENT

1. Clap or tap these measures.

2. Name these notes. Then sing these measures using the names of the notes.

REVIEW QUESTIONS

1. What is a scale?
2. What is the main difference between a major scale and a minor scale?
3. What is the purpose of a key signature?
4. What are the three most important chords in a key or scale?
5. What is the difference between a chord built on the seventh degree of a scale and a seventh chord?

Singing and Playing Instruments

Singing is clearly the main means of making music in elementary schools. Everyone is born with a voice, and no special technique is required to use it at a rudimentary level. It is also a very personal means of self-expression. Furthermore, a huge body of vocal music exists, especially of songs that are within the singing capabilities of elementary school students.

Singing by Classroom Teachers

Because they lack confidence in their ability to sing, many classroom teachers are not at all sure that they can or should sing for, or even with, their students. How important it is that they sing?

To begin, yes, singing is important! Through singing people express feelings with a sensitivity and subtlety not possible on any instrument. Singing is basic to an education in music, and it is an integral part of music education at the ele-

51

mentary school level. Although learning to sing like a professional requires much training and skill, most people can learn to sing simple songs with a minimum of instruction.

Do classroom teachers need to be able to sing? It's not mandatory, but it really helps if they can and will sing—even just a little bit—with their students. If teachers urge their students to sing, but don't sing themselves, they are tacitly giving their students a message: "Singing is good for you, but I, as your teacher, can't or won't do it." When classroom teachers sing along with their students, it makes a huge difference. Remember, students expect their music teacher to sing, but this is not necessarily so in the case of their classroom teacher. A little participation in singing by the classroom teacher says to them that music is not confined to the music room or only to people who have had special training in music.

Elementary education majors are not vocal music majors, and they seldom can sing nearly as well. But that really doesn't matter to elementary school students; they are not music critics! In fact, it can be argued that the trained style developed by voice majors is *not* the best model for young students. As long as one can sing with reasonably accurate pitch and a clear tone, that's all that is needed.

Improving Singing

What can future teachers who are not music majors do now to improve their ability to sing? Following a few simple steps can improve the sound of your singing.

1. Stand or sit erect. Sitting in a slouched position allows little room for air in the lungs. And an adequate air supply is necessary for a good singing tone.

2. When you inhale, your abdominal wall should move out, not in. The lungs expand below the rib cage; lifting the shoulders hardly increases the amount of air you can inhale.

3. As you sing a long tone or phrase, your abdominal wall should slowly move in. You can check this by touching your hand on your abdomen. The abdominal wall should also be slightly firm, because those are the muscles that control the breath.

4. Your throat and neck should be relaxed. Think of singing *through* your vocal cords (larynx), not *with* them. Focus your attention on your abdominal muscles, not your throat.

5. Your mouth should be open at least half an inch.

6. Think of projecting the sound through your forehead, not down in your throat. Furthermore, imagine that your sound is being projected all the way across the room to some one or some object that you see there.

7. Practice these steps on single syllables such as "loo" and "ah." Then try singing simple phrases of music while retaining a good flow of projected sound.

Singing with Accurate Pitch

What should do you do if you suspect your singing is not very accurate? Here are some suggestions.

1. Place a finger or hand over one ear while singing. This will allow you to hear yourself much better.

2. Women often have trouble with notes that seem to be too high for them to sing. You need to think about using what might be called your "head" or "little girl" voice. That is, try projecting the sound more through the cheeks and forehead and lightening up the quality. To find this voice, you can practice siren-like slides from low notes to higher notes. Then you should notice how the quality and physical effort required change as the sounds become higher.

3. Try working alone with a keyboard. Sing a note that is comfortable for you and sustain it. Then find that note on the keyboard as you hold the note. For women, those notes are often around or just below the middle of the keyboard; for men those notes are eight white keys lower. Once you find it, listen to the sensation when what you are singing and the note you are playing seem to agree. It might remind you of the sun coming out from behind the clouds, except in this case it's tonal clouds. It helps if you keep one hand on your ear as you do this activity.

4. Next, play one note higher and have your voice move up to that note. Repeat the process for several more notes, each time making sure that what you sing agrees with what you are playing.

5. Keep this activity up for no longer than ten minutes or so at a time. It may need to be repeated over a period of several different days. You should soon notice a definite improvement in your ability to sing a song more accurately.

Playing Instruments

Having at least a minimal skill in playing classroom instruments such as recorder, keyboard, or Autoharp can be very helpful in teaching music. Each of these instruments offers the opportunity to understand more about music.

Because skills are best learned over a period of weeks or months, they are introduced early in the book. Sections on furthering skills on these instruments are included at the end of most of the subsequent chapters to encourage skill development throughout the course.

Keyboards and Mallet Instruments

Keyboard/Piano.   Some elementary schools have electronic keyboards available to enhance the students' musical education. Many students will already have electronic keyboards at home; about four million of them are sold in the United

States each year.* In addition, many families own a piano, and many children in the upper grades take piano lessons.

Keyboard experience in elementary schools is quite different from private piano instruction that some of you had when you were young. It does not equip you to play anything more than very easy melodies. Rather, the value of a keyboard experience is to help you understand various pitch relationships and to experience working with the pattern of keys on the keyboard and bars on mallet instruments. Because the pattern of black and white keys is tactile and clearly visible, it is easy to see and feel where the half and whole steps are.

The first step in playing these instruments is to find designated pitches. Review what was said about finding pitches on the keyboard in chapter 5 and the pattern of two and three black keys. This task is easier on most mallet instruments, because the name of the pitch appears on each bar. If you are unfamiliar with finding pitches on a keyboard, practice locating notes such as D, F♯, E♭, A, B, A♭, and C♭.

The keys on a keyboard or piano should be depressed with the fleshy part of the tip of the fingers, and *not* the very tip of the fingers near the fingernails. The forearm should be parallel to the floor and even with the keyboard, and the wrist straight. Then you should "let your fingers do the walking" with decisive movements. The finger should be released from the key after it is depressed, unless you want the note to continue sounding.

Place your right thumb on middle C (the key to the left of the two black keys nearest the center of the instrument). Next, place your four fingers over the next four white keys to the right. Practice playing the five keys individually by moving your fingers independently. When you play them in order ascending, you will be playing C-D-E-F-G.

Next, place the thumb of your left hand on middle C, and play the notes to the left below your thumb. The notes descend as you play them, and will be C-B-A-G-F.

As you play notes with your right and then your left hand, say the note names to yourself.

At this point you can try playing a simple song with your right hand like, "Merrily We Roll Along." Begin on E with the third finger (counting your thumb as '1'). Hardly move your hand as your fingers sound the notes of this song.

You can also play "Merrily We Roll Along" on the metallophone or similar instrument.

When you play the five white keys in order with your right hand, C-D-E-F-G, you are sounding the first five notes of the C major scale. Play the first five notes of the D major scale. Move your thumb to the right one note to D. Then instead of playing the white key F, play the black key just to its right. That will be F♯. The five notes will be D-E-F♯-G-A. Notice that the two patterns sound alike, except that the second one is a bit higher. Also notice that the intervals between the notes when you start on C and when you start on D and use F♯ are exactly the same:

* National Association of Music Merchants, Carlsbad, CA, 2003.

MERRILY WE ROLL ALONG

Mer - ri - ly - we   roll a - long,   roll a - long,   roll a - long.

Mer - ri - ly we   roll a - long   o'er the deep blue   sea.

whole step, whole step, half step, whole step. It's an important concept in music. The tonal center of a piece of music can be changed. You may wish to play "Merrily We Roll Along" starting on F♯ by keeping the pattern of whole and half steps. Let your ear be your guide in making sure you are playing the correct pattern of whole and half steps.

Mallet Instruments.   The best way to use a mallet is to have it strike the bar lightly with a somewhat relaxed hand and wrist, and then immediately to raise the mallet off the bar. If you don't, then the bar will make only a muffled sound and not ring.

Recorder

The recorder is a simple wind instrument made of wood; very inexpensive plastic models are also available. Of the several sizes available, the soprano recorder is the most practical for classroom use. It can play almost all the songs that elementary school children sing, although it actually sounds one octave higher than the notation indicates.

Children
playing
recorders

Although not difficult to play in terms of producing sounds, the recorder takes time to learn. It cannot be mastered in a couple of minutes as an incidental music activity. For this reason, suggestions for learning to play the instrument appear at the end of many subsequent chapters in this book.

Hand and Finger Positions.   The recorder is played straight in front of the mouth, with the left hand covering the hole on the underside and the first three holes on the top. The thumb of the right hand goes under the instrument to hold it steady, and the fingers of that hand cover the remaining holes. Certain models of recorders have two small holes for the little finger, and they are covered easily with that one finger. By covering the holes completely with the padded part (not the tip) of the finger, the player prevents air leaks that cause wrong notes, squeaks, or no sound at all. The fingers need only to be firm enough to cover the holes. Squeezing the recorder with the fingers doesn't help; actually, it slows the movement of the fingers. When your fingers are not covering the holes, they should remain only an inch or so above the holes; pointing unused fingers at the ceiling doesn't help either.

Tonguing.   The recorder is played by inserting it slightly between the lips, holding it at a 45° angle to the body. Sounds should be started with the tongue against the back of the teeth and air *gently* released with the syllable "doo." This action is called *tonguing,* and it produces a clear start or "attack" for the tone. The amount of movement by the tongue is quite small. Only the tip of the tongue moves a little bit.

Sounds should not be started by a huffing and puffing action. That is tiring and doesn't provide a clean, smooth beginning to the sounds. Each phrase is started with the tongue, as well as all the notes that are not slurred. A slur is produced by playing two or more different pitches with one continuous breath after the initial tonguing action.

Fingering.   Beginners often start on the note B (middle line of the treble clef), which is played with the thumb and first finger of the left hand. It is also easy to add A (second finger) and then G (third finger). You can play the first three notes of "Are You Sleeping" by starting on G and ascending, or the first three notes of "Three Blind Mice" by starting on B and descending.

A fingering chart for recorder is presented in Appendix B. In such charts an open hole looks like o and a covered hole looks like •. A few holes are half covered to indicate that the hole should be only partially covered. The top of the recorder is at the top of the fingering chart, with the lower half at the bottom.

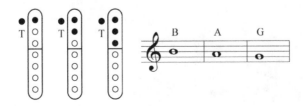

Putting It All Together.   Because the action of the tongue and breath have an important impact on how the music sounds, practice playing the series of notes with one breath and lightly touching the tip of the tongue to just behind the tip of your front teeth. These eight notes should be played like one note that is eight counts long, except for the tiny action of the tongue.

Practice the following music to become more familiar with playing the recorder.

In many elementary schools recorder is introduced to all students for a limited number of classes. Then, students are invited to come to an elective recorder ensemble that meets outside of class or school time. In this way, interested students can have more practice and instruction so they can play more songs.

Here is a three-note version of "Merrily We Roll Along" for you to play.

MERRILY WE ROLL ALONG

Autoharp

The Autoharp and similar instruments like the Chromaharp are ones on which you can easily play chords. It contains strings that are strummed and buttons that are held down so that only the notes in a particular chord will sound. Most Autoharps have fifteen chord buttons, which are the main chords of the more commonly used keys.

Chromaharp

The Autoharp is played while seated and the instrument laid on a table or arm of a classroom chair with the longer end closest to the body. Most people are right-handed, so a crossing pattern is best for them in which the buttons are held down with the *left* hand and the strings strummed with the *right* hand. Left-handers usually prefer strumming with the left hand and holding buttons with their right hand. Actually, it makes no difference in the music, and often teachers may have one child hold the buttons while another strums.

Movement of the hand while strumming is away from the body, so that the low strings sound first. Otherwise, the accompanying chords will sound strange. The motion should be fairly fast, to present individual notes from standing out. Usually the player uses a pick to save wear and tear on the fingers and fingernails. A hard plastic pick produces a more brilliant sound than a felt pick or a rubber pencil eraser. The type of pick used can vary according to the nature of the song.

The pattern of strumming is partly a matter of choice. The important thing is to have the strums occur in rhythm with the beats. Usually the first beat of the measure is played more forcefully than the other beats. Sometimes not all the strings are strummed on the less important beats in a measure. A four-beat measure may be played with strokes on the first and third beat, or just one on the first beat. Again, it depends on the nature and tempo of the song. The faster the tempo, the less strumming will be needed.

Often you will see letters above the notes in a song. These letters are for the chords to be played by an Autoharp, guitar, or piano. The advantage of the Autoharp is that pushing just one button will automatically dampen the sound of the strings by pressing felt pads against the strings that are not in the chord. A person playing the piano must depress each key in a chord in order to sound the chord, and a guitarist has to move his or her fingers to the appropriate place on each of the six strings of the instrument to sound the chord.

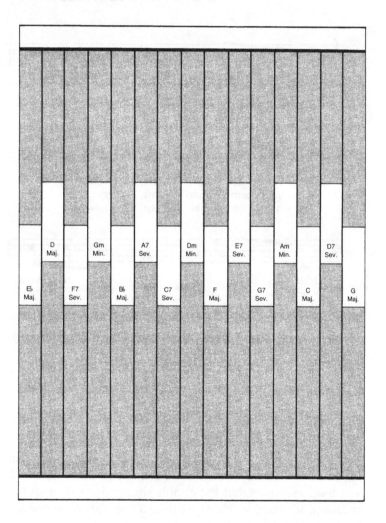

Autoharp bars

"Down in the Valley" is a good song for learning about chord changes and using the Autoharp. As you can see in the music, the letters for the chords appear above the line of melody. The song uses only two chords, F and C7. It is possible to play the chord indicated only when a letter appears. But that would be quite a sparse accompaniment! You could also strum just once in each measure, and that would be minimal. It would sound better if you strum the designated chord on each beat, with the first beat of the measure played louder than the second and third beats. Probably no chord should be strummed on the three pick-up notes that start the song. The F chord should be strummed before the song begins to give the class the starting pitch.

DOWN IN THE VALLEY

To illustrate that the designated chords are the correct ones, you can try playing just the F chord throughout the first two lines. You will hear in the second and third measures that the chords simply don't fit with the melody. Musically speaking, it's comparable to wearing a dress shoe on one foot and a sneaker on the other.

> ## Coda
>
> The better you can sing, the more likely you will be willing and able to help young students. Practically everyone can improve in their ability to sing by working on the suggestions offered in this chapter. Developing the ability to use keyboard and mallet instruments, plus a recorder and Autoharp, will also help you build your feelings of competence in music. The same is true of your ability to read music notation, even if only at a rudimentary level.

SKILL DEVELOPMENT

Make sure that you have acquired the technical skills required for the instruments presented in this chapter.

1. Play the following music examples on a keyboard and then on a mallet instrument.

2. Sing "Down in the Valley" with the Autoharp in the key of C. To do this, play C instead of F and G7 instead of C7.

3. Clap or tap the following rhythm patterns.

4. Name the following notes and sing them.

REVIEW QUESTIONS

1. Why is singing by a classroom teacher important?
2. What physical actions enable you to have more breath available for singing?
3. Describe four actions that you take to help yourself to sing more accurately on pitch.
4. What is the value of learning keyboard instruments in a music methods class?

5. How should a player strike a bar on a mallet instrument?

6. Why should you tongue notes when playing the recorder instead of starting and stopping them with your breath?

7. What happens when the player holds down a bar on the Autoharp that causes only the notes of the chords to sound?

HELPING TO TEACH MUSIC

Music specialists need help in teaching music to the students. It's not during the time they are in front of classes that they need it. Instead, they need it during the many hours that pass each week between the thirty or forty minutes they have with the students. No matter how effective they are during the once-a-week music class, the impact of a lesson is greatly reduced by the time a week has gone by. A little follow-up and reinforcement can accomplish a lot in terms of what the students remember and can do in music. The only way music classes taught by specialists are going to be reinforced is by classroom teachers.

The chapters in part III deal with initial teaching procedures for classroom teachers to help students experience rhythm, singing, listening, playing instruments, creative activities, and moving to music.

A small minority of classroom teachers are responsible for all the music instruction their students receive. These chapters are especially important to elementary education majors who someday will find themselves in a situation where they must provide music instruction. They will then have a basic knowledge and skills to draw upon.

These chapters also include skill development activities on the recorder, keyboard, and Autoharp, as well as singing.

7

Teaching Rhythm

- Experiencing the Beat
- Perceiving the Steadiness of the Beat
- Tempo
- Long and Short Durations
- Sound and Silence
- Meter
- The Notation of Rhythm

Every sound has four aspects: tone quality, pitch (degree of high or low), loudness, and duration (rhythm when consecutive sounds are involved). Because rhythm is intertwined with the other components of music, a music class should not deal exclusively with it. But some of the time it should receive special attention. Not only is rhythm interrelated with other aspects of music, it is itself made up of different components: beat, meter, tempo, and so on. Helping children to understand these components through experiencing them is an important goal in teaching music, and it is the basis for the teaching suggestions that follow.

The songs and activities presented in this chapter are described with the help of music notation. It is provided mainly for the information of teachers, not elementary school students. Youngsters need to sense aspects of rhythm in many musical situations before being asked to learn its written symbols.

Experiencing the Beat

In music there only a few instances of inherently logical learning sequences that need to be followed if learning is to be successful. But rhythm is one such instance. To understand rhythm, however, children must first feel the beat, because that ability is basic to learning others aspects of rhythm.

Most children usually require many experiences with the beat before they sense it consistently and accurately. This awareness is not a skill that can be acquired in a lesson or two; it must be reinforced over a span of months. Reviewing it can be brief, and it can be integrated with learning other aspects of rhythm, but it also needs to take place.

Here is one way in which a teacher can help students to feel the beat.

> How many of you have felt your heartbeat or taken your pulse? If you haven't, do it now. Touch your throat with your fingertips on one side of your voice box and your thumb on the other side, like this. . . . Then press backward gently until you can feel the strong pulse in your throat. . . . Can you feel it? . . . Notice that it's very even and steady: beat, beat, beat. The beat in music is like that. In fact, it can be called a pulse, too.

Sensing the beat seems to happen best when one just goes along with the flow in a relaxed atmosphere. And it seems to happen more easily in group situations. There's something captivating about a group of people clapping or dancing along with the music. A teacher may play a march on a CD while the children tap or clap along with the music. When most of the children demonstrate a sense of marking the beat, at that moment the teacher should say in a positive tone of voice something like, "There! Now you're feeling the beat of the music!"

Some music educators advocate starting children in kindergarten and primary grades with rhythmic experiences that involve the use of large muscles. This is a questionable view. Marching in time to music is a seemingly simple large-muscle activity. But dancing or marching to the beat is a skill that a few adults never seem to acquire well, so it is unrealistic to expect most children to be able to do this in the primary grades. Rather, it appears that children execute rhythm more easily through speech patterns or by smaller muscle movements such as hitting sticks together or clapping.

Perceiving the Steadiness of the Beat

When children begin to sense the beat, they need to be made aware of its steady nature. Although the desire for a steady beat may appear to be a natural inclination, it sometimes is not with children. Like most human behavior, it is probably learned. Much concentration is required to maintain a beat that doesn't speed up or slow down as it moves along.

Perceiving a steady beat can be taught in several different ways. One is with the use an electronic metronome with a light that blinks and produces a clicking sound with the beat. The children can clap or chant with the metronome. Sometimes youngsters do not realize that they are rushing a tempo until they see and hear their deviations from the blinks and clicks. The routine of letting the children alternately listen to four beats, then clap or tap four, is effective in helping them experience the steadiness of the beat.

Chanting short phrases is another way to develop a sense of the beat. Phrases for chanting can be found in many places: school cheers, rhymes, verses of songs, and lines made up by the teacher or class members. As the children become accomplished at chanting them, they can be divided into two groups, with different phrases being recited at the same time, or with a particular rhythm being chanted, or in staggered order like a round.

Children can be asked to make up their own chants and rhymes to reinforce their sense of the beat. Youngsters often devise their own rhymes when jumping rope or engaging in other play activities. You can have children who know them teach them to the class.

The following example shows how a teacher can help the children feel the steadiness of the beat.

> Here's a song that I'm sure you'll like. It's "The Bus." If you know it already, help me sing it. [The teacher sings the first verse and a few children join in.]

THE BUS

2. "The wheels on the bus go 'round and 'round . . ."

3. "The horn on the bus goes Toot, toot, toot . . ."

4. "The money on the bus goes Ding, ding, ding . . ."

5. "The wipers on the glass go Swish, swish, swish . . ."

Good! Now, remember how you've been learning to feel the beat of the music? Let's sing the song again and see if you can feel its steady beat. When you do, show us by clapping with the beat. [The teacher hums the starting pitch and indicates when to begin by making a motion of the hand or head or by emphasizing an intake of breath. The children start together and clap the beat as they sing "The Bus."]

"Are the beats in the song even or uneven?" [Several students respond that the beats are even.]

Children enjoy acting out the words to "The Bus," even though the traditional motions don't occur on every beat but in a "short short long" pattern beginning in the second full measure. Other actions are possible with a song such as this. Once the children have succeeded in clapping accurately, they can walk to the beat. They can chant the words with special emphasis on the syllables that occur on the beat, or they can tap the beat on simple rhythm instruments such as drums or rhythm sticks.

It's important to emphasize the beats and to recite the lines vigorously and with a steady, rhythmic beat. Energetic speaking should not be confused with shouting or forcing the voice. Rather, each word should be sounded decisively, especially the syllables that coincide with the beats, and the words should "bounce along" in singsong style.

Tempo

When children can feel the beat and recognize its regular nature, they are ready to listen for the speed of the beats—the tempo. It can be experienced in several different ways. The children can:

1. Sing the same song at different tempos while keeping the beat steady.

2. Listen to short excerpts of pieces that contain several changes of tempo.

3. Tap, march, or clap along with pieces that have different tempos.

The students can also listen to pieces in which the tempo gradually changes. For example, *The Little Train of Caipira* by the Brazilian composer Heitor Villa-Lobos begins with the train standing still. Then it starts up slowly, rolls merrily along, and finally winds down at the end of its journey.

Emphasize the fact that tempo is *the speed of the beats, not the speed of the notes.* Music can have a slow tempo in which many rapidly moving notes are performed. And the opposite can happen: a piece of music with a fast tempo may have notes that change slowly.

Long and Short Durations

In the following lessons the teacher uses the rhythm patterns of a song to show the differences between the number of notes on a beat and the beat itself. In the process, students can observe that notes are of varying durations, and that these durations are judged in relation to the beat. The important point to be learned is that the beat is the unit of time measurement in music.

The song "Are You Sleeping?" (page 33) clearly illustrates the three common note/beat combinations: one note for one beat, two notes of identical length occurring in one beat, and one note lasting for two beats. The song also establishes a strong sense of beat by featuring the consecutive one-beat notes before any other note values are heard.

In music class on Monday you learned a new song, "Are You Sleeping?" Today let's sing it again, while we clap the beat. [A few children may be uncertain in their clapping, but they make an attempt to follow their classmates or the teacher.]

You did a good job of keeping your beats even, class. The beats have to be even, because that's how we keep track of the passing of time in music. The beat helps us decide how much time should go by on the long and short notes.

Now let's say the words while we clap the song again. We want to find out if the words and notes are always just as long as the beats. Think about it as we do the rhythms now. [The children clap and chant with the teacher, who then invites their observations by questions such as these: "Did our words always match our claps? Were some of the words longer than the beats we clapped? Were some of the words shorter?" The teacher helps the class to discover, for example, that there are two notes to a beat on the words "Morning bells are."]

The song "Are You Sleeping?" can also be used to help the class discover similarities among the various rhythm patterns. The children can find out for themselves that in this song there are identical rhythms for each pair of consecutive phrases: the first and second ("Are you sleeping"), the third and fourth, and so on. A few observant children may notice that the rhythm for the lines "Brother John" and "Ding, dong, ding" is the same. The class can also be divided to demonstrate different patterns, with some of the children sounding the pattern of "Morning bells are ringing" while the others produce the rhythm for "Ding, dong, dong." They can sound the patterns by clapping, tapping on a drum, hitting rhythm sticks, or playing other rhythm instruments. They can also sing on one pitch using a neutral syllable such as "tah" or "lah."

An excellent technique for making children aware of rhythms is to help them discover the patterns of words in names. Children are curious to find out what rhythm patterns can be made from their own names. Here is one way in which this can be done.

Did you know that the name of every person in this class has a rhythm pattern? David, let's use you name as an example. It goes:

Da - vid *Smith*

The name "David" has two syllables so it seems to divide into two notes in one beat, just like the "morning" in "Are You Sleeping?" The word "Smith" is just one sound, so it's like one note, which takes up one beat. Let's all say "David Smith" in a rhythmic way, with lots of energy. [The class chants the name, and David seems pleased. The teacher then puts other children's names into patterns, pointing out that some names require three or four syllables within one beat,

Jen - ni - fer *Ar* - den   *Jer* - e - mi-ah *Hart* - man

and that others require an "upbeat" because the first syllable is not accented.]

Di - *ane*   *Rich* - ard - son.]

Sound and Silence

A good way to emphasize the continuity of the music during moments of silence is to let the children make decisive motions during the rests. In the song "If You're Happy," the teacher introduces the children to rests by asking them for silent action—moving hands as if to clap, but not striking them together—during those places of "organized silence."

Another technique is to sing a song in which portions of the melody are replaced with actions or silence. "Bingo" is a good example.

The song "Bingo" doesn't tell us much about the dog, but we can make the music interesting by playing a game with his name. As you can see, I've printed BINGO five times on the board, not in a line, but one above the other, like layers in a cake. Before we play the game, let's review the song by tapping the beat as we sing.

BINGO

Here comes the game! We'll sing the song five times. Each time, trade a clap for one letter in Bingo's name. The first time, clap for the letter B, the second time for B and I, and so on. I'll help you by circling the letter that you're going to replace with a clap. [The class sings the song five times.]

Now, let's make it more tricky. Sing "Bingo" five more times, but instead of claps, just think the notes silently in your head. When you think of the letters of Bingo's name, keep your thoughts moving at exactly the same speed as the music. Keep that beat going even in your mind.

Echo-clapping is an excellent means of teaching children to listen carefully to the interplay between sound and silence. Here is an example of how a teacher might do this.

I'll tap out a pattern on the drum, and you tap it back to me with your rhythm sticks. Listen carefully, and start tapping when I give you the signal by nodding my head.

As the children get better in imitating rhythms, the patterns can be lengthened and made more difficult.

Meter

Elementary school students should gain a concept of meter and develop the ability to recognize and perform various patterns. The learning process is more effective if students in their singing and playing are encouraged to emphasize the notes on the first beats of measures by making them a bit louder.

In the following lesson the teacher points out the patterns of strong and weak beats, and introduces the term "meter."

You've been learning about the beat in music for several weeks now. Can you clap the beat to "Eency, Weency Spider" as we sing the song? [The class sings the song, clapping with vigor.]

EENCY, WEENCY SPIDER

The een-cy, ween-cy spi-der went up the wa-ter-spout.

Down came the rain and washed the spi-der out.

Out came the sun and dried up all the rain, And the

een-cy, ween-cy spi-der went up the spout a-gain.

You made your claps nice and even, so they all sounded alike. But did you know that in music some beats are usually stronger than others, so they're sounded louder? And those strong and weak beats happen in a pattern. Sing "Eency, Weency Spider" again while I clap the beats. But this time, listen to my clapping to see which beats are stronger. [The class sings the song while the teacher claps the beat, emphasizing the first beat of each measure.]

This time sing "Eency, Weency Spider" while you clap the beats. The pattern is STRONG-weak, STRONG-weak, so be sure to make a difference in the strength of your claps. [The class claps and sings the song, following the teacher's example by exaggerating the loudness and softness of alternating beats.]

There's a word for the pattern of beats. It is *meter.* The meter of "Eency, Weency Spider" is STRONG-weak, STRONG-weak. Each pattern has two beats in it, so we'll call it "two-beat meter."

This time when we sing the song, keep on sounding the notes on the first beat a little stronger than the others. Notice that I said a little stronger. If you make too much difference, the song won't be smooth and musical.

In addition to clapping and tapping various meters and recognizing them when performed by teachers, children can listen to a recording of music that has a clearly felt beat. They can tap along and decide whether the music seems to be in a two- or three-beat pattern. Marches are an easy choice for two-beat meters, and minuets from Haydn and Mozart symphonies are clear choices for three-beat meter. But there are hundreds of examples of each type of meter, including the song "America."

The Notation of Rhythm

The experiences described to this point have had the children experience rhythm; no music notation was involved. And it's a fact: Music existed for thousands of years without any system of notation, and that condition continues today for much of the folk/ethnic music around the world. Music notation is a useful and important development, and students should over time learn to use it, at least at a rudimentary level. But it is important to remember that music is organized sounds. Notation is one way—and a limited one at that—of preserving and representing those sounds. It can indicate the basic rhythmic pattern of the sounds, as well as their pitch. The more subtle and expressive aspects of music lie beyond the capabilities of notation.

The notation of rhythm can be introduced to children in the primary grades through the use of "stick notation." The advantage of this notation is its simplicity; all the distracting symbols are eliminated. Initially, stick notation is limited to quarter and eighth notes, which can be represented by just stems and beams. A short vertical line can represent a quarter note, and two stems can be connected by a beam for eighth notes. Notes are not placed on a staff. As the children become competent with these two symbols, others can be added.

Children can use rhythm syllables along with stick notation. Rhythm syllables help students to "name" a note value, and can reinforce the association between what they see and what they hear. Several syllable systems are available, all of which work if taught consistently. The most commonly used is to call a quarter note "tah" and an eighth note "ti" (pronounced "tee"). Here is an example:

Pattern in conventional notation:	♩ ♩ ♫ ♩	
Pattern in stick notation:	| | ⊓ |	
Rhythm syllables for the pattern:	ta ta ti ti ta	

In the following lesson the teacher presents quarter and eighth notes in stick notation. At this stage, the two types of notes are not mixed in the same pattern.

> Today we'll learn a way to picture some rhythm patterns. First, I'll draw a straight line that stands up. . . . This is a picture of a note that takes up one beat. Here's a pattern of four lines standing up. . . . This means beat-beat-beat-beat. Let's read what the pictures tell us to do. For every note pictured by a line, say "tah." Rea-dy, go: "Tah tah tah tah." [The class says the "tahs" with the teacher.]

Good! Now try to read the picture at a different speed, a little faster. The tempo this time is beat-beat-beat-beat. Rea-dy go: "Tah tah tah tah."

The rhythm syllable "ti" is introduced in much the same way as "tah" is in the preceding example.

The notation for rests can also be introduced in a simple form with a quarter rest represented by a Z shape. Because syllables are being spoken, it is a good idea to represent rests with a softer sound like a puff as if blowing out a candle. Or silent motions can be used, such as turning the palms of the hands out.

When notation is initially introduced, only one more note value is needed to complete a basic rhythm vocabulary: the symbol for a note lasting two beats, which is usually represented by a half note. It can be the same in both stick and conventional notation. It can be said "tah-ah," with the "ah" occurring on the second beat of the note.

The transition from stick to conventional notation is simple because of the similarity between the two types. All that is needed is the addition of heads to the half, quarter, and eighth notes. When children demonstrate that they understand stick notation, the change to conventional notation can be made.

As they progress from one grade to the next, students will of course encounter more notational symbols than the few introduced here. The additional symbols will be learned more easily if a solid foundation has been established in the primary grades. And that foundation is built largely on experiences with music.

Coda

Rhythm is the lifeblood of music. It's as natural to most music as breathing. That's why it is the most logical element to deal with first. Experiencing rhythm is the way to begin understanding rhythm. After students have become well grounded in experiencing the various aspects of rhythm, then "pictures" of rhythm in the form of notation can be introduced.

Projects

1. Select two songs or two instrumental pieces of music with quite different tempos. Develop a plan of how you would teach the concept of tempo to a primary grade class.

2. Assume that the class can sing "My Country 'Tis of Thee." Describe how you help students to determine that the meter has three beats in each measure instead of two or four.

3. Notate the rhythmic pattern of these names:

   Jennifer Hopkins

   Ron Whitimore

   Mandy Roberson

   Latisha Brockington

SKILL DEVELOPMENT

SLEEP, BABY SLEEP

German Folksong

Sleep ba-by sleep,   sleep ba-by sleep.   Moth-er shakes the dream-land tree and

from   it   falls   a   dream   for   thee,   sleep   ba - by sleep.

Using the song "Sleep, Baby Sleep," do the following:

1. Tap the rhythm of the notes. Be sure to maintain a moderate, steady tempo and observe the rests in doing this.

2. Say the names of the notes in rhythm.

3. Say the names of the notes in rhythm as you finger the notes silently on your recorder.

4. Play the song. Make the notes as smooth and songlike as possible by just touching the tip of your tongue to the tip of your upper front teeth for a split second at the start each new note.

5. If you have a keyboard available, play the song on it.

6. Play the song on a mallet instrument.

7. Although it is a bit high, sing the song using the names of the notes instead of the words. Use your recorder or keyboard to establish the starting pitch. Make sure you use a light "head voice" to reach the correct pitches.

8. Sing the song again, but this time with the words.

9. If you have an Autoharp available, play the G chord on the first and third beats of the measure as members of your methods class sing the song.

REVIEW QUESTIONS

1. Describe three different ways in which you could help the children experience the beat.

2. How can teachers help students to sense and understand that beats in music are usually steady?

3. What are some actions that teachers can take to help students understand the concept of tempo?

4. How can teachers help students learn that the beat of the music and the notes that are sounded are not the same thing?

5. What can the children do to keep the sense that rhythm going when there are rests in the music?

6. What are the advantages of "stick notation" when first introducing students to music notation?

8

Singing in Elementary School Classrooms

It is traditional to describe the quality of children's voices with words such as "light," "free," and "clear." These words are as good as any, although none truly describes the charming quality of the sound. Children in elementary school, especially those in the primary grades, are not big enough physically to produce a full, rich tone; they just do not have the vocal mechanism or breath capacity for it. To sing more loudly, they must "force" the quality of their voices and produce a distorted sound that's often out of tune. The result is a quality closer to shouting than to singing. If continued, such singing can injure the voice.

Children's Singing

Unfortunately, there are not many good examples of children's singing for them to emulate. The best source is probably the ancillary CDs for the elementary book series, which were mentioned in chapter 3, and concert works for children's voices. The quality of the children's singing on those recordings is a good model for children.

Even young children can appreciate the difference between singing and talking. Vowels are sustained in singing, but not in speaking. In fact, the vowels in singing should be thought of as being connected to one another in a continuous stream until the conclusion of a phrase. This will need to be worked on in a variety of songs over a period of weeks. One simple procedure is to sing a song or phrase on a neutral syllable instead of with words. When the flow of singing tone has been achieved, the song should be sung with words and with the same stream of sound maintained. If a steady flow of sound is not achieved, the result is a chopped style in which each syllable is separated briefly from the next, giving a barking, disjointed effect.

When correctly produced, children's singing gives an impression of being floated out, not forced. It is as though the breath being used for singing would support a feather fluttering a few inches away from the mouth. To achieve this, you can apply the suggestions for singing procedures in chapter 6. Have the students stand or sit erect. Standing is an excellent way to attain a straight spine that allows for sufficient breath. The breath should be inhaled as if it's being directed to the area below the rib cage, so that the wall of the abdomen moves *out* as the breath is taken *in* and slowly moves *in* as air is expelled. The expansion needed for the breath comes not from puffing up the chest or raising the shoulders, but rather from moving the diaphragm down toward the waistline.

The mouth should be quite open. The actual height of the opening varies according to the word being sung. Except for the wall of the abdomen, there should be little tension, especially in the throat. The attention of the singers should be on maintaining a steady flow of air, not on manipulating the voice box. The idea should be to sing *through* the larynx, not *with* it.

Some children force their voices in an effort to sing higher or lower than their comfortable ranges, but such singing should be discouraged. As youngsters mature and learn to sing better, their ranges will slowly expand. For many children and adults, a range of about one octave is about the limit for comfortable singing and pleasant sound. With some practice and instruction a child's top vocal range can be extended. The typical range for first graders is about middle C to G or A above. For sixth grade students the range has increased to A below middle C to about F an octave and a half higher.

Teachers should not move the starting pitch of a song lower to make it easier to sing. Elementary school students simply do not have vocal cords large enough to allow them to sing more than about one note lower than the printed version in the music book. The CD of a song is pitched as printed in the book.

Boys' voices do not normally begin to change until the middle school grades. It is not unusual for some of the boys to acquire a brilliance and power not found in girls' voices. This is the age of boy sopranos and boy choirs, a tradition in English church music.

Introducing a New Song

When presenting a new song to a class, promote those aspects that are most likely to attract the interest of the students. In the following lesson the teacher builds on the children's interest in babies.

> Today we're going to learn a song that a mother might sing to her baby to help it fall asleep. I'll bet that some of you have little brothers and sisters who have trouble falling asleep sometimes. Maybe your mother sings to them to help them feel sleepier.

HUSH, LITTLE BABY

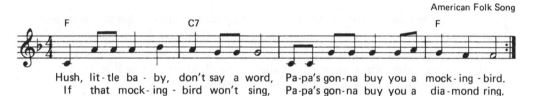

American Folk Song

Hush, lit-tle ba - by, don't say a word, Pa-pa's gon-na buy you a mock-ing-bird.
If that mock-ing - bird won't sing, Pa-pa's gon-na buy you a dia-mond ring.

A song may be introduced by first teaching the students a repeated portion of it. For example, in the song "All Night, All Day" (p. 83) the words "All night, all day" are sung to exactly the same music each time the phrase appears. The words "Day is dying in the west" and "Sleep, my child, and take your rest" are sung to the same melody, which is merely a more elaborate version of the first four half notes.

In other cases the children might first learn the words and then say them expressively. Or they might start by listening to the CD of the song. On other occasions they might learn part or all of a song on the bells or some other simple instrument prior to singing it.

Starting a Song

Teachers in elementary school do not usually conduct students when they sing. Conducting is used only when performing in public. Not only is conducting unnecessary, it can be distracting. The students find it difficult to look at their music book and the teacher at the same time.

Verbal commands are a far more effective way to help a class start a song together. The particular words used are not crucial. What matters is that the same routine be followed consistently so that the students become accustomed to it. Before starting to sing a song, they need to know

1. the pitch of the first note,

2. the tempo, and

3. when to start.

The pitch can be given by singing the first note on a neutral syllable or by sounding it on a recorder or keyboard. The teacher then sings or speaks *in the tempo of the song* a phrase such as "Rea-dy, sing," or "Rea-dy go." These directions are usually given on the two beats before the song starts. If a song begins with a pick-up note of less than one beat, the music starts at the appropriate moment after the signal. Here is an example of one such beginning:

Should men use falsetto voice when starting or teaching songs to students in the primary grades? They can, but the falsetto tone quality doesn't seem to help the children all that much. Although hearing pitches sounding one octave lower in the normal range for a man may bother some children a bit a first, they soon get used to it. And it is the sound that mature males usually use.

Teaching a Song

A song can be taught in several different ways. The choice depends on the nature of the song and the interests and abilities of the students and teacher. In the primary grades, most songs are taught by rote. That is, the teacher sings or plays on a CD the song or phrase while the children listen, and then they attempt to sing it. This procedure is repeated until the entire song is learned. The length of the phrase sung for the students depends on their abilities and the difficulty of the music. If a song is quite short, it may be sung without interruption. Longer songs are usually broken into phrases.

For example, the song "All Night, All Day" is probably too long to be learned in one segment. The teacher may find it helpful, however, to sing or play the entire song for the children at first, to give them an idea of how it goes. Rote teaching begins when the teacher sings "All night, all day" (if the children are young and inexperienced) or "All night, all day, angels watching over me, my Lord" (if the students are older and more experienced). The phrase is sung twice for the students before they attempt to sing it themselves. When that phrase is learned satisfactorily, the teacher moves on to the next phrase and repeats the procedure just described. With each new phrase, previously learned phrases are included at least once in the children's response. At this point the song may be set aside for the rest of the period. It can be refined on subsequent days.

Most of the work toward improving the singing of a particular song is done on the spot without prior planning. The teacher hears what the children sing, and takes that as a basis for deciding what needs work. The extent to which a teacher is able to do this depends on his or her training and ability in music.

ALL NIGHT, ALL DAY

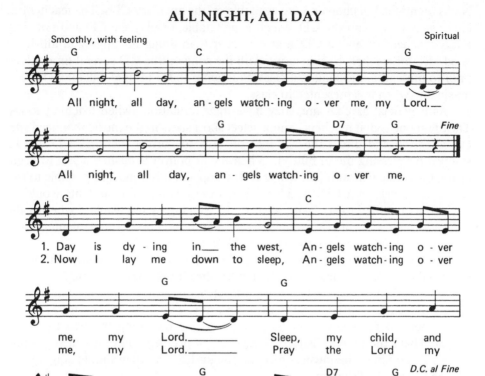

Here is how one teacher attempts to identify and correct the places where the students are not singing accurately.

> Your tone quality was just right that time. But there's one thing we can improve. We didn't all get the third note right. It's the one after "night." Listen while I sing the first three notes very slowly. [The teacher sings the three notes.]

> Now, while you sing the same notes, hold your hand in front of you like a shelf, like this, and move it up and down as you think the pitch of the notes goes. If you think a sound goes up, move your hand up. If you think a sound goes way up, move your hand up toward the top of your head. Show me with you hand where you think your voice should go. Rea-dy sing . . .

Teaching Songs from CDs

What if a teacher still thinks he or she can't sing at all well, even after trying the activities suggested in chapter 5? Fortunately, all the songs in the music series books mentioned in chapter 3 are available on the ancillary CDs. The teacher can either sing along with the CD, which is preferable, or play the CD and not sing. Every teacher can play a CD, and it's better than doing no singing at all! It's a good idea for teachers to sing along with the song on the CD several times alone prior to presenting the song to a class. Practicing ahead of time will allow for better singing when it is presented in class.

As beneficial as CDs are, they have their limitations when teaching songs. The main one is that teachers cannot select short spots in the music that need special attention and direct the children on how to correct them. A CD can be stopped by pressing the ▣ button. When the ▣ button is pushed again to begin again, the music will start just where it was stopped; it is almost impossible to isolate a few notes on a CD. And even if it were possible, the students would be unclear about when to start and what to do. Singing by the teacher, whether the music or classroom teacher, is much better. Let the CD be a complementary, supplemental activity to a song the students have learned.

The success of teaching songs using CDs requires that high-quality equipment be available. Poor equipment greatly reduces the effectiveness of using CDs.

When a CD is used, it helps if the teacher first introduces the words to the song. If the children are unable to read the words, they may be presented by rote. It also helps if the students do not sing with the recording the first time it is played. That's the time to listen. On subsequent playings, they should sing softly so they can listen to the music. Once the song is learned, they should sing it without the CD some of the time.

Rounds

A *canon* or *round* is a song in which the same music is sung by a different section of a group starting at different times. Only certain songs can be sung as rounds, for reasons that are beyond the scope of this book. Several rounds are included in the music series books. They look like other songs, except for the numbers above the staff that indicate when sections are to enter. A round can be repeated as often as desired, but usually the melody is sung two or three times.

"Good Night" is a typical round. It has three lines, so it will sound best when performed by three groups of singers. The second group starts at the beginning of the song when the first group begins singing the second line. The third group starts when the first group gets to the third line. The rendition of a round is balanced, with the first group singing the first line alone at the beginning, and the last group singing the last line alone at the end.

Rounds are taught much like other songs. Three points should be kept in mind, however. The students should:

1. Know the song well, and should be able to sing it in unison without help from the teacher.

2. Maintain a steady tempo as they sing a round. The tendency is to speed up, which messes up the round. It may be necessary for the teacher (and the

GOOD NIGHT

class, too) to clap a steady beat as they sing it in parts. A round should not become a musical race!

3. Not cover their ears in an effort to avoid the sound of the other groups. The musical attractiveness of a round is the harmony that's created as the different groups enter. Blocking out the singing of the other groups negates the point of a round.

If the class has little experience with rounds, the teacher may sing the second part alone while the entire class sings the first part. (The teacher may need to practice this first!) When the class is first divided, it's best to try the round in two parts. When that is successful, three parts can be tried.

Part Singing

The most noticeable change from primary to upper grades in terms of singing is the addition of songs in parts. In one sense, part singing begins with the singing of rounds, but in such songs all students are singing the same melody. Starting with a few songs in third or fourth grade, teachers can introduce music with additional parts.

Rounds are an effective first step in teaching singing in parts. A more advanced use of the principle of rounds is singing two songs that can be sung simultaneously, or what are usually called *partner songs*. For example, "Dixie" and "Yankee Doodle" can be sung at the same time, as can the rounds "Three Blind Mice" and "Row, Row, Row Your Boat." A surprising number of songs can be combined, and books containing rounds and partner songs are available.

An "echo" song is like a round, but instead of a continuous melody, it features short statements or fragments.

FOLLOW ME

Traditional

A more advanced step in teaching part singing is to present a song in which the second part is sung on one note or chanted. Such a part is easier to learn and to maintain than a second melody. "Chicka-Hanka" (page 87) contains a line consisting of only one pitch. The words "chicka-hanka" are intended to imitate the sounds of an old steam engine puffing. The second part presents a rhythmic challenge, but if the singers start each phrase at the right time and accent the syllable "hank," they can sing it correctly. A few students can also perform the line on rhythm instruments such as sandblocks, woodblocks, or maracas to add variety.

CHICKA-HANKA

Track Laborer's Song

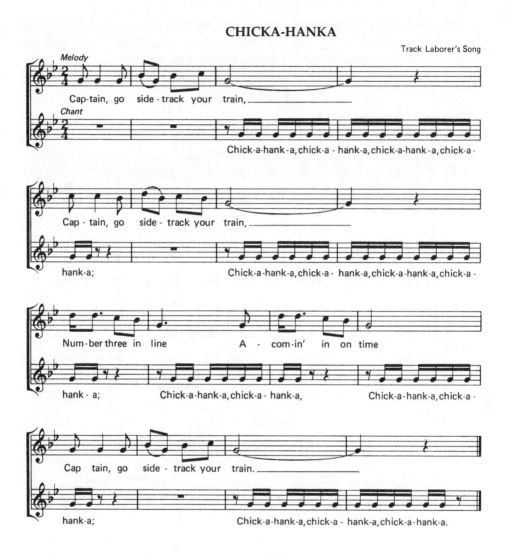

Another way to introduce part singing is to insert a few pitches that move parallel to the melody at the interval of a third or its inversion, a sixth. If the added part also has the same rhythm as the melody, it is relatively easy to learn. Initially, it may be wise to introduce a part in thirds (or sixths) for only a phrase or two of a song.

In "Marianina" the last few measures provide an optional part in small notes. Such short additional phrases are a good way to inject part singing into a song.

The first and third lines of "Marianina" are identical, and the second and fourth are similar. Several phrases appear in *sequence;* that is, the same melodic pattern recurs at a different pitch level. Noticing such points of similarity will help the students to learn the music more quickly.

When the class is comfortable singing the last few notes of "Marianina" in thirds, they can be asked to sing the first five lines entirely in thirds, with the exception of the last note of line 2, where a fourth sounds better.

MARIANINA

Words adapted by Mary Val Marsh

Italian Folk Song

Source: Mary Val Marsh et al., *Spectrum of Music*, Book 4. 1980, Macmillan.

Helping Out-of-Tune Singers

Many children in kindergarten and first grade seem unable to sing in tune. In fact, about one-third or more of all first graders have some trouble in this regard. The problem gradually disappears for most children, so that by the end of fifth grade that percentage has dropped to about 10 percent. It is encouraging to observe that with music instruction the difficulties with out-of-tune singing are greatly reduced. Less encouraging is the fact that in the meantime they may be acquiring negative attitudes about their musical interests and abilities. Like adults, children tend to dislike activities they don't do well. Likewise, the opposite is true: They enjoy activities in which they succeed.

Why do children so often have trouble singing on pitch when they enter first grade? There are several reasons.

1. Many parents do not sing to their children. Research data indicate that the amount of music activity in the home has much to do with the child's musical capacities upon entering school. Children who have had a limited music background simply need time and experience to gain the ability to sing on pitch.

2. Some children have not yet gained the concept of high and low pitch. They do not understand what they are to do with their voices.

3. Some children seem unable to pay attention long enough to learn a song. It is performed for them, but they fail to concentrate when listening or trying to sing.

4. Some children have not learned the muscle movements necessary to make their voices change pitch accurately. They tend to drone within a narrow pitch range, because they are unable to get the voice to sing higher (or occasionally lower).

5. Some children cannot hear the difference between pitches. True monotones—those who are unable to distinguish between pitches at all—are rare, something on the order of 1 percent. It is true that some people hear pitch more accurately than others, but almost everyone can learn to carry a tune.

6. A few children have vocal problems such as nodules on the vocal cords that prevent them from singing well. The nodule condition can be corrected with therapy and/or surgery. If a teacher suspects nodules on a child's vocal cords—a condition that makes the voice sound husky—the child should be encouraged to sing only softly or to stop singing entirely until a medical examination can be conducted.

7. A few children demonstrate good pitch discrimination except when they themselves sing. Apparently they lack the normal aural feedback of their own voices. Many of these children can eventually succeed in instrumental performance.

What can be done to help out-of-tune singers? To begin with, they should never be given the idea that something is seriously and irrevocably wrong! After all, most such children will eventually overcome the problem. Children who have trouble carrying a tune should not be singled out in front of their peers. The teacher should not bend over them and sing into their ears, nor should the youngsters be asked to sing in front of the group or to remain silent because their singing doesn't "contribute to the class." If they volunteer to sing alone, they should be encouraged to do so. But teachers should not mislead them by saying, "That's fine!" when in fact their singing is poor. It is more productive and honest to offer such comments as, "I'm glad you volunteered to sing for us," or "Your words were clear and easy to understand." Even in first grade, children can sense when their singing is faulty. The attitude of the teacher should be, "Let's work to make it better."

Probably the best way to help out-of-tune singers is to work with them privately or in a small group. This can take place during recess or lunch period, so long as the children do not regard the sessions as punishment.

Music specialists differ somewhat on how to help nonsingers. Some teachers believe the first step should be to help these children discover what it sounds like to be in unison with a given pitch. That is what the teacher in this example is trying to do. In this case the teacher sings the pitches, but they may also be played on a keyboard.

> Josh, sing what you think is your best note—the one that feels most comfortable for you and sounds best. When you find it, hold it while I sing that same note. . . .
>
> Okay. Now listen carefully to how it sounds when you and I are exactly together on that note. The two sounds seem to agree. Try it again. . . . That's the idea. . . . Now, let me sing the note again and you match it. . . . Better. Do it again. . . .
>
> Now let's move up one note from the pitch we've been singing. Think of moving your voice up just a short step.

If the child is able to move up a step and match pitch, then another note, perhaps the next step higher, can be attempted. Sometimes it helps if the child rather than the teacher plays the note on the keyboard instrument. Also, the child may find that putting a hand over one ear helps focus attention on his or her own voice.

Other music specialists have observed that children in the first grade seem to have two types of voices, a "chest" or "speaking" voice and a "head" or "singing" voice. The singing voice is about five notes higher than the speaking voice. After the children learn to recognize the difference between the two voices, they can be encouraged to use the singing voice for music. A teacher might say to a child who is droning in a chest voice, "That's your speaking voice. Now try it with your singing voice." Both the pitch-matching procedure and the singing-voice procedure appear to work when applied consistently.

After the sensation of unison pitch matching or using the singing voice has been experienced, other techniques can be tried.

1. Ask the child to imitate a siren by gradually raising and lowering the pitch level of his or her voice. This promotes the concept of changing pitch level without requiring the child to match exact pitches.

2. Invite the student to indicate with his or her hands the approximate pitch level of what is being heard or sung. One pattern can be sung to the words "Bounce my ball." As the words are sung, the child makes a bouncing motion with his or her hands, palms down, but with the height above the floor regulated by the relative pitch levels. A wide interval, even an octave, works well in this routine, because the rhythmic flow gives a feeling of energy and momentum, and the sudden leap in pitch encourages vocal flexibility.

Bounce   my   ball!

3. Give the out-of-tune singer extra practice on the echo patterns that are sung in music class to help all children sing pitches more accurately.

4. Record the out-of-tune singer during these practice sessions if the child does not become self-conscious. Listening to oneself on a recording makes self-evaluation more objective.

5. Suggest that the out-of-tune singer make up a short tune to sing. Sometimes a child who sings on only one pitch will make up tunes that require singing a variety of pitches.

6. Ask the student to imitate the sound of a cuckoo—the descending interval of a third found in so many children's songs around the world.

7. Invite the out-of-tune singer to pick out familiar tunes at the piano or on the bells. These instruments provide visual and physical reinforcement of the distance between pitches.

Some children may need special help for several months. Some may achieve the unison sensation once or twice, only to lose it by the next day. Patience is needed to help those who find it hard to sing on pitch. Efforts at helping them are well worth a teacher's attention, however, because their outlook toward music in later years will benefit from early correction of singing difficulties.

Selection of Songs

The songs in the music series books are graded and selected for elementary school students, but a teacher can be flexible in borrowing music recommended for another grade level. There is nothing "written in stone" about placement of songs according to grade level. Four factors seem to determine where songs are placed. One is the length of the song. Young children are more likely to lose interest when a song is long, so most material suggested for primary grades is short.

A second factor is the amount of repetition in a song. If lines or phrases are repeated, that makes learning easier. An example of such a song is "Old Mac-Donald," in which the response "Ee-i-ee-i-o" appears after each phrase of the text.

OLD MACDONALD

Children can learn the nonsense phrase quickly and then chime in on it as the entire song is sung by the teacher or played on a CD. The remainder of the song presents only a limited number of musical ideas. "Old MacDonald had a farm" and "On that farm he had some chicks" are sung to the same melody. The "chick-chick" segment is sung entirely on one note.

The song "John the Rabbit" features a two-word refrain that stays on the same pitch six times. Students can join in on the "oh yes" statement with enthusiasm.

A third factor in the placement of songs according to grade level is the text. If possible, it should involve something that children have experienced. This is why

JOHN THE RABBIT

many songs in primary grade music books deal with topics of home, school, and adult occupations that are visible in the community, such as firemen and school bus drivers. The words of the text should be understandable to the children. Long, complicated words should be avoided, unless they are vital to the text.

A fourth factor in song selection is how musically complex the song is. Singing in parts is seldom attempted before the third grade, so songs that depend on two or more simultaneous melodic lines are best introduced in the upper grades. Rounds, a good preparation for part singing, are often introduced in primary grades.

CODA

Singing is basic in music. For this reason, classroom teachers should do what they can to help their students learn to sing in a competent manner. Granted, most teachers do not feel particularly skilled when it comes to singing, but a high level of skill isn't needed. A clear tone with reasonably accurate pitch is enough. The fact that the teacher sings and is able to help his or her students learn to sing better can make a huge difference in how children feel about music and how much they learn.

PROJECTS

1. Select one song in this chapter. Practice singing it, using the suggestions for improving your singing, especially getting in your "head" voice. Be sure to start on the right pitch by checking with an instrument. If possible, record yourself singing the song. At first, you may be disappointed in the sound of your voice. But sing the song several times again, trying each time to make it better.

2. Practice demonstrating the difference between saying words and singing them. To do this, select a phrase from a song you know; "My country 'tis of thee" is one possibility. First, say the words. Next, sing them by sustaining the various vowel sounds. Finally, think of how you would describe what you did, to make singing instead of speaking, to a class of elementary school students.

3. Practice starting a song for a group of singers (maybe even your elementary methods class!). Make sure you follow the procedures suggested in this chapter.

SKILL DEVELOPMENT

Learn the note "low E" on the recorder. It is fingered:

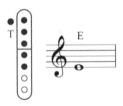

1. Practice fingering the following phrases silently in rhythm on your recorder as you name the notes.

2. Play each of the measures on your recorder. Try to keep your fingers rather relaxed and do not lift them more than one inch above the holes when they are not in use. Start slowly, and then gradually increase the speed with which you play the notes.

3. Practice the rhythm of the following measures on the syllable "tah."

REVIEW QUESTIONS

1. Why shouldn't children be urged to sing at a very loud dynamic level?
2. What can teachers do to help their students develop the difference between talking and singing?
3. What is the approximate vocal range of children when they are first graders?
4. What steps should teachers follow when starting students on a song, including those that they know?
5. What are the disadvantages of teaching a song from a CD?
6. What conditions should be met to sing a round successfully?
7. How is singing in parts introduced to elementary school students?
8. What steps can teachers use to help students who have difficulty singing with accurate pitch?
9. What makes some songs more suitable for primary grades and others more suitable for upper grades?

Teaching about Melodies

- Concept of High and Low
- Melody
- Pitch and Instruments
- Melodic Steps and Leaps
- Phrases
- Teaching Major and Minor
- Teaching the Notation of Pitch

Because singing is such an integral part of music in the elementary schools, it is an area where the contributions of classroom teachers are needed and helpful. Although they may not be able to do everything that is presented here, classroom teachers can very likely do some of them.

Concept of High and Low

The word "pitch" itself is not very important to elementary school students, but gaining a concept of high and low certainly is. This process is made a bit more difficult for teachers, because "high" and "low" are sometimes used by people to describe how loud a sound is. For example, they sometimes talk about "turning the volume down low" on a radio or TV.

In this lesson the teacher is helping children to associate the pitch level of sounds with the terms "high" and "low."

For the past few music lessons, we've been calling sound "high" or "low" or "medium." Now here's a problem for you to solve. I'm going to play some notes on the keyboard, and you tell me how high or low they are. What should we call this sound: high, low, or medium?

[The class responds that the note is high.]

What about this sound: high, low, or medium?

[The class responds that the note is low.]

That was pretty easy. The first sound was much higher than the second. Now you'll hear two more sounds. Here's the first one: high, low, or medium?

[The class, guessing the answer ahead of time, enthusiastically replies, "Medium!"]

What about this sound: high, low, or medium?

[The class hesitates, then a few children propose that the sound is medium.]

DeVon, the class says both sounds are medium. Does that mean those two sounds are the same? [If DeVon answers incorrectly, the teacher plays the two sounds again and asks another child to compare the two sounds.]

One sound is higher and one is lower, even though both of them are sort of medium. When we decide how high or low a sound is, our answer depends on the other sounds around it. A tall person doesn't seem so tall when he stands with other tall people. But when he stands with short people, he seems even taller! Sounds are like that when we describe how high or low they are.

The echo-singing of two-note patterns is one way to help children concentrate on pitch, especially the "cuckoo" interval (descending minor third in musical terms). The taunt "Johnny has a girlfriend" is one example of this interval. In the following lesson, the children imitate the "cuckoo" interval sung to them by the teacher. In this example the teacher sings the notes. They could be sounded on a recorder or on a keyboard, but singing is preferable.

> Today we're going to sing little bits of songs back and forth. Listen carefully as I sing, then you sing the notes back to me. Do all of you know about a bird called a cuckoo? It's a bird that sings a short two-note call. Let's start by imitating the sound of a cuckoo. Listen to me first; I'll sing the cuckoo call two times.

> Cuck-oo,   cuck-oo

> Now all of you sing the cuckoo call twice after I sing it." [The class sings the pattern.] "Good! I think some of you are ready to sing the cuckoo song back to me all by yourself. I'll go around the class and give a chance to as many of you as I can. Michele, let's start with you. Listen carefully and sing back what I sing.

If the interval is being repeated many times in succession, the teacher should change the pitch level occasionally. Continual use of the same pitches is tiring for both the teacher and the children.

Simple games can be devised to help children become more aware of pitch levels. The teacher may:

1. Play or sing pairs of pitches and ask individuals to tell which pitch is higher.

2. Invite various children to "play teacher" by sounding the pairs of pitches and deciding whether the responses of their classmates are correct.

3. Sound an interval twice in succession. For the first hearing, the children should notice which sound is higher and which is lower. When the interval is repeated, they should show with their hands or other body movement which pitch is which. For example, for the low pitch in the second pair, they might crouch or put their hands on their toes, and for the high pitch they might put their hands above their heads. Asking the children to close their eyes during this game encourages careful listening and discourages copying other children.

4. Pass out six or eight bells (one to each child) in random pitch order. Then invite them to discover the relative pitch of each bell and arrange themselves in order from low to high.

Some songs are especially good for aiding children in developing a sense of pitch. In the song "Tony Chestnut," the opening four notes outline a chord, and the second portion of the first line is a descending scale. The actions that accompany the singing emphasize the play on words that is apparent in the boy's name: On the syllable "To(e)," bend over and touch the toes; on "-ny," touch the knees, on "chest," straighten up and touch the chest, and on "nut," touch the top of the

TONY CHESTNUT

Traditional

To - ny Chest-nut, touch your fin - gers to the ground, To - ny Chest-nut, way up high.

head. On the words "Touch your fingers to the ground," wiggle the fingers while moving the arms and hands to the toes for the beginning of the next line.

It is only a short extension of the high-low concept to the notion of melodic lines ascending or descending ("going up" or "going down"). In "Tony Chestnut" the children can discover that the first five notes ascend and the next several notes descend. Simple pictures can be drawn and posted to provide visual reinforcement for the idea of pitch direction.

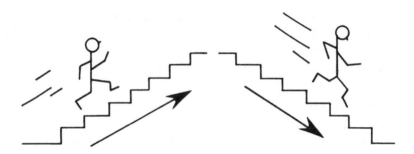

Melody

A verbal definition of melody, such as "A melody is a cohesive series of pitches," is largely wasted on children in elementary school, partly because the definition itself contains words that need to be defined. Knowing a few basic music terms is valuable, however, because a word can say something more precisely and clearly than a description like "a bunch of notes that seem to belong together."

Here is how a teacher might help a class understand what the word "melody" means.

The other day you learned a song called "Tony Chestnut." Let's stand up and sing it again, with the actions. [The class sings the song.]

Did you notice the direction that your hands moved on the first four notes? You made them go higher, because that's the way the notes sound at the beginning of this song. In what direction do the notes move on "Touch your fingers to the ground?" Sing it and show me. [The class members move their hands in a downward direction.] That's right! The notes get lower; they go down.

Because you're listening to the music so well, I think I'd better ask you to do something harder. Sing the song using only the sound "loo" without the words. Then tell me if it's still the same tune. Think what your answer is going to be as you sing. [The class sings the song with "loo."]

Okay now. Did you still sing the tune for "Tony Chestnut" when you didn't sing the words and just sang with "loo"? [The class responds, with some disagreement among the children about whether or not they did.]

You're both right—in a way. The words are needed if someone wants to know how the whole song goes. But a person who already knows the song would recognize what you were singing just from hearing the *melody* you sang with "loo."

That word "melody" is an important word in music. Every song has its own melody, it's own special group of high, medium, and low notes—with certain places where the tune gets higher or lower or stays the same. When notes seem to belong together, they make a melody. The melody for "Tony Chestnut" is what you sang with "loo," and it's the same no matter what words you put with it.

Here is one way in which a teacher can emphasize the sense of cohesiveness that is necessary if successive pitches are to be perceived as a melody.

I'm going to sound some pitches on the bells, but I'll do it without looking or thinking. [The teacher randomly strikes bars in no recognizable rhythmic or melodic pattern.]

Is that the melody you'd like to sing? [The consensus is "no."] No, because the notes don't seem to seem to belong together. Think of our class right here. You belong together; you do things together. You're not just 24 children who get thrown into a room to ignore one another. The notes in a melody have something to do with one another, and that's what makes a melody sound good, instead of just being a bunch of scattered notes.

Pitch and Instruments

Most of the melodic instruments played by children in the primary grades are of the simple keyboard type. Although they don't have keys to be depressed as on a piano, the bars of the xylophone, metallophone, and similar instruments are arranged with the pitches in the same horizontal pattern. This creates confusion for some children. After getting accustomed to describing pitches with "high/low" words and actions, they are now told that "high" is to their right on the instrument they have in front of them. In other words, the terms for vertical alignment are now employed for horizontal alignment.

One aid in overcoming this inconsistency is a simple xylophone instrument called the Step Bells, which is shown on the next page. The pitches on it follow the horizontal keyboard arrangement and ascend from left to right, but they do so with each pitch raised in stair-step fashion. In this way, children are better able to relate the vertical and horizontal aspects of pitch arrangement. If step bells are not

Step bells

available, a metallophone or other xylophone-like instrument can be propped up on a table or hung on the wall so that the bars are viewed vertically.

In this lesson the teacher encourages the children to notice certain facts about pitch and instruments.

> Julie, would you please take the mallet and strike each bar on the Step Bells? Go from the one nearest the table up to the one that's highest off the table. [Julie plays the bells in ascending order.]

> Class, what was the order of the pitches that Julie played? Did they move from high to low, or low to high? [The class reports hearing the low-to-high direction.]

> That's right, low to high. Kevin, you try the bells this time. Start with the bar highest off the table and play them in order moving toward the table top. [Kevin plays the Step Bells in descending order, and the class notices the high-to-low direction.]

When the children understand pitch relationships on the Step Bells or on a vertically positioned instrument, they can move on to instruments that have the keyboard arrangement on a horizontal plane. The transition can be aided by having the children discover that high and low pitches can be determined by their placement to the right or left, and by the relative length of the bars, with the longer bars being lower.

Some songs in the music series books have optional parts for instruments. These can contribute to the students' understanding of pitch and melody, but they shouldn't be allowed to consume too much class time. The children's singing should have first priority, and classroom instruments are limited in their ability to enhance this skill. Bell-like instruments sound pitches an octave higher than the voice. Their percussive tones do not provide as good a model for singing as instruments like the flute or violin, which can sustain sounds. Although classroom instruments are not the best aids for developing pitch discrimination and vocal tone, they do provide variety within the music class, and introduce children to the vast and rewarding world of instrumental music.

Melodic Steps and Leaps

As children grow in their understanding of melody, they should begin to notice the relative closeness of pitches to one another. Intervals of a whole or half step are referred to as being one *step* apart. Larger intervals are described as *leaps*. In the following lesson the teacher helps the class decide whether an interval is a step or a leap. The song is shown below.

> Last week you learned a song called "The Little Chickens." Let's sing it again today to see how well you remember it. Here's the starting note: Rea-dy sing. [The class sings the song.]

> That's good! Now we're going to find out how far one note is from the next one. Listen to the first five notes of "The Little Chickens" while I play them slowly on the bells. As you listen, decide if the notes are "next door" to each other, which is a *step*, or if they're farther apart than that, which is a *leap*. [The teacher plays the first five notes, then helps the class to discover that they move up by step.]

> So we have five notes, each one a step away from its neighbor. What about the notes on the words "chickens"? [The teacher plays the two notes, which happen to be the "cuckoo" interval or descending minor third. The class discovers that the interval is a leap.]

The teacher can proceed through the song, asking the children to decide whether various intervals form a step or leap. Variations of this procedure include singing the intervals, asking the children to sing or play the intervals, and showing, by the use of hand motions, the relative distance between steps and leaps.

The teacher can try other intervals on subsequent days. Intervals smaller than the "cuckoo" pattern are somewhat more difficult for children who have trouble discerning pitch differences. Intervals in which the notes are quite far

LOS POLLITOS ("The Little Chickens")

Mexican Children's Song

Los pol - li - tos di - cen: pi - o, pi - o, pi - o,
Hear the lit - tle chick - ens peep - ing, peep - ing, peep - ing,

cuan - do tie - nen ham - bre, cuan - do tie - nen fri - o.
when___ they are hun - gry, when___ they are cold.___

apart are also difficult, not because they are hard to hear, but because children with a limited singing range simply have trouble reproducing widely separated pitches. For variety, the teacher can play pitch patterns on an instrument such as a recorder or keyboard.

Phrases

Phrases in music are like phrases in language: they are logical groupings of sounds or words that stand together as a single idea. On a page of a book or magazine, phrases are marked off by commas, semicolons, and periods. In music, stopping places are also indicated with varying degrees of conclusion, primarily through the choice of notes and chords at phrase endings. If a song is well written, the phrases of the text and of the music will coincide.

Noting the similarity of phrases in speaking and in singing helps to reinforce the concept of phrases.

> Phrases in music are like phrases in speaking. You've been phrasing ever since you learned to talk—and you didn't even know you were so talented! When you talk, you don't run all your words together or say them all in the same way. Remember when you learned patterns in rhythm? You discovered that people don't talk like a machine "with-all-sounds-exactly-alike." You make certain sounds stronger or higher, and you group them in certain ways so that other people will understand what you mean.

Children in primary grades can learn whether phrases are alike or different. In the song "Tony Chestnut" (p. 100) they can sing the song and then decide how many phrases there are. Further examination will help them see that two phrases are identical until the halfway point, and then they differ.

Students can also begin to sense the statement-answer phrase patterns that appear in many songs. Often one phrase seems to present the first half of a musical statement, and the second phrase seems to respond to it. This pattern can be seen in both "All Night, All Day" (page 83) and "Tony Chestnut."

Teaching Major and Minor

Recognizing the difference between major and minor in songs contributes to learning about music. An easy first step in learning to compare the difference in sound between major and minor keys is to sing a simple song like "Go Tell Aunt Rhody" in both keys. The original version is provided here.

The teacher can use the song if available in a book, or copy it and pass out photocopies, or project it on an overhead projector.

> Here's a song that uses notes arranged in a certain pattern called *major*. The song looks pretty simple. Let's sing it. I'll go first. [The teacher either sings it or plays a recording of it, and then the class sings the song.]

GO TELL AUNT RHODY

Pennsylvania Dutch Song

Go tell Aunt Rho - dy, go tell Aunt Rho - dy,

go tell Aunt Rho - dy, the old gray goose is dead.

> That's the way! You either have good memories from singing this song before, or you're turning into good sight-readers. You've just performed this song the way it's usually heard, which is major. Now let's change its character by singing it in minor. It's not really hard to do. Listen to the sound of the major scale for "Go Tell Aunt Rhody." [The teacher play the first five notes on a keyboard or similar instrument.]

> Just lower the third step of the scale by one half-step. Listen to the sound of minor scale. [The teacher plays the first five notes, with the third note lowered one half-step, which is E♭.] That lowered note happens to be the note the song begins on. I'll play the first three notes of "Go Tell Aunt Rhody" in minor so you can hear how minor sounds.

Other familiar songs in minor can be pointed out, and some of them can be sung. Experiencing a number of songs in minor helps the students to get the quality of minor in their ears.

Often songs in minor keys have the seventh step of the scale raised one half-step to help establish the tonal center. For this reason it's not unusual to see an occasional ♯ or ♮ in songs that are in minor. "Tum-Balalaika," for example (see page 106), contains several C♯s, as well as parts that move in thirds for several measures.

Teaching the Notation of Pitch

A note is a printed symbol that serves two purposes. By its appearance it indicates how long a particular sound should last, and it also shows how high or low the sound should be. This latter function of notes is described here, and the length of notes in the next chapter.

TUM-BALALAIKA

Jewish Folk Song
Arranged by Mary Val Marsh

Boys: Maid - en, maid - en, can you ex - plain, What can
Girls: Fool - ish boy, I can___ ex - plain, A stone can

grow with - out an - y rain? What___ can burn for
grow with - out an - y rain. True love can burn for

man - y a year? What___ can cry, and shed not a tear?
man - y a year. A sad heart can cry, and shed not a tear.

Refrain

Tum - ba - la, Tum - ba - la, Tum - ba - la - lai - ka, Tum - ba - la,

Tum - ba - la, Tum - ba - la, Tum - ba - la - lai - ka, Tum - ba - la,

Tum - ba - la, Tum - ba - la - lai - ka, Tum - ba - la - lai - ka,

Tum - ba - la, Tum - ba - la - lai - ka, Tum - ba - la,

Tum - ba - la - lai - ka, Tum - ba - la - lai - ka, Tum - ba - la, tum!

tum, Tum - ba - la, tum, Tum - ba - la, Tum - ba - la, tum!

Children do not need to begin learning music notation by looking at conventional notes. Rather, the use of a one- or two-line staff, with notes placed in relative positions around those lines, is a good beginning step. Here are two examples of such notation.

A one-line staff is enough for melodies that have only a few notes close together in pitch. A two-line staff is better if the melody contains five adjacent levels of pitch. The clef sign, bar lines, and key signature are missing, because they are not needed at this point. Here is how a teacher could introduce the notation of pitch.

> I think you're ready to look at pictures of different notes. First, let's start by putting down two lines that run along together sideways. One step is the distance from a line to the next space, or from a space to the next line. With two lines, we can show five steps. [The teacher draws lines on the chalkboard and inserts the word "step" between them.]

STEP

—— STEP ——

STEP

—— STEP ——

STEP

> Now I'll put some notes on the lines and spaces, and you tell me how far apart the notes are, and whether the sound moves higher or lower. Here's an example. [The teacher draws a note head under the bottom line and another slightly to the right and on the bottom line.]

> The interval moves up a step, doesn't it? It will sound like this. [The teacher plays an ascending whole step on the metallophone. Then another note is added in the space above the second note, and the class comments that it is higher by one step.]

> Very good reading! Now, let's see if you can play on the bells the notes I put on the board. [The teacher draws two more notes, one on the upper line and another on the space above it.]

Kelly, here are five bells, arranged by step from lowest to highest. That means the bell on your left is the sound for the lowest spaced note on the board. First, play all your notes in order from low to high as I point to them on the board. [Kelly plays the notes.] Wonderful! Now I'll point to two notes on the board and see if you can play them on the bells.

The students should sing with each pattern after hearing it on the bells. Next, they may try to sing directly from the notation, but this is usually more difficult than singing by imitation or playing the pattern on an instrument. They may also come to the board individually to draw or point to notes for the class to perform.

Should students learn to read music? Clearly, that is desirable. But note reading is a skill that requires considerable time to develop for most elementary school students. Granted, some students take piano lessons or in other ways are exposed to notation and learn to read it to some extent. And there is a program involving electronic keyboard that has been designed for use by elementary school classes. It is the *Music in Education* program developed by the Yamaha Corporation. Keyboards help in learning notation because of the visual benefit of seeing the pattern of whole and half steps.

Music education has a long history of debating the relative merits of two systems of teaching music reading through singing. One is the traditional solfa syllables—*do, re, me, fa, sol, la, ti,* and then *do* again. The other way is to use of numbers for the notes in a scale; "1" is the first step of the scale, "2" the second, and so on. Both are successful, *if practiced consistently and persistently.* Probably the music specialist with take the lead in this matter, but classroom teachers may follow up and have their students practice on days when they don't meet with the music specialist.

The value of both the solfa syllables and numbers is that they help provide a sense of relative distance from one pitch to another. The triad built on the home note of a scale is 1-3-5, and a triad built on the second note of the scale is 2-4-6, and so on. In solfa syllables the triad on the first note of the scale is *do-mi-sol,* and the triad on the second note of the scale is *re-fa-la,* and so on. Students already understand the relationship among numbers, but they are not quite as singable as the solfa syllables; "seven" must be sung as "sev'n," for example. The disadvantage of the solfa syllables is that they need to be learned first, and then a pattern like *do-mi-sol* will be helpful. Both of these patterns are only aids in learning to read. Students can also practice singing on a neutral syllable. In fact, the more complex the music is, the less useful numbers or syllables become.

CODA

Most classroom teachers are not going to have the main responsibility for teaching their students to sing better and to use music notation. But if teachers understand some of the basic procedures, then they are more likely to follow up on the efforts of music specialists. Classroom teachers truly can make a noticeable difference in how well their students learn to sing.

PROJECTS

1. Make ten pictures containing pairs of objects, one that makes low sounds and the other that makes high sounds. Use objects that will be recognizable by children in the primary grades.

2. Using the song "Los Pollitos," list the steps you would follow in guiding elementary school students to recognize phrases in the music.

3. Find two songs in one of the music series books available in the music library. Decide how you would help students to hear the differences between the two songs.

4. Choose one of the songs you selected for the previous project. Listening to its CD, learn to sing it without someone helping you.

SKILL DEVELOPMENT

To play the song "Tom Dooley," you will need to learn the note low D. It is fingered:

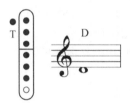

The recorder will squeak or not sound on low notes if you blow too hard. Make sure that all the holes are covered and blow gently. If you have trouble getting low D, play G, then low E, and then low D. Practice these patterns:

Here is the song "Tom Dooley."

1. Tap or clap the rhythm of the notes. Pay careful attention to the syncopation in measures 1, 3, 5, and 7. The second note occurs half-way through the first beat. Also make sure that the dotted half note gets three beats. The beats of the song move at a brisk pace.

2. Read through the song on the syllable "tah."

3. Read the note names of the song in rhythm as you finger the notes on your recorder. Notice that measures 1, 3, and 5 are exactly alike, which makes the song easier to learn.

4. Sing the song, first with letter names, and then with the words. Finger the notes as you sing.

5. Practice playing the song on the recorder. Breathe where you see the comma just above the staff. Work especially on measure 7, because it is different and contains several eighth notes in a row.

6. Play the song on a keyboard with your right hand. Play D with your thumb, E with the second finger, G with the third, A with the fourth, and B with your little finger.

7. Play the song on a mallet instrument.

REVIEW QUESTIONS

1. What procedures can a teacher follow to help students gain a concept of high and low pitches?

2. What interval seems to be nearly universal among children and children's songs?

3. Why is the song "Tony Chestnut" an especially good one for helping children to learn about pitches in music?

4. How can a teacher help students understand the cohesive nature needed for a group of notes to be considered a melody?

5. Why are Step Bells useful in helping children to understand how pitches are arranged on a keyboard or mallet instrument?

6. How might a teacher help students comprehend phrases in music?

7. What steps can a teacher follow to help students learn the difference between major and minor?

8. How might a teacher introduce the notation of pitch?

9. Which is preferable, learning to read music using numbers or solfa syllables? Does it make a difference which is used?

Listening to Music

Often people turn on a radio or CD player and say that they are "listening" to music as they study or jog or talk to friends. To most people in America today, music is used as a sonic background, which is certainly valid, of course. But having music as a background for other activities is not listening as musicians use that word. To most of them, listening means giving the music undivided attention, keen concentration, and contemplative thought. Because most people do not normally listen carefully to music in that way, music instruction in elementary schools needs to include experiences that help children listen in a more mentally active and analytical manner.

Unfortunately, several factors in American life work against the idea of careful listening.

1. Music is so pervasive in America that no one can pay careful attention to all, or even most, of it. The sounds emanating steadily from supermarkets, radios, airports, CD players, and so forth provide so much aural stimuli

that people find it hard to listen carefully. They simply fall into the habit of tuning out many, if not most, of the sounds that they hear every day.

2. Popular music is generally short and simple. Art or "classical" music tends to be longer and more complex, which requires much more concentration.

3. People expect most popular music to be loud. They are not accustomed to noticing music that does not capture their attention by being quite loud.

4. Most popular music contains little in the way of developing themes, which is a feature of art music.

Listening should be a part of all activities involving music. Children and adults need to listen as they sing a song or move to music. Virtually every class-room activity described in this book calls for careful listening in addition to the other activity. Students need to be reminded that they should listen as they sing, listen as they move to music, listen as they create music. Music exists in sound, and the only way sounds are perceived is through listening.

Listening to Concert Music

It is impossible to change society and significantly reduce the amount of music people hear each day, and that probably would not be desirable even if it were possible. What is possible, however, is to teach children to listen to different types of music in different ways. Much of the music they hear each day need be given only superficial attention, because it does not contain subtle or sophisticated uses of sounds. What they need to learn is to treat concert or art music in another way, to put on a different "set of ears" for it. Here are some suggestions for teach-ing this different approach for listening to music.

1. Before playing a musical work, try to do something to get the students interested in it. This could be telling something about the composer, type of music, a feature to listen for, or providing a visual aid such as puppet or a picture—anything that might serve to catch their interest.

2. Make sure you sound interested and enthusiastic about listening to the work.

3. Avoid talking too much. Two minutes should be long enough before the music is played. Limit background information to only what will help the students listen to the music.

4. Have the students become involved in listening. For example, they could

   • count the number of times a theme is heard;

   • decide if there are distinct melodies or sections and if they contain a pattern;

   • follow a "listening guide";*

* Available in the *Adventures in Music Listening* series by Leon Burton, Charles Hoffer, and William Hughes. Miami: Warner Bros. Publications, 1996, 1997, and 1999. The series has three books: kin-dergarten and primary (29 works), intermediate (20 works), and upper elementary (25 works). Each level has a teacher edition with CD and a student book that calls for student involvement. The kindergarten/primary book also has a "big book" with pictures related to the musical works.

- answer questions about the work, which are written on the chalkboard or handout;
- look at two or three pictures or graphics and decide which one best represents the music; and
- create a "doodle map" in which they draw their impressions of what they heard as the music plays. (If two parts of a work are quite different, their maps should reflect this fact.)

5. Keep the time when music is playing to two minutes or less with students in the primary grades, and only moderately longer with students in the upper elementary grades. Long works can be played, but they should be paused at appropriate places and the students given new information or instructions before resuming with the work.

6. Limit the number of features that the children are expected to notice in a single listening session. It's better to select a limited number of features and examine them more thoroughly. Kindergarten and first grade children may be able to attend to only one feature at a time. It is a good teaching procedure, however, to present a short work again and ask the youngsters to notice one or two additional features.

7. Play a work enough times for them to become familiar with it. The children should hear it often enough to recognize it, remember it, and enjoy it as one of their pieces. It should not be played so frequently that they tire of it, however. It can be interspersed with other selections to reflect a balance between familiar and unfamiliar music.

The teacher attempts to follow these suggestions in this example.

> Let's listen to a patriotic song from the Revolutionary War. Who can name some famous Americans who were living during those years? [Tony raises his hand and mentions George Washington and Benjamin Franklin.]
>
> That's right! The song was written by a man named William Billings, who made his living tanning leather but who loved music. His tune is so good that a composer 175 years later came along and used it as a melody for a piece of music for orchestra. His name was William Schuman. The tune has a name, a boy's name, "Chester." Schuman makes it easy for you to hear it, because the piece opens with a melody. Listen to it very carefully. When I pause the music, I'll ask you whether this would be a good piece of music to march to. [The teacher plays the first 47 seconds of "Chester."]
>
> How many of you think that would be a good piece to march to? Raise your hands. How many think it's *not* really marching music? [A majority of the class doesn't think it's good marching music.]
>
> I agree with most of you. I don't think it would be easy to march to "Chester." Did you notice that it seems to divide itself into four long phrases or lines? I'll play it again, and let's listen for those phrases. I'll write 1 2 3 4 on the chalkboard, and then I'll point to the number when the phrase comes

up in the music. [The teacher plays the opening 47 seconds again and points out the four phrases as they are heard in the music.]

So far, "Chester" has seemed like a pretty calm piece, hasn't it? Well, wait until Tuesday when you get to hear more of "Chester." It suddenly changes character and becomes very fast and lively.

When the class meets again, it could listen to the opening 47 seconds again, but the music would continue into the lively, brilliant section that uses melodic fragments from "Chester." The students could follow a "listening guide" or create a doodle map as they listen.

Program Music

Instrumental music that has nonmusical ideas associated with it, called *program music,* is attractive to children because it usually suggests images. Children need to realize, however, that instrumental music cannot truly tell a story. Only words, which can be sung in a song, are able to relate a specific message. Instrumental music can offer only general impressions. They are so general, in fact, that different stories can be made to go with the same instrumental work. When students become preoccupied with listening for certain events in the music, they are probably not listening to the work as a piece of music. Furthermore, they are apt to assume that all instrumental music is incomplete, and therefore not interesting, unless it has a story associated with it.

When program music is to be played for a class, the teacher might present it with an explanation similar to this:

Today we're going to hear a short piece called "Circus Polka." This piece by a man named Stravinsky is *not* trying to tell us any details about the clowns and animals and trapeze artists. Instead, he is giving us his impressions of a circus. The piece might remind you of a circus, but you won't be able to say, "Now he's telling us about the lion trainer," or "There's the music about cotton candy." Let's also listen to the meter of music. See if you can feel it in twos or threes.

Listening to Melodies

To many children, "melody" is synonymous with "song." As they move to the upper grades of elementary school, they should begin to understand that a melody can be more than a singable tune. When a melody is conceived as the basis for a longer work of music, it is called a *theme.* In instrumental music, the theme need not be songlike; in fact, it may be quite unsingable. It can be remembered by the mind, but sometimes when it is intended for instruments it may be too complex or too awkward to be sung without much practice and skill.

The second movement of a symphony or concerto usually features melodies, and such music, if not too long or complicated, is attractive to elementary school students. Here is how a teacher might present the second movement of Mendelssohn's Symphony No. 4 ("Italian").

Here's a part of a symphony by a man named Felix Mendelssohn. He lived in Germany about 150 years ago. The melody sounds almost like a song. To help you remember it, I'll play the beginning for you twice. But the melody doesn't start right away. First there's a short introduction for about 10 seconds. Okay, here we go. Listen carefully, because this music is not loud. It won't grab your attention like a lot of the music you're used to does. [The teacher plays the opening 45 seconds of the music twice.]

To appreciate Mendelssohn's later treatment of the melody, listeners must be able to remember its original sound, so committing the theme to memory is important. Teachers can aid that process by asking the students to participate in a limited way.

I'm going to play those beginning 45 seconds once more. This time, hum along softly with the orchestra. That will help you remember the melody.

The class needs to realize that symphonic music is generally longer than a song. This means that the listeners need to notice not only the melody itself, but also changes in the theme and the transitional music between themes. The teacher might continue:

The first melody in the music by Mendelssohn is sort of like a song that has four two-measure phrases. Can everyone hear that? Let's all hum it once more. I'll hold my fingers to show you the phrases. You can do it with me if you want to. [The teacher plays the music again and the students hum along.]

Good! Now it's starting to sound familiar to you, so this time I'll let the CD play longer. See if you can keep track of the four phrases as the song is repeated three more times. The first two phrases get changed quite a bit, but you'll recognize them. The notes are going to move evenly downward by a step. [The teacher plays about two minutes of the movement.]

On another day the teacher may want to continue working with the second movement of Mendelssohn's Symphony No. 4.

I hope you remember the melody that Mendelssohn composed for the second movement of his "Italian" Symphony, because we're going to listen to it some more today.

You'll hear the melody four times. But then the music gets kind of a "Halloween" feeling, because the instruments sort of quietly sneak around. Then you'll hear something different. That's when I want you to raise your hands. I'll stop the CD and ask you what's different about the music. [The students discover that the contrasting section is in major and has a rich full sound.]

Following the same basic procedure, the teacher can help the class notice other melodic features in this movement. Perhaps most obvious to most listeners is the fact that the main theme is accompanied by continuous "walking" notes in the low strings each time it appears. A somewhat harder point to notice is that the two-note figure near the end—the one that serves to unify the movement—is derived from the theme.

Skillful manipulation of themes is prevalent in much of the music heard in concert halls. In fact, it is the basis for many forms used in music.

Orchestral Instruments

Elementary school students should be introduced to the instruments used in a symphony orchestra at some point, usually around fourth grade. If students can recognize the sounds of most instruments in the orchestra or band, it helps in listening to instrumental music. No longer is the sound of a clarinet just another sound. It becomes a clarinet, and its sounds are therefore more meaningful.

There are four groups or families of instruments: strings, woodwinds, brasses, and percussion. All string instruments, except the harp, produce sound when a horsehair bow is drawn across a string or when the string is plucked. This family shares the same basic shape, as can be seen in the photographs. The strings on the instruments are held up from the hollow wooden body by a wooden bridge. The function of the body is to amplify the sound of the strings.

Violin

Both right and left arms and hands are important in playing string instruments. The fingers of the left hand determine the pitches by pressing the strings against a fingerboard. The shorter the amount of string allowed to vibrate, the

Bass viols

higher the pitch. Advanced string players rock their left hand rapidly back and forth, a motion called *vibrato,* to add warmth to the sound. The tone quality is also affected very much by how the bow is drawn across the strings.

It is important to remember that all sounds are made by molecules in the air vibrating against each other and then striking our eardrums. So for all instruments, including the voice, sounds are produced when something vibrates. These vibrations are visible on the strings when low pitches are being sounded; the vibrations are too small and fast to be seen on higher pitches.

The harp produces sound when its strings are plucked. The modern harp has several pedals that make it possible to change the pitch of strings and sound more notes.

All woodwinds make sound with the player's breath. And all originally had wooden bodies; the flute acquired a metal body about 100 years ago. The clarinet, oboe, and bassoon use reeds, which are cut from bamboo-like material that has been carefully shaped. The oboe and bassoon use two reeds wired together, and the clarinet uses one reed that is clamped on a mouthpiece. The sounds of the flute are produced when the player blows across a mouthpiece at just the right angle and speed of breath. Then the outgoing air streams collide with the incoming air stream, which produces the sound.

All woodwinds change pitch by opening and closing holes, either with the fingers or by the fingers operating key mechanisms. Sounds are started and stopped by the player's tongue. One of features of woodwind instruments is their distinctive tone qualities, whereas string instruments have a rather homogeneous timbre.

All brass instruments are made of metal. Players produce sounds by buzzing the membranes of their lips into a small cup-shaped mouthpiece as they blow. Brass instruments include trumpet, French horn, trombone, and tuba. They all function in a similar way, but differ significantly in size. The tuba is the largest and produces the lowest sounds of the brass instruments. The trumpet, French horn, and tuba change pitch through the use of valves, which change the length of the tubing. Trombones use a slide for this purpose. As with the woodwinds, sounds are started and stopped with the player's tongue. Brass instruments can alter their sounds through the use of a variety of mutes that can be inserted into the end or bell of the instrument. French horn players normally do this with their hand.

The percussion family contains a wide variety of instruments, but they all have one thing in common: They produce sound when they are struck (usually with sticks) or rattled. Drums are the most familiar percussion instruments. They consist of a hollow ring covered with plastic or animal skin and are sounded with sticks or the fingers and hands. They come in a wide variety of sizes but do not produce definite pitches. Kettledrums or timpani are the large drums that look like large copper bowls; they are tuned to specific pitches.

The xylophone and similar instruments have wooden or metal bars in the pattern of the piano keyboard. They are played with sticks, called mallets, and come in a variety of sizes.

A sizable number of less frequently heard instruments are also part of the percussion family. They include cymbals (large metal discs that are struck together), tambourine (a covered wooden ring with small metal discs in it), triangle, chimes, maracas (dried gourds that are shaken), wood block, claves (pronounced *clah-vays*—thick wooden pieces that are struck together), castanets (small hollowed out pieces of wood that are clicked together), as well as bells of various types and the gong.

Clarinets and
bassoons

Trumpets

Trombones and tuba

French horns

Timpani

An excellent way of acquainting students with instruments is to have students who are in the local middle or high school band or orchestra give brief (five minutes or so) demonstrations to the class. These presentations should include showing the instruments and telling how sounds are made on them. They can conclude with the secondary school student playing a song that elementary school students know from their music series books. Even though the playing level of the instrumentalists may not be very advanced, elementary students will almost always be impressed.

If such demonstrations cannot be arranged, several CDs and videotapes or DVDs are available that demonstrate orchestral instruments. One outstanding concert work that features instruments is Benjamin Britten's *Young Person's Guide to the Orchestra.* Its theme, originally by a seventeenth-century English composer named Henry Purcell, is a variation for each section of the orchestra. The work concludes with a lively fugue (a work with much imitation based on one theme) in which the theme (subject) is played by each section of instruments before being combined with Purcell's theme in long notes.

Orchestras and Bands

The symphony orchestra consists of about 100 players, of which half play string instruments. Other instruments have only one to four players on each. The typical seating arrangement is shown on the following page.

A concert band includes all the woodwind, brass, and percussion instruments found in the orchestra, but no strings except maybe one string bass. It also includes several instruments not usually heard in orchestras, such as saxophones in several sizes and baritone horns or euphoniums. The size of a band can vary between 50

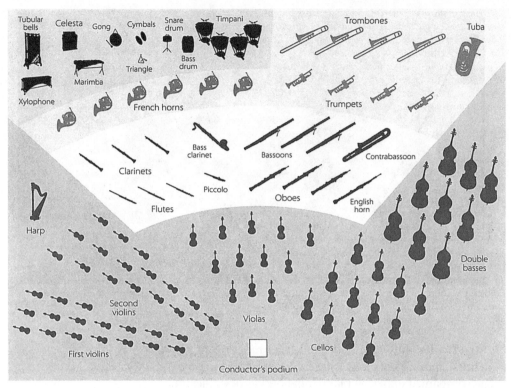

The instruments of the symphony orchestra are grouped into four families according to the way they produce sound: strings, woodwinds, brasses, and percussion. This illustration shows a typical seating plan, although exact number and placement of the instruments can vary.

to 100 players. Marching bands are usually larger than concert bands and feature versions of wind and percussion instruments that can be heard better outdoors.

Conductors of orchestras and concert bands stand on a podium so they can be seen more easily by the players. They also usually use a stick or *baton* in their hand to make their conducting gestures more visible. They look at (or occasionally have memorized) a copy of the music called the *score* that shows what every instrument part is playing; the players in the band or orchestra see only their own part.

Choral Groups

Elementary schools often have a volunteer choral group that meets before or after school and is led by a music specialist. Usually these groups sing music in unison or two parts.

High school and adult choral groups generally sing music that involves four voice groupings. The *soprano* is the higher female voice, whereas the *alto* is the lower female voice. The *tenor* is the higher male voice, and the *bass* (pronounced "base") is the lower male voice. Choral groups can vary greatly in size. They

Gainesville Youth Chorus-Concert Choir

stand when they sing and often have memorized the music. A large amount of choral music exists that is unaccompanied, or *a cappella*. Other choral works are accompanied either by piano, pipe organ, or orchestra.

Informal Listening

There are many opportunities in elementary school classrooms for listening to music in a nondirective way. These situations should not replace the more organized listening activities that have been presented in this chapter. Rather, they are supplementary. Their purpose is to help students hear music in an unobtrusive way.

When are those times for casual listening to music? Any time the students are in a quiet or studying situation. In the lower grades, these times may be during breaks or "rest" periods. Teachers may play music at a rather soft level. In the upper grades, these times could be when they are working in workbooks or doing quiet reading.

The music chosen for such occasions should be of concert quality. It may be from recognized composers, but it can also include musicals and music other than currently popular music, which is often distracting to the students.

One highly successful classroom teacher had a group of about a dozen CDs that she would play for her fifth grade class throughout the year during study times. The students soon learned the names of the works and/or composers of these CDs. She would then rotate the choice of music among the students in the class. She made a point of asking students who normally would not have made any such requests to choose a selection, which encouraged a greater sense of participation.

Listening to Live Performances

Listening to music should not be confined to recorded music. There is at least one big advantage to listening to someone performing music in a live performance. Hearing someone perform in your presence has a much greater impact than listening to a CD or watching a videotape or DVD; there is something attention grabbing about it. For this reason, teachers should have students who take piano lessons perform for the class every so often. Recess periods when the weather restricts going outside is one such logical time.

When students perform for their peers, it is crucial to establish a positive situation prior to the performance. Teachers need to talk briefly about how everyone should be supportive of all the performers; no negative remarks should be permitted! After all, it can be pointed out, many of them are not able to perform at all themselves!

Quite often music specialists will arrange for students in their music classes to attend a children's concert by an orchestra or band at a location other than the school. Sometimes a local high school performing organization will come to the elementary school to present a performance. Students need to be instructed in the clearest possible terms about their behavior at these performances. They should learn proper concert etiquette, including:

1. To applaud by clapping only at the conclusion of a work. Applause is also in order when the conductor enters after the group is seated. Verbal comments are out of order!

2. To listen to the music quietly. There should be no talking or wiggling around as music is being played.

3. If the performance takes place at a location other than their school, remind the students that they are representing the school and good behavior before, during, and after the event is expected.

CODA

Young people today grow up surrounded by music. It is so pervasive that they learn not to pay attention to it. For this reason, both music specialists and classroom teachers have their work cut out for them in helping students to improve their listening skills. That is why elementary school students need guidance in listening. But the effort is well worth it in terms of enabling students to hear more of what musical works have to offer.

PROJECT

Examine one of the teacher's edition books for each grade level, 1–5, for works included primarily for listening. Analyze the nature and number of the suggestions provided for helping students to listen. Also notice the length and nature of the musical works selected and how they change as the grade level becomes higher.

SKILL DEVELOPMENT

A new note is introduced for the recorder, F♯. It is fingered:

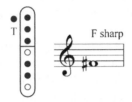

Up to this point, as each successive hole was covered, the pitch became lower. The note F♯ is different, because the first finger of the right hand does not cover its hole, but the second and third fingers cover their respective holes.

Practice the following patterns.

"Kum Ba Yah" is probably familiar to you. It starts on the low D you learned in the previous chapter and includes F♯.

KUM BA YAH

African Folksong

1. Tap or clap the rhythm of the notes. Pay careful attention to the dotted eighth/ sixteenth note. The dotted eighth note takes up three-fourths of the beat, leaving only one-fourth for the sixteenth note, which is quite a difference.

2. Say the note names in rhythm while you silently finger them on the recorder. Notice that measures 1 and 5 are identical.

3. Play the song. Try to make your playing as songlike as possible by quickly touching your tongue to the back of your front teeth to begin notes.

4. Sing the song using the note names.

5. Sing the song with the words.

6. Play the melody on a keyboard with your right hand. Play D with your thumb, F♯ with your second finger, and A with your fourth finger. Move your thumb up slightly to play the E at the end of the first line, and then move it back to D to start the second line.

REVIEW QUESTIONS

1. Why don't most people listen carefully to the music they encounter in their everyday lives?

2. List six actions that teachers can take to get students to listen to music carefully.

3. Why is it a good idea to play a piece of music several times on different days for the students?

4. What is program music? Can music really tell a story? Why is program music often used in elementary schools for listening purposes?

5. What are the four families of orchestral instruments? Why is it a good idea to learn about the instruments of the orchestra in elementary school?

6. What are some actions elementary school teachers can take to acquaint their students with instruments?

7. What are the differences between a concert band and a symphony orchestra?

8. What opportunities are available in the elementary school classroom for having students hear music in a nondirective way?

9. Why is it a good idea to have elementary school students listen to live performances of music?

10. What points are essential for proper concert etiquette?

Tone Quality and Playing Instruments

Every sound, every person's voice, and every type of musical instrument has a unique tone quality. The musical term for the quality of a sound is *timbre* (pronounced *tam*-bur). The quality of sounds, both vocal and instrumental, is one of the four basic elements of music; rhythm, loudness, and pitch are the others.

Exploring Sounds

Children can learn much about timbre and sounds by following their natural curiosity and exploring different sources and ways of producing sounds. Because of its large size and easy availability, the piano is a logical instrument on which to explore the nature of sound. Children can do the following:

1. Feel the vibrations by putting their hands lightly on the piano's soundboard (it's on the underside of a grand piano or the back of an upright piano) or on the strings after notes have been played.

131

2. Observe that the lower strings are thicker and longer than the shorter and higher strings.

3. Watch the strings moving like a blur after the keys have been depressed. The larger, lower strings are more suitable for this purpose.

4. Watch the felt hammer strike the string and notice how it must immediately leave it if the string is to sound freely.

5. Hold down the sustaining pedal (the one to right) while they tap the string with different objects such as a pencil or triangle beater.

Teaching about Tone Qualities

Children are often only vaguely aware of the differences in tone colors. One way to begin to get them thinking about timbres is to compare them on a same-different basis.

> Today let's notice the quality of the sounds we hear. We'll do it by playing a game. On the table in the back of the room there are several rhythm instruments. José, why don't you go back there by the table. Look over the class to make sure no one is turning around and watching you. Then play two different sounds, one after the other. You can play them on different instruments or on the same instrument. Then, call on someone in the class to tell if the qualities of the two sounds were same or different. [José plays several pairs of sounds, each time calling on a different student to ask whether or not the timbres were alike.]

The game can continue as other children take turns producing sounds that are available around the classroom: tapping or scraping against flower pots, window shades, the chalkboard, and so on.

Another way to stress the uniqueness of tone qualities is to ask the children to identify, without looking, the voice of a child who is speaking. To prevent identification of the voice by its location rather than its quality, the teacher can ask the children to stand in a circle but face outward. The teacher then stands in the center of the circle and taps a child on the shoulder to say a designation word or phrase in a normal manner. The children should not try to fool one another by disguising their voices, because that destroys the point of the activity. Following this activity the teacher might conclude with something like these words.

> You see, you can recognize people just by hearing their voices, even though they're saying the same words. How can you do that? Because each person in the whole human race has a somewhat different quality of voice. You don't get mixed up at home listening to your mother, father, brother, or sister speaking, even when they're in a different room, because each person's voice has a quality all its own.

For a variation of this game, the children can divide into teams. The winner is the first team to guess, without looking, the identity of every speaker on the other side.

Basic Voice and Instrument Types

Children in the primary grades can learn to recognize basic types of instruments and voices. The process is not difficult, because they are likely to have some experience doing this from preschool experiences or watching television. The basic instruments probably are the piano, violin, clarinet, trumpet, and snare drum. The basic types of voices are male (bass-baritone) and female (soprano).

In about the third grade, students can begin to compare families of instruments according to how they produce sounds—winds, strings, and percussion. They can also learn that the way in which an instrument is played can also alter its sounds. They can discover this fact with classroom instruments.

> I'm going to pass out three different types of sticks for the metallophone. Lauren, here's one that has a hard head. Leon, this one is medium, and Melissa, here's a soft one. The three of you go to the metallophone and take turns striking bars. The rest of us will compare the tone quality that we hear when the different types of sticks are used.

Similar changes of tone quality can be observed on the Autoharp when played with different picks.

A good way to encourage children to investigate tone qualities and types of instruments is to ask them to make simple instruments at home from inexpensive articles they find around the house: a piece of an old garden hose, empty cereal cartons, tin cans, bottles, pie pans, combs, and so on.

A few guidelines can be provided to prevent the project from becoming an exercise in junk collecting. If the instrument is a percussion type, it should have a clear and easily heard tone, plus the capability of withstanding repeated striking or shaking. If it's a wind or string instrument, it should be capable of producing at least three distinct pitches with a reasonably clear quality.

Here is a list of simple instruments that can be constructed with the help of a teacher or parent.

Drum:	Remove both ends of a gallon can. Cut two circles from a tire inner tube, making them somewhat larger than the ends of the can. With a paper punch, make holes about 2½ inches apart around the edges of the rubber circles. With leather strips, lace the heads onto the drum by running the strips back and forth between the two circles.
Triangle:	On a steel rod about 18 inches long, measure 6 inches from each end and bend the rod in a vice until the ends nearly touch, forming a triangular shape. Attach a cord to one corner of the triangle, and hold the instrument by the cord when playing. Use a large spoon for a beater.
Sand Blocks:	Cut two wood blocks about 3″ × 5″ × 1″. Attach a knob to the large side of each block. Cut two pieces of heavy sandpaper

large enough to cover the side of each block opposite the knob, and long enough to fold over onto the ends of the block. Attach the sandpaper with thumbtacks or staples. To play, hold each block by its knob and scrape the rough sides together to produce a brushing sound.

Maracas: Wash two empty half-pint milk, yogurt, or cream cartons. Place dried beans or metal nuts inside and staple the top closed.

Rhythm Sticks: Cut dowel rods, about 3/8-inch thick, into lengths of about 14 inches.

The students should be able to answer questions about their homemade instruments.

1. Can it produce both high and low pitches? If its pitch is limited, is its range basically high or low?

2. Does its sound tend to be loud or soft? How much variation in loudness is possible on your instrument?

3. Can a sound be held on it for a while, if desired?

4. Can notes be played on the instrument one right after another in rapid succession?

5. Does the sound have a ring or is it dull?

6. Is the tone quality especially suitable for a certain type of song?

7. Is it more appropriate for playing a tune or for accompanying?

Children may be invited to discover that certain songs suggest a particular voice quality. Songs in the music series books, for example, sometimes ask the youngsters to imitate animal sounds or other effects like the howling of the wind. These words or sounds are attempts to infuse different vocal qualities in the music.

Songs about instruments are helpful because they imply certain tone qualities. The "German Instrument Song" includes a simple instrument part containing four pitches. Of the five instruments mentioned in the song, a set of bells can play the instrumental part in the first verse. The next two instruments can also play their respective verses as written, with the recorder assuming the role of the pipe. Chords are suggested for the fourth instrument—the Autoharp—which is not at its best playing a melody. The drum, which can't play pitches, is given an independent rhythm part to add interest to the song. If no instruments are available, the students can make up sounds and words for those parts, as the teacher has them do in this example:

> We don't have the instruments mentioned in this song, so we'll just have to make the instrument sounds ourselves. What would be a good sound or word for the bell? Rasheed? [He suggests "ding," and that seems acceptable to the class.]
>
> All right, let's say "ding" for the bell. Who has an idea for the fiddle? Rachel? [She suggests "zing," which seems agreeable to the other students.]

GERMAN INSTRUMENT SONG

English words by Tulla Statler

German Folk Song

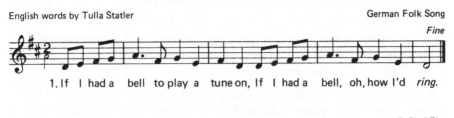

1. If I had a bell to play a tune on, If I had a bell, oh, how I'd *ring.*

(Instrumental)

2. If I had a fiddle, fiddle, fiddle,
   If I had a fiddle, how I'd *bow.*

3. If I had a pipe to play a tune on,
   If I had a pipe, oh, how I'd *blow.*

4. If I had an Autoharp to play on,
   If I had an Autoharp, I'd *strum.*

5. If I had a drum that I could play on,
   If I had a drum, oh, how I'd *beat.*

6. Now we have a tune to play together,
   Now we have a tune, oh, how we'll *play.*

Source: Bennett Reimer et al., *Music*, Book 3. 1975, Silver Burdett.

That's a good sound, and it rhymes with "ding" for the bell. Now, what about the pipe to blow on? Jason? [He suggests "toot," which is not liked by some of the other students.]

What other sound might work for the pipe? Casandra? [She suggests whistling the notes for the pipe.] How many of you prefer "toot"? . . . How many prefer whistling? . . . [The class favors whistling.]

Okay, let's sing the first verse with "ding" for each note of the bell, the second with "zing" for each note of the fiddle, and the third with whistling for each note of the pipe.

Sound Effects in Stories

Children in primary grades like to add sound effects to stories they know. This also helps to increase their consciousness of tone qualities. For example, "Jack and the Beanstalk" could be orchestrated in this way:

Jack climbing up:	ascending pattern on bells
Jack climbing down:	descending pattern on bells
Giant:	large drum or low notes
Hen cackling:	castanet
Harp:	Autoharp
Chopping beanstalk:	woodblock
Beanstalk falling:	cymbals and drums

As the students gain experience in associating sound effects with a story, the teacher can move on to more sophisticated music.

Many compositions feature sounds by associating them with a story. Sergei Prokofiev's *Peter and the Wolf* includes a part for a narrator, who tells how a boy with the help of some animal friends captures an angry wolf. Various instruments play tunes specially associated with the characters: Peter, Grandfather, a duck, a cat, a bird, some hunters, and of course the wolf. The music is imaginative and charming. On the first hearing the children can concentrate on the story, because they will be interested in the outcome. On subsequent hearings they can concentrate on the sounds of the various instruments.

Tone qualities are always associated with objects, animals, and personalities, of course. Students should also experience abstract music that consists of sounds. Electronic music came into being in the twentieth century. Such music often lacks melody and harmony, as well as meter. Instead, it exists as an organized series of sounds. At the very least, these compositions demonstrate the imaginative abilities of the composers.

A good combination of tonal effects and conventional music is Carlos Chavez's *Toccata for Percussion Instruments*. In this work, Chavez successfully exploits rhythms and the possibilities offered by the variety of percussion instruments.

Playing Classroom Instruments

Classroom instruments used with students in elementary schools often include several instruments that are not conventional orchestral or keyboard instruments. They are easy to play and do not require much prior instruction or effort to learn, at least at a rudimentary level. The more common ones are described below and pictured on page 138.

In kindergarten and first grade much of the instrument playing is done by the teacher. Gradually, the children are introduced to playing short phrases and easy parts on an instrument. The guideline to follow in selecting or creating instrumental parts for primary- grade school children to play is: *keep it simple.* At first only one or two instruments should be played at the same time.

Classroom Rhythm Instruments

Instruments that are shaken:

Maracas: Rattles, often in pairs, that are shaken to produce the sound of loose pellets inside a dried, hollow gourd or plastic imitation gourd

Sleigh bells or jingle bells: Small spherical bells attached to a strap or frame and shaken

Tambourine: A skin or plastic membrane stretched across a wooden hoop rimmed with metal discs that produce a jangling sound when the instrument is shaken, struck on the corner with the knuckles, tapped with the fingers, or played with mallet

Instruments that are scraped:

Guiro (pronounced *Gwee*-roh): A notched gourd that is scraped with a stick

Sandblocks: Flat metal or wooden surfaces over which sandpaper is stretched to create a scratching sound when they are rubbed together

Instruments that are struck:

Castanets: Two small wooden cup-shaped pieces struck together against the leg or palm of the hand, or held in one hand and tapped together by the fingers, or (if attached to a handle) struck together by a whip-like motion of the player's hand

Claves: Two cylindrical wooden sticks, one of which is supported lightly in the hand and struck with the other stick

Coconut shells: Two hollow half-spheres that can be struck together on their open ends, hit singly on a flat surface, or struck on the outside with a mallet

Cymbals: Large metal discs struck together, or suspended singly and hit with a stick or brush

Drum: A skin or plastic membrane stretched over a frame and struck with the hand, fingers, or beater

Finger cymbals: Two small metal discs struck against each other or their edges to produce a high-pitched bell-like sound

Rhythm sticks: Two dowel rods that are hit against each other

Temple blocks and wood block: Wood blocks struck with a mallet to produce a hollow, resonant sound

Triangle: A three-sided suspended metal frame struck with a beater to produce a clear metallic sound.

Studio 49 instruments: xylophones, metallophone, hand drums, cymbals, tambourines, triangle, maracas, claves, wood block, and sleigh bells

An example of how instruments can be worked into music instruction can be seen through the song "Are You Sleeping?" (see page 33). The song is in the key of F. That pitch can be sounded on the first beat of each measure throughout the song. If the child playing the instrument senses the beat clearly, he or she can think (and even say softly), "Play, rest, play, rest," and so on. If that does not work, the teacher can point to the child each time the note is to be sounded.

The suggestion in the preceding paragraph—that the teacher direct the child each time the note is to be played—is typical of the amount and type of help that needs to be given when children first begin to play instruments. Much of a teacher's attention will need to be devoted simply to keeping the player on the beat so that an incorrectly played part does not confuse the singers. To limit the amount of distraction, it is important that the class have the song learned thoroughly before an instrumental part is added. Also, it is often necessary to take a minute or two of class time to let the instrument player practice the part, even though that part may seem extremely simple to the teacher.

The teacher should give each child an equal opportunity to play instruments. This means that the less musically able youngsters, as well as the talented stu-

---

Classroom Melody Instruments

Melody instruments are able to play pitches, which means that they can play melodies.

Glockenspiel and bells: Metal strips arranged like a keyboard that sound when struck by a mallet. In a set of resonator bells, each bar is mounted on a separate hollow block that can be removed from the set for individual use.

Xylophone: Similar to the glockenspiel except that its bars are made of wood and mounted on resonating devices

Recorder (and songflute, flutophone, Tonette): Wind instruments with finger holes that can be covered in various combinations to alter the length of the air column and thereby change the pitch

Piano: A keyboard instrument capable of producing 88 pitches, each sounding by the action of a felt hammer hitting against strings

Electronic keyboard: A short keyboard that produces electronically synthesized sounds when its keys are depressed

---

dents, must have a chance to play. It is advisable to select the more able students to perform the part the first time or two it is played. This gives the class an idea of how the music should sound, and helps the other students learn the part so they can play it better when their turn comes.

Keyboard Instruments

Keyboard or mallet instruments can also be used to contribute to understanding features of songs. "The Inch Worm" (page 178) contains several patterns that can be understood better when they are played on the keyboard or mallet instrument.

In "The Inch Worm" the notes of the melody are exactly the same the first time we sing "two and two are four" and "four and four are eight." But the next two times we sing those words, they've changed so that the word "are" is higher each time. Ron, come to keyboard and help me play the note that changes each time. [Ron comes to the keyboard and is shown the notes B♭ and A. He practices them a couple of times in the rhythm of the song, while the teacher sings softly with him, ". . . are four." The quick rehearsal continues with the same notes but with the teacher singing ". . . and eight."]

Good, Ron! Now help us, class, by singing only "Two and two" (rest rest rest), "four and four" (rest rest rest). Be really silent on the rests so you can hear Ron's part. He's playing a *half step*, when the notes are close together. Here's your starting note, class. . . . Rea-dy sing.

Some children have started to take piano lessons by the time they are in the grades 3 and 4. These children should be given the opportunity to play with and for the class. Such an activity reinforces what they have learned, demonstrates to the other children the practical advantages of piano study, and contributes to the music class. Even children not studying piano can be taught to play a simple one-finger part like the one repeated-note accompaniment suggested for "Are You Sleeping?".

Tone qualities are an important component of music. To help children appreciate and understand their potential, teachers need to employ a variety of procedures through which elementary school students can discover and experience timbre in music.

PROJECTS

1. Choose a story like *The Three Bears* that children in primary grades are likely to know. Then plan a series of musical sound effects to accompany the story.

2. Find a song in one of the music series books that includes a part for instruments. Listen to the ancillary CD of the song, which will probably include instruments but not the classroom instruments suggested in the teacher's edition. If you can play the CD in a place where you can make sounds, add the part for each of the classroom instruments suggested and play along with the recording.

3. Think of an elementary classroom that you have observed. Make a list of the sounds that can be made from objects around that room.

4. Make up a list of sounds that can be made with one's body (omitting inappropriate ones, of course). They can include tongue clicks, clapping and slapping, stomping feet, and various vocal sounds.

SKILL DEVELOPMENT

The new note is high C, and it is fingered:

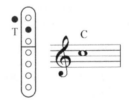

Practice the following patterns.

The song "Bingo" is familiar, because it is presented in chapter 7. The challenge is to play the notes on the recorder at the usual tempo.

BINGO

(For autoharp, transpose to F major)   American Folk Song

There was a farm-er had a dog, And Bin-go was his name-O. B-I-N-G-O, B-I-N-G-O, B-I-N-G-O, and Bin-go was his name-O.

1. Read through the song saying the names of the notes while fingering the notes on your recorder. Try to keep your hands and fingers relaxed.
2. Play the first line at a rather slow tempo. Then play the first line at a quicker tempo. Then play it at about the same speed as when the song is sung. Be sure to tongue each note; avoid starting notes with your breath.
3. Play the second and third lines at a rather slow tempo. Then play them at a quicker tempo, and finally play them at about the tempo the song is usually sung.
4. Play the entire song, maybe slower at first, but then at the usual tempo.
5. Play "Bingo" on a mallet instrument.

REVIEW QUESTIONS

1. What can children learn about sounds by exploring a piano?
2. What actions can a teacher take to help students hear different tone qualities?
3. What questions should elementary school students be able to answer about any instrument they make?
4. What is an especially good work for demonstrating the use of musical instruments to enrich a story?
5. Describe four classroom instruments that produce sounds by being struck.
6. Describe three classroom instruments that can play melodies.

Creating Music

- Value of Creative Activities
- Types of Creativity in Music
- Creating with Existing Music
- Creating Original Music
- Sound Explorations
- Improvising
- Orff-*Schulwerk* Techniques

The word "creative" is a troublesome one, because people have used it in so many different ways. For our purposes let's define it as "a thought, product, or action that is original to the person who creates it." According to this definition, a child who makes a sand castle is being creative, even though a million other children have made sand castles. A child who copies another person's sand castle is not being creative.

Value of Creative Activities

There is no disagreement about the value of creative efforts of people such as Beethoven, Edison, and Michelangelo. But what about the value of the creative efforts of most people, especially those of youngsters? Is a child struggling with the tone bells in some way to be compared with Beethoven? Are the painted paper plates that students bring home from school as valuable as paintings by Rembrandt and Cezanne?

143

From the standpoint of inherent artistic worth, the phrases on the bells and the painted paper plates are of virtually no value. However, creative activities are included in music instruction not for the artistic product that may result, but rather for the benefits that accrue to students through the act of creating.

And what are those values? For one, they encourage individuals to express their own musical thoughts. When trying to create music, people are drawing on their own ideas and manipulating an art form in a personal way. This is an enriching experience. Music involves learning not only to reproduce or listen to what others have created, but also to organize sounds for one's own satisfaction. Children should have opportunities to try out their musical ideas.

A second reason for creative activity is the fact that what a student makes seems valuable to him or her. A tune that fourth-grader Amy creates by hitting certain bars on a xylophone is meaningful to her because probably she has produced a pleasant system of sounds that no one else has produced. These sounds can be heard and reproduced by her and others, but by creating something that is uniquely hers, she has contributed to her self-image as a productive and competent person.

A third value of creative effort is the contribution it makes to the learning of music. When a person is creating music, whether it be a one-measure repeated pattern containing two pitches or an entire choral work, the mind is engaged in much trial and error in thinking about sounds and how they can best be organized to express what the person has in mind. When people are trying to create music, they are thinking intently about sounds and their organization, which is the essence of music. In short, they are thinking much harder about music than when studying what someone else has composed or performed.

Types of Creativity in Music

There are two types of creative experience in music: *composing* and *improvising*. The difference between these activities is the amount of thought and planning that goes into the creative effort. Composing implies careful, thoughtful preparation of music. Such preparation means either writing the music down on paper or preserving the composition on tape or CD.

A person who improvises, on the other hand, makes up music extemporaneously without much prior planning. The performance setting is likely to be casual, with no attempt to preserve the musical result. Improvising is usually based on preexisting guidelines (rarely written down) for the type of music being performed, so the performer-improviser does not make up music out of thin air. Both composing and improvising are important in the world of music, and they can be incorporated in an initial form into elementary school classrooms.

Creating with Existing Music

The idea of asking students to create music may seem like an unrealistic hope. How can youngsters do that when they can hardly sing an entire song accurately? The answer is: They should not be asked to do so, unless the creative effort is structured, and unless the teacher provides much help. A basic rule for guiding creative activities is: *Start with short, simple tasks in which the students have a limited number of options.* When they succeed in simple creative efforts, then they can move on to more complicated and longer creative efforts.

Changing Existing Music

One way to introduce creativity in music instruction is to add original ideas to songs the children know. A song like "Jump Down, Turn Around" is a good one for adaptation. Because it is short and simple, elementary school students will find it easy to try out ideas.

JUMP DOWN, TURN AROUND

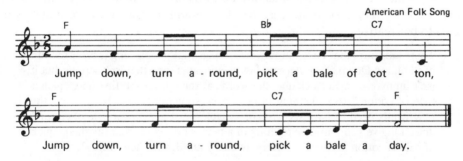

"Jump Down, Turn Around" can be varied in four ways: rhythm, timbre, pitch, and dynamic level, as well as combinations of those four elements. Here is one possibility:

> You've been singing "Jump Down, Turn Around." Now, I am going to play the song on the bells for you, but I'll make some changes in it. Some of the notes will be higher or lower than we've been singing them. It won't be a mistake, because I'm making the changes on purpose. Listen and tell me where I made a change. [The teacher plays the two notes on "cotton" one octave higher. The children identify the spot in the music that was changed.]

> Now see what you can do to make some changes in the song all by yourselves. The important thing about these changes is that they will be *your* ideas; they will come from inside your heads. Remember that you're going to change only how high or low some of the notes are. Each of you can change just one note and keep everything else the same.

> I'll give you a minute or so to think through silently to yourself *one* change in the pitches of "Jump Down" that you would like to try. When you have your

change in mind, you can sing it or play it for us, and then we'll all do it together. Okay, think of your change for a minute . . . Latisha, what change did you think of? [Latisha sings "pick a bale of cotton" with all notes on the same pitch.]

The teacher should react positively to Latisha's version, even though it involves more than one note. The teacher should replay it on the bells to make sure everyone understands what was altered.

The rhythm of "Jump Down, Turn Around" can also be altered. A repeated pattern can be added and clapped by the students. Here is a two-measure possibility:

Changing Words

In addition to altering an element in the music, the class can also vary the words. Elementary school students often do this on their own anyway, and many times they are very good at it. It is, therefore, a logical place for encouraging students to be creative.

There are songs that have funny words, songs that people sing just for the fun of it. "Jump Down, Turn Around" is an enjoyable song that isn't serious, but it isn't funny either. Let's change the words at the end of the first line, "pick a bale of cotton," to something else—maybe something silly. Remember, the new words need to have six parts or syllables, just as "pick a bale of cotton" does. I'll give you a minute to think of a new set of words that fit where "pick of bale of cotton" is now. . . . Terry, what's your idea for new words?

"How about 'pet a noisy fat cat?'"

All right, here's how the new words go: "Jump Down, turn around, pet a noisy fat cat." Let's sing them in the song to see if they work. [The class sings the song with the new words.]

In addition to changing the words and altering the various musical elements, the students can think up short introductions, conclusions, and short repeated patterns *(ostinatos)*. Actually, a one- or two-measure ostinato figure can be extended to serve as an introduction or coda to the song.

Adding Chants

Another way to work with an existing piece of music is to add a chant—a rhythmic line with little variation. "This Old Hammer" suggests the idea of a hammer pounding. Here is one way to develop a chant:

You probably noticed that "This Old Hammer" has a steady quality. Why don't each of you make up a chant that you can repeat again and again while the rest of the class sings the song. All your pattern really needs is a strong

THIS OLD HAMMER

rhythm. Remember, *keep it short*. We'll sing through the song again, so that you can get ideas for a short phrase that might make a good chant. [Class sings "This Old Hammer."]

Who has an idea for a chant? Scott?

"How about '*Ham-mer, ham-mer, ham-mer?*'"

Sounds good! Let's try it. The six of you sitting near the window say his chant. The rest of you sing the song. [The class sings the song with six students singing Scott's chant.]

The teacher, after a few hints to the class, may be able to elicit from them another chant, spoken at first, and then pitched on one note. The note D is a good one, because all the phrases in the song begin and end on that note.

A chant, performed alone at the beginning and end of the song, makes a fitting introduction and concluding section. It sets the mood at the beginning of the song and reinforces it at the end. When combined with well-controlled changes in dynamic level, the chant has a dramatic effect.

Ostinato Parts

A chant must be spoken or vocalized in some manner, but an ostinato can either be played on an instrument or sung. Its characteristic feature is a persistent repeating of a rhythmic or melodic pattern. (The word "ostinato" in Italian liter-ally means "obstinate" or "stubborn.") A simple figure derived from a song is effective, and choosing a pitch level is easy if the song is not complicated. In "Swing Low, Sweet Chariot," the note C is selected to stand out in the ostinato because it is in both of the important chords of the song. An ostinato can be used for an introduction or closing section, as is true of a chant.

Creating Original Music

Many children in primary grades engage in spontaneous singing. A child playing alone may sometimes be heard humming or singing quietly. This impro-vised singing is a natural creative act and should be encouraged.

> Elizabeth, I heard you singing about the rain that we've been having today. It's a good idea to sing about things. Do you suppose that you could sing your song about the rain for me and the class? [Elizabeth agrees, but does not sing the same tune that the teacher heard. She does not repeat the words sung before: "Wet rain, go away. I want to play."]

That's a nice song, Elizabeth. Does anyone else have a song about the rain?

The fact that Elizabeth did not repeat her previous song exactly is typical. The previous singing was a fleeting musical expression that she didn't try to remember. But by asking her to sing it, the teacher has encouraged Elizabeth and indicated to her classmates that creativity is valued.

Sound Explorations

Elementary school students have a natural curiosity about their surroundings, including sounds. They can be encouraged to explore the classroom for its sound-making possibilities. They can rap pencils against flowerpots, chair legs, and ventilator grillwork; they can crinkle paper, hit chalk erasers together, and so on. They should not overlook the possibilities for making sounds with their bodies—clapping, stomping feet, snapping fingers, clucking tongues, hissing, whistling, rapping knuckles, and so on, as was mentioned in chapter 11.

> There are all sorts of ways to make sounds right here in our room. I'll give you a couple of minutes to go around the room on your own and find two different ways to make sounds. Remember what your two sounds are, then come back and we'll make a list of all those ways. [The students go about the room testing different ways of making sounds.]
>
> All right, now let's make that list of ways to make sounds. I'll ask each of you for one way to make a sound. Dennis, what was one way you found? [Dennis suggests tapping on the table with a pencil. The teacher notes the idea on the board and asks other students for their ideas.]
>
> That's quite a list. But even though we have a good list of ways to make sounds, we don't have music. If we're going to make the sounds into music, we need to decide first what sounds we're going to use. They should be sounds that all of us can make. Ebony, what sound do you think we should make first?
>
> Slapping the leg. [The teacher puts a 1 by that suggestion on the board.]
>
> Gary, what's you choice?
>
> Stomping a foot on the floor. [A 2 is written by the suggestion. The teacher continues for several more students.]
>
> Now, how do you want to arrange these sounds so that we can have a piece of music made up of just sounds? [The class decides on the order, with each sound heard four times in succession before moving on to the next one.]

Many things can be done with just five sounds. They can be arranged into certain patterns like: Sound 1, Sound 2, Sound 1, Sound 3, Sound 1, Sound 2, Sound 1. The degree of loudness can be varied, and more than just four notes of equal length can be tried. The sounds can also be changed so that other sounds the students uncovered can be used.

As the students progress in their ability to organize sounds, they can begin to evaluate their sound pieces and to decide what can be done to make them better.

Improvising

Another way to encourage creativity in music is to ask the students to improvise measures or short phrases in response to musical statements provided by the teacher or another student. Initially these efforts will probably consist of short rhythm patterns that are clapped or tapped. The statement sets the tempo and style of the response. The individual student responds in kind.

> I'll clap a short pattern. You "answer" my pattern by clapping a pattern of your own. Don't just clap my pattern again. Think of something different, something of your own. But be sure to keep the tempo the same. I might clap

> and you might answer.

> See how it goes? The nice thing about this is that there aren't any wrong answers! So don't be afraid to clap whatever comes into your head as long as it's in the tempo. Let's start with you, Ginny. Here's the statement. I'll clap it twice. The second time you join in right after the statement is finished. Ready? Here it is.

As the students improve at improvising, they can work in pairs, with one student thinking up a statement and the other improvising an answer. The material can gradually be increased in length and extended to include other than three or four beats to the measure. The activity can also be expanded into a game. A rhythmic statement is agreed on by the class. The first, third, and other odd-numbered members of the class clap it alone when their turn comes, while the second, fourth, and other even-numbered members of the class improvise responses individually. The object of the game is to keep the rhythm going without a break until everyone in the class has participated.

The technique of providing students with statements and having them make up responses can also be used with melodic phrases. A musical statement like the following can be played or sung, with the student responding by singing or by playing on an instrument.

Orff-*Schulwerk* Techniques

Many American music specialists have adopted various practices from Orff-*Schulwerk,* a method of music instruction that was developed under the direction of the twentieth-century German composer Carl Orff and assisted by Gunild Keetman. One aspect of the *Schulwerk* (which in German means "school work") involves clapping, chanting, and other means of producing rhythm patterns. The Orff practices also encourage children to improvise and create music. The methods suggested earlier in this chapter are very consonant with the *Schulwerk* ideas: Give children a limited number of options in a highly structured situation. In fact, it is so structured that the initial efforts at making up music may be limited to two pitches in a pattern only four beats long.

An integral part of Orff-*Schulwerk* is a number of high quality instruments that are suitable for classroom use. Mallet instruments not only have a quality sound, they also have removable bars. With the unwanted bars gone, a child can't hit an "off limits" pitch. Music in two or more parts is encountered early, and ostinatos are a prominent feature.

The five-note pentatonic scale is used often in the Orff-*Schulwerk.* That scale has no half steps, which avoids those potential dissonances and the melodic tendencies of intervals a half step apart. Initially, the bars that are not removed should be the first and fifth notes of a scale. Other bars can be added later to form a pentatonic scale.

Initial efforts should also be confined to two or three different instruments playing at the same time, one of which may be a drum. The teacher should hear each instrument alone first before attempting to combine them. When early experiences have been successful, the music can become more complex and longer.

CODA

It would be unfortunate if elementary school students never had a chance to try creating some music. Their education in music would be missing something valuable. Fortunately, one does not need to have been a music major in order to help students do simple creative things in music. Classroom teachers can make a real contribution in this area.

PROJECTS

1. Think up changes in "Jump Down, Turn Around" that involve changes:
   a. of notes, or
   b. in the rhythm, or
   c. in the levels of dynamics, or
   d. a combination of the elements.
   Be prepared to play or sing your version to your methods class.
2. Create a "sound piece" with others in your methods class.
   a. Individually think of two sounds that you find around your classroom.
   b. Make a list of the sounds that others find.
   c. Decide on at least five that you want to use.
   d. Decide on a rhythm pattern that consumes four beats for each sound.
   e. Decide on an order or pattern for the five sounds: e.g., *A B A C A B A*
   f. Try different rhythm patterns that consume four beats and different orders for the appearance of the sounds.
   g. Try five different sounds, and create another sound piece.
   h. Create a short introduction and a short coda for your new piece.
3. Practice statement/answer patterns.
   a. Begin with one person thinking of a rhythm pattern as a statement and another creating an answer. Be sure to keep the beat steady with no break between the statement and its answer.
   b. Then move on to simple melodic patterns that consume four beats.

SKILL DEVELOPMENT

The new note is high D. It is fingered:

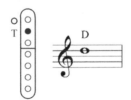

It requires that you uncover the thumb hole under the left hand. Practice playing these patterns.

"Canon" by Thomas Tallis, a sixteenth-century English composer, has you play all seven notes that you have learned thus far. It is a canon—a somewhat more sophisticated round—so it can be played in two, three, or four parts. The numbers indicate where the parts enter. Notice that it consists of only quarter notes, so the rhythm couldn't be simpler.

TALLIS' CANON

Thomas Tallis, c. 1567

1. Read through "Canon" saying the note names while fingering the notes on your recorder.
2. Play the song through, making it as smooth as possible and avoiding starting notes with your breath.

3. In your methods class, play the song in two parts, then three, and then four parts.

4. Sing "Canon" in two parts, then three, and then four parts. The first time sing note names, and then sing it with the words.

5. Play "Canon" on a keyboard with the right hand. Play the opening G with the thumb and cross your second finger over to play the F♯. In the second measure of the second line, play the first A with the second finger, but then switch to the third finger for the next A. That will make it easy to play the low D and finish the song without moving your hand. As you play a piano or keyboard, be sure to keep your wrist from collapsing. Keep a straight line from your elbow to your hand.

REVIEW QUESTIONS

1. Why is it valuable for elementary school students to engage in creative activities?

2. What are the differences between composing and improvising?

3. What are three ways in which students can alter an existing piece of music?

4. What is an ostinato? How can ostinatos be helpful in having students create music?

5. How can teachers guide students to make up a musical composition out of the sounds they can find around their classroom?

6. What actions can teachers take to help students improvise?

7. What are the basic features of the Orff-*Schulwerk* approach?

8. What is special about the instruments that have been created for use with the Orff-*Schulwerk* approach?

9. Why is the pentatonic scale favored in the Orff-*Schulwerk* approach?

Music and Movement

- Fingerplays
- Role of Imitation
- Moving in Structured Situations
- Action Songs
- Moving to Musical Elements
- Singing Games
- Folk and Social Dancing
- Dramatizations

Because movement is a natural human response to music, children should be encouraged to move to the musical sounds they hear. Experience with movement provides a change of activity in the music lesson, and this variety is often beneficial to the learning process. Furthermore, because motion is overt, teachers can easily tell by the students' actions whether or not they are involved with the music.

Fingerplays

A fingerplay is a series of finger, hand, or arm motions performed rhythmically to depict the images suggested by a song or rhyme. Most youngsters have enough manual dexterity to perform fingerplays competently, and children enjoy the muscle manipulation required to act out a story with their hands.

The value of muscle movement was noted many years ago by Friedrich Froebel, the German educator who established the kindergarten/nursery school

trend early in the nineteenth century. He believed that children begin to understand the things they imitate. His idea that children learn through play was reinforced as he went about the countryside observing peasant mothers and their
young children. He collected their fingerplays and games and used them in his
own teaching.

The following fingerplays are known to most teachers and children: "The
Eency Weency Spider," "This Old Man," "Here Is the Beehive," "Ten Little Indi-
ans," and "Where Is Thumbkin?" The motions of these songs are varied and each
is sung to a standard tune that is merely recited. Young children seem not to tire
of these and similar songs.

Role of Imitation

As with fingerplays, children's first experiences with moving the whole body
to music can be imitative. Following the motions of a leader helps to stimulate the
youngsters' own ideas. By thinking aloud, "What can we do here?" and then
quickly showing appropriate motions while encouraging the children to do the
same, teachers help them learn that movement can be spontaneous and that many
different motions are possible.

Imitative movement need not occur simultaneously with the teacher's
motions. Instead, the children can follow a teacher's movements in echo fashion.
Youngsters will understand the procedure if told that the class is "taking turns"
with the teacher.

The song "Are You Sleeping?" (p. 33) is ideal for echo-type motions, because
each of the four phrases is repeated before the next one occurs. Echo-clapping is
a good introduction to the procedure because only one type of motion is
involved. A teacher can sing through the song, clapping with the words in measures 1, 3, 5, and 7 and signaling for the class to clap in the same way at measures
2, 4, 6, and 8.

As the children become more adept at waiting for their turn and repeating a
phrase accurately, a teacher can change motions for each new phrase and then
change them within a single phrase. If desired, the song text can be replaced with
specific directions, as in this version of "Are You Sleeping?," to be sung to these
words and performed in place from a standing position:

Step the beat now,	(children imitate)
Turn a-round,	(imitate)
Clap your hands to-geth-er,	(imitate)
Step once more,	(imitate)

After seeing the teacher lead the group with different motions, a child may be
invited to lead with other ideas. The youngster's movements may in fact be
exactly like the teacher's previous actions, but the child will be pleased to be
named "leader," and enjoyment is one goal of the activity.

Moving in Structured Situations

When children first attempt to move freely in a large area, they need to know that their actions are guided by rules. They must find their own space and respect the space of others. They should not touch other people unless the teacher suggests that they do so. Their attention needs to be on the music, so that their motions reflect what they hear. As they gain experience in self-direction and attentive listening, they are becoming better prepared to work with partners and participate in large-group endeavors.

Limits also help to focus the children's attention on what they are doing. They respond well to requests that are phrased as challenges: "How far can you reach with your elbow?" "In how many ways can you move your foot?" "Can you touch your nose to your shoulder?" Such suggestions may appear confining, but they actually encourage imaginative movement.

Teachers should be aware of the limitations inherent in the physical setting and plan accordingly. Actions that require a child to move from one place to another—*locomotor* activity as opposed to the "in place" nature of *axial* or *non-locomotor* activity—must occur in a safe environment. Children in stocking feet can slip on tile floors, and rubber-soled shoes, especially on a carpet, make skipping and certain other movements difficult. If space is very limited, some children can be assigned to provide the music while others move; then the groups can trade roles.

Action Songs

In contrast to fingerplays, which appeal to young children, action songs are enjoyed by older as well as younger ones. Motions should be decisive and energetic, unless the music is gentle in character. When students move with energy, they feel more confident and tend to duplicate the rhythm accurately, which increases their enjoyment of music.

"Johnny Works with One Hammer" is strongly rhythmic and ends with movement of the entire body. The children's own names can be substituted for "Johnny" to involve them more in the music. The singers pound with one fist for "one hammer" and with two fists for "two hammers." Unless the students are able to move confidently from a standing position, they should remain seated as they do this song, because the "three hammers" verse requires balancing on one foot and tapping with the other, "four hammers" calls for jumping (to tap with both feet), and "five hammers" requires jumping plus nodding the head.

Here are some suggestions that can be adapted for managing action songs:

1. Be firm and consistent about the students stopping movements when the music stops. That makes the activity more manageable and also makes both the beginning and ending of a song clear.

2. Help the students develop lateral balance by choosing activities that involve both sides of their bodies for foot-tapping, finger-snapping, waving, wink-

JOHNNY WORKS WITH ONE HAMMER

American Folk Song

John - ny works with one ham - mer, one ham - mer, one ham - mer.

John - ny works with one ham - mer, Now he works with two.

2. Johnny works with two hammers (etc.) . . . Now he works with three."

3. Johnny works with three hammers (etc.) . . . Now he works with four."

4. Johnny works with four hammers (etc.) . . . Now he works with five."

5. Johnny works with five hammers (etc.) . . . Now he takes a rest."

ing, and so on. A song such as "Hokey Pokey," with its references to "right" and "left," is a good choice to reinforce the concept of equal body sides.

3. Promote spatial orientation by helping students produce sounds through body movement at different levels: a foot tap at floor level, a thigh slap called a "pat" or *"Patsch"* (a German word for which the plural is *"Patchen"*), a clap at waist level, and a finger snap at shoulder level. If some children cannot snap, a bouncing motion of the hand is a good substitute. Let students make up rhythm patterns of these four motions and apply them as accompaniments to songs.

4. To encourage buoyancy in skipping, choose music (or provide a drum beat) in 6/8 meter:

5. Solicit ideas from the children for altering a song text or adding extra verses to provide more actions.

6. Prepare a repertoire of animal motions to propose for songs that mention animals.

   Elephant: lean forward from the waist, clasp hands together near the knees, and swing arms sideways

   Pony: prance by stepping in place, lifting each knee high with the toe pointed down

Horse: gallop forward while slapping one hip

Bear: keep knees slightly bent and walk with legs apart, shifting weight from side to side and holding limp wrists against chest

Frog: squat with hands touching floor between legs and jump forward

Duck: squat with feet apart and bottom almost touching floor, waddle forward by shifting weight onto alternate legs

Butterfly: cross wrists and wave hands gently

Penguin: walk stiffly with knees straight, toes out, and arms held stiffly against sides

7. Do not impose a specific story on the music if the composer did not do so! The students can still move expressively to the music, whether it implies specific images or not.

8. Remember that props such as scarves to wave and balls to bounce are not necessary for experiencing movement. In fact, they may distract the students' attention from the bond between the music and their response to it.

"Stretching Song" is a good choice for young children. The words clearly describe the recommended actions, and the actions correlate well with the pitch levels in the melody. Besides, the bending and stretching is fun!

STRETCHING SONG

Words and Music by Eunice Boardman

1. I'm stretch-ing ver - y tall, And now I'm ver - y small. Now tall!
2. My hands I stretch out wide, Be-hind me they will hide. Now wide!
3. My hands I stretch up high, Now on the floor they lie. Now high!
4. Now with my head I shake, Now not a move I make. Now shake!
5. Now all the girls and boys Don't make a sin-gle noise! Sit down!

Now small! Now I'm a ti-ny ball.
Now hide! I put them at my side.
Now lie! Now   way up to the sky.
No move make! Now my whole bod-y I shake.
No sound! And dream of man-y toys.

Moving to Musical Elements

Elementary school students can demonstrate recognition of what's happening in the music by their actions. Initially, this can be as simple as stopping a motion when the music stops. Then they can be asked to recognize opposites in the music: high/low, up/down, loud/soft, heavy/light, fast/slow, right/left, forward/backward, in/out, over/under, and so on. By asking students to change motions when they hear particular features in the music, teachers can assess their understanding of musical concepts such as beat, tempo, meter, pitch, duration, dynamic level, timbre, and form.

Singing Games

Unlike action songs, which focus on individual efforts, singing games require cooperation and similar motions from the participants. Singing games are more structured and take place in a particular formation, often a circle on the floor. One of most successful to have the students pass an object (balls, pencils, erasers, etc.) to the beat of the music in two beats to the measure.

> Class, now that you're sitting on the floor in a circle, we can try a little game with music. Show me you know which hand is your left hand by raising it. [The students raise their left hands, and the teacher helps a few that raised their right hand.] Now lay you left hand your knee facing up. Touch you left hand with your right hand on the first beat. On the second beat move you right hand over to the right and touch your neighbor's left hand. [The teacher plays a march and the students keep the beat, touching first their left hand and then their neighbor's left hand.]

When they can do this in rhythm, they can then pass an object from their left hand to their neighbor's left hand in the rhythm of the music. Many variations of this basic game can be created. For instance, they could pick up an object on "1," lay it down on "2," clap on "3," and put it in their neighbor's left hand on "4."

Teachers can consider the following in planning singing games in which the students are not seated:

1. If partners are required, the selection process should do no harm to any child's self- image.

2. If the children must move sideways in a circle while touching, they may rest their hands on the neighbors' shoulders or place one hand at each neighbor's elbow. Youngsters are apt to stretch the circle and pull at other people if they are holding hands, and if they link elbows they are pulled too close to move freely.

3. Cooperation is an important goal of singing games. This may be a new idea for a youngster who thinks a singing game is a contest to see who can sing loudest or move fastest in order to "win." Teachers should emphasize that the purpose of the activity is to do something together, not to win.

Folk and Social Dancing

Movement in dancing is organized even more strictly than in singing games. To give the students a repertoire of dance music, teachers can play CDs of folk songs appropriate for dancing, or have the class sing typical square dance songs.

The most direct way to introduce dance steps is simply to go through them while everyone is standing in a circle. The teacher can guide the activity by describing the steps and demonstrating them as in the following examples.

> *Polka:* Here's an easy dance pattern. Watch me do it first in slow motion: step to the right, put the left foot close to it, step to the right again, and hold. Got it? Do it with me, a little faster. *Right* step *right* hold, *left* step *left* hold, *one* and *two* hold, *pol-* ka *step—, pol-*ka *step—, now-*we'll *stop.* You're off to a good start!

On another day a teacher might review the dance movements presented to the class earlier, and then introduce additional easy steps.

> *Waltz:* Let's do a dance in three-beat meter today. We need to make each step even, like this: *right* slide right, *left* slide left, *one* two three, *one* two three, *fast-*er now, *one* two three, *now-*you-are-*waltz-*ing! Get-*rea-*dy-to-*stop.* That's the way, class! This is a good dance with "O My Darling Clementine." Let's sing it as we waltz around again. [The class waltzes and sings.]

If the members of a class need to be in partners for a dance, they can be asked to count off by twos, with one group being the "Blues," for example, and the other being the "Oranges." If the students wear identifying patches of color, prepared in advance by the teacher, it will be easier to keep their places and the dance activity will proceed more smoothly.

Students are often interested in basic square dance movements and learn them easily. In this example the teacher is demonstrating the do-si-do.

> For the do-si-do, you need to form two lines that face each other. Leave a little more room between neighbors . . . that's the way. Now, each of you hold your forearms crossed in front of you, then skip forward so that opposite people meet in the center. Go around each other with right shoulders close, always facing forward, then move backward with left shoulders close, still skipping, and return to your places. Keep your arms folded through all of this. We'll try it to a good skipping song like "Here We Go 'Round the Mulberry Bush."

The students need to realize that dancing involves more of the body than just the feet and legs. Teachers can demonstrate various ways in which to position the arms, in addition to folded arms that the students have already experienced. Partners may want to try these possibilities: clap their own or their partner's hands, raise joined hands while walking into a circle and lower them while backing out, face in opposite directions and link elbows, join crossed hands in the "skaters' position," join both hands and turn back to back to "wring the dishrag," make arches for people to go under, create a star formation with joined hands of other dancers, and proceed around in a circle in a "shake hands" manner to form a "grand chain" or "grand right and left."

Dramatizations

Dramatization means acting out a story through movement. It implies at least a rudimentary plot and a degree of character development. Mime is a good example of drama that can be conveyed by movement alone.

Most elementary music series books include stories to be acted out to music. These dramatizations range from simple children's tales for young groups to scenes from operas and musicals that can be enacted by older children.

Meaningful experiences with movement require attention to its four components: *time*—the sense of orderly progression through past, present, and future; *space*—the realm of line, direction, and distance; *weight*—the feeling conveyed by varying degrees of emphasis; and *idea*—the concept or object being described by the movement.

Coda

The goal of movement is to provide physical experiences that lead elementary school students to perceive the music and respond to it with pleasure, intellectual recognition, and physical ease.

PROJECTS

1. Practice singing and doing one of the fingerplays suggest earlier in this chapter.

2. Sing through "Are You Sleeping?" with the words for movement. Then sing and step through the actions indicated in the song.

3. Make up a new set of words and actions for "Johnny Works with One Hammer." If possible, perform the new version for your methods class.

4. Locate a movement activity in one of the music series books. Either verbally or in writing describe it to the other members of your methods class.

SKILL DEVELOPMENT

The new note on the recorder is F♮. Like F♯ it involves leaving a hole open. It is fingered:

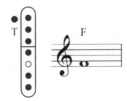

It may seem like it's not necessary to cover those two holes below the first finger. But if they are not covered, F♮ will be quite out of tune.

Practice the following patterns that involve F♮.

The new song is "Hanukah."

HANUKAH

Jewish Folk Song

1. Tap or clap the rhythm of the song. Notice that the first and third lines are alike, and that the second line is very similar, being one step lower.

2. Say the note names for line 1 as you finger the notes on your recorder. Then say and finger the notes for line 2. Next, do the same for the fourth line. Finally, say and finger the notes for the entire song.

3. Play "Hanukah" on your recorder. It may help if you learn one line at a time before attempting the entire song.

4. Sing the song using note names, and then sing it with words.

5. Sing the song accompanied by the Autoharp following the chord symbols above the staff.

6. Learn three simple chords on a piano or keyboard. Here is the I or tonic chord in the key of the song, C.

Next, the IV or subdominant chord (F) in the key of C.

And finally the V7 or dominant seventh chord (G7) in the key of C. It is not in root position and its fifth is missing so that it is easier to play.

Practice playing these three chords using the fingers indicated. Barely move your hand in doing so. When you can play the chords, sing "Hanukah," and play the chords on the keyboard according to the letters above the staff.

REVIEW QUESTIONS

1. What is a fingerplay? Why are fingerplays a good way to introduce students to the idea of moving to music?

2. What are echo-like motions in music? Why are they helpful in teaching students about music?

3. What are action songs? Why are action songs a good way to help students move to music?

4. Describe some of the folk dances that can be used in elementary schools.

5. Describe actions that elementary school students can do to depict various animals.

ENRICHING ELEMENTARY SCHOOL CLASSROOMS WITH MUSIC

Music can be a great help to classroom teachers. It can contribute to the teaching of language arts, social science, mathematics, and science by adding a different dimension, a richer view of the subject being studied. There are literally hundreds of ways to involve music with the teaching and learning of other subjects. Chapter 14 suggests a few examples of the possibilities in each of the major areas of the curriculum.

Chapter 15 suggests some of the uses of music in helping to manage classrooms and contribute to a more relaxed atmosphere. Chapter 16 examines the needs of students with disabilities and how music can contribute to their educational experience.

Enriching the Curriculum with Music

- Sources for Bringing Music into the Classroom
- Language Arts and Reading
- Music and Social Studies
- Music and Mathematics
- Music and Science
- Music and the Arts
- Music and Physical Exercise

Classroom teachers can make the study of other subjects in their classrooms more interesting and richer by incorporating music. This chapter points out a few of the many possibilities for taking advantage of the benefits of involving music.

Sources for Bringing Music into the Classroom

Because they must guide their students in learning a variety of subjects, classroom teachers do a great deal of planning. Music is only one of many areas that they need to think about. For this reason, they can often use some help in getting ideas for enriching the learning in other subjects with music. Where can they go for such help?

Music Specialists: It is hoped, as described in chapter 2, that the music specialist will offer suggestions for using music in response to the classroom teacher telling him or her what will be covered in various subjects. In fact, if suggestions are not forthcoming from the music specialist, the classroom teacher should ask for some. Classroom teachers are certainly entitled to such help from music specialists.

Music Book Series: Another major source is the elementary music series books described in chapter 3. As helpful as these books are, their focus and organization are on music. They often attach ideas for incorporating activities from other subjects to enrich the study of a particular aspect of music. This is only logical and fair, because they are, after all, music books. However, this is *not* the approach or need of classroom teachers who come to a subject from the opposite direction. Instead of asking, "How can (social studies, language arts, etc.) contribute to the students' learning of music?", classroom teachers ask, "How can music contribute to the students' learning of this topic in (social studies, language arts, etc.)?"

Are the elementary music series books, therefore, of little use to classroom teachers? Absolutely not! Whereas their scope and sequence are based on musical topics, they are—fortunately—thoroughly indexed. Their indices include words that relate to subject matter taught in the classroom. As classroom teachers plan for various subjects, they can look under likely certain words in the index of the music series book to find appropriate songs, music, or activities for their grade level. The series books may vary slightly in their indexing of topics, but many of them will list music from various countries for use in social studies, list poetry that can contribute to language arts, and so on. Classroom teachers will usually find many more suggestions than they have time to use.

Music for Learning Materials: A third source are songbooks and CDs designed specifically to help students learn in subjects ranging from reading to science to social studies. Some of these songs are or were popular songs, a few are from Broadway musicals, some are adaptations of folk songs with new words, but a great many of them were created by musicians for classroom use. They are not likely to be songs that appear in elementary music series books or that will be taught by music specialists, unless requested by classroom teachers. Musically speaking, these songs may not be of great value, but one doesn't need an art song by Franz Schubert to learn the times tables or how to sound out words when learning how to read.

Where does one find such material? A search of the Internet reveals a few. One currently excellent site is www.songsforteaching.com. Other sites are also available, and undoubtedly others will appear in the future. Songbooks and music books are available on www.amazon.com.

This chapter offers examples in six areas about how music can contribute to the learning of other subjects.

Language Arts and Reading

Singing and speaking have much in common. Both of them involve the mental processing and organizing of sounds. Both appear to call for quite similar skills. And both are learned in a similar way. For these reasons, music can play a valuable role in helping students in improving their language-making abilities.

Development of Speech and Singing

None of us remembers how we learned to talk. We're sure we never had any lessons, except for a few youngsters who, after they were in elementary school, had help in correcting their pronunciation of certain sounds. So how did we learn how to speak? By the simple process of listening to others, initially our parents, and imitating what they said. This rote process begins very early life, when before they are one-year old, infants become more aware of and their brains respond to some spoken sounds and not to others. At around 21 months of age many children begin saying words and soon language develops at an amazing pace. They put together thoughts and express them in words with a skill that seems beyond logical explanation. Like the bee who flies in spite of the fact that it doesn't have wings of sufficient size to do so, youngsters aren't concerned with rules and niceties of speech. They just do it—and they learn in the process.

Children learn to sing in much the same way. They hear someone singing, and they imitate it. But there is an important difference between speaking and singing. All children except those who are deaf have the benefit of hearing people talk. Many children do not have the benefit of hearing people sing on any regular, normal basis. The fortunate ones whose families do sing are far more likely to be able to sing on pitch when they enter school than those who don't.

The ability of children to process sounds and use language is retained to a high degree until around the age of 10, after which it gradually declines. Many youngsters learn to speak English and also learn to speak Spanish or Korean to their grandmother or other relative who has much difficulty learning English. To them, being bilingual is easy! Adults can also learn to be bilingual, but it takes more effort, and they rarely learn to speak the second language without an accent.

The ability to speak and knowledge of a large number of words is essential in learning to read. Children know the word "house," and then—and the order is important here—they learn that a particular group of letters represents "house." If their spoken vocabulary does not include "house," they will find learning to read that word very difficult, if not impossible. The "ear it before they eye it" principle holds true in both language and music.

Does practice in processing musical sounds aid in processing verbal sounds? The answer is, "Very likely." When children learn to listen and imitate sounds carefully, it does seem to make a difference. If this were not true, why is it that when children are taught foreign languages, their language teachers often have them sing songs in the language being studied? Clearly, these teachers have discovered that music is an excellent way to reinforce learning a language.

> We've been learning about vowels lately, haven't we? You know, singing about them will help us to remember them even better. You all remember the song "Bingo." Let's change its words! Let's substitute the five vowels for the letters in Bingo's name. The new version of the song goes like this:
>
> The vowels of the alphabet
> I know them all by name, oh!

a-e-i-o-u
a-e-i-o-u
a-e-i-o-u
I know them all by name, oh!

We can sing just as we usually do with "Bingo." We'll leave off one vowel with each verse. Let's sing the vowels! Rea-dy sing.

Many other songs are available that deal with vowels and consonants, blends, digraphs, and diphthongs, and letters of the alphabet.

Reading and Singing Words of Songs

Just about every song has a text that has been coupled with a melody. Both classroom and music teachers can (and should) help the students with the words. Students can read the words aloud together, or individual students can do so. The same skills in recognizing the sounds of words that are used for teaching reading can be extended to reading the words in songs. Song texts also present a chance to add an element of rhythm to the words.

The words of the round "Good Night" are more vivid when they are said with rhythmic emphasis. Instead of being said without inflection and expression, the first word of each measure can be slightly emphasized.

The texts of songs also have punctuation, which guides the singer and reader in how a song is divided into logical phrases for both text and music. "Good night to you all" forms a logical thought, as does "May angels around you their silent watch keep." The four appearances of "good night" are each separated slightly from the others.

In this example the teacher seeks to make the students more aware of the logic of the text and music.

You may not think about it, but you don't say all the words you say in exactly the same way. Only talking machines do that, and they are not all that interesting to listen to. Look at the words to the round "Good night." Which words do you think should be made stronger than others? Felicia? [Felicia says that "Good" and "you" should be emphasized.]

Who else has thought of words that should be made stronger? Jordan? [Jordan suggests "Night" and "all."] Why those words, Jordan? [He answers that they are the first beats in the measures of music and—besides—"all" has a "thing" following it.]

Jordan is right. The first beat after each up/down line is normally emphasized. And there is the mark we call a "comma" after "all." Let's read the words in rhythm. But let's give the first words following the measure bar line more emphasis, and notice where the marks we call punctuation appear. [The class says the words in a rhythmic manner by placing more emphasis on the first beats of measures.]

Another point to have students notice is the rhyme scheme used in many songs. In "Good Night" the final word of the first two lines ("sleep" and "keep") rhyme. In fact, the texts of most songs can be considered poems. They often have a metrical quality, which is one reason for reading them in rhythm. They also frequently have rhyme schemes.

In this example the teacher asks the class to read the poem "Everyone Sang" by Siegfried Sassoon.

> Everyone suddenly burst out singing;
> And I was filled with such delight
> As prisoned birds must find in freedom,
> Winging Wildly across the white
> Orchards and dark-green fields; on—on—and out of sight.
>
> Everyone's voice was suddenly lifted;
> And beauty came like the setting sun;
> My heart was shaken with tears; and horror
> Drifted away . . . Oh, but Everyone
> Was a bird; and the song was wordless; the singing will never be done.

Teacher: Craig, does the poem have a form or pattern?

Craig: Well, it has two stanzas. Is that form?

Teacher: Yes, very good, but keep looking. What do you notice about the first two lines of each stanza?

Craig: They're sort of alike. Both lines have the words "everyone . . . suddenly." Um . . . and both of the second lines begin with "and," so I guess there's a plan.

Teacher: Good. Now, Claudia, are there any lines where the sounds of the words or first letters of words contribute to the effect of the poem?

Claudia: Ah . . . you have three "W" words where it says "winging, wildly, across the white."

Teacher: Good for you! Another way to unify a poem is through rhyme. Is there some rhyme in this poem, Naomi?

Naomi: Yeah. In the first stanza the last words on a line sometimes rhyme, like "delight," "white," and "sight" . . . And the same thing happens in the second stanza.

Teacher: So the poet is thinking about the sound of words as well as their meanings. It there anything similar about what a poet and a composer do when they work? Vanessa?

Vanessa: Well, music is sounds, and a poem is partly sounds, so I guess they do some things the same.

The teacher can point out an even more basic similarity between the two arts: Good music and good poetry invite the listener to return to the work and explore its fuller meaning. The initial attractiveness is not an end in itself, but rather a promise of further reward as a person probes for the deeper significance of the poem or piece of music.

Many songs are available for helping students with words and syllables, rhymes, word families, and the manipulation of phonemes and syllables. In addition, many teachers have found that elementary school students really enjoy *rap* and chanting, and a wide selection of such music for educational purposes is available.

Most music teachers have little enthusiasm for rap. The element of melody is virtually absent, and the same rhythm patterns are repeated again and again. So musically it isn't very satisfying, even if it does sell a lot of CDs. Many of the popular rap CDs also have texts that are totally inappropriate for elementary school students. But the concept of rap is what is being discussed here; its musical value is not the main concern. The question is, "Can rap help students learn?" Almost all indications point to a positive answer to that question.

What are rap's virtues in terms of helping students learn? Its foremost attribute is that elementary school students usually enjoy raps, and so learning becomes fun rather than a chore. Its repeated phrases help some students master language fluency. And it certainly provides a change of pace in the classroom. Finally, students can be encouraged to develop their own raps, which helps them build self-confidence and encourages creative thinking.

Music and Foreign Languages

As has been pointed out, children are quick to learn and pronounce words in different languages. Music books and classes include music from a variety of countries. Some of the ancillary CDs for the music series books include not only the songs, but also have a native speaker pronouncing the words for the students. The pronunciations are also in phonic spellings in the teacher editions of the books, but they are usually not as accessible for the students.

Today let's practice a song that you started in music class yesterday. It's "La Bamba." First, let's review the words. Do you remember what language we will be using? Allison? [Allison responds that the language is Spanish.] That's right, Allison. Let's listen to the speaker on the CD as she says the words. Listen carefully. [The teacher plays the portion of the CD in which the native speaker says the words for the students.]

Let's practice saying them once more before we sing the song. Only we'll have two of you say a phrase, and then another two, and so on. Ray and Heather, let's hear the two of say the first phrase. Rea-dy begin. [Ray and Heather say the phrase in Spanish. Then other pairs of students are called on.]

Now I think we're ready to sing the song. [The teacher strikes the starting note on the bells, and then sings in the tempo of the music "Rea-dy sing." [The class sings through the song.]

Many songs and other materials are available in a wide variety of languages. The most common are Spanish and French, but songs in several African languages are also available, as well as music from other parts of the world.

Music and Social Studies

Because music exists in every part of the world and has existed in every age of civilization, music seems a "natural" for inclusion in the study of the various areas of social studies. Indeed, it is difficult to think of an area that would *not* be suitable for the inclusion of at least some music. Consider these groups of topics:

Home and Community: Hearing lullabies is one of the first contacts with music that many children have. In addition, there are many places in the community where people encounter music. These range from musical events to music in films and television and on the radio. Many songs about family and animals are also available.

Various parts of the United States: There are many songs and musical works that have regional associations within America. Some of them are associated with occupations (e.g., cowboys, railroad workers) and some with geographical features (e.g., "Roll on Columbia," *The Grand Canyon Suite*).

Different historical periods: Such music ranges from music associated with the settling of the western part of the United States (e.g., "Little Sod Shanty") to different periods in history.

Different countries around the world: The amount of music from other countries and cultures in the music series books is extremely large. Also more and more music materials are becoming available via the Internet. Finding music from other parts of the world is hardly the problem, however. The problem is that there is so much that no one, even if he or she devoted an entire life to it, could ever know more than a portion of it. There is so much available and so little time to learn about it! What can teachers (both classroom teachers and music specialists) do about it?

1. Emphasize that music is an important part of life in every part of the world.

2. Explain that just as people speak different languages, they have different musical "languages." For this reason, their music often will *not* sound like the music that is familiar to us. It is going to seem strange, almost like listening to someone talking in a foreign language.

3. Explain further that just as we want people to respect our language and music, they want us to respect theirs. No language or music is superior to another. It's easy to think that one's own language and music is better, of course, because it's the one we know. Encouraging an attitude of respect for people and their cultures that are different from us is perhaps the most important action teachers can take in this matter. An accepting, inquisitive attitude is useful for the study of every type of music, whether learned in school or encountered in the future.

4. Inform students that in a world with instant communication and jet planes, not to mention the immigration of people from other nations to the United States, part of being a good world citizen involves knowing something about some of the other types of music of major areas throughout the world.

Here is an example of how one classroom teacher introduces a song from another culture.

SAKURA

Japanese Folksong

Cher - ry bloom, cher - ry bloom, Gent - ly sway - ing in the air,
Sa - ku - ra, Sa - ku - ra, Ya - yo - i - no so - ra wa.

Sweet the fra - grance ev - 'ry - where, Pet - als soft and col - ors bright,
Mi - wa - ta - su Ka - gi - ri Ka - su - mi Ka Ku - mo - ka

Float - ing clouds that seem to say: Come and see,
Ni - o - i - zo i - zu - ru I - za - ya

come and see, Come and see the cher - ry bloom.
I - za ya' Mi - ni - yu - ka - un.

Teacher: I told your music teacher, Mrs. Morgan, that we're studying Japan and Asia, and I understand that she started a new song from Japan with you. It's called "Sakura," and it's about cherry blossoms. Let's sing it with the CD so it's fresh in our minds. Here we go. [Teacher plays CD of "Sakura" as the students sing along.]

Notice that it has a simple, kind quality. Ashley, does it sound like an American song?

Ashley: Oh, no. It sounds different.

Teacher: Greg, Ashley says that "Sakura'" sounds different. Why do you think it sounds different?

Greg: I don't know. Maybe it just seems simpler.

Teacher: Lacy, why do you think it sounds different?

Lacy: Well, I don't think too many American songs are about sweet smells. And the music just sounds different.

Teacher: It does sound different, and we would expect that—right—because Japan is in a different part of the world and has a different way of life. It's good to know that the Japanese have really nice music, like a lot of other countries. And to me, it does seem simpler and gentler than a lot of music we hear.

Music and Mathematics

The music series books at the primary grade levels include songs that involve counting and numbers. In addition, there are many songs and raps available for multiplication and division, as well as addition and subtraction and fractions. Here's one example that's sung to the tune of "Shortenin' Bread":

/   /   /   /
Twenty-one, twenty-one, twenty-one, twenty-one,

/   /   /   /
Three times seven is twenty-one.

/   /   /   /
Twenty-eight, twenty-eight, twenty-eight, twenty-eight.

/   /   /   /
Four times seven is twenty-eight.

A more musically interesting song that talks about numbers and measuring is "Inch Worm." Because it has two voice parts, it is more appropriate for students in the fourth or fifth grade.

THE INCH WORM

Words and Music by Frank Loesser

Two and two are four, four and four are eight; That's all you have on your busi-ness-like mind. Two and two are four, four and four are eight; How can you be so blind?____

Refrain

Two and two are four, Four and four are eight,

Inch worm, inch worm, mea-sur-ing the mar-i-golds,

Eight and eight are six-teen, Six-teen and six-teen are thir-ty two.

You and your a-rith-me-tic, you'll prob-a-bly go far.____

Two and two are four, Four and four are eight,

Inch worm, inch worm, mea-sur-ing the mar-i-golds,

Eight and eight are six-teen, Six-teen and six-teen are thir-ty two.

Seems to me you'd stop and see how beau-ti-ful they are.

Music and Science

Many songs and musical works can be found that refer to natural objects and phenomenon like the weather. Most of them are more poetic than factual. For example, *Clair de Lune* by the French composer Claude Debussy gives a beautiful and sensitive impression of moonlight (which is what the title means in English), but it doesn't offer any factual information about the moon.

The same is true of *The Planets* by the English composer Gustav Holst. The idea that stimulated Holst's music was the names the planets. But that actually doesn't make them useless for purposes studying about planets. The music provides a different and interesting way of thinking about the planets; the factual data about them can be found in books and other sources. Here is how a teacher might introduce Holst's music.

> You've learned a lot of facts about the planets and the solar system. Now, let's switch to a different way of thinking about them. Listen to some music by a composer named Holst who wrote about the planets. He wrote this music in 1915 and called it *The Planets*. It has seven sections or movements, one for each planet. Why seven instead of nine planets? Because he left out Earth, and Pluto wasn't discovered until 15 years after Holst wrote the music.
>
> But Holst wasn't interested in telling us how many miles away a planet is, or what kind of atmosphere it has. Instead, he was attracted by the names of the planets, which come from the names of ancient Roman gods. One of the sections of *The Planets* is called "Mars, the Bringer of War," and another is called "Mercury, the Winged Messenger." Usually you see pictures of Mercury with wings on his helmet and his feet. Maybe you've seen him on TV. He's the character you see in the ads for sending flowers to people in other cities.
>
> Now I'll play one of the sections of *The Planets*. See if you can tell the Roman god it's named for. I'll play either Mars or Mercury, but I'm not telling you which one. Listen carefully, and then decide which it is. [The teacher plays the movement titled "Mercury."]
>
> *Teacher:* Alberto, which section was that: Mars or Mercury?
>
> *Alberto:* The music was pretty fast, so I think it was Mercury.
>
> *Teacher:* You're right. It was Mercury.
>
> In a day or two we'll listen to Mars. It will remind you of some of the music from the movie *Star Wars*.

Music is, of course, a natural for learning about sound. Acoustics can be a very challenging subject at an advanced level, but some of the principles of sounds can be introduced in elementary school. At the kindergarten and primary level, children can examine the piano and other instruments to discover how their sounds are made. As mentioned in chapter 11, they can see the strings of the piano vibrate and test what happens when pedals are depressed or when the keys are held down. They can also discover that longer bars on mallet instruments are lower in pitch than the shorter ones, that the thicker and longer strings create lower sounds, and that a large drum usually makes a lower sound than a small one.

Students in fourth and fifth grade can tune water glasses. The idea is to take eight glasses or bottles that are exactly alike and fill them with different amounts of water so that they sound a scale when they are struck. The pitch of each glass can be checked against a keyboard instrument. Once tuned, the students can play simple tunes on them.

From this experience students can learn a basic principle of acoustics: All things being equal, the shorter or smaller the amount of material that is allowed to vibrate, the higher the pitch will be. In the case of the water in glasses or bottles, it is the amount of glass not covered by water.

Music and the Arts

There are several ways in which studying the arts can be enriched by references to music. In this example the teacher is helping students understand the concept of form in architecture and music.

> We've learned how to see the patterns in lines of poems, and I think you have done this with Mrs. Johnson in music class with lines of songs. Today let's look at patterns in a different place: In architecture, in buildings. In your books you have a picture of the Chartres Cathedral near Paris.
>
> Look carefully at the Cathedral. Who can point out something about the pattern or design of it? Michael?
>
> *Michael:* It has two towers, one on each side of the Cathedral. It has a balanced pattern.
>
> *Teacher:* That's right; the Cathedral is evenly balanced. Monica, what do you see in the center of the Cathedral about halfway up?
>
> *Monica:* Well, it looks like a big round window.
>
> *Teacher:* Yes, it's called the "rose window." What about the doors and the doorways? Sharonda?
>
> *Sharonda:* The middle door looks like it's a little bigger . . . and the doorways have lots of decorations around them . . . and they're shaped like an upside-down "U" with a point at the top.
>
> *Teacher:* Excellent! Now what about the up-and-down pattern of the Cathedral?
>
> *Sean:* It has sort of three layers, and then the towers are on top of that.
>
> *Teacher:* All right! Now how could we represent the pattern of the Cathedral in letters like you have lines in poetry and in music? [Most of the class responds by saying "*A B A*."]

Chartres Cathedral near Paris, France

Music and Physical Exercise

Music can make physical exercise easier and more enjoyable. The fact that thousands of jazzercise classes take place every day across the country and that so many exercise classes use music testifies to this fact. So do chants that soldiers often say as they march.

On days when the students don't have a physical education class, teachers can ask them to stand and do various motions and stretches in place to the accompaniment of a lively musical piece. They can also march and clap and do similar activities in place. Taking a few minutes to do such activity to music provides a good break from sedentary work. The physical activity can rejuvenate students both physically and mentally.

There are also many songs about health practices for younger children. They include such topics as brushing teeth, eating the right foods, and getting enough sleep. Some are included in the music series books, whereas others are listed on Internet resources.

CODA

Music can very easily enrich other areas of the curriculum. To incorporate music requires only a small amount of planning and knowledge or skill in music. Several resources are available to teachers for involving music in the learning of the other subjects, making it easy for teachers to use music in various ways to enrich the subject matter or motivate learning. There is a wealth of information waiting to be utilized.

ACTIVITIES

1. Examine the indices of one of the elementary music series books. Notice how it classifies materials that can be used with other areas of the curriculum. Report your findings to your methods class.

2. Use the Internet to find music materials that can contribute to the students' learning in other areas of the curriculum. Share your findings with your music methods class.

3. Select a song in one of the elementary music series books. Decide on two different ways in which you could use the words to help students learn about language.

4. Create a few verses in rap style that will help students learn multiplication, addition, or subtraction.

5. Select a song in a foreign language from the elementary music series books. Listen to it on the ancillary CD. Practice saying its words, as well as learning the melody of the song. If time permits, teach the song to others in your methods class.

6. Select one piece of music, either a song that students can sing or a piece for listening, that could be used in conjunction with a social studies lesson. Then decide how you could incorporate it into a lesson.

7. Take eight identical water glasses. Fill them with the necessary amounts of water to create a scale. Check the pitches of the scale with a mallet instrument or keyboard.

8. Look through the elementary music series books for pictures or artworks that reveal a pattern.

SKILL DEVELOPMENT

The new note on the recorder is low C. It is fingered:

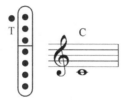

Practice the following patterns that include low C. Remember to blow very gently when playing that note.

Follow these steps with the song "Scarborough Fair:"

1. Clap or say "tah" for the rhythm of the notes. Make sure to observe the rest in the third measure and the dotted quarter/eighth-note pattern in the third measure.

2. Say the note names as you finger the notes on your recorder.

3. Play the song on your recorder. Hint: You may wish to learn it one phrase at a time before attempting the entire song.

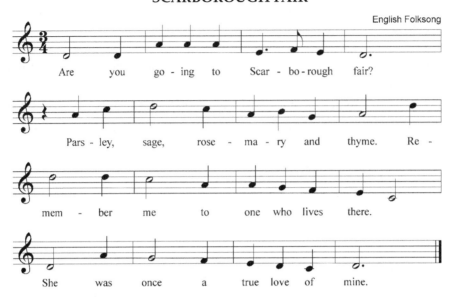

SCARBOROUGH FAIR

English Folksong

Are you go - ing to Scar - bo - rough fair?

Pars - ley, sage, rose - ma - ry and thyme. Re -

mem - ber me to one who lives there.

She was once a true love of mine.

4. Sing the song using the note names, and then sing it with the words.

5. Play the song again on the recorder. Try to make it as smooth and songlike as you did when you sang it.

6. Play the melody of the song on a keyboard or piano. The first phrase can be played without moving your hand by starting with your thumb on D. Start the second phrase with the second finger on A. Start the high D on the third phrase with the little finger. When you get to the A in the third line, change to the little finger for the second A. Conclude the fourth phrase by playing the low D with the thumb and crossing your first finger over to play the next to last note, C.

REVIEW QUESTIONS

1. In what way are the approaches of the elementary music book series and the needs of classroom teachers different?

2. In what ways are learning how to speak and learning to sing similar?

3. Explain the educational principle, "Ear it before you eye it."

4. Can rap contribute to students' learning of language skills? If so, in what ways?

5. What actions should both classroom and music teachers take to help students develop the right attitude toward music from non-Western cultures?

6. In what ways can music contribute to learning in mathematics?

7. In what ways can teachers relate "form" in music to "pattern" in the visual arts?

Music and the Classroom Atmosphere

- Music and Classroom Routines
- Contributing to the Learning Process
- Building Confidence and Self-Esteem

In addition to helping students learn in most subject-matter areas, music can play a very beneficial role in aiding teachers in the day-to-day management of their classrooms. Music can also help in developing the students' self-esteem and attitudes, which in many cases are as important as their academic progress. It's no secret that some students come to school from home situations that would challenge anyone to function normally. Unfortunately, these students cannot leave all their problems outside the school door. They carry them over into classrooms, where they can present real challenges for teachers.

Music and Classroom Routines

Starting the School Day

Imagine that you are nine years old and in fourth grade, and it's your first day of school in the fall. You finally find your classroom. You know only a few of the students, and you have a new teacher whom you don't know. The room isn't really noisy, because most of the students feel a bit uncomfortable and a bit scared, just as you do. The atmosphere isn't warm or inviting. Then, the teacher speaks out firmly, "Boys and girls, it's time to get started."

Now imagine the same situation, except that relaxing music is being played. The setting becomes warmer and more comfortable. When the music stops, you know that the school day has started. The teacher can then smile and quietly say, "Welcome to the fourth grade." Music has made for a more friendly classroom setting and provided a clear beginning of the school day.

Two or three generations ago many American school children began every school day by singing a song that began with the words, "Good morning to you! Good morning to you! We're all in our places with bright shining faces." These words may strike you today as dated and quaint, but the song provided a clear starting point to the day, saved teachers the trouble of telling students to take their seats, and maybe helped children who carry more than their share of burdens to forget a few of them for a few moments. Isn't singing a song a nice way to start the school day? Are there "good morning" songs available today? There certainly are, both in the music book series and in materials listed on the Internet. Starting the day with a song is an idea that has much merit.

The value of singing the same song, or alternating between two or three songs, is that students really get to know them. They become the musical equivalent of an old pair of shoes—comfortable and familiar. Some schools start the day with the students singing a patriotic song, which is also an excellent idea. Unfortunately, "The Star-Spangled Banner" has a wide range and is not easy to sing. "My Country 'Tis of Thee" and "God Bless America" are much easier. "America, the Beautiful" is probably the most satisfying song from a musical point of view, but it is a bit more difficult for young children to sing.

Transitions

Changes of activity, such as when students are divided into small groups to work on projects, often are times when the classroom can become noisy and teachers need to raise their voices to be heard. Music can be played for smoother, quieter transitions. Playing music usually has a calming effect or there may be situations in which music can be used to cover some of the sound of the students talking. Music can certainly help make transitions between activities orderly and fun. For example, students can recite a short chant that involves actions such as snapping their fingers or stomping their feet in rhythm.

/   /   /   /   /   /
Hey! Hey! Snap away! [snap, snap]

/   /   /   /   /   /
Hey! Hey! Stomp away! [stomp, stomp]

/   /   /   /   /
This is how we do it [silent beats]

/   /   /   /   /   /   /   /
Every day! [snap, stomp, snap, stomp, snap-stomp]
                              (together)

The fact that actions are involved requires students to pay attention—and lets the teacher know if a student is not involved. Such transitional activities are especially useful in the primary grades.

Short songs can be sung to facilitate transitions. Sometimes new words can be made up to familiar children's songs. For example, these words can be sung to "Mary Had a Little Lamb":

Everybody take your seat,
Take your seat, take your seat,
Everybody take your seat,
Now we'll sit right down!

Class, we need to end our group meetings on how the Native Americans lived and come to our seats. As you come back, let's sing our "take your seat" song. [In this situation the teacher does not provide starting directions, he or she just starts singing and the students join in.]

The same tune can serve to make other transitions easier:

Everybody clear your desk,
Etc.

Everybody go to lunch,
Etc.

Everybody quiet now,
Etc.

Teachers and students can make up words to go with different tunes for other transitions in the classroom day. Even if the words don't match the music particularly well, it doesn't matter. Music still makes for smoother, more pleasant transitions. That's so much better than teachers barking out commands. Using music helps improve the classroom atmosphere. Guaranteed.

Contributing to the Learning Process

Children and adults today expect things to happen quickly; Americans tend to get bored easily. For example, the maximum length of a shot on a television show is four seconds; for MTV and many commercials it's much shorter than that. Now, imagine that you are a child and have to sit in school learning math or reading or geography for a long time. Wouldn't you appreciate a break? That's what this teacher is providing.

We've been working hard at reading, haven't we? Let's take a couple of minutes break. Stand up by your seat. I'll play "The Hokey Pokey" CD. You can do the motions, but just stay right where you're standing. We'll just do them in place, and then we can get back to reading with more energy! [The teacher plays "The Hokey Pokey," which calls for shaking arms and legs.]

Other "music breaks" are also possible: singing a song, listening to a CD, having a student who studies piano play for the class, marching in place to a march, and so on.

Educators and psychologists have known for many decades that attention and energy for a task tend to dissipate as it continues. The first ten minutes of an activity normally produce more learning than the next ten minutes, which in turn results in more learning than the next ten minutes, and so on. A break of some type increases the chances of the amount of learning that occurred in the first ten minutes happening again. Breaks, therefore, are not time wasted. Rather, they are good investments in helping students learn.

There are times when a class seems unresponsive and sleepy. Yes, music can help in this situation, too. The breaks cited above can be inserted to stimulate the class, or lively music can be played. Adding these types of breaks is better than chiding the students for not being more actively interested in learning.

Building Confidence and Self-Esteem

The old saying is true: Success breeds success." And—sad to say—failure tends to breed failure. Some children seem to realize at a very young age that school is not for them. Experienced first-grade teachers can usually spot those children who will probably fail or drop out of school in later grades. Can music help children to build confidence and self-esteem, which then increases their chances of succeeding in school—and in life?

Yes, it can help. To begin with, music is another avenue of mental activity, another "intelligence," to use Howard Gardner's term.* Students have different modes or strengths in how they learn. Some children are more gifted verbally (and they usually do well in school), others are more visually oriented, others seemed inclined to music and auditory stimuli, others are more talented in math and quantitative subject matter, others in mechanical tasks, and others excel in psychomotor skills. The more of these modes teachers utilize, the better the chances of helping more students.

Music will be the favorite subject for some students. For a few of them, it may be the only subject in which they succeed. For them, therefore, the more music, the better. It is hoped, of course, that all elementary school students feel that they are competent in music. But for a few students, music may be their school "life preserver."

Songs can encourage self-esteem and positive attitudes in all students. Singing a song about being polite or feeling good will not in and of itself make students be polite or feel happy. *But it can't hurt!* And who knows? Singing and thinking about being polite and feeling happy just may make a difference. At least the students will have thought about such things for a few minutes. And singing a cheerful

* Gardner, Howard. *Frames of Mind* 10th ed. (New York: Basic Books, 1993).

song is certainly better than not singing at all, or having to deal with what seems to some students to be one tedious task after another.

Elementary school students should learn songs, such as "The More We Get Together," which encourage good feelings and a sense of togetherness.

THE MORE WE GET TOGETHER

A day that's special for all children is their birthday. The chances are that this day will not fall on a day when the class has music with the music teacher. For this reason, classroom teachers should be prepared to lead the class in singing "Happy Birthday" for the student. All children should be recognized on their birthday and given the attention it rightfully brings them.

CODA

Music is itself an academic subject, but it can also contribute to the learning of other subjects. It can also help create a more relaxed, cheerful, and alive atmosphere in classrooms. In addition, music can help students to feel better about themselves and life in general, which in turn will help them learn.

SUGGESTED ACTIVITIES

1. Examine the music series books and locate a song that would be good for starting the school day.
2. Create a chant that you could use for transitions in the classroom.
3. Create a set of words to a familiar children's song that can be used to make transitions in the classroom smoother.

SKILL DEVELOPMENT

The last new note introduced in the book is B♭. It is fingered:

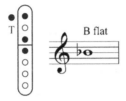

Practice the following patterns to become familiar with it.

"Coventry Carol" includes both the new note, B♭, and F♯. It concludes with B♮. Follow these steps in learning it.

COVENTRY CAROL

Old English Carol

Lul - lay, thou   lit - tle   ti - ny   child,

bye, bye, lul - ly,   lul - lay.   Lul -

lay,   thou   lit - tle   ti - ny   child,

bye, bye, lul - ly,   lul - lay.

1. Say the names of the notes as you finger them. Don't forget that a dotted half note gets three beats, and that twice it is tied to another half note, for a total of five beats.
2. Play the song. You may learn it phrase by phrase.
3. Sing "Coventry Carol" with the words.
4. Play the song on a piano or keyboard. Start with your thumb on G and cross your second finger over to play the F♯s. Play all the B♭s with your third finger.
5. Play the melody on a mallet instrument.

REVIEW QUESTIONS

1. What are the benefits of starting the school day with music?
2. What are the benefits of singing a "good morning" song?
3. What are some characteristics of a good chant or song to use during transitions of classroom activity?
4. Why is music an especially important activity for students who come from undesirable home situations?
5. Is singing songs about good behavior or feeling happy a good idea? Why, or why not?

16

Music and Special Learners

- The Mentally Retarded
- The Physically Challenged
- The Visually Impaired
- The Hearing Impaired
- The Speech Impaired
- The Learning Disabled
- The Emotionally Disturbed

Almost all children can learn to enjoy music and participate in it to some degree. In fact, music can be of particular value to children who are handicapped in their ability to hear, see, think, move, or respond.

The federal government has mandated a "free appropriate public education" for all students with disabilities with the passage of Public Law 94-142 in 1975. The law was renamed the Individuals with Disabilities Act in 1990, and an amended version was passed in 1997. The law requires that children with disabilities not only be involved in a school setting, but also placed in "the least restrictive environment"—that is, with nonhandicapped children of comparable age and ability. This practice is called *mainstreaming.* For this reason, most classrooms are likely to include one or more handicapped learners.

When changes in the music program are needed for special learners, the alternations most often involve the rate of learning and in some cases the scope of what is learned. The child with a disability may take quite a bit longer to accomplish the same amount of learning as other children. Nor can every handicapped child succeed at every task. Students with physical disabilities may not be able to participate in some activities that involve movement. Retarded children may never be able to conceptualize some aspects of music, but most are able to participate in music and enjoy the experience.

The Mentally Challenged

Several terms have been devised to classify varying degrees of mental retardation, but they all refer to below-average intellectual ability. The mentally challenged students who are mainstreamed into regular classrooms are likely to be only mildly retarded, and they can do many things in music. They learn more slowly and in smaller increments, however, and they require more repetition. Their attention span is short. Because they are less able to generalize, concrete learning experiences are more effective. Their language ability is limited, so reading and writing is not successful in most cases.

Mentally challenged children are usually quite receptive to music, and a teacher can enhance their enjoyment by keeping these points in mind when teaching them:

1. Choose songs with repetition in words and music, and a text that has concrete imagery.
2. Base the learning on active participation. A song with motions requires the student to pay attention to the words, and helps the teacher assess how well the child is understanding.
3. Keep verbal directions and explanations short and to the point.
4. Change songs and activities frequently.
5. Praise each student frequently, by name, for specific accomplishments.
6. Do not confine instruction to simple tasks that the students can always do; they need to be challenged at times.

Self-image and confidence can be encouraged by hearing their name. Severely retarded children who are unable to speak show alertness when their names are spoken. Teachers may need to speak or sing the name directly in front of the child, and bend down or touch the child lightly to make contact. Songs can be altered by substituting the name of a child in the class. For example, "Little David, Play on Your Harp" can become "Lori Gibson, Play on Your Harp."

Students who can associate their names with letters will enjoy the song "Initials." The words should be adapted, of course, to accommodate the needs of children with limited mobility.

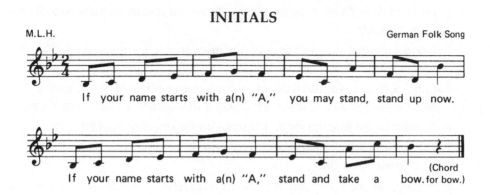

The Physically Challenged

Sometimes termed "orthopedically impaired," these students are limited in mobility and may lack coordination. Physical activity in music may be altered to accommodate orthopedic disabilities, but it should not be eliminated. A child in a wheelchair can participate by moving rhythmically while others march with the music. Musical instruments can be adapted for playing, too, even to the extent of hitting a bell with a beater held between the teeth. In such cases the instrument's height may need to be adjusted, or other arrangements made for the student's comfort. Most physically disabled children who are not in other ways deficient are ingenious in thinking up ways to overcome their disability. With a little help, they can do nearly everything that other class members do, but sometimes their participation takes a different form.

The Visually Impaired

Students with vision problems are usually able to function well in music classes, probably because their condition has required them to listen carefully and remember what they hear. Their limitation in music involves reading printed music and other visual materials. Braille, an international system of reading through the fingertips by feeling embossed dots on paper, has a code for music as well as for letters and numbers. But few children in elementary school have learned to read music in Braille, and the system is slow, even for people who have learned it.

Another area in which students with limited sight encounter difficulty is in moving to music. They cannot see how others move, so they cannot imitate movement. They must also contend with the possibility of physical injury when they move in an unfamiliar setting.

Teachers should keep these points in mind when teaching students with visual limitations:

1. Remember not to rely on instruction by visual means; explain verbally for these students.

2. Encourage the students to identify instruments by touch as well as by sound.

3. Label bells and Autoharp buttons with tactile symbols or Braille letters. The student may be able to make the letters if the teacher doesn't know them.

4. Prepare raised-line drawings, if special duplicators are available.

5. Use wide-lined staff paper and large print to help partially sighted children read music notation.

6. Arrange for vision-impaired students to practice parts on an independent basis so that they are prepared ahead of time for the music class.

7. Assign a sighted partner to help a sight-impaired student in activities that involve moving about the room.

8. Do no ask visually impaired children to cover their ears.

The Hearing Impaired

In clinical terms, "deaf" refers to profound hearing loss, whereas "hard of hearing" describes less severe impairment. Very few children hear nothing at all. Some are unable to hear pitches in certain ranges, and others cannot hear soft sounds. With the improvement of hearing technology, the trend today is to develop whatever hearing potential a child has, rather than to rely completely on lip reading or signing. Fewer than 50 percent of speech sounds are visible, so lip reading is limited in effectiveness, and signing is limited by the small number of persons who can communicate using it.

A hearing aid amplifies the sound entering the ear, and so it must be fitted to the individual by a specialist. Teachers need to know a student's hearing ability with the aid, because it's with the aid that the student will be functioning in classes. Although they are remarkable devices, hearing aids are limited in terms of the distance at which they can pick up sounds and their fidelity for reproducing timbres. Like listening to music over the telephone, hearing through an aid provides less richness of sound than normal hearing does. Loud sounds must never be produced directly into a hearing aid, because the device has already been calibrated to provide the best sound level for that student's needs.

Although most sounds are transmitted to the brain through the ears, vibrations are also felt through other parts of the body. The tactile sense complements the ear, and it's the reason that students with hearing problems are encouraged to touch sound sources. Hearing-impaired persons can learn to feel a difference between high and low pitches, and this helps them to sing. Hearing-impaired students have been taught to play conventional wind instruments such as the clarinet and saxophone, on which pitches can be located without acute hearing.

As might be expected, hearing-impaired students exhibit poor speech development as a result of their auditory limitations. Often what they try to say is difficult to understand and lacking in inflection. For this reason, working on language and words in music class can be helpful.

Teachers should remember these points when teaching students with hearing problems:

1. Do not startle the students by touching them after approaching from outside their range of vision.

2. Do not speak when turned away from the class, as when writing on the chalkboard.

3. Speak directly to the student, even if it means bending down in the case of small children.

4. Speak clearly with normal fluency and inflection, but do not talk loudly.

5. Encourage the students to talk, not merely gesture. Feel free to correct their speech or to admit that you do not understand what they said, but do so in a positive and constructive manner.

6. Use visual as well as verbal symbols to indicate the beginning of a song and similar activities.

7. Do not expect a high degree of timbre discrimination.

8. Encourage hearing-impaired students to touch sound sources directly, so they can feel the vibrations and sense the beat.

9. Do not ask hearing-impaired students to close their eyes.

The Speech Impaired

Communications disorders are evident in poor articulation, stuttering, voice irregularities, unnatural pitch range, and use of faulty word sequence. The fact that music helps overcome stuttering and stammering was mentioned in chapter 1. Music is helpful in aiding over 92 percent of all such speech problems.* Perhaps it is successful because vocal music treats speech in a way that differs from the students' usual experience with language. In singing, vowels are sustained, and the rhythmic flow of the music encourages fluency of expressing other nonverbal sounds. Other songs contain echoes, which are beneficial in providing phrases to be imitated. Needless to say, all musical experiences related to speech for students who are not proficient in speaking should be undertaken in a relaxed and non-threatening atmosphere.

---

* Richard M. Graham, comp., *Music for the Exceptional Child* (Reston, VA: Music Educators National Conference, 1975), p. 35.

The Learning Disabled

This category as defined in the *Federal Register* includes any "disorder in one or more of the basic psychological processes involved in understanding or in using language, spoken or written, which may manifest itself in an imperfect ability to listen, think, speak, read, write, spell, or do mathematical calculations."[*] These are students of average or above average intelligence, although at times they exhibit characteristics of mental retardation. It takes them longer to organize information that comes to them from two or more senses, and they are slower at making judgments, evidently because they are trying to process information that has become distorted before they can sort it out. Some of them have trouble judging distances and direction, so they cannot play catch with a ball, for example. Some cannot use two senses at the same time, so they cannot simultaneously sing and walk. Others have a poor concept of time, so they have little sense of past or future. Still others fail to remember for more than a few seconds.

Children with learning disabilities often have one sense that is stronger than the others, and some are quite talented in music. When possible, teachers should work with the stronger capability to build the student's confidence and then seek to improve performance in the weaker areas. The student should learn one point thoroughly before attempting another.

These students do not profit from repetition to the extent that mentally retarded children do, because the same drill may elicit a different response each time.

Teachers should follow these guidelines in teaching learning disabled students:

1. Get the student's attention before trying to communicate.

2. Present only one directive at a time.

3. Limit the number of choices offered to the student.

4. Use visual materials that are uncluttered with distracting images or printing.

5. In action songs, be ready to help the student identify right and left sides or recall the sequence of motions when patterned responses are called for.

6. Expect short attention spans, or overattention, as when the student seems unable to break the spell of interest in a prior activity.

7. Do not pressure a learning-disabled student for a response before he or she is ready to respond. If there has been a pattern of responding impulsively, encourage the student to take time to think.

8. Praise the student for specific accomplishments, especially in matters involving attentiveness, sequencing, and problem solving.

9. Maintain order and consistency in classroom operation.

---

* *Federal Register* 42(August 23, 1977) 42478.

The Emotionally Disturbed

This handicap features an inability to learn that cannot be explained by intellectual, sensory, or health factors. Emotionally disturbed children exhibit inappropriate behavior or feelings under normal circumstances and have difficulty working with others. Their antisocial behavior may take the form of withdrawal, hyperactivity, clowning, defiance, or aggression. Students who are antisocial generally have a poor opinion of themselves and feel insecure, despite frequent displays of bravado. They seem unconcerned about any future rewards or penalties their actions may bring.

Music instruction can help both withdrawn and aggressive students. Music by its nature is a different language. Furthermore, music classes and activities are relatively short, so music is a break from the school routine for them. In addition, music often calls for a degree of social interaction, which many emotionally disturbed students need.

Teachers can reinforce a student's progress toward emotional stability in several ways:

1. Choose songs with texts that contribute to a positive self-image and encourage sensitivity to others.

2. Plan activities to accommodate a short attention span.

3. Limit the number of choices available to the student. Often such students feel more secure when they are simply told what they will be doing.

4. Plan carefully for any activities involving movement.

5. Recognize that for no apparent reason these students will have good and bad days.

6. Try behavior modification techniques, which reinforce desirable behavior through a system of rewards.

7. Find time to help the student on a one-on-one basis, because individual attention is often what is needed and wanted by the student.

CODA

Helping students with disabilities is demanding and difficult. Even with good support services in terms of counseling and materials, the responsibility for the disabled students' learning and well-being falls largely on the classroom teacher, who must be knowledgeable, patient, understanding, and resourceful. A patient attitude on the part of the teacher may be the most important factor in ensuring that the music experience will be enjoyable and productive for both teachers and students.

SUGGESTED ACTIVITY

1. Observe a classroom in which some of the students have one or more disabilities. Notice their behavior for one hour. Also look for the actions on the part of the teacher to help these students. Write up your observations.

SKILL DEVELOPMENT

The song "Coventry Carol" appears here in a two-part version.

1. Because the melody was learned in the preceding chapter, concentrate now on the new harmony part. When the methods class meets, divide into two groups and have each play the song in one part. Trade parts occasionally.

COVENTRY CAROL

Old English Carol

Lul - lay, thou   lit - tle   ti - ny   child,

bye, bye, lul - ly,   lul - lay.   Lul -

lay,   thou   lit - tle   ti - ny   child,

bye, bye, lul - ly, lul - lay.

2. Conclude your skill development with a performance. Your methods class can play "Coventry Carol" on the recorder in two parts, with some of the class singing the melody. Trade roles several times.

REVIEW QUESTIONS

1. What is mainstreaming? Why is it likely that both music and classroom teachers will encounter students who are being mainstreamed for part or all of the school day?

2. Why is it desirable with mentally challenged students to substitute their names in songs or sing a song that includes their initials?

3. Should physically disabled students be encouraged to move to music? Why, or why not?

4. Why are students who are visually impaired often better listeners than students without visual limitations?

5. Why are hearing aids more useful in helping students with hearing problems than signing or lip reading?

6. Why is it likely that students who stutter rarely do so when they sing?

7. What actions can a teacher take to help a student with an attention-deficit disorder, which is a type of emotional disability?

Appendix A
Music Books

Elementary Music Series Book Publishers

Making Music (K–6) © 2002. Glenview, IL: Silver Burdett/Scott Foresman. Scott Foresman. 1900 East Lake Avenue, Glenview, IL 60025. www.sbgmusic.com

Share the Music (K–5) © 2003. New York: Macmillan/McGraw-Hill School Division. Two Penn Plaza, New York, NY 10121. www.mhschool.com

Music Expressions (K–5) © 2004. Miami: Warner Bros. Publications. 15800 NW 48th Avenue, Miami, FL 33179. www.music-expressions.com/Default.aspc

Jump Right In: The General Music Series (1–3). Chicago: GIA Publications. 7404 South Mason Ave. Chicago, IL 60638. www.giamusic.com

Books on Music and Other Subjects

Ardley, N. (1991). *Science Book of Sound*. New York: Harcourt Brace.

Bates, K. L. and N. Waldman, illustr. (1993). *America the Beautiful*. New York: Atheneum.

Cole, J., ed. (1999). *Best Loved Folktales of the World*. Econo-Clad Books.

Goodkin, D. (1997). *A Rhyme in Time: Speech Activities and Improvisation for the Classroom*. Miami: Warner Bros. Publications.

Hamilton, V. with L. and D. Dillion, illustr. (1995). *Her Stories: African American Folktales, Fairy Tales, and True Tales*. New York: Scholastic Trade.

Prelutsky, J. and M. So, illustr. (1997). *The Beauty and the Beast: Poems from the Animal Kingdom*. New York: Alfred A. Knopf.

Rosen, M., ed. and W. Goldberg, illustr. (1992). *South and North, East and West: An Oxfam Book of World Tales*. Cambridge, MA: Candlewick Press.

Spier, P., illustr. and F. S. Key. (1992). *The Star-Spangled Banner*. New York: Doubleday.

Books on Music and Movement

Bennett, P. D. and D. R. Bartholomew. (1997). "Folk Song Games" in *Song Works 1*, Belmont, CA: Wadsworth Publishing Company.

Brophy, T. (2002). *I've Got to Move!* Miami: Warner Bros. Publications.

Burton, L. H. and T. Kudo. (2000). *SoundPlay: Understanding Music through Creative Movement*. Reston, VA: MENC-The National Association for Music Education.

Choksy, L. and D. Brummitt. (1987). *120 Singing Games and Dances*. Englewood Cliffs, NJ: Prentice-Hall.

Froseth, J., A. Blaser, and P. Weikart. (1993). *Music for Movement*. Chicago: GIA Publications.

Weikart, P. (1988). *Movement Plus Rhymes, Songs, and Singing Games*. Ypsilanti, MI: The High/Scope Press.

Weikart, P. (1996). *Rhythmically Moving*. Ypsilanti, MI: The High/Scope Press.

Appendix B
Recorder
Fingering Chart

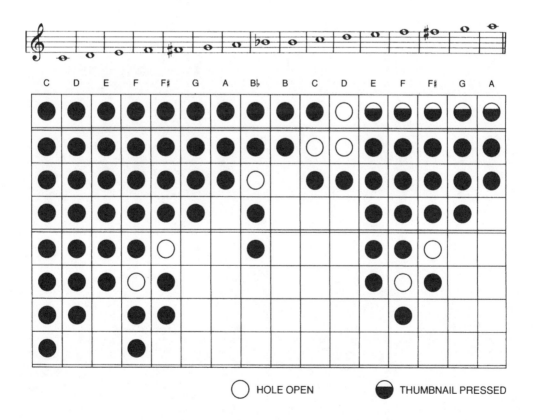

Glossary

accent	sudden loudness at the beginning of a musical sound
accidental	a sharp, flat, or natural within a composition to indicate a pitch not in the key signature
action song	a song that can appropriately involve the body in addition to singing
alto	the lowest women's singing voice
Autoharp	an instrument with metal strings, which the player strums with one hand while depressing a button with the other to sound the desired chord
bar	a measure in rhythmic notation
barline	the vertical line that separates each bar or measure from adjacent measures
bass	in vocal music, the lowest men's singing voice
bass clef ($\mathcal{9}$)	the clef in which F below middle C is positioned on the fourth line from the bottom of the staff
beam	a straight, heavy line connecting the stem ends of consecutive notes that would otherwise have individual flags
beat	the recurrent throb or pulse in music, which is the unit by which the passing of time is measured
bells	metal strips arranged in keyboard fashion on a supporting frame that are struck with a mallet; in some sets, the bells can be removed for individual use
borrowed pattern	a rhythm pattern in which the note values represent durations different from those indicated by the meter signature; such patterns are identified by a number above the altered portion
canon	a composition in which the imitation between two or more lines in not always at the same pitch level

207

castanets	two small, wooden cup-shaped pieces struck together against the leg or palm of the hand, or held in one hand and tapped together with the fingers, or (attached to a handle) struck together by a whip-like motion of the wrist.
chamber music	instrumental music for small groups involving only one player on each part
chord	the simultaneous sounding of three or more pitches
chord function	the role or function of a chord in a particular key
chromatic notes	notes altered by a sharp, flat, or natural
claves	two cylindrical wood blocks that are struck together; pronounced *clah*-vays
clef	a sign placed on the staff to show the exact pitches of the notes
coda	a concluding section that is not essential to the form of a piece of music
composing	developing an original musical work
compound meter	meter in which the beat subdivides in three background pulses
consonance	the effect of simultaneous sounds that the listener considers agreeable or pleasant
contour	the "shape" of a melody created by the ascending and descending notes
counterpoint	the simultaneous sounding of two or more equally distinct melodic lines
crescendo *(cresc.)*	becoming gradually louder
cymbals	large metal discs that are struck together or suspended singly and hit with a mallet or steel brush
da Capo *(d.c.)*	a term directing the performer to return to the beginning of the music
decrescendo *(decresc.)*	becoming gradually softer
descant	a contrasting line to a song, usually at a higher pitch level
diminuendo *(dim.)*	becoming gradually softer
dissonance	simultaneous sounds that the listener considers clashing or harsh
dominant chord	the chord built on the fifth step of a major or minor scale
dominant seventh chord	a four-note chord built on the fifth step of a scale, with an interval of a seventh between its root and top note
dotted note	a note followed by a dot that increases the value of the note by one half
drum	an instrument consisting of a skin or plastic sheet stretched over a frame and struck with a stick or the hand
dynamics	the varying levels of loudness and softness
echo clapping	performing a rhythmic pattern by immediately imitating another person's performance of it

eighth note	a note with a solid head connected to a stem with a flag
ensemble	a group of musicians; also, the effect of unity achieved when they perform together
fine arts	the body of subjects, including music, visual arts, theater, and dance, that are pursued for their aesthetic, artistic qualities
finger cymbals	two small metal discs struck against each other
finger plays	a series of finger, hand, or arm motions performed rhythmically to depict the images suggested by the song or rhyme
flag	the short curved line extending from the end of the stem of a note
flat	a symbol (♭) indicating that the pitch should be lowered by one half step
form	the design or plan of a piece of music
glockenspiel	small metal strips arranged in keyboard fashion and struck with a mallet
guiro	a notched gourd scraped with a stick; pronounced *gwee*-roh
guitar	a flat-bodied six-stringed instrument that is plucked to produce notes
half note	a note with an open head connected to a stem
half step	the smallest pitch interval on a keyboard instrument
hand signs	a system of signals conveyed by using various hand positions to represent the different pitch syllables
harmonic minor scale	a minor scale in which step 7 is raised so that it is one half step away from the keynote
harmony	the effect created when pitches are sounded simultaneously
improvisation	creating music spontaneously, often within accepted guidelines
interpretation	the style of musical expressiveness when performing it
interval	the distance from one pitch to another
inversion	turning an interval or melody upside down, so that what ascended now descends, and so on
irregular meter	beat patterns that do not follow a regular pattern
jingle bells	small spherical bells attached to a strap or frame and shaken
key	the tonal center of a piece of music, usually named for the scale on which the music is based
key center	the tonic or pitch around which the music is based
key signature	the sharps or flats at the left of the staff indicating that certain notes are to be consistently raised or lowered one half step unless indicated by a natural sign
keyboard	an arrangement of five black and seven white keys that is repeated for several octaves
keynote	the tonic note or note around which the music is centered
locomotor activity	actions that require movement from one place to another

ledger lines	short horizontal lines indicating the pitch of notes too high or too low to be placed on the staff
major key	the effect created when steps 3–4 and 7–8 are one half step apart
major scale	an eight-tone scale with half steps between 3–4 and 7–8
maracas	rattles, often in pairs, that are shaken to produce the sound of moving pellets
measure	the notation indicated by vertical lines for one unit of a metrical pattern
melodic minor scale	a minor scale in which steps 6 and 7 are raised one half step when ascending and lowered when descending
melody	a series of consecutive pitches that form a cohesive musical entity
meter	the grouping of beats according to the relative emphasis
meter signature	the two numbers placed at the beginning of a piece of music that indicate the metrical pattern and the type of note that equals one beat
metallophone	an instrument consisting of metal bars arranged in keyboard fashion that are placed on a frame and struck with a mallet
middle C	the C nearest the middle of the keyboard; also the note that is halfway between the bass and treble clefs
minor key	the effect created when the third step above the keynote is lowered one half-step
mixed meter	the changing of meter signatures within a musical work
modulation	changing the key within a piece of music
music	the art of organized sound
music consultant	a music specialist whose role is not primarily to teach classes but to provide help to teachers
music reading	the ability to perform music from looking at music notation
music specialist	a teacher who holds a certification in music and whose job is teaching music
music supervisor	an administrator certified in music who provides leadership for the music program
natural	a symbol (♮) that cancels a sharp or flat previously applied to a note
natural minor scale	a minor scale in which there are half steps between 2–3 and 5–6
nonlocomotor activity	actions that do not require movement from on place to another
note	a sign placed on the staff to indicate the pitch and duration of a musical sound
note value	the duration of a note in terms of the beat
octave	the interval between a note and the nearest pitch with the same letter name
Orff-*Schulwerk*	techniques for learning music devised by the German composer Carl Orff

ostinato	a short pattern of notes or rhythm that is repeated persistently
parallel keys	major and minor keys that share the same keynote; e.g., C major and C minor
partner songs	two songs that can be sung simultaneously because they are identical in key, harmonic structure, and length
Patsch	German for a thigh slap
pentatonic scale	a five-note scale in which every note is either a whole step or one and one-half steps away from its closest neighbor, like the black keys on a keyboard
phrase	a logical group of sounds
piano	(1) the term for a soft dynamic level; (2) a large keyboard instrument capable of producing eighty-eight pitches
pickup note	an unstressed note, usually a beat or less in length, that begins a phrase or piece of music
pitch	the highness or lowness of a musical sound
primary chords	the chords most commonly used in a major or minor key—I, IV, and V
program music	instrumental music associated with a story or nonmusical idea
quarter note	a note with a solid head and a stem
range	the upper and lower pitch limits of a voice, instrument, or a piece of music
recorder	a wind instrument on which pitches are determined by opening and covering holes
register	the general pitch level of a song
relative keys	major and minor keys that share the same key signature; e.g., C major and A minor
rest	a period of measured silence in music
rhythm	the sense of orderly motion as music progresses
rhythm syllables	a word system that assigns a certain syllable to a particular note value
root	the note on which a chord is built and the note that gives the chord its name
rote	learning by imitating another person
round	strict imitation occurring between two or more lines of music throughout the song
sandblocks	flat metal or wood surfaces over which sandpaper is stretched to create a scratching sound when two are rubbed together
scale	a series of pitches ascending or descending according to a prescribed pattern of intervals
sequence	the immediate repetition of a musical phrase at successfully higher or lower pitch levels

seventh chord	a chord of four pitches, each a third apart
sharp	a symbol (♯) indicating that a pitch should be raised one half step
sightreading	the ability to look at music notation and translate its symbols into sound
simple meter	meter in which the beat subdivides into two background pulses
singing game	a structured group activity in which the players perform similar motions in a particular formation, often a circle
sixteenth note	a note written as a solid head connected to a stem with two flags
sleigh bells	small spherical bells attached to a strap or frame and shaken
slur	a curved line connecting two or more notes of different pitch, indicating that there should be no separation between them; in vocal music it also connects notes that are to be sung on a single syllable
solfeggio (Italian), *solfège* (French)	use of *do, re, mi* syllable system for identifying pitches
soprano	the highest women's singing voice
staff	the five lines and four spaces on which notes are placed
step	an interval in which one note is adjacent to the other both in alphabet letter name and in the position of their note heads on the staff
stick notation	a simplified form of rhythm notation in which unnecessary symbols are eliminated
subdominant chord	the chord built on the fourth step of the scale
syncopation	the placement of an accented note where it is not usually expected, or the removal of an accented note where it is expected
tambourine	an instrument having a skin or plastic sheet stretched across a wooden hoop rimmed with metal discs that produce a jangling sound when it is shaken or struck
temple blocks	wood blocks struck with a mallet to produce a hollow, resonant sound
tempo	the rate of speed at which beats recur
tenor	the highest men's singing voice
theme	a melody that is structurally important because of its role in a work of music
third	the interval from one note to another when there is only one alphabet letter between the names of the two notes; e.g., C to E
tie	a curved line connecting two or more notes of identical pitch to indicate that they should be combined into one continuous note
timbre	the tone quality of an instrument or voice; pronounced *tam*-ber
time signature	the meter signature, which is the two numbers at the beginning of a piece that indicate the number of beats in a measure and what note equals one beat

tonal center	the tonic, which is the pitch around which the piece of music is built
tone color	the tone quality or timbre of a voice or instrument
tonic	the pitch on which a scale or piece of music is built
tonic chord	the chord built on step 1 of a scale
transposition	performing an entire piece of music in a key different from the original
treble clef (𝄞)	the clef in which the G above middle C is positioned on the second line from the bottom of the staff
triad	a chord containing three pitches a third apart
triangle	a three-sided suspended metal frame struck with a metal beater to produce a clear, metallic sound
unison	the musical result of two or more sounds produced simultaneously at exactly the same pitch level
upbeat	an unstressed note, usually the last beat of a measure, that begins a musical phrase
value	the duration represented by a particular note
water bottles	a set of glass containers, each holding a level of water that will produce a specific pitch when a bottle is tapped
whole note	a note with an open head and no stem
whole step	an interval as wide as two half steps
wood block	a block of wood struck with a mallet to produce a hollow, resonant sound
xylophone	wooden bars arranged in a keyboard fashion and mounted on a frame that are struck with mallets

Song Index

Index

Vocabulary Mastery 1

Using and Learning the Academic Word List

LINDA WELLS

Ann Arbor
The University of Michigan Press

⊗ Printed on acid-free paper

2010   2009   2008   2007   4   3   2   1

ISBN-13: 978-0-472-03073-6
ISBN-10: 0-472-03073-6

Acknowledgments

Many thanks to all those who have encouraged and supported me in this project. I am grateful for your unwavering energy, enthusiasm, and advice. A huge thank you especially to my editor, Kelly Sippell, for her continuing friendship and editorial guidance, and to Bob Carocari for his support and patience throughout. Many thanks also to the staff at the University of Michigan Press for their hard work, and to all the students and colleagues who have contributed to this volume in one way or another over the years. To all, my heartfelt thanks.

The author and publisher would like to acknowledge the original sources of material reproduced in this text.

AWL List

Permission granted by Averil Coxhead to use the Academic Word List in the appendix and in the book's subtitle.

Unit 1

Unit-opening photo courtesy of Kreutz Photography for photo of Lance Armstrong, 2005 Tour de France.

Adapted excerpts from *It's Not about the Bike* by Lance Armstrong with Sally Jennings (New York: The Berkley Publishing Group, Penguin Putnam, 2001), 214–15; *Every Second Counts* by Lance Armstrong with Sally Jenkins (New York: Broadway Books, Random House, 2003), 156–59; and *Bike Racing 101* by Kendra and René Wenzel (Champaign, IL: Human Kinetics, 2003), 204–5.

Photos courtesy of the Library of Congress and photos.com.

Unit 2

Unit-opening photo courtesy of iStockphoto.com

Adapted excerpts from *Through a Window: My Thirty Years with the Chimpanzees of Gombe* by Jane Goodall (Boston: Houghton Mifflin, 1990), 18–20; *The Deluge and the Ark* by Dale Peterson (Boston: Houghton Mifflin, 1989), 323–24; *The Man Who Listens to Horses* by Monty Roberts (New York: Ballantine / Random House, 1997), 31–36.

Photos courtesy of photos.com and Getty Images.

Unit 3

Unit-opening photo courtesy of Getty Images.

Adapted excerpts from *The Diary of a Young Girl: The Definitive Edition* edited by Otto Frank and Mirjam Pressler (New York: Bantam / Doubleday / Random House, 1997), 175–76; *The Importance of Anne Frank* by John Wukovits (New York: Lucent, 1999), 48–49; *Anne Frank: The Biography* by Melissa Muller (New York: Metropolitan Books / Henry Holt, 1998), 303–6.

Photo courtesy of Judy Dean.

Unit 4

Unit-opening photo courtesy of photos.com.

Adapted excerpts from *The Hungry Ocean* by Linda Greenlaw (New York: Hyperion, 1999), 143–45; *The Riverkeepers* by John Cronin and Robert F. Kennedy, Jr. (New York: Touchstone / Simon and Schuster, 1997), 177; *An Inconvenient Truth* by Al Gore (Emmaus, PA: Rodale, 2006), 164–68.

Photos courtesy of photos.com. Chart courtesy Rodale from *An Inconvenient Truth*.

Unit 5

Unit-opening photo courtesy of NASA.

Adapted excerpts from President John F. Kennedy's address at Rice University on the Nation's Space Effort, September 12, 1962, Houston, Texas, available at *www.jfklibrary.org/Historical+Resources/Archives/Reference+Desk/Speeches/JFK/*; *A Man on the Moon* by Andrew Chaikin (New York: Penguin, 1994), 205–6, 208–9; and *Moon Shot* by Alan Shepard and Deke Slayton with Jay Barbree and Howard Benedict (Atlanta, GA: Turner Publishing, 1994), 329–30.

Photos courtesy of NASA and the Associated Press.

Unit 6

Unit-opening photo courtesy of the Library of Congress.

Adapted excerpts from *Seabiscuit* by Laura Hillenbrand (New York: Random House / Ballantine, 2001), 70; "Tribute to a Hero" by Oscar Otis, *Los Angeles Times*, March 3, 1940; "The Great Depression" in *The National Geographic Almanac of World History* by Patricia S. Daniels and Stephen G. Hyslop (Washington, DC: National Geographic Society, 2003), 291–92.

Photos courtesy of photos.com and the Associated Press.

Contents

To the Teacher

Teachers and students alike realize that strong vocabulary skills are necessary for academic success. Specifically, students need to know the vocabulary they will most frequently encounter in their academic studies in order to successfully complete their reading and writing assignments. This book, *Vocabulary Mastery 1*, teaches students the words they need to know to succeed in their academic work. These words come from the Academic Word List (AWL) developed by Averill Coxhead ["A New Academic Word List," *TESOL Quarterly* 34, no. 2 (2000): 213–38]. The Academic Word List resulted from Coxhead's analysis of a broad corpus of academic texts—about 3.5 million words—from 414 academic texts in 28 topic areas. Out of this corpus, Coxhead selected the 570 word families that occur most frequently in academic texts. *Vocabulary Mastery 1* teaches these word families.

Learning vocabulary involves more than simply recognizing a word. In order to truly know a word, students must:

- **Have multiple exposures to the word.** Nation [*Teaching and Learning Vocabulary*, Newbury House, 1990] concluded that a word needs to be encountered anywhere from five to more than 16 times before it is learned. The readings and exercises in *Vocabulary Mastery 1* provide students with multiple exposures to the target vocabulary. Activities that require student to do outside reading also increase their exposure to the target vocabulary.

- **Know more than the meaning, spelling, and pronunciation of a word.** Students must also learn the grammar of the word, the words it frequently occurs or collocates with, the associations a word has, the frequency with which it occurs, and its register. *Vocabulary Mastery 1* uses an effective interactive approach that develops both explicit and implicit word knowledge. The exercises in this book provide students with word knowledge that is explicitly taught (spelling, meaning, pronunciation, and collocation). It also provides numerous encounters with words to help students develop their own implicit, contextual knowledge (association and register) of words.

- **Be familiar with other members of a word's family.** By learning some or all of a word family, students are able to use the correct form of a word within a particular context. Every unit in *Vocabulary Mastery 1* contains exercises that focus on word families and derivations.

- **Understand collocations.** Knowledge of collocations makes word use more natural. Exercises teach some of the more common collocations of the target vocabulary. More important, though, these exercises raise students' awareness of collocations, which may help students notice collocations when they occur and build their own knowledge of collocation.

- **Know that one word can have different meanings used in different contexts.** Exercises show the different meanings of a target word in the appropriate contexts. Students are encouraged to use a dictionary to help them learn these different meanings.

- **Learn to focus on the words they want to learn.** The readings and exercises in *Vocabulary Mastery 1* contain 200 words from the AWL. To aid students in learning, the target vocabulary in each unit is marked in **bold.** Other AWL vocabulary in the readings is underlined. AWL words that occur in exercises are marked only if they are target words. Words and idioms that occur infrequently but are needed to understand the text are glossed in the margins.

The readings and vocabulary appear in an order so that skills and concepts are built upon as students progress through the book.

In addition to academic vocabulary, this text helps students develop the critical-thinking skills necessary for academic achievement. Activities in each unit require students to think about and analyze what they have read. In addition, writing assignments require students to think critically about what they have read as they learn and practice skills they will need in their academic classes. These skills include: answering questions and supporting answers with concrete examples, interpreting a chart and answering questions about it, ordering information chronologically and writing paragraphs that give that information, making a schedule based on information given, analyzing and writing about a problem they select, summarizing, giving an opinion, and identifying causes and effects.

Vocabulary Mastery 1 has six units, each on a particular high-interest theme. Each of the six units is divided into:

- **Vocabulary Preview 1 and 2.** These exercises help students and teachers discover how much target vocabulary is already familiar.

- **Reading Preview.** These questions are designed to activate students' prior knowledge of the topic.

- **Introduction to the Readings.** An introductory reading about the topic provides background information about the readings that follow.

- **Three short readings on a theme or topic that contain 15 target words from the Academic Word List.** At least one reading is biographical or autobiographical, and the other readings are non-fiction. The variety of readings exposes students to the target words in different writing styles and voices. In addition to the target vocabulary, all of the readings expose students to a number of other words from the AWL and recycle AWL words already learned.

- **Comprehension Check.** This series of True/False questions determines how well students understood the Introduction and Readings.

- **A list of 15 target vocabulary words from the Academic Word List.**

- **Ten vocabulary-based activities that include:**

  ➤ Understanding Words
    —Word Parts: suffixes, prefixes, and roots
    —Word Relationships: synonyms, antonyms, collocations, and analogies
    —Word Families Chart: a target word and its most commonly used derivatives
    —Word Meanings: multiple meanings of a word
    —Word Forms and Derivatives

  ➤ Understanding Words in Context
    —Using Words Correctly
    —Making Inferences
    —Constructing Sentences

  ➤ Using Words in Communication
    —Reading activities that encourage research and outside reading about the topic
    —Writing activities that ask students to react, summarize, and give an opinion

  ➤ Critical-Thinking Questions
    —Questions to be used for writing assignments or class discussion

The exercises and activities in *Vocabulary Mastery 1* give students the opportunity to study academic vocabulary in two important ways. Students encounter each word as a discrete language unit and also within natural contexts as part of a whole language system. An Answer Key for all exercises is available at *www.press.umich.edu/esl/*.

I hope that you and your students find this textbook is a useful and enjoyable way to learn vocabulary from the Academic Word List. Good luck in your endeavors!

To The Student

Vocabulary Mastery 1 will help you learn the vocabulary words that you will need to know in order to do well in your academic studies. These words come from the Academic Word List (Coxhead 2000). This list contains 570 words that are most commonly used in academic reading. These words may be different from the words you hear and use in your everyday life, but by learning these words along with a basic 2,000-word vocabulary, you will be able to understand more than 85 percent of your academic reading assignments. Here are some suggestions for using this text. Your teacher may have others.

1. Start by finding out how much vocabulary you already know by doing the Vocabulary Preview exercises in each unit.

2. Go over the list of words in the Word Study section of the unit, and cross out the words that you already know.

3. Use your dictionary to find the meanings of words you do not know. Write these in a vocabulary notebook or make vocabulary cards. (See How to Make Vocabulary Cards on page xv for some ideas.) By the time you finish this textbook, you will have your own academic learner dictionary or set of academic vocabulary cards.

4. Read the introduction and readings in the unit. Check your dictionary for words that are not listed on your vocabulary list that you need to know to understand the reading.

5. As you read, check to see whether you understand what you are reading. Ask yourself: Did I understand what I just read? Which sentence or word is giving me a problem? Why? What or who can help me understand this? Can I ask a classmate or my teacher to help me?

6. Answer the Comprehension Check questions, which will show you how well you have understood the introduction and readings. The questions here are answered with True or False. If you have trouble answering these questions you may want to reread the introduction and readings.

7. Once you feel like you understand the introduction and readings, do the activities in the Word Study section.

8. When you have finished all of the activities in the Word Study section, check your answers in the online Answer Key.

9. Reread the introduction and readings to find out if they have become easier to understand.

10. Use outside materials such as books, magazine articles, videos, and films to help you learn more about the topic in each unit. Your local library and the Internet are good places to find outside material. For example, the film *Apollo 13* might be a fun and interesting way to learn more about NASA and the Apollo Project.

Completing this textbook will help you to learn the words you need for academic success. Good luck in your studies!

How to Make Vocabulary Cards

Vocabulary cards are an easy way to study and review new vocabulary words. Make your own vocabulary cards by following these directions.

1. Use one card for each word. You can buy inexpensive index cards at most supermarkets or drugstores.

2. Write each vocabulary word on the front of a card.

3. Write the meaning or meanings of each word on the back of the card in English. You might also want to write the meaning in your native language if you are learning English.

4. Add other helpful information on the back of the card. You might want to include:
   • how the word is pronounced
   • an example sentence for the word
   • a picture that helps you remember the meaning of the word
   • other members of the word's family
   • words that collocate or often appear with that vocabulary word

5. Keep your cards in a box or put them on a ring. Practice with the cards for a few minutes every day. Look at the word on the front of the card, and see if you can remember its meaning. Check the definition on the back of the card to see if you are correct.

6. When you know a word well, move the card to the back of the box. If you don't know a word, keep it near the front where you will practice it often.

7. Review the vocabulary words frequently. This will help you remember and master these important academic vocabulary words.

Professional Cycling

Vocabulary Preview

These sentences contain information from the readings. Fill in the blanks with the word that best completes each sentence.

individual   participate   percent   physically   survive

1. To win the Tour de France, a cyclist must _____ three weeks of very difficult bicycle racing.

2. The cyclists are quite thin: only about 3 or 4 _____ of their total body weight is fat.

3. The riders who _____ in the race train all year to prepare for the Tour de France.

4. Riders must be mentally and _____ strong in order to finish the race.

5. The _____ who finishes all 21 days with the lowest total time wins the race.

Look at the way the underlined words are used in the sentences. Match each word with its meaning or definition.

1. He <u>estimated</u> that it would take about three hours to ride his bicycle 50 miles.

2. Riders use computers and heart rate monitors to collect <u>data</u> while they race and train.

3. Athletes who are paid or win prize money in sports are <u>professionals</u>. Amateurs aren't allowed to make any money.

4. It is hard for riders to <u>sustain</u> such a fast pace for three weeks.

5. A rider can win or lose the Tour de France by a few seconds, even on the <u>final</u> day of the race.

_____ 1. **estimated**   a. the last one

_____ 2. **data**   b. a person who does something for money

_____ 3. **professional**   c. to continue, to maintain

_____ 4. **sustain**   d. information

_____ 5. **final**   e. calculated roughly or approximately

Reading Preview: What Do You Already Know?

Circle the correct answer. If you don't know the answer, guess.

1. Lance Armstrong is

   a. an astronaut

   b. a famous cyclist

   c. a cancer researcher

   d. originally from France

2. Lance Armstrong is probably best known for

   a. wearing only yellow cycling shirts

   b. surviving cancer

   c. winning the Tour de France seven years in a row

   d. coaching young cyclists

3. Lance started bicycle racing

   a. because he wanted to get in shape

   b. when he was a teenager

   c. so he could win prize money

   d. because he wasn't a good student

Introduction to the Readings

(1) Lance Armstrong was born in 1971 in Plano, Texas. He was a natural athlete. He joined a swim club when he was 12 and began swimming seriously. At age 13 he entered an IronKids Triathlon. In a triathlon, the athletes compete in three sports: biking, swimming, and running—three sports that Lance was good at. He won his first triathlon easily and, by age 16, was competing **professionally.** Bicycling soon became his only sport, and during his senior year in high school, Lance trained with the U.S. Olympic cycling team. He began cycling on a full-time basis and competed in the 1989 junior world championships. In 1991 he was the U.S. National Amateur Champion, and he **participated** in the 1992 Olympic games in Barcelona (Spain). Lance's first professional race was the 1992 Classico San Sebastian. He finished in last place, 27 minutes behind the winner, but he refused to quit. That race showed Lance's attitude toward life: Don't quit, no matter what. That attitude helped him **survive** the next big challenge in his life.

(2) In 1996 Lance was the top cyclist in the world. But in October of 1996, he found out that he had cancer that had already spread to his lungs and brain. Even though his doctors gave him a less-than 50 **percent** chance of **surviving,** he did **survive.** He lived through two difficult surgeries and chemotherapy. He was able to start riding and training again just five months after his cancer was discovered. He began racing again in 1998.

(3) Lance has achieved amazing things since his recovery from cancer. He is the only person to win the Tour de France seven times in a row—winning in 1999, 2000, 2001, 2002, 2003, 2004, and 2005. In addition to cycling, Lance **established** the Lance Armstrong Foundation. This organization provides services and support to cancer patients, cancer survivors, and their families. His "don't quit" attitude continues to give hope and to inspire fans and cancer survivors everywhere.

Reading 1: The Tour de France

Excerpt adapted from *It's Not About the Bike: My Journey Back to Life* by Lance Armstrong and Sally Jenkins (New York: Berkley Publishing Group, 2001): 214–15.

(4) It would be easy to see the Tour de France as just another sports event: 200 riders cycling through France, mountains included, over three weeks in the heat of the summer. There is no reason to attempt such a thing. It's a contest in suffering. But for reasons of my own, I think it may be the greatest <u>challenge</u> in the world. To me, of course, it's about living.

Cyclists crossing the Mirabeau Bridge in Gap, France, during Tour de France, 1951.

(5) A little history: the bicycle was invented during the industrial revolution and the first Tour was held in 1903. Of the 60 racers who started, only 21 finished. The event immediately interested the people of France. An **estimated** 100,000 people lined the roads into Paris to watch the race, and there was cheating right from the start: drinks were spiked,* and leaders hoping to slow other riders down threw tacks and broken bottles onto the road. These early riders carried their own food and equipment. Their bikes had just two gears, and they used their feet as brakes. Mountain stages were introduced in 1910 (along with brakes) when the cyclists rode through the Alps, despite the fear of attacks from wild animals. In 1914, the race began on the same day that the Archduke Ferdinand of Austria was shot. Five days after the finish of the race, World War I began.

> ***spiked:** to add a drug or dangerous substance to a drink

(6) Today the race depends on technology. The bikes are so light you can lift them overhead with one hand, and the riders are equipped with computers, heart rate **monitors,** and even two-way radios. But the essential test of the race has not changed: who can best **survive** the difficulties and find the strength to keep going? After my own battle with cancer I couldn't help feeling it was a race I was made for.

Reading 2: Winning Is in the Details

Excerpt adapted from *Every Second Counts* by Lance Armstrong and Sally Jenkins (New York: Broadway Books, Random House, Inc., 2003), 156–59.

(7) There was no mystery or miracle drug that helped me win the Tour de France in 1999. It was a matter of better training and technique and my experience with cancer and willingness to make the sacrifices. If you want to do something great, you need a strong will and attention to detail.

(8) The Tour is basically a math problem. A 2,000-mile race over three weeks that's sometimes won by a difference (or margin) of a minute or less.

How do you move yourself through space on a bicycle, sometimes steeply uphill, at a speed **sustainable** for three weeks? Every second counts.

(9) Riders have to be willing to look at any small part of their body or bike to find extra time. Once you reach a certain level, everyone is good and trains hard. The difference is who is more willing to find the smallest bits of time. You have to become a slave to **data.** You have to measure literally every heartbeat, and every bite you eat, down to every spoonful of cereal. You have to be willing to look too thin, with your body-fat around 3 or 4 **percent,** if it made you faster. If you weigh too little, you wouldn't have the **physical resources** to produce or <u>generate</u> enough speed. If you weigh too much, your body is a burden.* It is a matter of power to weight.

> ***burden:** something that is heavy and difficult to carry

(10) Who knew when you might find a winning difference in December, during equipment testing? You might find another fraction of time in your position on the bike, or in a helmet, or in the composition of a wheel. The winning is really in the details. It's in the details that you get ahead. And in racing, if you aren't getting ahead, you might as well be going backward.

Reading 3: Stage Racing

Excerpt adapted from *Bike Racing 101* by Kendra and René Wenzel
(Champaign, IL: Human Kinetics, 2003), 204–5.

(11) To win a stage of any race, a rider must have the lowest **accumulated** time over all stages. For each stage completed, her finishing time is recorded and added to her times for <u>previous</u> stages. The list of all the riders who have completed all stages so far, organized in order of total time, is called the general classification, or GC. A rider must complete every stage in order to place in the **final** GC.

(12) Each stage has an **individual** winner, and each day has a GC leader. After the first stage, the stage winner **automatically** becomes the <u>overall</u> race leader and is given a special jersey (in the Tour de France, it's the yellow jersey or *maillot jecene*). If that same rider wins the next stage or finishes in close enough time to that stage's winner, she keeps the lead and the leader's jersey. If the current leader loses enough time that another rider <u>achieves</u> the lowest total time, the jersey goes to the other rider. The current stage winner may not be the current overall leader. That depends on the amount of time the riders in the GC make or lose against one another. Stage racing is exciting because a great ride by a competitor or a terrible ride by the current race leader can overcome a multi-minute lead even in the final stage of the race.

(13) The most famous example of a last-stage comeback* happened during the 1989 Tour de France. Frenchman Laurent Fignon,

*comeback: recovering a lead or a return to success

looking for his third Tour de France win, went into the final stage in Paris feeling reasonably certain he could hang on to his 50-second lead over American Greg LeMond during the short 24-kilometer (15-mile) finishing time trial.* LeMond won the three-week race by just eight seconds as Fignon crossed the line exhausted. LeMond's look of joy and Fignon's <u>collapse</u> off his bike equal any great moment in sports.

*time trial: a race that is timed. The fastest time wins.

⊚ Comprehension Check

Did you understand the readings? Mark these sentences true (T) or false (F).

_____ 1. The Tour de France began in France a little more than 100 years ago.

_____ 2. During the Tour de France, cyclists ride all the way around France, a distance of about 2,000 miles, in three weeks.

_____ 3. The route of the Tour de France is flat and follows the coastline of France.

_____ 4. Modern technology has made the Tour de France much safer and easier.

_____ 5. Armstrong won the 1999 Tour de France because he trained hard and paid attention to data and small details that helped him ride faster.

_____ 6. Cyclists have to watch their weight carefully to find the best balance between strength and body weight.

_____ 7. The GC winner is the rider with the lowest total time at the end of each day.

_____ 8. Laurent Fignon won the 1989 Tour de France by only a few seconds.

Word Study

Target Vocabulary

accumulate	final	physical
automate (automatically)	individual	professional (professionally)
data	monitor	resource
establish	participate	survive
estimate	percent	sustain (sustainable)

Word Parts

Words are made up of different parts. The *root* or *stem* is the part of the word that carries the main idea or basic meaning. A *prefix* is a part that is added before the root. A *suffix* is a part that is added after the root. Prefixes and suffixes change or add to the meaning of the root. English has many prefixes and suffixes. Look at these examples.

	Prefix	Root	Suffix	Meaning
nonsense	*non-* meaning "not"	*sense*		not making sense
overlook	*over-* meaning "above"	*look*		to ignore, to look at from above
predict	*pre-* meaning "before"	*dict* from the Latin word *dicere* meaning "to say"		to know or tell something before it actually happens
lightness		*light*	*-ness* meaning "a condition or quality of something"	the quality of being light
slowly		*slow*	*-ly* meaning "in a certain way"	in a slow way or manner
annually		*annual*	meaning "in a certain time period"	happening every year

Exercise 1: Prefixes and Suffixes

A. Underline the prefix or suffix in each word, and then write the word in the correct column. Some words may contain a prefix and a suffix. The first one has been done for you.

breakable   happiness   overachieve   previously
densely   nonperishable   <u>over</u>eat   quickly
dryness   nonviolent   precede

non-	over-	pre-	-able	-ness	-ly
	overeat				

B. Do you know any other words that have these prefixes or suffixes? Add them. Compare your answers with another student. Did you learn any new words?

Exercise 2: Word Meanings

Use what you know about prefixes and suffixes to match each word on the left with the correct meaning on the right. The first one has been done for you.

__k__	1. **overeat**		a.	rapidly, speedily
_____	2. **previously**		b.	a feeling of pleasure and contentment
_____	3. **densely**		c.	to be lacking water or moisture
_____	4. **breakable**		d.	to do much more than is expected
_____	5. **happiness**		e.	to be crowded together or packed tightly
_____	6. **quickly**		f.	at some time before
_____	7. **dryness**		g.	peaceful, not violent
_____	8. **overachieve**		h.	to come in front of or earlier than something
_____	9. **nonviolent**		i.	will not spoil or go bad quickly
_____	10. **nonperishable**		j.	able to be broken
_____	11. **precede**		k.	to eat too much

Word Relationships

Words can be related to each other in different ways. Words can be *synonyms*, *antonyms*, or *compounds*. Words can also belong to the same *category*. Read these definitions.

Synonyms are words that have almost the same meaning. Synonyms for *cold* are *chilly, freezing, nippy, cool,* and *frosty*.

Antonyms are words that have opposite meanings. The words *cheap, inexpensive, reasonable,* and *economical* are antonyms for the word *expensive*.

Compounds are a combination of two or three words that have a particular meaning when they are used together as a fixed phrase. Some compounds are written as one word *(babysitter, online)*; others are written as separate words *(full time, industrial revolution)*.

Words can also belong to the same *category*. For example, the words *apple, banana, orange,* and *cherry* all belong to the category *fruit*. The words *green, red, blue,* and *yellow* all belong to the category *color*.

Exercise 3: Synonyms

A *synonym* is a word that has basically the same meaning as another word. Draw a line from each word on the left to its synonym(s) on the right. The first one has been done for you.

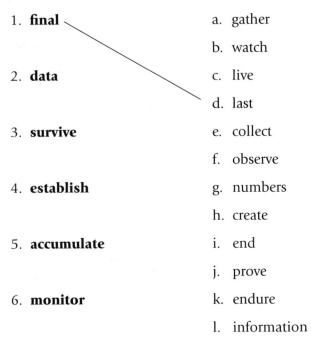

1. **final**

2. **data**

3. **survive**

4. **establish**

5. **accumulate**

6. **monitor**

a. gather

b. watch

c. live

d. last

e. collect

f. observe

g. numbers

h. create

i. end

j. prove

k. endure

l. information

The Grammar of Words and Word Families

When you learn a new word, you should pay attention to the *grammar* of the word. What part of speech is it? If the word is a noun, is it a countable noun or an uncountable noun? If it is a verb, is it a regular verb or an irregular verb? Is it an adjective or an adverb?

Words belong to *word families*. A word family is made up of all the grammatical forms of a word. These forms are also called *derivatives*. Remember that a word family may not always contain every part of speech. Look at the word family for the word *individual*.

Noun (n.)	*individual, individualism, individuality*
Noun (person) (n.)	*individual*
Verb (v.)	*individualize*
Adjective (adj.)	*individual, individualistic*
Adverb	(adv.) *individually*

Exercise 4: Word Families

Use these words to fill in the word family chart. Follow the example given. Some words may be used more than once.

accumulate	automate	establish	estimate	final (2x)
accumulation	automatic	established	estimation	finalist
accumulative	automatically	establishment	estimator	finalize
	automation			finally

monitor (3x)	participate	percent	physical (2x)	professional (2x)
monitorial	participant	percentage	physicality	professionalism
	participation	percentile	physically	professionally

resource	survive	sustain
resourceful	survivable	sustainable
resourcefully	survival	sustained
resourcefulness	survivor	sustenance

Noun	Noun (person)	Verb	Adjective	Adverb
accumulation	——	accumulate	accumulative	——
automation	——	automatic	automatic	automatically
establishment	——	establish	established	——
estimate estimation	estimator	estimate	——	——
final	finalist	finalize	final	finally
monitor	monitor	monitor	monitorial	——
		participate	——	——
percent	——	——	——	——
physicality	——	——	physical physicality	physically
professional	professionalism	——	professional	professionally
resource resourcefulness	——	——	resourceful	resourcefully
survival	survivor	survive	survivable	——
sustenance	——	sustain	sustainable sustained	——

Exercise 5: Word Forms

Complete each sentence with the correct form of the word.

1. Any rider who uses drugs is _____ out of the race.

   automatic   automaton   automatically   automation

2. Lance _____ himself as the best cyclist in the world by winning the Tour de France seven times in a row.

   establish   establishment   established   establishing

3. It was a very close race. The three _____ crossed the finish line within seconds of one another.

   final   finalists   finalize   finally

4. At the end of each day, the _____ winner is the person with the day's fastest time.

   individual   individualize   individualism   individually

5. America's natural _____ include coal, oil, natural gas, and timber.

   resourcefulness   resourceful   resourcefully   resources

6. It takes great _____ and mental strength to survive an exhausting race like the Tour de France.

   physical   physicals   physically

Understanding Words in Context

Exercise 6: Word Meanings in Context

For each meaning, find the word in the reading for that meaning and write it on the line. The number in parentheses is the number of the paragraph where the word occurs. The first one has been done for you.

1. took part in (1) __participated__

2. approximately, about (5) _____

3. devices that measure and record information about the body (6) _____

4. having to do with the body (9) _____

5. things that one has and can use (9) _____

6. always happens as a normal result of something else (12) _____

7. one particular person (12) _____

Collocations

Words that often appear together, or that are usually associated with one another, are called *collocations.* You can think of them as **word friends.** Take the word *mountain.* Some words that collocate with the word *mountain* are:

bike   *mountain bike*

pass   *mountain pass*

peak   *mountain peak*

Can you think of any other words that collocate with *mountain*? How about *climbing, road, stream,* and *view*?

Exercise 7: Collocations

Match the four words with their common collocations, or the words they often appear together with. Write the combinations on the lines provided. Can you think of any other words that collocate with these? Add them. One has been done for you.

decision	natural	raw
exam	offer	scientific
entry	physical	transmission
financial	processing	weapon

1. automatic   _automatic transmission_ _____

   _____

2. data   _____

   _____

3. final   _____

   _____

4. resources   _____

   _____

⌾ **Using Words in Communication**

Exercise 8: Reading for Details

1. Re-read *Reading 3: Stage Racing.* Read the table, and then answer the questions.

	Stage 13 July 19		Stage 14 July 20		Stage 15 July 21	
Rank after Stage 14	122.5 miles		118.92 miles		98.9 miles	
	Stage Time	**Total Time**	**Stage Time**	**Total Time**	**Stage Time**	**Total Time**
1. Lance Armstrong	<u>5:17:16</u>	55:34:01	5:33:16	61:07:17	4:29:26	65:36:23
2. Jan Ullrich	5:17:09	55:34:16	5:33:16	61:07:32	4:30:06	65:37:30
3. Alex Vinokourov	5:17:26	55:35:02	5:32:33	61:07:35	4:31:33	65:39:08

1. The time "5:17:16," which is underlined in the table, can be read and written as "5 hours, 17 minutes, and 16 seconds." Write out the other stage times for Stage 13 in the same way.

   _____

   _____

2. Who was the individual winner of Stage 13? Who was in second place? Who was in third?

   Winner _____

   Second place _____

   Third place _____

3. Which rider was the GC winner after Stage 13? _____

   What was his total time? _____

Exercise 9: Writing

Put these events in order, beginning with Lance's childhood. Then use this information to write one or two paragraphs about Lance Armstrong. The first one has been done for you.

_____ is the only person who has won the Tour de France seven years in a row

_____ participated in his first professional race in 1992 and finished last

_____ trained with the Olympic cycling team when he was a senior in high school

_____ found out that he had cancer in 1996

_____ participated in the Barcelona Olympics in 1992

_____ continues to help other cancer patients and cancer survivors through the Lance Armstrong Foundation

___1___ was born in 1971 in Plano, Texas

_____ survived two cancer surgeries and chemotherapy

_____ joined a swim club when he was 12

_____ was the top cyclist in the world in 1996

_____ won his first triathlon when he was 13

_____ started training again only five months after his cancer was diagnosed

_____ began competing in races again in 1998

Exercise 10: Critical Thinking

These questions will help you develop your critical thinking skills. Critical thinking helps you understand and evaluate information. It helps you reach reasonable conclusions from the information that is given. Ask yourself these questions as you work on your answers: What information in the reading supports my answer? What other information do I have to support my conclusion? Where can I get more information about the topic?

1. How is the Tour de France of today different from the first Tour de France? Do you think the race is easier now? Why or why not? Give examples from the readings to support your answer.

2. Lance Armstrong says that "the winning is really in the details." What does he mean by that? Support your answer with details from the readings.

Talking to the Animals

⟳ Vocabulary Preview

Preview 1

These sentences contain information from the readings. Fill in the blanks with the word that best completes each sentence.

capable   communicate   construct   contexts   implements

1. Jane was surprised to see wild chimpanzees make and use _____ to remove ants from their nest.

2. Another scientist, Wolfgang Kohler, has also seen chimps _____ towers out of boxes and then climb up one of the towers to reach food.

3. Allen and Beatrice Gardner showed that chimpanzees were _____ of learning a human language.

4. Washoe, a chimpanzee, learned signs for objects and ideas and was able to use these signs in the correct _____.

5. After years of observation, Monty Roberts was able to _____ with horses by using their non-verbal body language.

Preview 2

Look at the way the underlined words are used in the sentences. Match each word with its meaning or definition.

1. In each group of horses, there is one <u>dominant</u> female. She acts as the leader and teaches the younger horses how to behave.

2. Monty <u>identified</u> patterns of behavior that horses use to communicate with one another.

3. Jane Goodall was one of the first people to make physical <u>contact</u> with wild chimpanzees.

4. By the time Loulis was eight, he had <u>acquired</u> and was able to use 58 signs correctly.

5. Charles Darwin's theory of <u>evolution</u> states that living things change and develop gradually over time.

_____ 1. **dominant**   a. to touch something or someone

_____ 2. **identify**   b. a process of slow change over time

_____ 3. **contact**   c. more powerful or important than others

_____ 4. **acquire**   d. to recognize or know

_____ 5. **evolution**   e. to learn or develop a skill or habit

Reading Preview: What Do You Already Know?

Circle the correct answer. If you don't know the answer, guess.

1. Jane Goodall did NOT discover that chimpanzees

   a. make and use tools

   b. live alone

   c. hunt and kill animals for meat

   d. communicate with a variety of sounds and gestures

2. Until recently we thought that humans were different from animals because

   a. humans can learn and understand language

   b. humans can make and use tools

   c. humans can think and talk about the past, present, and future

   d. all of the above

3. Scientists have discovered that

   a. chimpanzees do not communicate with one another

   b. chimpanzees can learn a new language

   c. horses and humans do not communicate with one another

   d. chimpanzees and other animals cannot make or use tools

Introduction to the Readings

(1) Humans and animals have lived together on the earth for hundreds of thousands of years. We have always been interested by what makes us as humans different from other animals. Is it our ability to make and use tools? Is it the way we learn and use language? Or is it our ability to think in terms of past, present, and future time? Scientists also want to know what animal behavior can teach us about human behavior. Are we as different from other animals as we think, or are we a lot like them? The readings in this unit explore these ideas.

(2) The first reading is by primate <u>researcher</u> Jane Goodall. Jane has been observing the chimpanzees in Gombe, Africa, since 1960. She thought that learning about chimpanzees, which are <u>similar</u> to humans, could help us better understand our prehistoric ancestors and ourselves. During her time with the chimps, Jane saw some surprising things. She watched the chimps making tools from grass and then using these tools to gather insects. This was a <u>major</u> discovery because for many years scientists thought that humans were the only species that made tools. Jane also discovered that chimpanzees would hunt and kill smaller animals for food. Until then, scientists thought that chimps ate mostly fruits, vegetables, and insects. Since that first year in Gombe, Jane Goodall has continued to make discoveries about chimpanzees and their behavior.

(3) The second reading tells about an interesting experiment by <u>psychologists</u> Allen and Beatrice Gardner. The Gardeners wanted to see if a chimpanzee named Washoe could learn a human language. Their experiment showed that Washoe was <u>capable</u> of learning American Sign Language. In fact, she could even teach it to other chimpanzees! Another trait that scientists thought separated humans from animals—our ability to learn a new language—turned out to be false.

(4) The third reading is by Monty Roberts, the "horse whisperer." Monty is known all over the world for his ability to quickly and gently train abused, difficult, and dangerous horses without using violence. Throughout his life, Monty has watched and learned the way wild horses **communicate** non-verbally with one another. He uses this horse body language to train horses without using force or fear. This <u>method</u>, which Monty calls "join-up," is based on <u>mutual</u> respect and clearly <u>defined</u> expectations. A horse must be allowed to fail, but she cannot be allowed to be lazy. She must also be shown how to succeed at what humans are asking her to do. If the horse meets or goes beyond what is expected of her, she is rewarded. Monty has shown that his <u>method</u> can be used successfully with humans, too. He and his wife have taken in and raised nearly 50 troubled children. Most of these young people have gone on to lead happy and successful lives.

Reading 1: Making and Using Tools

Excerpt adapted from *Through a Window: My Thirty Years with the Chimpanzees of Gombe* by Jane Goodall (Boston: Houghton Mifflin Company, 1990), 18–20.

(5) When I first read about human **evolution,** I learned that only our species was **capable** of making tools. This was one of the **definitions** of being human. However, Wolfgang Kohler's <u>classic</u> experiments showed how captive chimpanzees could stack boxes and then climb these **constructions** to reach fruit hanging from the ceiling. They could also join two short sticks to make a pole long enough to rake in fruit that was out of reach.

(6) It was one thing to know that chimps in a lab could use **implements,** but it was quite another to find that this was a naturally <u>occurring</u> skill in the wild. This is one of the events I witnessed. Gigi, a large female chimpanzee, <u>found</u> a nest of army ants—a delicious food for chimpanzees. When she saw the nest, she broke a long straight branch from a bush, <u>removed</u> the side branches, and then carefully <u>removed</u> the bark until she had made a smooth

tool about three feet long. She reached her hand into the ant's nest until the ants began to swarm out. She quickly stuck her tool into the nest, waited a moment, and then pulled it out, covered by ants. She pulled the stick through her hand, pushed the ants into her mouth, and crunched vigorously. As the ants poured out of the nest, Gigi climbed a nearby tree, and reaching down with her stick, continued her meal.

(7) Figan, another chimp, began to "fish" for ants as well, but after ten minutes he ran away to pick off the ants that had crawled up his arms and legs. His brother, Faben, picked up the tool, but after fishing for only a <u>couple</u> minutes, he too gave up.

Reading 2: The Washoe Project

Excerpt adapted from *The Deluge and the Ark* by Dale Peterson
(Boston: Houghton Mifflin Company, 1989), 323–24.

(8) In 1960 Allen and Beatrice Gardner, <u>psychologists</u> at the University of Nevada, **acquired** a young chimpanzee named Washoe. They wanted to know whether Washoe could learn human language. The Gardners knew American Sign Language (ASL), a language for the deaf <u>consisting</u> of signs that **function** as words or **concepts.** The Gardners provided Washoe with a supportive and stimulating <u>environment</u>. They played with her, fed her, bathed her, and signed to her in ASL whenever **appropriate.** They used several <u>techniques</u> to teach and encourage her to sign.

(9) By 1969, Washoe had a vocabulary of 30 <u>definite</u> signs that stood for objects (toothbrush), actions (open), and <u>abstract</u> qualities and **concepts** such as "sweet," "funny," and "sorry." Once Washoe had **acquired** a vocabulary of eight or ten signs, she began producing original combinations. When she wanted to go outdoors, Washoe would stand near the door and sign, "You me out." She signed "open food drink" to refer to the refrigerator, and "listen dog" at the sound of a barking dog.

(10) Other chimps entered the <u>project</u>, and <u>finally</u> Washoe adopted an infant, Loulis. Loulis was given no lessons in language, but by the time he was eight he made 58 signs in the correct **contexts.** How did he learn them? Mostly by copying Washoe. One day, for example, Washoe began signing food! in great excitement. She had seen a human <u>approaching</u> with a bar of chocolate. Loulis watched. Suddenly Washoe went over to him, took his hand, and shaped it into the sign for food. Another time, in a <u>similar</u> context, she made the sign for chewing gum—but with her hand on his body. On a third occasion Washoe picked up a chair, took it over to Loulis, set it down in front of him, and made the chair sign three times. The two food signs became part of Loulis' vocabulary but the sign for chair did not. <u>Obviously</u>, food was more important to a young chimp than a chair!

Reading 3: "Join-up"

Excerpt adapted from *The Man Who Listens to Horses* by Monty Roberts
(New York: Ballantine Publishing Group, Random House, Inc., 1997), 31–36.

Monty Roberts with a horse he helped by listening to the animal.

(11) I **identified** a <u>phenomenon</u> that I called "join-up." I was <u>convinced</u> that it could remove the natural barrier between the horse and man. I stood in the middle of a pen with a young wild horse. He was too nervous to step toward me, but his attention was on me. I used the same body language as the **dominant** mare in a family group. I asked him to go, so I could later ask him

to come back and "join-up" with me. I moved quickly toward the horse, squared my shoulders, and looked him in the eye. He began running around the pen, as far away from me as possible. I used my posture—shoulders <u>parallel</u> to his body, eyes locked on his—to keep him running. Then I used the signals that I had seen in the wild. I allowed my eyes to drop back to his neck, and he slowed down. I let my eyes drop back to his shoulder, he slowed a bit more. He began to look over at me. I looked him in the eye, and his speed increased immediately. He was reading me. He knew we were **communicating** in his language.

(12) I waited for his inside ear to open into me, for him to start licking and chewing, and then to duck his head and run along with his nose a few inches off the ground. This meant "let me back in; I don't want to run away anymore." When this happened it was time for me to become **passive,** to let this horse come in and "join up" with me. I avoided eye **contact** and turned my shoulders away from him. Immediately he stopped and faced me. I <u>maintained</u> my position. He stepped toward me. I waited. Then he walked right up to me, not stopping until his nose was inches from my shoulder. I couldn't speak. It was magic. This horse trusted me. I was no longer an enemy. I was his safety zone.

Comprehension Check

Did you understand the readings? Mark these sentences true (T) or false (F).

_____ 1. Humans are the only animals that can make and use tools.

_____ 2. Chimpanzees in a lab make tools, but wild chimpanzees don't.

_____ 3. Jane observed chimpanzees make and use a tool to get food.

_____ 4. The Washoe Project proved that chimpanzees could not learn American Sign Language.

_____ 5. Loulis learned sign language from another chimpanzee.

_____ 6. Loulis only learned signs for things that were important to him.

_____ 7. Monty watched horses and learned their body language so he could communicate with them and train them.

_____ 8. Monty acted like a dominant mare in order to get the colt to trust him.

_____ 9. The technique of "join-up" is only successful with horses.

Word Study

Target Vocabulary

acquire	construct (constructions)	evolve (evolution)
appropriate	contact	function
capable	context	identify
communicate	define (definition)	implement
concept	dominate (dominant)	passive

Word Parts

Exercise 1: Suffixes

When the suffix *-ity* is added to a word, a noun is formed. This new word means "a quality or state of being." For example, if *-ity* is added to the word *prosper,* the new word *prosperity* is formed. Prosperity means "to be doing well financially, to have more than enough money."

> <u>Example</u>: The 1980s and 1990s were a time of *prosperity* in America. Most families owned at least one car, and some families had two or three.

A. Add the suffix *-ity* to these words, and write the new words on the lines provided. Spellings may need to be changed.

capable   passive   mental   final   individual

_____   _____   _____   _____   _____

B. Complete each sentence with the correct new word.

1. "No, you cannot stay out all night," she said with _____.

2. Leakey knew that Jane had the right _____ to spend days quietly watching the chimps and recording what she saw.

3. Dominance and _____ are opposite behaviors.

4. New computers have the _____ to process data very quickly.

5. She was very fashionable and showed great _____ in the way she dressed and wore her hair.

Word Relationships

Exercise 2: Antonyms

An *antonym* is a word that means the opposite of another word. Draw a line from each word on the left to its antonym(s) on the right.

1. **dominant**

2. **remove**

3. **obvious**

4. **capable**

5. **appropriate**

a. add

b. obscure

c. passive

d. subtle

e. incompetent

f. recessive

g. inappropriate

h. unsuitable

i. incapable

j. bring

Exercise 3: Word Families

Use these words to fill in the word family chart. Follow the example given. Some words will be used more than once.

acquire	appropriate (2x)	capable	communicate	concept
acquired		capability	communicating	conceive
acquisition		capably	communicative	conceptual
			communication	

construct (2x)	contact (3x)	definition	dominant	evolution
construction		definable	dominate	evolutionary
constructive		define	domination	evolve

function (2x)	identify	implement (2x)	passive (2x)
functional	identity	implementation	passively

Noun	Noun (person)	Verb	Adjective	Adverb
acquisition	——	acquire	acquired	——
——	——	aproprate	appropriate	——
capability	——	——	capable	capably
communication	——	communicate / communicative	communicating	——
concept	——	conceive	conceptual	——
construction	——	construct	constructive	——
contact	contact	contact	——	——
context	——	——		
definition	——	define	definable	——
domination	——	dominate	dominant	——
evolution	——	evolve	evolutionary	——
function	——	function	functional	——
Identity / identification	——	identify	——	——
implement / implementation	——	implement	——	——
passive	——	——	passive	passively

Exercise 4: Word Forms

Complete each sentence with the correct form of the word.

1. How would you _____ "human"? What things make us different from all other animals?

   definition   define   defining   definitive

2. The _____ of equal rights for all people, no matter what their race or gender, is quite new.

   conceive   concepts   conceptual   concept

3. Jane discovered that simple, _____ clothes—shorts with pockets, a long-sleeved shirt, a hat, and sturdy boots—were best for working in the jungle.

   function   functional   functioning   malfunction

4. Monty used a communication _____ he called "join-up" to train young horses.

   technician   technique   technical   techniques

5. The Gardners _____ several different techniques to try to teach Washoe sign language.

   implement   implementation   implements   implemented

Understanding Words in Context

Exercise 5: Constructing Sentences

Use each set of words to write a sentence. Use all the words given. No additional words are needed. Add punctuation. The first one has been done for you.

1. learned / and / Washoe / in / context / signs / them / correct / used / the

   <u>Washoe learned signs and used them in the correct context.</u>

2. with / signals / to / another / Monty / horses / communicate / identified / another / that / use / one

   _____

3. construct / to / food / chimpanzees / tools / them / help / get

   _____

4. evolved / a / humans / ancestor / and / apes / common / may / from / have

   _____

5. button / is / function / what / this / of / the

   _____

Exercise 6: Using Words Correctly

Some words have more than one meaning. Read the three common definitions of the word contact.

A. /kontaekt/ v: to meet with, write to, or telephone someone

B. /kontaekt/ v: to physically touch someone or something

C. /kontaekt/ n: a person in an organization or profession who you get help or information from

Look at the way the word **contact** is used in each sentence. In the space given, write the letter of the meaning that best fits the way the word is used in that sentence. Why did you choose that meaning? Write your reason on the line given.

_____ 1. A cloud of dust rose as Neil Armstrong's foot made *contact* with the moon's surface.

Reason: _____

_____ 2. The anthropologist Louis Leakey was probably the most important *contact* Jane made in Africa. He helped her with her work at Gombe in a number of ways.

Reason: _____

_____ 3. I'll be in *contact* with Sarah later this week. We're planning to meet for lunch on Friday.

Reason: _____

_____ 4. We will *contact* Mr. Jones as soon as we have his test results. What's the best number to reach him at?

Reason: _____

_____ 5. Close physical *contact* is very important for babies. They are happiest when they are being held.

Reason: _____

Exercise 7: Making Inferences

The meaning of a word can often be ***inferred*** or guessed at from the information in the surrounding words or sentences.

> <u>Example</u>: Jane thought that learning about chimpanzees, which are <u>similar</u> to humans in many ways, could help us better understand our prehistoric ancestors and ourselves.
>
> From the information given, the word <u>similar</u> means
>
> a. be different from
>
> b. be like
>
> c. be exactly the same as
>
> d. be the opposite of

The correct answer is *b.* because if learning about chimpanzees helps us understand humans and their ancestors, chimpanzees must in some ways be like humans and their prehistoric ancestors.

In each exercise, infer the meaning of the underlined word or phrase by using information from the surrounding words and sentences.

1. Wolfgang Kohler's experiments showed how captive chimpanzees could stack boxes and then climb these <u>constructions</u> to reach fruit hanging from the ceiling. They could also join two short sticks to make a pole long enough to rake in fruit that was out of reach.

   In this context, the word *constructions* means

   a. a pile of things

   b. something that is made or put together

   c. a method for stealing food

2. By 1969 Washoe had a vocabulary of 30 definite signs that stood for objects (toothbrush), actions (open), and abstract <u>concepts</u> such as "funny" and "sorry."

A *concept* must be

a. a feeling or idea

b. an object

c. an action or gesture

3. I moved quickly toward the young horse, squared my shoulders, and looked him in the eye. He began running around the pen, as far away from me as possible. I used my <u>posture</u>—shoulders parallel to his body, eyes locked on his—to keep him running.

The word *posture* means

a. a movement toward something

b. the way a person holds and moves his or her body

c. a way of staring or looking at something

4. I waited for his inside ear to open into me, for him to start licking and chewing, and then to <u>duck</u> his head and run along with his nose a few inches off the ground.

In this sentence the word *duck* means

a. to turn away

b. a kind of bird that can swim

c. to drop or lower

5. Monty has observed and learned the way wild horses <u>communicate</u> <u>non-verbally</u> with one another. He uses this horse body language to train horses without using force or fear.

Non-verbal communication is

a. a spoken language

b. violence and force

c. body language

Using Words in Communication

Read the article, and answer the questions that follow.

An Animal Communicator

We've all seen animals communicate with one another: barking, chirping, meowing, and growling. If you have a pet, you probably feel like you can communicate with your pet, too. However, a 61-year-old woman named Donnetta Zimmerman, claims to be a true "animal communicator." She says that she is able to talk to animals and understand them when they talk back to her.

According to Zimmerman, she began talking to family pets as a child. She had poor hearing and found it difficult to talk to people, but her pets always listened to her. About 30 years ago, she began to put her abilities to use helping other people understand what their cats, dogs, birds, and, yes, even fish, were thinking and feeling. At that time, people thought that being a "pet communicator" was kind of weird, so Zimmerman rarely talked about her work.

Now, however, Zimmerman does about four sessions or "readings" a week. Pet owners tell her what they want to know, and then she works with the animal. She gently touches the animal (or its aquarium, if it's a fish), while she asks questions. The animals answer her, but not as you might expect. Zimmerman says the answers come to her in quick, mental images rather than words or sounds.

What kinds of things do pet owners want to know? Usually they just want to know whether their animals are healthy and happy. Sometimes they want to know why their pet is misbehaving. Zimmerman can usually ask enough questions to find out why. She says that animals usually have a very logical explanation. The cat isn't using the litter box in the basement anymore because it's too dark in the basement. Or the dog may be biting at someone because the dog doesn't like the smell of perfume on the person. Explanations like these can help pet owners understand their pets and make them happier.

Some animals even have their own story to tell. Zimmerman says that animals that have been rescued will always tell her that they now have a home. Many of them are very grateful to their new owners. They tell Zimmerman that they are happy to always have food and to be treated well.

As you might expect, Zimmerman has pets of her own. She currently lives with 10 cats. She likes dogs very much, and she says that they enjoy "talking," but she's not home enough to keep them happy. However, her cats are more independent and are always happy to talk with her when she gets home. What do they talk about? Zimmerman says that her cats are like spoiled children. Each cat tells her all the bad things the other cats did to him or her while she was gone.

1. Who is Donetta Zimmerman, and what does she do? _____

   _____

2. How long has she been doing this job? _____

3. What do most people want to know from their pets? _____

   _____

4. How does Donetta get answers to the questions she asks? _____

   _____

5. Does Donetta have any pets of her own? What do they tell her? _____

   _____

6. Write one question you would like to ask Donetta. _____

   _____

Exercise 9: Writing

Think about what you read for Exercise 8. Fill in the information that follows. Then use this information to write a short paragraph about what you read. Be sure to use your own words. Do not copy from the article.

1. I read about _____.

2. I learned that (give at least three examples):

   a. _____

   b. _____

   c. _____

3. I thought this was interesting / boring (circle one) because _____

   _____

   _____

Exercise 10: Critical Thinking

First, answer these questions by yourself. Then share your answers with a partner. Decide on one answer for each question. Be prepared to explain your answers to the class.

1. How did Loulis learn sign language? How do you know? Give some examples from the readings to support your answer.

2. What things make humans different from other animals? In your opinion, do these things make us smarter than animals? Why or why not?

3

Living in Hiding

Vocabulary Preview

These sentences contain information from the readings. Fill in the blanks with the word that best completes each sentence.

documents   **excluded**   **normal**   **obtain**   **register**

1. People had to _____, or sign up with, local officials to get the papers they needed to buy food and other supplies.

2. You needed two special _____, a registration card and a ration card, to buy most food items.

3. There was a shortage of food and other supplies. Some things were impossible to _____, even with a ration card.

4. Life in hiding was not _____. Anne and her family depended on their friends to bring them food and books and news from the outside world.

5. By law, Jews were _____ from movie theaters, restaurants, libraries, and public parks.

Look at the way the underlined words are used in the sentences. Match each word with its meaning or definition.

1. The Frank family's new <u>accommodations</u> were on the top floors of the annex at the back of the building where Mr. Frank had his business.

2. Many Jewish people have traditionally worked in banking and <u>finance</u>.

3. People in the <u>labor</u> camps worked to produce supplies for the German military.

4. If you <u>reverse</u> the letters in the word *but* you have the word *tub*.

5. The government <u>issued</u> identification papers that people had to carry with them at all times.

_____ 1. **accommodations**

_____ 2. **finance**

_____ 3. **labor**

_____ 4. **reverse**

_____ 5. **issued**

a. work

b. to arrange in the opposite order; to go the opposite way

c. a room or building where people can live

d. put out or distributed

e. having to do with money, investments, and banking

Reading Preview: What Do You Already Know?

Circle the correct answer. If you don't know the answer, guess.

1. Anne Frank

   a. was a Jewish girl, born in Frankfurt, Germany, in 1929

   b. her family went into hiding for more than two years; Anne kept a diary during this time

   c. died in a Nazi concentration camp in 1945

   d. all of the above

2. Anne's family

   a. helped many Jewish families leave Europe and go to Israel

   b. hid in a small area behind her father's business offices

   c. helped other Jewish families by bringing them food and supplies

   d. none of the above

3. Anne wanted to be

   a. a biologist

   b. an actress

   c. a famous writer

   d. a high school math teacher

4. The Frank family lived in hiding

   a. with several other Jewish families

   b. in the cellar underneath Mr. Frank's business office

   c. for only a few weeks before they were arrested

   d. with the help of Mr. Frank's secretary and employees

Introduction to the Readings

(1) During World War II, Adolph Hitler, the Nazi leader of Germany, planned to kill all Jewish people living in Europe. By the end of the war, he had killed six million of them. This killing is known as the Holocaust. In the Holocaust, Jewish men, women, and children were picked up and sent by train to <u>concentration</u> camps. Most camps were **labor** camps where the prisoners made <u>equipment</u> and supplies for the German **military.** Six of the camps were death camps built for the purpose of killing Jews. People who were strong enough to work in the **labor** camps were allowed to live, but many of them soon died from lack of food, illness, or the cold. Anyone who was too young, too old, or too sick to work was killed quickly. Many people were killed by poison gas.

(2) Hitler invaded the Netherlands, which is also called Holland, in 1940. He began to take action against the Jews there. All Jews were <u>required</u> to **register** with the local officials. A large black "J'" was stamped onto their identity cards, and they had to wear a large yellow star on their clothes. Their activities were very **restricted:** they could not go to restaurants, movies, libraries, or public parks. They could not ride in cars or use streetcars or bicycles. They were not allowed to be out on the streets between 8 PM and 6 AM. Jewish children could only attend separate Jewish schools. Jews were no longer allowed to run their own businesses. They could not work for the government or for businesses owned by Dutch (people who live in Holland) Christians. These rules **excluded** Jewish people from the rest of Dutch society.

(3) By June of 1942, the situation for the Jews in Holland was bad—people were being taken from their homes and sent to **labor** camps in Germany. Many people went into hiding to avoid this fate. Anne Frank was a Jewish girl living in Amsterdam at this time. She received a diary as a gift for her 13th birthday on June 12, 1942, and wrote in it from June 12, 1942, until August 1, 1944. Anne's diary tells the story of her family's time in hiding.

(4) Otto Frank, Anne's father, knew that the situation for Jewish people was getting worse. Mr. Frank owned a building where he had his business. Business offices **occupied** the front of the building, but there were empty rooms in an annex (or addition) in back of the building. He prepared the rooms as a hiding place for his family, moving in furniture and household <u>items</u>. Several of Mr. Frank's employees, including his secretary, Mies Geip, helped him get the annex ready.

(5) On July 5, 1942, Anne's 16-year-old sister, Margot, was told that she would be sent to a **labor** camp in Germany the following day. That night the Frank family packed some clothing and a few other belongings. They went into hiding in the annex on July 6, 1942. Hermann van Pels, Mr. Frank's business <u>partner</u>, and his wife and 16-year-old son, Peter, moved in a week later. One more person, Fritz Pfeffer, joined the group on November 16,1942. Miep Geis and her husband Jan, along with other "helpers," visited the annex daily, bringing them food, supplies, books, and news from the outside world.

(6) On August 4, 1944, the hiding came to an end. All eight people living in the annex were arrested. Four days later they were sent to a **labor**

🕂 = labor or concentration camps; ☠ = "death" camps.

camp in eastern Holland. In September, they were moved to Auschwitz, one of the biggest death camps in Poland. The following month, Anne and her sister Margot were sent to a camp in Germany, Bergen-Belsen. Sometime in late February or early March of 1945, both sisters became sick and died. The war in Europe ended on May 7, 1945. Of the eight people who had lived together in the annex, only Mr. Frank <u>survived</u>. The seven others were killed or died from disease in the camps.

(7) When Mr. Frank returned to Amsterdam on June 3, 1945, he went to live with Mies and Jan Geip. In August, he learned that both of his daughters had died. After the arrests in 1944, Mies had <u>found</u> Anne's diary on the floor of the annex. She had kept it, hoping to return it to Anne when the war was over. When Mies heard that Anne had died, she gave the diary to Mr. Frank. Anne's diary was first <u>published</u> in 1947.

Reading 1: The Secret Annex

Excerpt adapted from *The Importance of Anne Frank* by John Wukovits
(New York: Lucent, 1999), 48–49.

(8) The two families quickly settled into a routine in their new **accommodations.** <u>Constructed</u> in 1635, the building housing the Secret Annex could be entered from three separate doors. A door on the right led to a warehouse on the ground floor. By stepping through the middle door, a visitor would walk to the main office. A hallway opened to a second office. From this office a hallway led to the entrance to the Secret Annex in the rear of the building.

(9) After passing through the entrance, a person could either turn right and enter the Frank's living <u>area</u>, or move straight ahead to the steps to the fourth floor, which the van Pelses **occupied.** The Franks had two bedrooms— a larger one used by the parents and a smaller one for the girls. The washing room with the toilet, which all seven shared, was on the Franks' floor. Directly

overhead were the van Pelses' quarters—a huge family room that also served as a kitchen/dining <u>area</u> and as a bedroom for Mr. and Mrs. van Pels, and Peter's room. A ladder stretched from Peter's room to an attic, which was used to store food.

(10) Various arrangements were made to <u>ensure</u> a steady, if not <u>varied</u>, supply of food. To **obtain** most <u>items</u>, a person needed to have a government-**issue**d ration card (a document that limited what you could buy), which gave permission to **purchase** the <u>item</u>. Early on, therefore, Miep's husband had gathered the seven ration cards from the members of the Annex and exchanged them for new ones forged* by a secret Dutch organization working against the Nazis. This enabled Mies Giep to walk into a store and **purchase** food with the fake ration cards. Since wartime cuts off many **sources** of supplies, she had to make the best of what she could find.

*forged: to make a fake copy of a document or painting

Reading 2: Going Underground
from Anne's diary, January 28, 1944

Excerpt adapted from *The Diary of a Young Girl: The Definitive Edition,* edited by Otto Frank and Mirjam Pressler (New York: Bantam Books, 1997), 175–76.

(11) Going underground has become routine. There are many resistance groups that forge identity cards, provide **financial** support to those in hiding, organize hiding places and find work for people who go underground. It's amazing how much these unselfish people do, risking their own lives to help and save others.

(12) The best example of this is our own helpers, who have managed to pull us safely through so far and will hopefully bring us safely to the shore. They have never said a word about the burden we must be, never complained that we're too much trouble. They come upstairs every day and talk to the men about business and politics, to the women about food and wartime difficulties, and to the children about books and newspapers. They put on cheerful

The house hidden by the trees is the Anne Frank House in Amsterdam.

expressions, bring flowers and gifts for birthdays and holidays, and are ready to do what they can. That's something we should never forget; while others <u>display</u> their heroism in battle, our helpers prove theirs every day by their good spirits and affection.

(13) The strangest stories are making the rounds, but most of them are really true. For <u>instance</u>, Mr. Kleiman reported this week that a soccer match was held. One team <u>consisted</u> entirely of men who had gone underground, and the other of eleven **Military** Policemen. In one city, new registration cards were issued. In order for people in hiding to get their rations (you have to show your card to **obtain** your ration book or else pay for a book), the registrar asked those in hiding to pick up their cards at a <u>specified</u> hour, where the **documents** could be collected at a separate table.

(14) All the same, you have to be careful that things like these don't reach the ears of the Germans.

Yours, Anne

Reading 3: Courage to Help

Excerpt adapted from *Anne Frank: The Biography* by Melissa Muller
(New York: Metropolitan Books/Henry Holt, 1998), 303–6.

(15) I've been asked how I <u>found</u> the courage to help the Franks. This makes me uncomfortable. Why do people ask this? Why do people hesitate when the time comes to help others?

(16) It took me a long time to understand. Children are told: "If you are good and well-behaved, everything will work out for you later in life." The **reverse** of this is: if you get into trouble you must have behaved badly and made mistakes. It's that simple. Everyone gets the life he or she deserves. If we really believe this, it's easy to mind our own business and not help people in need. But is it that simple?

(17) My life taught me better. I was born in Austria before World War I. When I was nine, we didn't have enough to eat. Relief action to help starving children had been organized. In December 1920 my parents took me to the train, said good-bye, and left me. They had no other choice, but I did not understand until much later. I was hungry and sick and very lonely. What had I done to deserve this? I experienced how people can find themselves in difficulty through no fault of their own. That was what was happening to the Jews in World War II. It was only natural for me to help as much as I could.

(18) When we are shocked to think that six million people were killed and we ask ourselves, "How could this happen?" we should remember the indifference of **normal** human beings. If not for the apathy* of people every- | *apathy: lack of interest or concern
where, the horrible death camps could never have taken place.

(19) To my sorrow I wasn't able to save Anne's life, but I was able to help her live two years longer. In those years she wrote the dairy. Through her diary Anne really does live on. She stands for the triumph of the spirit over evil and death.

Comprehension Check

Did you understand the readings? Mark these sentences true (T) or false (F).

_____ 1. The Frank family's hiding place was in an annex at the back of Mr. Frank's business.

_____ 2. The van Pels family had a living area, a bathroom, and two bedrooms downstairs.

_____ 3. If a person had enough money, he or she could buy as much food as he or she wanted.

_____ 4. The people who helped the Franks were risking their own lives.

_____ 5. Resistance groups helped people go underground, find jobs, and get new identification cards.

_____ 6. Six million people died during the Holocaust.

_____ 7. Mies Giep believed that it was important to help people who were in trouble.

Word Study
Target Vocabulary

accommodate (accommodations)	labor	purchase
document	military	register
exclude	normal	restrict
finance (financial)	obtain	reverse
issue	occupy	source

Word Parts

Look at these prefixes and suffixes.

	Prefix	Root	Suffix	Meaning
exclude	**ex-** meaning "out of" or "outside"	*claudere* from the Latin word meaning "to close"		to keep outside of
unhappy	**un-** meaning "not" or "the opposite of"	*happy* meaning to feel lucky or fortunate		to feel the opposite of lucky or fortunate
estimation		**aestimare** from the Latin word meaning "to value or judge"	**-ation** meaning "the action or process"	the process of valuing or judging
hopeful		**hope** meaning "a feeling or belief that something will happen"	**-ful** meaning "to be full of" or "have the quality of"	full of hope

Exercise 1: Prefixes and Suffixes

A. Underline the prefix or suffix in each word, and then write the word in the correct column. Some words may contain a prefix and a suffix. The first one has been done for you.

exceed   accommodation   cheerful   registration

unselfish   exportation   documentation   unsustainable

resourceful   uncomfortable   expand   careful

ex-	un-	-ation	-ful
exceed			

B. Do you know any other words that have these prefixes or suffixes? Add them. Compare your answers with another student. Did you learn any new words?

Exercise 2: Word Meanings

Use what you know about prefixes and suffixes to match each word on the left with the correct meaning on the right. The first one has been done for you.

__f__	1. **exceed**	a. to become greater or larger in size
_____	2. **accommodations**	b. good at finding ways to solve problems
_____	3. **cheerful**	c. papers that provide proof of something
_____	4. **registration**	d. generous, giving
_____	5. **unselfish**	e. happy, pleasant
_____	6. **exportation**	f. to go beyond an amount or limit
_____	7. **documentation**	g. a room to stay in, work in, or live in
_____	8. **unsustainable**	h. to do something with attention and thought
_____	9. **resourceful**	
_____	10. **uncomfortable**	i. the process of sending goods to another country
_____	11. **expand**	
_____	12. **careful**	j. cannot be kept up or continued for very long

k. the process of officially recording something or officially signing up for something

l. difficult, painful, not pleasant or easy

Word Relationships

Exercise 3: Antonyms

An **antonym** is a word that is opposite in meaning to another word. The words *hot, steamy,* and *boiling* are all antonyms for the word *cold.* Draw a line from each word on the left to its antonym on the right.

1. **automatic**		a.	sell
2. **occupy**		b.	first
3. **final**		c.	vacate
4. **forward**		d.	individual
5. **group**		e.	manual
6. **normal**		f.	reverse
7. **exclude**		g.	unusual
8. **purchase**		h.	include

The Grammar of Words and Word Families

Exercise 4: Word Families

Use these words to fill in the word family chart. Follow the example given. Some words will be used more than once.

accommodation	document (2x)	exclude	finance (2x)	issue (2x)
accommodate	documentary (2x)	exclusion	financial	issuer
accommodating	documentation	exclusive	financially	
			financier	

labor (2x)	military	normal (2x)	obtain	occupy
labored	militant (2x)	normality	obtainable	occupant
laborer	militarily	normalize		occupation
	militia	normally		occupier

purchase (2x)	register (2x)	restrict	reverse (3x)	source (4x)
purchaser	registered	restricted	reversal	
	registrant	restriction	reversible	
	registrar	restrictive	reversibly	
	registration			

Noun	Noun (person)	Verb	Adjective	Adverb
accommodation	——	accommodate	accommodating	——
documentation document documentary	——	document	documentary	——
exclusion	——	exclude	exclusive	——
finance	financier	finance	financial	financially
issue	issuer	issue	——	
labor	laborer	labor	labored	——
military militia	militant	——	militant	militarily
normality	——	normalize	normal normally	normally
——	——	obtain	obtainable	——
occupation	occupant occupier	occupy	——	——
purchase	purchaser	purchase	——	——
registration register registrar	registrant	register	registered	——
restriction	——	restrict	restricted restrictive	——
reverse reversal	——	reverse	reverse	reversibly
source	source	source	source	——

Exercise 5: Word Forms

Complete each sentence with the correct form of the word.

1. The prisoner's diet was _____ to stale bread, thin soup, and sometimes potatoes.

   restrict   restriction   restrictive   restricted

2. Unemployed people can receive _____ support from the government.

   finance   financier   financial   financially

3. Jewish prisoners were used as _____. Every healthy man, woman, and
   child worked for hours a day in the camps.

   labor   labored   laborers   laboring

4. The government _____ special cards, called ration cards, which people had to use to obtain food.

   issue   issues   issued   issuing

5. A constant _____ of tension was the fact that there was no privacy in
   the Annex. It was almost impossible to be alone.

   sources   source   resources   resourceful

6. No one was allowed to make noise during the day, so Anne studied and
   wrote in her diary to keep herself quietly _____.

   occupy   occupied   occupant   occupation

Understanding Words in Context

Exercise 6: Words in Context

Complete each sentence with one of these words. Change the word form by adding -s, -ed, -ial, or -ing if necessary.

finance   issue   normal   obtain   reverse   source

1. I don't normally feel tired in the morning. Actually the _____ is true: I usually feel energetic.

2. Oil and gas continue to be the main _____ of income for many oil-rich countries.

3. Most college students try to get some kind of _____ aid to help pay their tuition.

4. I lost my library card, but the library _____ me a new one right away.

5. _____ tickets for the Friday night show was impossible, but I did get tickets for Saturday night.

6. _____ business hours are 9 to 5, Monday through Friday. The office is closed on Saturday and Sunday.

Exercise 7: Collocations

Remember that **collocations** are word friends, or words that often appear before or after one another. Take the word *school* as an example. The words *bus, cafeteria, day, trip,* and *after* collocate with *school: school bus, school cafeteria, school day, school trip,* and *after school.*

A. Can you think of other words that collocate with *school*? Add them.

_____

B. Match the four words with the words they often appear together with. Write the combinations on the lines provided. One has been done for you.

agency	**course**	**in**	**problems**
aid	**direction**	**official**	**resistance**
church	**home**	**policy**	**school**

1. financial   __financial aid_____

      _____

2. government   _____

      _____

3. group   _____

      _____

4. reverse   _____

      _____

Using Words in Communication

Exercise 8: Reading

A. Find a short article or story about a person who survived the Holocaust. Go to the library or use the Internet to locate information. Follow these steps as you look for information.

    1. Start by finding information about the main topic: **Holocaust survivors.**

    2. Narrow your search by looking for **memoirs, biographies,** or **stories,** about **Holocaust survivors.**

    3. If you would like to find information about a young person, try looking for **children who survived the Holocaust** or **child Holocaust survivors**.

B. Read your article, then fill in as many blanks as you can about the survivor.

    1. Survivor's name _____

    2. Place of birth _____

    3. Date of birth (month/day/year) _____

    4. Age at the end of the Holocaust (1945) _____

    5. Number of people in family _____

    6. Family members who survived the Holocaust _____

    7. What was their life like during the Holocaust? _____

       _____

       _____

    8. What was interesting or surprising to you? _____

       _____

       _____

    9. Write one question you would like to ask this person. _____

       _____

Exercise 9: Writing

A. Imagine that you have to live in hiding without a television, radio, iPod®, computer, or other electronics. You cannot make any noise at all from 9:00 AM to 6:00 PM every day except Sunday. What would you do all day? Fill out the chart.

9:00 AM	
10:00 AM	
11:00 AM	
12:00 PM	
1:00 PM	
2:00 PM	
3:00 PM	
4:00 PM	
5:00 PM	
6:00 PM	

B. Now, write a short dairy entry for the same day.

_____

_____

_____

_____

_____

_____

_____

_____

Exercise 10: Critical Thinking

First, answer these questions by yourself. Then share your answers with a partner. Decide on one answer for each question. Be prepared to explain your answers to the class.

1. Re-read the Introduction to the Readings and the rules that the Jews in Holland had to follow. Do you think these rules cut Jewish people off from their Dutch neighbors? Why do you think Hitler wanted to isolate the Jews? Explain your answers.

2. Imagine what life would be like hiding in the Secret Annex. List five things you think Anne and the others might have done to make sure they were not discovered.

Saving Our Water

Vocabulary Preview

These sentences contain information from the readings. Fill in the blanks with the word that best completes each sentence.

consumers   evidence   factors   global   regulations

1. Global warming, acid rain, and pollution are all _____ that contribute to the death of coral reefs.

2. _____ limit the number, size, and type of fish that fishermen can legally catch.

3. In 17 years of swordfishing, Linda Greenlaw says that she has seen no _____ of overfishing. If this is true, why are there fewer fish in the ocean than ever before?

4. American _____ should buy U.S.-caught fish, because U.S. fishermen catch fish legally.

5. Scientists agree that there is a definite link between _____ warming and the death of coral reefs.

Preview 2

Look at the way the underlined words are used in the sentences. Match each word with its definition.

1. The police have the <u>authority</u> to arrest or fine anyone who breaks the law.

2. What can you do to protect the <u>environment</u>—to protect the quality of the air, the water, and the land?

3. The <u>welfare</u> of the oceans and rivers affect all of us. All living things need clean water to drink.

4. <u>Chemicals</u> affect the water in the ocean and the life of coral plants and shellfish.

5. It was <u>legal</u> for Jimmy Blake to fish for and catch sturgeon, but it was against the law to catch striped bass.

_____ 1. **authority**

_____ 2. **environment**

_____ 3. **welfare**

_____ 4. **chemical**

_____ 5. **legal**

a. a state of health and wellness

b. a material that is made by mixing two or more substances together

c. within the law; allowed by law

d. the right to command or control people or their actions

e. the natural world of land, sea, air, plants, and animals; our surroundings

Reading Preview: What Do You Already Know?

Circle the correct answer. If you don't know the answer, guess.

1. The world's oceans are unhealthy because of

   a. global warming

   b. overfishing

   c. industrial pollution

   d. all of the above

2. Most American commercial fishermen/fisherwomen

   a. obey government regulations and observe boundaries

   b. can't make a living by fishing

   c. do not care about the environment

   d. make a lot of money

3. Global warming

   a. does not affect ocean life

   b. is causing the temperature of the ocean to rise

   c. creates colder winters and more snowfall

   d. is not related to greenhouse gases produced by cars and industries

4. What percentage of the earth's surface is covered by water?

   a. 33 percent

   b. 65 percent

   c. 71 percent

   d. 86 percent

Introduction to the Readings

(1) Water is one of our most important <u>resources</u>. Nearly 71 percent of the earth's surface is covered by water, causing astronauts orbiting the earth to name it "the blue planet." The human body is <u>approximately</u> 65 percent water. Water is needed for life. Oceans and rivers supply us with drinking water, food, and power. In addition, oceans and rivers have provided humans with the opportunities to explore and travel. It is difficult to imagine human history without oceans and rivers. However, the <u>impact</u> of the growing world population and our increasing use of fossil fuels is <u>affecting</u> the health of the world's oceans, rivers, and lakes. The readings in this unit discuss some of the important <u>issues</u> facing the world's rivers and oceans today.

(2) The first reading is by Linda Greenlaw. She has been fishing commercially for nearly 25 years and is perhaps the only <u>professional</u> female swordfish captain to fish off the Grand Banks in Nova Scotia. Her work and her <u>income</u> depend on having <u>adequate</u> numbers of fish in the ocean. At the same

> ***conservationists:** people who want to protect the environment and living things from harm, loss, or change

time, many scientists and conservationists* worry that the oceans are being "fished out"—that there are too many people catching too many fish, too fast. They fear that soon there may be no fish left in the oceans. Some groups have tried to create less demand for fish by refusing to buy or eat it. This reading gives a commercial fisherwoman's point of view on the overfishing issue.

> ***pollution:** substances that harm the water, air, or atmosphere
>
> ***sewage:** waste from homes and factories that is carried away by water in pipes called *sewers*

(3) The second reading is from a book called *The Riverkeepers*. The Hudson River Fishermen's Association was <u>founded</u> in 1966 and later became known as Riverkeeper. The group included fishermen as well as others who lived along the Hudson River. They were all concerned about what was happening to their once beautiful river. Pollution* was killing it. New York City was dumping 1.5 billion gallons of raw sewage* into it every day, factories were dumping **chemicals** and waste

into the river, and power plants were killing millions of fish every day. The association decided to use two little-known laws—the Rivers and Harbors Act of 1888 and the Refuse Act of 1899—to find and prosecute the Hudson River's polluters. These two laws made it **illegal** to pollute American waters and gave a reward to whoever reported the <u>violation</u>.

(4) Since 1966, Riverkeeper has tracked down hundreds of polluters, taken them to court, and forced them to spend hundreds of millions of dollars cleaning up the Hudson. Today the Hudson is one of the healthiest bodies of water on earth, and the Riverkeeper organization has inspired others to act as "waterkeepers" on more than 150 waterways around the world. The reading here is one of the early cases Riverkeeper became <u>involved</u> in.

(5) The <u>final</u> reading is about global warming and the harmful effect it is having on the world's coral reefs. In order to understand this reading, we need to understand the **process** of global warming. **Global*** warming is the gradual increase in the temperature of the atmosphere closest to the earth. The temperature of the atmosphere near the earth's surface is warmed through a natural **process*** called the "greenhouse effect." <u>Visible</u> light travels from the sun to the earth and passes through a blanket of "greenhouse" gases made up of water vapor, carbon dioxide, methane, nitrous oxide, and ozone. Infrared radiation, which we cannot see but can feel as heat, is reflected off the planet's surface toward space. Some of this heat is trapped by the greenhouse gases and reflected back toward the earth. This reflected radiation, or heat, keeps the earth at an average temperature of about 60 degrees Fahrenheit (16 degrees Celsius). Most living things on earth can live at this temperature.

*global: having to do with the whole earth

*process: a series of things that happen in order and result in change

(6) In the last 100 years, growth in industry, agriculture, and <u>transportation</u>, and the increased use of fossil fuel has produced more greenhouse gases. This increase in the amount of greenhouse gases is trapping more heat in the earth's atmosphere* and causing its temperature to rise. During the

*atmosphere: the layer of air and other gases around a planet

past century, the earth's atmospheric temperature has risen 1.1 degrees Fahrenheit (0.6 degrees Celsius). Melting snow and ice from the polar caps has caused the sea level to rise by several inches.

(7) The earth's atmosphere and the oceans also affect one another. As heat causes ocean water to evaporate* into the atmosphere, tiny particles of salt are left in the air. Water vapor condenses* around these particles to form fog and clouds. Eventually, some of this water vapor returns to the earth as rain, and brings with it other chemicals and particles that are present in the atmosphere. As you will read, some of these chemicals are changing the acidity of water in the oceans, and this change is killing the coral reefs.

> ***evaporate:** to change from a liquid into a gas
> ***condense:** to change from a gas into a liquid

Reading 1: Fishing or Overfishing?

Excerpt adapted from *The Hungry Ocean* by Linda Greenlaw
(New York: Hyperion, 1999), 143–45.

(8) No matter what **equipment** you have, you can't catch fish if they're not there. And the only way to know whether the fish are at home or not is to put the fishing gear in the water. I guess that's why what I do is called "fishing." If it was easy, we'd call it "catching," and there would be more people doing it. Then, perhaps there would be a reason for the conservationists to advocate putting an end to commercial fishing. In 17 years of fishing, I have seen no **evidence** of fewer fish.

(9) I have always been happy to follow government **regulations** and to observe boundaries, believing that this will ensure the future of fish and fishing. What annoys me are the actions taken by groups such as the restaurant chefs who took swordfish off their menus to try to protect it. I wonder how these chefs can presume they know better than the fishermen and scientists who have been working together for years to keep the stocks of fishes strong. In my opinion, chefs should leave fisheries management to those who know more about swordfish.

(10) U.S. fishermen are among the most **regulated** fishermen in the world. Fishermen of my <u>generation</u> are conservation-minded. We also don't like that the public is given misinformation. If a problem with overfishing does develop, it is not the American fisherman who should be punished, but the fishermen from other countries who continually <u>exceed</u> their allowable catch limits. Fishing for a living is part of our country's history. **Consumers** should enjoy the fruits of the <u>labor</u> of law-abiding and conservation-minded fishermen without being made to feel guilty. Eat U.S.-caught fish! It's **legal**!

Reading 2: Fish Kills

Excerpt adapted from *The Riverkeepers* by John Cronin and Robert F. Kennedy, Jr.
(New York: Touchstone, Simon & Schuster, 1997), 177.

(11) In 1981, officers from the New York State Department of **Environmental** Conservation (DEC) charged commercial fisherman Jimmy Blakely with **illegally** catching 52 striped bass by net. Blakely claimed he caught the bass accidentally while fishing **legally** for another type of fish called sturgeon. The state agency fined Blakely the maximum, $250 per fish. With no money for a lawyer and facing the <u>prospect</u> of having to sell his home to raise the $13,000 fine, Blakely <u>contacted</u> John Cronin, a commercial fisherman working with the Hudson River's commercial fishermen and the state DEC. After a judge issued a fine of only $250, angry DEC officials banned winter netting for all fish species on the Hudson.

(12) There was irony* in Blakely's arrest. He had been arrested near the Indian Point power plant, which was **illegally** killing more than a million fish per day, yet the DEC officers had never issued the plant a single ticket. On the <u>contrary</u>, the DEC had shielded the energy company, even attempting to stop photographs of the high numbers of fish killed at the Indian Point plant in 1965. When the photos were **located** and <u>published</u> in *Sports Illustrated*, it <u>created</u> a national scandal* and led to congressional hearings on the fish kills and the withholding of evidence.

> ***irony:** an unusual or unexpected aspect of a situation

> ***scandal:** a situation that many people find shocking or wrong

(13) Have times changed? Unfortunately not. Many other fish kills have been reported in the <u>decades</u> since. The Clean Water Act and other laws are intended to protect public property and **welfare** and improve water quality by forcing polluters to pay. However, regulations alone will not accomplish these **objectives.** Only following the law will. Environmental law gives government the **authority** to stop pollution, but it cannot make the government exercise that authority.

Reading 3: Global Warming

Excerpt adapted from *An Inconvenient Truth* by Al Gore
(Emmaus, PA: Rodale, 2006), 164–68.

(14) Coral reefs, which are as important to ocean life as rainforests are to land animals, are being killed in large numbers by **global** warming. Many **factors** <u>contribute</u> to the death of coral reefs—pollution, destructive dynamite fishing in less-developed <u>regions</u>, and more acidic ocean waters. However, the most deadly cause of the recent, rapid destruction to coral reefs is believed by scientists to be the higher ocean temperatures due to global warming.

(15) Coral bleaching—the **process** that turns healthy multi-colored coral reefs into white or gray skeletons—<u>occurs</u> when tiny organisms living in the covering are <u>stressed</u> by heat and other **factors** and leave the coral. When they escape, the thin clear skin <u>reveals</u> the colorless skeleton beneath. The bleached

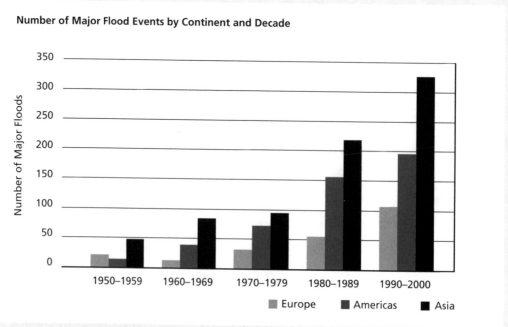

Number of Major Flood Events by Continent and Decade

Source: *An Inconvenient Truth,* page 106.

appearance usually precedes the death of the coral. The <u>link</u> between global warming and the bleaching of corals, considered **controversial** only 10–15 years ago, is now universally accepted.

(16) Corals—along with many other ocean life forms—are also threatened by the growth of carbon dioxide (CO_2) emissions* worldwide because up to one-third of these emissions end up sinking into the ocean and increasing the acidity of the water. We are used to thinking about the harmful effects of all the extra CO_2 in the atmosphere. But we now have to worry about the **chemical** <u>transformation</u> of the oceans as well.

*emissions: gases that are released into the air

(17) Acid resulting from all the extra CO_2 changes ocean water and <u>alters</u> the amount of carbonate and bicarbonate ions.* This, in turn, <u>affects</u> the levels of calcium carbonate in the oceans—and that is important because many small sea creatures routinely use calcium carbonate as the basic building block from which they make the hard <u>structures</u>—like reefs of shells—on which their lives depend.

*ions: electrically charged atoms

⟨◎⟩ Comprehension Check

Did you understand the readings? Mark these sentences true (T) or false (F).

_____ 1. Linda Greenlaw does not believe that the oceans are overfished.

_____ 2. Scientists, fishermen, and the government all want to ensure that there will be plenty of fish in the future.

_____ 3. It's unhealthy to eat swordfish.

_____ 4. The Indian Point power plant had to pay a huge fine for killing millions of fish.

_____ 5. The New York Department of Environmental Conservation stopped fishermen from netting fish during the winter.

_____ 6. Riverkeeper started out as a group of local people who wanted to clean up and protect the Hudson River.

_____ 7. Global warming is one of the factors causing coral reefs to die.

_____ 8. A decrease in the acidity of ocean water is killing coral reefs and shellfish.

_____ 9. Global warming occurs when the earth gets too close to the sun.

Word Study

Target Vocabulary

authority	equip (equipment)	locate
chemical	evident (evidence)	objective
consume (consumer)	factor	process
controversy (controversial)	globe (global)	regulate
environment	legal	welfare

Word Parts

Exercise 1: Suffixes

The suffix -*ment* is used to form nouns. These nouns refer to an action or process, the thing that is used to perform an action or process, the result of an action, or the place where an action occurs.

Match each noun containing the suffix -*ment* with the best definition. Write the letter of the definition in the space provided.

1. *environ* means *around,* so **environment** means _____

2. *elementum* means *a basic part or principle,* so **element** means _____

3. *docēre* means *to teach or to prove,* so **document** means _____

4. *equipper* means to *prepare for action* or to *make ready,* so **equipment** means _____

a. an official paper that shows or proves something

b. a single part of something that combines with other parts to make up a whole

c. a person's surroundings; the natural world around us

d. the tools or resources that will be needed to perform an action

Word Relationships

Analogies are comparisons between two sets of words. An analogy consists of four words, three of which are always given. The analogy is completed by adding a fourth word that completes the comparison.

Examples:

1. A kitten is to a cat as a child is to a/an _____.

   kitten : cat :: child : <u>adult</u>

2. Day is to light as night is to _____.

   day : light :: night : <u>dark</u>

3. A driver is to a car as a pilot is to a _____.

   driver : car :: pilot : <u>plane</u>

Exercise 2: Analogies

Use one of the target words from Units 1 to 4 to complete each analogy. Change the word form by adding a word ending if necessary.

1. mind : mental :: body : _____

2. stadium : sports :: bank : _____

3. many : crowd :: one : _____

4. goods : purchase :: food : _____

5. canvas : painting :: paper : _____

6. unknown : question :: know : _____

Exercise 3: Synonyms and Antonyms

Identify these pairs of words as synonyms (S) or antonyms (A).

_____ 1. locate/find   _____ 5. normal/typical

_____ 2. individual/group   _____ 6. appropriate/unsuitable

_____ 3. dominant/passive   _____ 7. legal/unlawful

_____ 4. process/method   _____ 8. controversial/arguable

The Grammar of Words and Word Families

Exercise 4: Word Families

Use these words to fill in the word family chart. Follow the example given. Some words will be used more than once.

authority (2x)	chemical (2x)	consumer	controversial	environment
authoritative	chemist	consume	controversially	environmental
authoritatively	chemistry	consumerism	controversy	environmentalism
authorization		consuming		environmentalist
authorize		consumption		environmentally

equipment	evidence	factor (2x)	global	legal
equip	evident		globalization	legality
	evidently		globalize	legalize
			globally	
			globe	

locate	objective (2x)	process (3x)	regulate	welfare (2x)
location	objectively		regulation	
			regulatory	

Noun	Noun (person)	Verb	Adjective	Adverb
authority authorization	authority	authorize	authoritative	authoritatively
chemical chemistry	chemist	——	chemical	——
consumption consumerism	consumer	consume	consuming	——
controversy	——	——	controversial	controversially
environment environmentalism	environmentalist	——	environmental	environmentally
equipment	——	equip	——	——
evidence	——	——	evident	evidently
factor	——	factor	——	——
globalization globe	——	globalize	global	globally
legality	——	legalize	legal	——
location	——	locate	——	——
objective	——	——	objective	objectively
process	——	process	process	——
regulation	——	regulate	regulatory	——
welfare	——	——	welfare	——

Exercise 5: Word Forms

Complete each sentence with the correct form of the word.

1. Laws _____ the places where fisherman can fish and the number of fish that they can legally catch.

   regulation   regulates   regulate   regulating

2. Photographs showing dead fish were used as _____ in the trial against the power company.

   evident   evidence   evidently   evidenced

3. Swordfishing takes special _____. The fish are so large and so strong that they easily break ordinary fishing gear.

   equipped   equipments   equip   equipment

4. One of the main _____ of Riverkeeper was to find and prosecute the people and businesses that were polluting the Hudson River.

   objective   objection   objectives   objects

5. Today commercial fishermen use radar and aerial searches to _____ schools of fish.

   location   located   locating   locate

Understanding Words in Context

Remember that *collocations* are words that often appear together. Match the four words with their common collocations. Write the combinations on the lines provided. Can you think of any other words that collocate with these? Add them. One has been done for you.

activist	**confidence**	**protection**
agency	**goods**	**rights**
case	**impact**	**warming**
challenge	**issues**	

1. consumer   *consumer confidence* _____

     _____

     _____

2. global   _____

     _____

3. legal   _____

     _____

4. environmental   _____

     _____

Exercise 7: Constructing Sentences

Use each set of words to write a sentence. Use all the words given. No additional words are needed. Add punctuation.

1. effect / is / that / earth's / the / atmosphere / greenhouse / a / process / warms

   _____

2. warming / water / global / the / balance / ocean / is / chemical / of / changing / of

   _____

3. of / controversial / overfishing / the / is / idea

   _____

4. to / are / factors / many / reefs / causing / many / die / coral

   _____

5. environment / do / can / help / consumers / what / to / the

   _____

Exercise 8: Reading

Read the article, and answer the questions in your own words.

Recycling

Recycling turns old, used materials into new products. Recycling is important because it prevents the waste of useful materials, reduces the consumption of raw materials, reduces energy usage and reduces the production of greenhouse gases. Glass, paper, aluminium, asphalt, iron, textiles and plastics can all be recycled. Food waste or garden waste is also recyclable through composting.

There are two common methods of recycling. In "curbside collection," consumers separate glass, paper, plastic, and metal materials. They leave these recyclable materials in front of their home or business where they are collected by a recycling vehicle. With a "bring" or carry-in system, the consumer takes the materials to a collection point. From there recyclables are sorted and separated into material types, and the material is cleaned.

After they are cleaned and separated, the recycled materials are manufactured into new products. Today many products are being manufactured with total or partial recycled content. Common household items that contain recycled materials include newspapers and paper towels; aluminum, plastic, and glass soft drink containers; steel cans; and plastic bottles. Recycled materials are also being used in new ways such as recovered glass in roadway asphalt (called glassphalt) or recovered plastic in carpeting, clothing, and park benches.

Purchasing recycled products completes the recycling loop. By "buying recycled," governments, businesses, and individual consumers make the recycling process a success.

1. What is recycling? _____
   _____

2. There are three main steps in the recycling process. What are they?
   _____

3. What kind of materials can be recycled? _____

4. Describe two common methods of recycling. _____
   _____

5. What kind of products are made with recycled materials? _____
   _____

6. What are three benefits of recycling? _____
   _____

Exercise 9: Writing

A. Some of the serious environmental problems we face today are listed. Choose a topic that interests you, and circle it.

- human overpopulation
- water pollution and water shortages
- air pollution
- global warming
- loss of plant and animal habitats
- endangered and extinct species of plants, animals, and fish

1. In your opinion, what are some of the causes of this problem?

   _____

   _____

2. Do you think this is a serious problem? Why or why not?

   _____

   _____

3. What can you do to help solve this problem? List three things.

   _____

   _____

4. What do you think will happen if this problem is not solved?

   _____

   _____

B. Use the information you wrote in Part A to write one or two paragraphs about your topic.

Exercise 10: Critical Thinking

A cause and effect relationship occurs when one event (the **cause**) leads to another event (the **effect**). The first event makes the second event happen. Here are some examples:

CAUSE ———→ leads to ———→ EFFECT

You touch something hot.	It hurts, so you pull your hand away.
You always eat too much.	You gain weight.
You sit in the sun all day.	You get a sunburn.

Global warming is a series of cause and effect events. Put the events that follow in the correct order. Write the number of the event in the space provided. Write number 1 next to the first thing that happens, number 2 next to the second event, and so on. Refer back to the introduction and readings for more information.

_____ a. Some heat is trapped by greenhouse gases and reflected back toward the earth.

_____ b. Increased amounts of greenhouse gases trap more heat in the earth's atmosphere.

_____ c. Melting snow and ice from the polar caps causes the sea level to rise by several inches.

_____ d. Visible light from the sun goes through a layer of "greenhouse" gases that surround the earth.

_____ e. Industry, agriculture, and the increased use of fossil fuel produce more greenhouse gases.

_____ f. The temperature of the earth's atmosphere rises.

_____ g. Infrared radiation is reflected by the earth's surface toward space.

_____ h. Reflected radiation heats the earth to about 60 degrees Fahrenheit.

5

Exploring Space

Vocabulary Preview

These sentences contain information from the readings. Fill in the blanks with the word that best completes each sentence.

challenged   **created**   **significant**   **simulations**   **technology**

1. Exploring space required the development of new science and _technology_.

2. The _simulations_ that the astronauts practiced in training prepared them for their experiences in space.

3. Many people felt that landing on the moon was important, but Neil Armstrong thought that man's first steps on the moon's surface were even more _____.

4. President Kennedy _____ the American people to explore space and go to the moon before the Russians did.

5. The moon was _____ when huge clouds of gas began to turn into solid matter.

Preview 2

Look at the way the underlined words are used in the sentences. Match each word with its definition.

1. There was political <u>conflict</u> between the United States and the Soviet Union during the Cold War of the 1950s, '60s and '70s.

2. The 1960s were a <u>decade</u> of optimism and excitement. America had a young, energetic President who wanted to explore space.

3. The <u>goal</u> of the space program was to land an American on the moon before the end of the 1960s.

4. The formation of the moon <u>generated</u> intense heat that turned the surface of the moon into boiling lava.

5. Most Americans watched a black-and-white television <u>image</u> of man's first steps on the moon.

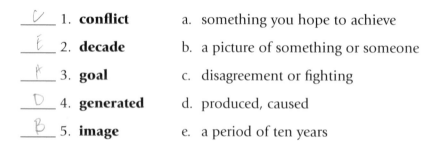

   _C_ 1. **conflict**   a. something you hope to achieve

   _E_ 2. **decade**   b. a picture of something or someone

   _A_ 3. **goal**   c. disagreement or fighting

   _D_ 4. **generated**   d. produced, caused

   _B_ 5. **image**   e. a period of ten years

Reading Preview: What Do You Already Know?

Circle the correct answer. If you don't know the answer, guess.

1. During the 1950s and 1960s there was a "space race"

   a. between China and the United States

   b. between China and the Soviet Union

   c. between the Soviet Union and the United States

   d. none of the above

2. Which American President pushed America's space program forward?

   a. President Clinton

   b. President Kennedy

   c. President Nixon

   d. President Reagan

3. Which American spacecraft were designed to fly to the moon?

   a. the Apollo series

   b. the Gemini series

   c. the Mercury series

   d. all of the above

4. How did the earth develop an atmosphere and oceans?

   a. through global warming

   b. volcanic gases from the moon traveled to the earth

   c. the earth's gravity and magnetic field held gases close to its surface

   d. none of the above

Introduction to the Readings

(1) During the 1950s and 1960s, the United States and the Soviet Union (now Russia) were in a Cold War. The two countries were not actually at war, but they were fighting over political views, <u>specifically</u> democracy and communism. The Soviets put the first man in space in Sputnik 1 in 1957. The first U.S. space program began on October 7, 1958, with <u>Project</u> Mercury. This was the beginning of the Space Race between the two countries.

(2) The **goals** of the Mercury program (1961–1963) were: (1) to send a spaceship with a man inside around Earth, (2) to see if man was able to <u>function</u> in space, and (3) to bring both man and spacecraft safely back to earth. However, on May 5, 1961, just three weeks after the first U.S. space flight, President John F. Kennedy announced that he wanted the U.S. to land a man on the moon before the end of the decade.

(3) <u>Project</u> Gemini was an <u>intermediate</u> step between the Mercury Program and the Apollo Program that would someday put a man on the moon. The main <u>objectives</u> of the Gemini missions (from 1965 to 1966) were: (1) to put two men and their <u>equipment</u> into space for long flights and observe what happens, (2) to learn how to "fly" a spacecraft by moving it around during orbit,* (3) to practice meeting and connecting to other <u>vehicles</u> in space, and (4) to improve methods of re-entry to Earth and landing.

*orbit: the circle around a planet, the moon, or the sun
*Command Module: the main spaceship that travelled to the moon
*Lunar Module: the . small spacecraft that would land on the moon. It was attached to the Command Module.

(4) The Apollo Program (1967 to 1975) was <u>designed</u> to land humans on the moon and bring them safely back to Earth. Six of the missions—Apollo 11, 12, 14, 15, 16, and 17—<u>achieved</u> this **goal** and carried out scientific experiments on the surface of the Moon. Neil Armstrong, on Apollo 11, became the first man to land and walk on the moon. Apollo 7, which tested the Command Module,* and Apollo 9, which tested both the Command Module* and Lunar Module,* were missions that orbited Earth. Apollo 8 and Apollo 10 also tested

equipment while orbiting the moon and returned with photos of the moon's surface. Apollo 13 did not land on the moon due to an accident that blew up one of the spacecraft's oxygen tanks. Luckily, the astronauts were able to use the Lunar Module as a lifeboat to travel safely around the Moon and back to Earth.

(5) The most recent space projects include:

Skylab (1973–1976)

Designed for long duration flights, the Skylab program hoped (1) to prove that humans can live and work in space for long periods and (2) to expand our knowledge of the sun.

Shuttle-Mir (1986–present)

The Shuttle-Mir program uses U.S. space shuttles and the Russian Space Station Mir. It allows astronauts from both countries to experience space and carry out scientific research together.

The International Space Station (1998–present)

The most complex engineering and construction project in the world is currently in space. The first crew arrived at the Space Station in 2000.

Reading 1: The Challenge of Space

Excerpt adapted from President John F. Kennedy's address at Rice University
on the Nation's Space Effort, September 12, 1962, Houston, Texas.

(6) If history teaches us anything, it is that man, in his quest for knowledge and progress, is determined. The exploration of space will go ahead, whether we join in it or not, and no nation that expects to be the leader of other nations can expect to stay behind in the race for space. We mean to lead it. We intend to be first. Our hopes for peace and security require us to make this effort, to solve these mysteries for the good of all men, and to become the world's leading space-faring nation.

(7) We set sail on this new sea because there is new knowledge to be gained, and new rights to be won and used for the progress of all people. For space science, like **nuclear** science and all **technology,** has no conscience of its own. Whether it will become a force for good or ill depends on man. There is no strife, no prejudice, no national **conflict** in outer space yet. Its hazards are hostile to us all. Its conquest* deserves the best of all mankind, and its opportunity for peaceful <u>cooperation</u> may never come again. But why, some say, the moon?

*conquest: the conquering or controlling of something

(8) We choose to go to the moon in this **decade** because that **goal** will organize and measure the best of our **energies** and skills, because that **challenge** is one that we are willing to accept, and one that we intend to win. Space is there, and we're going to climb it, the moon and the planets are there, and new hopes for knowledge and peace are there. Therefore, as we set sail, we ask God's blessing on the most hazardous and dangerous and greatest adventure on which man has ever embarked.*

*embarked: to start on something difficult or dangerous

Reading 2: A Man on the Moon

Excerpt adapted from *A Man on the Moon* by Andrew Chaikin
(New York: Penguin Group USA, Inc., 1994), 205–6, 208–9.

(9) If it hadn't been for the fact that everyone made such a big deal of it, Armstrong wouldn't have <u>focused</u> on the matter at all. To Armstrong the [moon] landing was the flight's greatest <u>achievement</u>, but to a public <u>unaware</u> of the **technology** of this journey, a landing was less meaningful than a foot-step. It was natural for them to want historic words for historic occasions. Now, on the moon, Armstrong knew he could delay no longer. As he thought about the first step he would take on the moon, he thought about the <u>inherent</u> paradox—a small step, yet a **significant** one—he knew what he would say.

Apollo 11 astronauts Buzz Aldrin and Neil Armstrong plant the American flag on the moon.

*mission control: the group of scientists and engineers on Earth that stayed in contact with the astronauts and helped them with any problems they had

(10) On the screen in mission control* a strange black-and-white **image** came into existence. The shadowy form of Neil Armstrong coming down the ladder. When Armstrong reached the bottom, he paused. Armstrong looked down at the moon's soil and described what he saw for the **benefit** of scientists on earth. "The surface appears to be very, very fine grained as you get close to it; it's almost like a powder…" In **simulations** his voice had been decidedly calm; now it was filled with excited curiosity.

(11) Grabbing the ladder, Armstrong turned and leaned outward. "Okay," he said, "I'm going to step off the Lunar Module now." Carefully, he lowered his left foot to the dust. He tested his weight, bouncing in the gentle gravity, and when he felt firm ground he was still, one foot on the Lunar Module and one foot on the moon. He spoke: "That's one small step for [a] man"—a pause—"one giant leap for mankind." Armstrong lowered his foot and stepped sideways, both hands resting on the Eagle's* landing gear. And at last, after bouncing up and down a few more times, he let go of *Eagle* and stood on the moon.

*the Eagle: another name for the Lunar Module

The Eagle has landed.

Reading 3: The Moon

Excerpt adapted from *Moon Shot* by Alan Shepard and Deke Slayton, with Jay Barbree and Howard Benedict (Atlanta: Turner Publishing, Inc., 1994), 329–30.

(12) The <u>data</u> from Apollo 17 and the other landing missions would keep scientists <u>intensely</u> busy for **decades.** What **emerged** is a picture of a moon that was born in tremendous heat, lived a **brief** life of boiling lava and collisions, then died geologically in an early, primitive stage.

(13) The moon was **created** some 4.6 billion years ago when great clouds of gas (called the solar nebula) began condensing* to form the sun, earth, and other planets and moons of the solar system. The nebula first condensed into chunks of space debris—from small pebbles to miles-wide boulders—that crashed together and formed these bodies.

> *condensing: the changing of a gas into a liquid

(14) Study of the Apollo data showed that, in the case of the moon, this <u>process</u> **generated** intense heat, which turned the lunar surface into a sea of molten lava. When the lava cooled, it became the moon's crust. Debris left over from the **creation** of the solar system continued to hit the moon, carving

out giant craters* and valleys and forming mountains by stacking up large piles of rocks.

> *craters: very large, round holes in the ground

(15) Scientists believed that the young earth went through the same <u>period</u> where meteorites hit it and there was volcanic activity for about half a billion years. Then the Earth and moon took different paths. The small moon's weak gravity could not prevent volcanic gases from escaping into

space. But the larger body, Earth, with strong magnetic and gravity fields, held onto its volcanic gases. These gases formed oceans and an atmosphere around the Earth, creating conditions for the development of life. The moon became a dead body where life could not exist.

🌀 Comprehension Check

Did you understand the readings? Mark these sentences true (T) or false (F).

_____ 1. The United States and the Soviet Union were fighting a war in 1958.

_____ 2. President Kennedy didn't believe that an American would ever land on the moon.

_____ 3. Exploring space would be an opportunity for scientists from many countries to work together peacefully.

_____ 4. Neil Armstrong felt that stepping onto the moon was more historic than landing a spacecraft on the moon.

_____ 5. The moon and the Earth were both created about 4.6 billion years ago.

_____ 6. Unlike the moon, the Earth was never volcanic.

_____ 7. Geologists consider the moon "dead," a place where nothing can live.

_____ 8. Gravity on the moon is the same as gravity on the Earth.

🌀 Word Study

Target Vocabulary

benefit	decade (decades)	image
brief	emerge (emerged)	nuclear
challenge	energy	significant
conflict	generate (generated)	simulate (simulations)
create (created, creation)	goal	technology

Word Parts

Exercise 1: Prefixes

Many English words that refer to number, distance, weight, or volume use prefixes from Latin and French. If you already use the metric system, you will be familiar with some of these common prefixes. Look at these words.

Prefix	Meaning
kilo- or **mille-**	**one thousand** or **1,000**
cent- or **cento-**	**one hundred** or **100**
deca-	**ten** or **10**
deci-	**one-tenth** or **1/10**
centi	**one one-hundredth** or **1/100**
milli	**one one-thousandth** or **1/1000**

Match each word with the correct definition. Use your dictionary if you need to.

_____ 1. **decade**

_____ 2. **decimal**

_____ 3. **centimeter**

_____ 4. **centipede**

_____ 5. **century**

_____ 6. **kilogram**

_____ 7. **kilometer**

_____ 8. **millennium**

_____ 9. **millimeter**

_____ 10. **millisecond**

a. a period of 100 years

b. 1,000 grams

c. one one-thousandth of a meter

d. a period of ten years

e. one one-thousandth of a second

f. a counting system based on the number 10

g. an insect with 100 legs

h. 1,000 meters

i. one one-hundredth of a meter

j. a period of 1,000 years

Word Relationships

Exercise 2: Related Words

Four of the words in each series have similar meanings. Cross out the word that has a different meaning. The first one has been done for you.

1. benefit   profit   ~~harm~~   advantage   gain
2. brief   lengthy   short   quick   small
3. energy   power   strength   stillness   drive
4. significant   important   boring   meaningful   matter
5. emerge   appear   leave   return   issue
6. generate   use   produce   make   cause

Exercise 3: Word Associations

Which topic is each of these words associated with? Write each word under the appropriate topic. Some words may be used more than once. Add one more word to each list.

chemical	generate	physical
communications	global	regulate
consume	labor	resources
data	military	survive
equipment	nuclear	sustainable

Conflict	_Energy_	_Technology_
_____	_____	_____
_____	_____	_____
_____	_____	_____
_____	_____	_____
_____	_____	_____
_____	_____	_____
_____	_____	_____
_____	_____	_____

The Grammar of Words and Word Families

Exercise 4: Word Families

Use these words to fill in the word family chart. Follow the example given. Some words will be used more than once.

benefit (2x)	brief	challenge (2x)	conflict (2x)	create
benefactor	briefly	challenger	conflicting	creation
beneficial		challenging		creative
beneficiary				creatively
				creativity
				creator

decade	emerge	energy	generate	goal
	emergence	energetic	generator	
	emergent	energetically		
		energize		

image	nuclear	significant	simulate	technology
		significance	simulation	technological
		significantly		technologically
		signify		technologist

Noun	Noun (person)	Verb	Adjective	Adverb
benefit	beneficiary benefactor	benefit	beneficial	——
——	——	——	brief	briefly
challenge	challenger	challenge	challenging	——
conflict	——	conflict	conflicting	——
create creation	creator	create	creativity	creatively
decade	——	——	——	——
emergent	——	emerge	emergence	——
energy	——	energize	energetic	energetically
generator	——	generate	——	——
goal	——	——	——	——
image	——	——	——	——
——	——	——	nuclear	——
significance	——	signify	significant	significantly
simulation	——	simulate	——	——
technology	technologist	——	technological	technologically

Exercise 5: Word Forms

Complete each sentence with the correct form of the word.

1. Large rocks and meteorites crashed into the moon's surface _____ large holes called craters.

   create   creation   creator   creating

2. One of the _____ of the space program was to land a man on the moon.

   goal   goalkeepers   goals   goal-oriented

3. None of the astronauts ever _____ just how beautiful the Earth was when seen from space.

   image   images   imagination   imagined

4. _____ physics is the branch of science concerned with the nucleus of the atom.

   nucleus   nuclei   nuclear   non-nuclear

5. The astronauts practiced situations that _____ what it would feel like to land and work on the moon.

   simulate   simulated   simulation   simulations

Exercise 6: Derivatives

The root of the word *benefit* comes from the Latin words *bene facere* meaning "to do good to." The following words all share that root: *benefit, benefactor, beneficiary,* and *beneficial.* Complete these sentences with the correct word. If necessary, change words by adding *-s, -ed,* or *-ing.*

1. The school had many wealthy _____, some of them had also been students there.

2. Several popular musicians performed at the _____ concert to raise money for hurricane victims.

3. We all know that a good diet, plenty of exercise, and enough sleep are _____ to a persons' health.

4. The will listed several _____ and what each of them would inherit after his or her death.

Understanding Words in Context

Exercise 7: Simplifying and Inferring

Sometimes a text is complicated. Writers often use more words than they need to. It is helpful to break the text into small parts and then restate each part more simply.

> <u>Example</u>: The exploration of space will go ahead, whether we join in it or not, and no nation that expects to be the leader of other nations can expect to stay behind in the race for space. We mean to lead it.

1. Break the text into whole thoughts:
   - The exploration of space will go ahead, whether we [the U.S.] join in it or not.
   - No nation that expects to be the leader of other nations can expect to stay behind in the race for space.
   - We [the U.S.] mean to lead it.

2. Rewrite or rephrase each part so it's easier to understand:
   - Other countries will explore space whether the U.S. does or not.
   - The U.S. can't be behind in the "space race" if we want to lead other countries.
   - The U.S. wants to lead the space race.

3. Combine the simpler sentences to help you understand the original text:
   Other countries will explore space whether the U.S. does or not. The U.S. can't be behind in the "space race" if we want to lead other countries. The U.S. wants to lead the space race.

Sometimes a writer does not make a point directly. Then the reader must *infer* or guess what the writer is trying to say by looking at the information that is given. What can you infer from the paragraph in item 3 above?

> a. The U.S. may not explore space.
> b. The U.S. wants to lead other countries.
> c. The U.S. does not want to lead other countries.

The correct answer is *b.* because we know that the U.S. wants to lead the space race, so we can guess, or infer, that the U.S. also wanted to lead other countries in 1962.

What can we infer from the passages that follow? Simplify the text first to help you understand its meaning.

1. We set sail on <u>this new sea</u> because there is new knowledge to be gained, and new rights to be won and used for the progress of all people. For space science, like nuclear science and all technology, has no conscience of its own.

   _____

   _____

   _____

   _____

   In this passage, what is *this new sea*?
   a. a new sea on the moon
   b. space science
   c. an unexplored sea on the earth

2. If it hadn't been for the fact that everyone made such a big deal of <u>it</u>, Armstrong wouldn't have focused on the matter at all. To Armstrong the moon landing was the flight's greatest achievement, but to a public unaware of the technology of this journey, a landing was less meaningful than a footstep.

   _____

   _____

   _____

   _____

   In the first sentence, what does *it* refer to?
   a. being the first person to travel to the moon
   b. being the first person to land a spaceship on the moon
   c. being the first person to step onto the moon's surface

3. In simulations Armstrong's voice had been decidedly calm; now it was filled with excited curiosity.

_____

_____

_____

_____

What can you infer about the how Armstrong felt about the simulations and about being on the moon?

a. Armstrong felt that the simulations were an ordinary part of his job.

b. Armstrong felt that the simulations were ordinary, but he was curious and excited about being on the moon.

c. Armstrong felt that the simulations and being on the moon were both not very interesting.

4. Then the two bodies took different paths. The small moon's weak gravity could not prevent volcanic gases from escaping into space. But the larger body, Earth, with strong magnetic and gravity fields, held onto its volcanic gases. These gases formed oceans and an atmosphere around the Earth, creating conditions for the development of life. The moon became a dead body where life could not exist.

_____

_____

_____

_____

_____

_____

_____

Why did the moon become a _dead body where life could not exist?_

a. The moon did not develop oceans or an atmosphere.

b. The moon's gravity was too weak.

c. Living things need volcanic gases in order to develop.

Using Words in Communication

Exercise 8: Reading

A. Choose a topic that interests you, and circle it.

- The Mercury, Gemini, or Apollo Programs
- Skylab
- The Space Shuttle
- The Shuttle-Mir Project
- The International Space Station
- The Hubble Telescope
- The moon landings
- An astronaut such as John Glenn, Neil Armstrong, or Sally Ride
- Another topic related to our solar system, the stars, or other planets

B. Go to the library or use the Internet to locate information. Write down this information for the book or article you choose.

Name of book or article:

_____

Author of book or article:

_____

C. Read a section of the book or the whole article at least two times. As you read, try to answer these questions.

1. What is the topic of the article or section of the book?

   _____

2. What are the main points of the article or section of the book?

   _____

3. Are there any words that you don't know? Write some of them here.

   1. _____

   2. _____

   3. _____

   4. _____

4. Use your dictionary to write a short definition for each word you wrote in Question 3.

   1. _____

   2. _____

   3. _____

   4. _____

Exercise 9: Writing

Think about the book or article you read for Exercise 8. Write a paragraph that describes what you read. Be sure to include the topic you wrote in Question 1, and the main points you wrote in Question 2. Write a second paragraph that gives your opinion about the book or article. Give at least two reasons why you feel that way.

Exercise 10: Critical Thinking

First, answer these questions by yourself. Then share your answers with a partner. Decide on one answer for each question. Be prepared to explain your answers to the class.

1. Exploring space is very expensive and there are many problems here on earth, problems like pollution, disease, poverty, and global warming. Do you think we should spend so much money to explore space? Or would it be better to spend money on problems here on earth? Support your answer with at least three specific reasons.

2. Space exploration can be very dangerous. List at least three of the dangers that you think astronauts face. Would you be willing to go into space? Why or why not? Support your answer with specific reasons.

6

Seabiscuit and the Great Depression

Vocabulary Preview

Preview 1

These sentences contain information from the readings. Fill in the blanks with the word that best completes each sentence.

coordination   economy   income   prohibited   task

1. During the 1920s, the _____ of most Americans was growing. People had enough money to buy cars, radios, and appliances.

2. The _____ Tom Smith had was to help horses heal after being injured.

3. Jockeys are incredible athletes. A good jockey needs great strength, balance, and _____.

4. The sale of alcohol was _____ in America during the 1920s.

5. The U.S. _____ crashed in October of 1929. This event started the Great Depression.

Look at the way the underlined words are used in the sentences. Match each word with its definition.

1. Cold causes matter to <u>contract</u> or become smaller, and heat causes it to expand or become larger.

2. He <u>invested</u> half his money in the stock market and half of it in real estate.

3. The increasing <u>volume</u> of goods imported from other countries has hurt American manufacturing.

4. War Admiral <u>pursued</u> Seabiscuit until the very last turn, and then he seemed to give up. Seabiscuit won the race by four lengths.

5. It took her a year to <u>recover</u> from the car accident, but she's able to walk normally now.

_____ 1. **contract**	a. the amount there is of something
_____ 2. **invest**	b. chase or run after
_____ 3. **volume**	c. to become healthy again
_____ 4. **pursue**	d. grow smaller
_____ 5. **recover**	e. to buy or put money into something

Reading Preview: What Do You Already Know?

Circle the correct answer. If you don't know the answer, guess.

1. Seabiscuit was alive and racing during the

    a. 1920s

    b. 1930s

    c. 1940s

    d. 1950s

2. People loved Seabiscuit because

    a. he had a hard life when he was young

    b. he was determined to win

    c. he wasn't beautiful or spoiled like most racehorses

    d. all of the above

3. Horseracing was popular during the Great Depression because

    a. it was free entertainment

    b. Americans loved horses

    c. people were allowed to gamble at the racetrack

    d. it wasn't very exciting

Introduction to the Readings

(1) In October of 1929, the American stock market crashed, and the country entered the Great **Depression**. Many people lost all the money they had **invested** in the stock market and were suddenly poor. As consumers, people had less money to spend, and the **economy** slowed down. Businesses cut their costs and, as a result, millions of people lost their jobs. Unemployment was at a record high of 25%. It was a terrible time in U.S. history.

(2) Life was not all bad, though. People <u>found</u> ways to escape the hard reality of daily life. The movies were very popular. About 85 million people went to the movies every week. The glamorous Hollywood films of the 1930s gave tired audiences a couple of hours of beauty and fantasy. Radio <u>dramas</u> were another way people could escape. Families sat around the radio to listen to programs like *The Lone Ranger* or *Little Orphan Annie*.

(3) Baseball and horseracing also became very popular forms of entertainment. People enjoyed the drama and excitement of horseracing. But there was another reason many people went to the races. Racetracks were almost the only place in the United States where gambling was <u>legal</u>. Some people bet on the horses in hopes of winning enough money to feed their families for a week or a month. A big win at the races could help a person out of poverty.

(4) The racehorse Seabiscuit was born on May 23, 1933. He became an American hero: a brave underdog who won when no one expected him to. Seabiscuit, a Thoroughbred, came from a family of famous racehorses. His sire (father) Hard Tack and grandsire (grandfather) Man o' War were both horses that broke racing records. Unfortunately, Seabiscuit didn't take after either of them. He was a small horse with what looked like weak knees and crooked legs. He was slow. And he was lazy—eating and sleeping were his two favorite activities. No one could have predicted he would become one of the most popular and successful racehorses of all time.

(5) After Seabiscuit's first two unsuccessful years of racing, Charles Howard, a self-made millionaire, decided to buy him. Howard's horse trainer, Tom Smith, thought the horse had something inside him that was special. He believed he could improve the little horse, and he did. Within months, Seabiscuit was winning races and setting track records. The little horse that no one ever expected to win was winning in a big way.

(6) One of Seabiscuit's most famous victories was on November 1, 1938, at the Pimlico racetrack in Maryland. Charles Howard had <u>finally</u> arranged for Seabiscuit to race against War Admiral, another famous grandson of Man o' War. War Admiral was the number one horse on the east coast, and Seabiscuit was the top racehorse on the west coast. The country took sides: Either you were for War Admiral (and the east coast) or you were for Seabiscuit (and the west coast). To many people, the beautiful War Admiral <u>symbolized</u> the rich, spoiled upper class. Seabiscuit, on the other hand, wasn't pretty and had had a tough life. He seemed to stand for the ordinary working man and the less fortunate.

(7) On race day, the whole country went crazy over the race. Forty million people listened to the race on the radio, and tens of thousands of fans watched at the track as "the Biscuit" beat War Admiral by four lengths (of a horse). The winning time was just over one minute and 56 seconds for one and three-sixteenths of a mile—a new track record at Pimlico.

(8) Seabiscuit thrilled fans for the <u>final</u> time when he came back to win the 1940 Santa Anita Handicap in record time. This win made Seabiscuit the top-earning horse in the world. He won $437,730 during his career. The 1940 Santa Anita Handicap was Seabiscuit's last and, some would say, greatest race.

Reading 1: The Racehorse

Excerpt adapted from *Seabiscuit* by Laura Hillenbrand
(New York: Ballantine Publishing Group, Random House, 2001), 70.

(8) A Thoroughbred racehorse is one of the world's most impressive animals. Weighing up to 1,450 pounds, he can <u>sustain</u> speeds of forty miles per hour. He swoops over as much as 28 feet of earth in a single stride and turns on a dime. His body is shaped to slip through the air with the ease of an arrow. His mind is fixed on a single command: run. He **pursues** speed with courage, pushing beyond defeat, beyond exhaustion, and sometimes beyond the limits of bone and muscle. In flight, he is nature's <u>ultimate</u> pairing of form and purpose.

catapult: a machine that launches or throws something

(9) To ride a racehorse is to ride a half-ton catapult.* It is one of the most difficult feats in sport. A study of the **elements** of athleticism <u>conducted</u> by Los Angeles exercise physiologists and physicians <u>found</u> that of all <u>major</u> sports competitors, jockeys may be, pound for pound, the best <u>overall</u> athletes. They have to be. To begin with, there are the demands on

balance, **coordination**, and reflexes. A horse's body is <u>constantly</u> <u>shifting</u>. On a running horse, a jockey does not sit in the saddle, he crouches over it, leaning all of his weight on his toes, which rest on the thin metal stirrups. When a horse is in full stride, the only parts of the jockey that are in contact with the animal are the insides of the feet and ankles—everything else is balanced in midair.

Reading 2: Tribute to a Hero

Excerpt adapted from "Tribute to a Hero" by Oscar Otis,
Los Angeles Times, March 3, 1940.

(10) Seabiscuit <u>found</u> the pot of gold at the end of the rainbow yesterday. He <u>emerged</u> the winner of the Santa Anita Handicap in new record time, 2:01 1/5 seconds for the mile and a quarter, and became the money-winning champion of the world by a **margin** of $60,000 in the most popular victory in the history of western racing.

(11) Seabiscuit is a super horse, one in a million, who was <u>purchased</u> by Charles Howard from the Wheatley <u>Stable</u>. Wheatley had used Seabiscuit chiefly as a workhorse to help train his more expensive horses. I first saw him at Bay Meadows in his first western race for Charlie Howard. It was a flat mile. Seabiscuit got left behind at the post and won in 1:36. I knew then he was a good horse and so did all who saw the race.

(12) Then Seabiscuit came to Santa Anita. He lost by a nose in the $100,000 to Rosemont. He tried again the next year and lost to Stagehand. In between races at Santa Anita, he became a <u>confirmed</u> traveler. He amazed everyone with his ability to win against the toughest competition after just getting off the railroad cars. He won races here, there, and everywhere. Until that fateful day here last year when Seabiscuit broke down in a race against the horse Today. Howard took the horse out of racing and sent him to his ranch to **recover.** Seabiscuit did, and he came back yesterday.

(13) Seabiscuit's rise to glory happened under trainer Tom Smith. It's **sufficient** to say that this silent man was once a cowboy in the rough-and-tough world of the rodeo. There he had the **unique task** of helping rodeo horses **recover** from injuries. Smith later worked at the racetrack and did so well that he was suggested as a trainer for the Howard <u>Stables</u>. It was a happy combination. Smith rebuilt Seabiscuit. The fact that after all his racing, traveling, and injuries Seabiscuit is a healthier horse today than the day he was <u>purchased</u> tells a lot about Smith and shows that Seabiscuit is a horse of iron.

(14) This story wouldn't be complete without the ovation given to Seabiscuit by the 74,000 at Santa Anita yesterday. It was the greatest race ever seen. The cheering at Santa Anita was from the heart—for the brave old fellow is the kind of an animal that once you see him run, see him try, see that great heart of his nearly burst in an effort to get down to the wire, stays in your heart for all time. There may be another horse to come along greater than Seabiscuit, but none will be as popular with the people, with the $2 fan, as Seabiscuit. He is a hero.

Reading 3: The Great Depression

Excerpt adapted from "The Great Depression" in *The National Geographic Almanac of World History* by Patricia S. Daniels and Stephen G. Hyslop (Washington, DC: National Geographic Society, 2003), 291–92.

(15) The 1920s were a <u>period</u> of great change in America. **Prohibition** was in full swing, making the sale or possession of alcoholic beverages <u>illegal</u>. Women had recently gained the right to vote. For the upper classes, life was a ball.

(16) Except among farmers, **income** was on the rise. The average rate in the rise of income among workers was about one <u>percent</u> each year. The wealthiest one <u>percent</u> of the population saw their income increase about eight times as fast. This new money fueled the economy. The less wealthy used the installment plan to pay for new cars, radios, and other <u>purchases</u>. The rich

Bread lines were common during the Depression.

paid cash. Much of the wealth <u>found</u> its way into the stock market. As prices rose, those who hoped to get rich bought stocks with money they had borrowed.

(17) Stock prices began to weaken in September 1929, but few **investors** seemed concerned. Then on October 21, prices began to fall more quickly. Nervous investors sold stocks in large **volumes.** Stock prices began to drop. Within a week, those who had borrowed heavily to buy stocks suddenly owed much more than they had. Many people <u>found</u> themselves penniless overnight.

(18) America's **economy** at the time prospered because of the confidence that the stock market would continue its upward surge. When it fell instead, consumer confidence fell with it. The economy entered a downward spiral. Jobs disappeared, and incomes fell, leading to less demand for goods. This caused the economy to contract or shrink. Many businesses failed, putting more people out of work. In 1930, the number of unemployed workers was five million. One year later, 13 million were jobless.

Comprehension Check

Did you understand the readings? Mark these sentences true (T) or false (F).

_____ 1. Thoroughbred racehorses are fast—they can run at speeds of 40 miles an hour.

_____ 2. Jockeys are not as fit as other athletes.

_____ 3. Seabiscuit was more beautiful than most racehorses.

_____ 4. People escaped from daily life by watching movies and listening to radio dramas.

_____ 5. Seabiscuit did not win many races when he was young, but he did win a lot of races as he got older.

_____ 6. Tom Smith was Seabiscuit's owner.

_____ 7. The Great Depression began in September of 1929 and ended on October 28, 1929.

_____ 8. Many Americans lost their jobs during the Great Depression.

Word Study

Target Vocabulary

contract	income	recover
coordinate (coordination)	invest (investors)	sufficient
depress (Depression)	margin	task
economy	prohibit (Prohibition)	unique
element	pursue	volume

Word Parts

Exercise 1: Prefixes

The prefix *mis-* means "wrong" or "done badly." Note the way the underlined words are used in the sentences. Then match each word with the correct definition.

1. The students started <u>misbehaving</u>, talking loudly, and throwing things at one another, as soon as the teacher left the room.

2. I <u>misplaced</u> my glasses. I can't find them anywhere.

3. Seabiscuit was <u>mistreated</u> by his first owner. He was raced too much and whipped too often.

4. I <u>misinterpreted</u> her smile. I thought she was being friendly, but she was only being polite.

5. Unfortunately, we were <u>misinformed</u>. We thought we could buy tickets at the door, but the show was already sold out.

6. The paper <u>misprinted</u> his name—it's spelled Smyth not Smith.

_____ 1. **misbehave**   a. to understand wrongly

_____ 2. **misplace**   b. to make a mistake in printing something

_____ 3. **mistreat**   c. to put something in the wrong place

_____ 4. **misinterpret**   d. to act in a way that is not acceptable

_____ 5. **misinform**   e. to treat badly or abuse

_____ 6. **misprint**   f. to give incorrect information

Exercise 2: Suffixes

The suffixes -ant (or -ent), -ist, and -er (or -or) mean "a person who. . . . or one who. . . . "
For example, a *student* is a person who studies, a *pianist* is a person who plays the piano, and a *worker* is one who works at a job.

Go back to the readings, and find words that have these meanings. The number of the paragraph where the word can be found is given in parentheses.

1. _____ (1), (18)   one who buys things or uses services

2. _____ (9)   a person who studies physiology

3. _____ (12)   one who travels

4. _____ (13)   a person who teaches or trains animals

5. _____ (16)   a person who makes a living by farming

6. _____ (17)   a person who invests money in something

Do you know any other words like this? Write them on the line.

_____

Word Relationships

Exercise 3: Synonyms and Antonyms

Identify these pairs of words as synonyms (S) or antonyms (A).

_____ 1. income/expense

_____ 2. depress/raise

_____ 3. contract/expand

_____ 4. pursue/chase

_____ 5. prohibit/ban

_____ 6. recover/heal

_____ 7. unique/ordinary

_____ 8. task/job

The Grammar of Words and Word Families

Exercise 4: Word Families

Use these words to fill in the word family chart. Follow the example given. Some words will be used more than once.

contract	coordination	depress	economy (2x)	element
contraction	coordinate	depressed	economic	elemental
	coordinator	depressing	economical	elementary
		depression	economist	
			economize	

income	invest	margin	prohibit	pursue
incoming	investment	marginal	prohibition	pursuer
	investor	marginalize	prohibitive	pursuit

recover	sufficient	unique	volume (2x)	
recovery	suffice	unique		
	sufficiently	uniquely		
		uniqueness		

Noun	Noun (person)	Verb	Adjective	Adverb
contraction	——	contract	——	——
coordination	coordinator	coordinate	——	——
depression	——	depress depressed	depressing	
economy	economist	economize	economical economic economy	——
element	——	——	elemental elementary	——
income	——	——	incoming	——
investment	investor	invest	——	——
margin	——	marginalize	marginal	——
prohibition	——	prohibit	prohibitive	——
pursuit	pursuer	pursue	——	——
recovery	——	recover	——	——
——	——	suffice	sufficient	sufficiently
uniqueness unique	——	——	unique	uniquely
volume	——	——	volume	——

Exercise 5: Word Forms

Complete each sentence with the correct form of the word.

1. Hydrogen is the lightest chemical _____.

    elements   elemental   elementary   element

2. During the Great Depression many businesses _____ by cutting jobs and laying off workers.

    economy   economics   economized   economists

3. Please leave wide _____ on both sides of the paper.

    margin   margins   marginal   marginalize

4. The number of chairs wasn't _____, so some people had to stand.

    suffice   sufficient   sufficiently   suffices

5. The Declaration of Independence states that every person is equal and has the right to "life, liberty and the _____ of happiness."

    pursue   pursuer   pursuit   pursuing

⊚ Understanding Words in Context

Exercise 6: Words in Context

Complete each sentence using one of the words that is given. Change the word form by adding -s, -ed, -ing, or -ly if necessary.

coordinate	**element**	**income**	**prohibit**	**unique**

1. Cigarette smoking is _____ in all restaurants, bars, and public places.

2. Many families have two _____; the husband and wife both work.

3. We need to _____ our schedules so we can all meet at 1:00 next Thursday afternoon.

4. She has a _____ style. She dresses differently from everyone else, but she always looks great!

5. How many _____ are listed on the Periodic Table?

Exercise 7: Constructing Sentences

Use each set of words to write a sentence. Use all the words given. No additional words are needed. Add punctuation.

1. than / car / A / is / economical / to / more / a / big / small / truck / drive

   _____

2. eye / light / The / pupil / the / bright / of / contracts / in

   _____

3. depressed / her / after / felt / died / husband / She

   _____

4. speed / Basketball / coordination / good / requires / and

   _____

5. the / invest / market / risky / stock / It's / to / in

   _____

Using Words in Communication

Exercise 8: Reading

Review the table, and answer the questions. Write your answers in complete sentences.

Seabiscuit's Race Record						
Year	Age	Race Starts	Win (1st place)	Place (2nd place)	Show (3rd place)	Earnings
1935	2	35	5	7	5	$12,150
1936	3	23	9	1	5	$28,995
1937	4	15	11	2	1	$168,580
1938	5	11	6	4	1	$130,395
1939	6	1	0	1	0	$400
1940	7	4	2	0	1	$96,850
Total		89	33	15	13	$437,740

1. How many years did Seabiscuit race? How old was he when he started racing? How old was he when he finished racing?

   _____

2. How old was Seabiscuit during his busiest race year? How many races did he run in?

   _____

3. How old was Seabiscuit when he had his most race wins? What year was this?

   _____

4. Which year was Seabiscuit's worst year? Why?

   _____

5. In which year did Seabiscuit win the most prize money? In which year did he win the least prize money?

   _____

6. How much prize money did Seabiscuit win during his racing career?

   _____

Exercise 9: Writing

Write at least two paragraphs about Seabiscuit or the Great Depression. You may use information from the Introduction to the Readings, the three readings, and the exercises in this unit. You can also go to the library or use the Internet to find more information. Be sure you write in your own words. Do not copy from a book, article, or website.

After you have written your paragraphs, skip a line and write where you found the information you used. Follow the examples given. If you use information from a book or magazine, write the author's name, the title of the book or magazine, the title of the magazine article, and the page numbers where you found the information.

> <u>Example</u>: Linda Wells, *Vocabulary Mastery 1*, x–xx.

If you use information from a website, write the website address (URL), the name of the website or web article, and the author of the website if there is one.

> <u>Example</u>: *www.seabiscuitonline.com/index1.asp*, Seabiscuit: An American Legend

Exercise 10: Critical Thinking

First, answer these questions by yourself. Then share your answers with a partner. Decide on one answer for each question. Be prepared to explain your answers to the class.

1. Seabiscuit was a hero to many Americans. Why do you think people loved him so much? Explain your answer.

2. According to the readings, how did the Great Depression start?

Appendix 1
Academic Word List

This list, compiled by Coxhead (2000), contains 570 word familes that are important for students to know to read texts and do well in academic settings. Words explicitly studied in this text as target words are set in **bold** and marked by the number of the unit in which they appear. Words that are not studied explicitly but occur in the text are set in ordinary type and marked by the number of the unit in which they appear. Words that occur in exercises are set in ordinary type with the number of the unit in which they appear in parentheses.

abandon
abstract Unit 2
academy
access
accommodate Unit **3**
accompany
accumulate Unit **1**
accurate
achieve Units 1, 5
acknowledge
acquire Unit **2**
adapt
adequate Unit 4
adjacent
adjust
administrate
adult
advocate Unit 4
affect Unit 4
aggregate
aid
albeit
allocate
alter Unit 4
alternative
ambiguous

amend
analogy Unit 4
analyse
annual Unit 1
anticipate
apparent
append
appreciate
approach Unit 2
appropriate Unit **2**
approximate Unit 4
arbitrary
area Units 2, 3
aspect
assemble
assess
assign
assist
assume
assure
attach
attain
attitude Unit 1
attribute
author Units 2, 3, 5, 6
authority Unit **4**

automate Unit **1**
available Unit 5
aware Unit 5
behalf
benefit Unit **5**
bias
bond
brief Unit **5**
bulk
capable Unit **2**
capacity
category Unit 1
cease
challenge Units 1, **5**
channel
chapter
chart Units 1, 2, 3, 4, 5, 6
chemical Unit **4**
circumstance
cite
civil
clarify
classic Unit 2
clause
code
coherent

coincide
collapse Unit 1
colleague
commence
comment
commission
commit
commodity
communicate Unit **2**
community
compatible
compensate
compile
complement
complex
component
compound Unit 1
comprehensive
comprise
compute Units 1, 2, 3
conceive Unit 2
concentrate Unit 3
concept Unit **2**
conclude
concurrent
conduct
confer
confine
confirm Unit 6
conflict Unit **5**
conform
consent
consequent
considerable
consist Units 2, 3
constant
constitute
constrain

construct Units **2,** 3
consult
consume Unit **4**
contact Units **2,** 4, 6
contemporary
context Unit **2**
contract Unit **6**
contradict
contrary Unit 4
contrast
contribute Unit 4
controversy Unit **4**
convene
converse
convert
convince Unit 2
cooperate Unit 5
coordinate Unit **6**
core
corporate
correspond
couple
create Units 4, **5**
credit Unit 5
criteria
crucial
culture
currency
cycle
data Units **1,** 5
debate
decade Units 4, **5**
decline
deduce
define Unit **2**
definite
demonstrate
denote

deny
depress Unit **6**
derive
design Unit 5
despite Unit 1
detect
deviate
device
devote
differentiate
dimension
diminish
discrete
discriminate
displace
display
dispose
distinct
distort
distribute Unit 3
diverse
document Unit **3**
domain
domestic
dominate Unit **2**
draft
drama Unit 6
duration Unit 5
dynamic
economy Unit **6**
edit
element Unit **6**
eliminate
emerge Units **5,** 6
emphasis
empirical
enable Unit 2
encounter

energy Unit **5**
enforce
enhance
enormous
ensure Units 3, 4
entity
environment Units 2, **4**
equate
equip Units 1, 3, **4,** 5
equivalent
erode
error
establish Unit **1**
estate
estimate Unit **1**
ethic
ethnic
evaluate Unit 1
eventual Unit 4
evident Unit **4**
evolve Unit **2**
exceed Unit 4
exclude Unit **3**
exhibit
expand Unit 5
expert
explicit
exploit
export
expose
external
extract
facilitate
factor Unit **4**
feature
federal
fee
file

final Units **1,** 2, 4, 6
finance Unit **3**
finite
flexible
fluctuate
focus Units 1, 5
format
formula
forthcoming
foundation Units 1, 4
found Units 1, 2, 3, 6
framework
function Units **2,** 5
fund
fundamental
furthermore
gender
generate Units 1, **5**
generation Unit 4
globe Unit **4**
goal Unit **5**
grade
grant
guarantee
guideline
hence
hierarchy
highlight
hypothesis
identical
identify Unit **2**
ideology
ignorance
illustrate Unit 4
image Unit **5**
immigrate
impact Unit 4
implement Unit **2**

implicate
implicit
imply
impose
incentive
incidence
incline
income Units 3, 4, **6**
incorporate
index
indicate
individual Unit **1,** 2
induce
inevitable
infer Unit 2, 5
infrastructure
inherent Unit 5
inhibit
initial
initiate
injure
innovate
input
insert
insight
inspect
instance Unit 3
institute
instruct
integral
integrate
integrity
intelligence
intense Unit 5
interact
intermediate Unit 5
internal
interpret Unit 6

interval
intervene
intrinsic
invest Units 3, **6**
investigate
invoke
involve Unit 4
isolate
issue Units **3,** 4
item Unit 3
job Unit 3
journal
justify
label
labor Units **3,** 4
layer Unit 4
lecture
legal Units **4,** 6
legislate
levy
liberal
licence
likewise
link Unit 4
locate Unit **4**
logic
maintain Units 1, 2
major Units 2, 6
manipulate
manual Unit 3
margin Units 1, **6**
mature
maximise
mechanism
media
mediate
medical
medium

mental Units 1, 4
method Units 2, 4
migrate
military Unit **3**
minimal
minimise
minimum
ministry
minor
mode
modify
monitor Unit **1**
motive
mutual Unit 2
negate
network
neutral
nevertheless
nonetheless
norm
normal Unit **3,** 6
notion
notwithstanding
nuclear Unit **5**
objective Units **4,** 5
obtain Unit **3**
obvious Unit 2
occupy Unit **3**
occur Units 2, 4
odd
offset
ongoing
option
orient Unit 5
outcome
output
overall Unit 1
overlap

overseas
panel
paradigm
paragraph Units 1, 2, 3,
    4, 5, 6
parallel Unit 2
parameter
participate Unit **1**
partner
passive Unit **2**
perceive
percent Units **1,** 6
period Units 1, 5, 6
persist
perspective
phase
phenomenon Unit 2
philosophy
physical Units **1,** 2
plus
policy Unit 3
portion
pose
positive
potential
practitioner
precede Unit 1
precise
predict Unit 1
predominant
preliminary
presume Unit 4
previous Unit 1
primary
prime
principal Unit 4
principle
prior

priority
proceed
process Units 1, 2, 3, **4,** 5
professional Units **1,** 4
prohibit Unit **6**
project Units 2, 5
promote
proportion
prospect Unit 4
protocol
psychology Unit 2
publication
publish Units 3, 4
purchase Units **3,** 6
pursue Unit **6**
qualitative
quote
radical
random
range
ratio
rational
react
recover Units 1, **6**
refine
regime
region Unit 4
register Unit **3**
regulate Unit **4**
reinforce
reject
relax
release
relevant
reluctance
rely
remove Unit 2
require Units 3, 5, 6

research Units 1, 2, 5
reside
resolve
resource Units **1,** 3, 4,
respond
restore
restrain
restrict Unit **3**
retain
reveal Unit 4
revenue
reverse Unit **3**
revise
revolution Unit 1
rigid
role
route Unit 1
scenario
schedule Units 3, 6
scheme
scope
section Unit 2
sector
secure Unit 5
seek
select
sequence
series Units 4, 6
sex
shift Unit 6
significant Unit **5**
similar Units 2, 5
simulate Unit **5**
site
so-called
sole
somewhat
source Unit **3**

specific Units 2, 5
specify Unit 3
sphere
stable
statistic
status
straightforward
strategy
stress Unit 4
structure Unit 4
style Unit 6
submit
subordinate
subsequent
subsidy
substitute
successor
sufficient Unit **6**
sum
summary
supplement
survey
survive Units **1,** 3
suspend
sustain Units **1,** 6
symbol Unit 6
tape
target Units 1, 2, 3, 4, 5, 6
task Unit **6**
team
technique Units 1, 2
technology Units 1, **5**
temporary
tense
terminate
text Units 1, 2, 3, 4, 5, 6
theme Unit 2
theory

thereby

thesis

topic Units 1, 2, 3 ,4, 5, 6

trace

tradition Unit 3

transfer

transform Unit 4

transit

transmit

transport Unit 4

trend

trigger

ultimate Unit 6

undergo

underlie

undertake

uniform

unify

unique Unit **6**

utilize

valid

vary Unit 3

vehicle Unit 5

version

via

violate Unit 4

virtual

visible Unit 4

vision

visual

volume Unit **6**

voluntary

welfare Unit **4**

whereas

whereby

widespread

Appendix 2
Expansion Activities

Unit 1: Professional Cycling (pages 1–21)

Cycling

1. If possible, find a video or check your local listings for replays of the Tour de France on the TLC channel on cable. Watch it as a class if possible.

2. If possible, ask students to attend a bicycle road race. Most local communities have a bike race or cycling event during the course of the year.

3. Ask students to investigate cyclists from their home countries and track their progress in races during the course of the term.

Cancer Survival

1. Ask students to learn more about different types of cancer and their survival rates.

Unit 2: Talking to the Animals (pages 22–43)

Jane Goodall

1. Ask students to find out more about Jane Goodall and her work with chimpanzees or to research other similar animal researchers.

2. If possible, get a video of the PBS show *Nature* that features Jane Goodall. It's called "Jane Goodall's Wild Chimpanzees" and is available at *www.pbs.org/wnet/nature/goodall/*. Watch it as a class.

Animal Whisperers

1. Ask students to watch the movie *The Horse Whisperer* starring Scarlett Johansson and Robert Redford or watch it as a class. Notice the things Robert Redford's character does to communicate with the damaged horse.

2. Cesar Millan is currently called the Dog Whisperer. He became popular after working with the dogs of celebrities like Will Smith and Oprah Winfrey. Learn more about Millan to find out the kinds of behavioral problems he seems to be able to fix in dogs.

3. Ask students to write about the connections with animals and pets that they have had. Do they have evidence that their pets communicate with them?

Unit 3: Living in Hiding (pages 44–65)

Anne Frank

1. In 2006, a movie called *Freedom Writers* was released; it's now available on DVD. The movie was based on a book called *The Freedom Writers Diary*, which told how one teacher introduced her students to books she thought they, as teenagers living in a drug- and gang-ridden zone, could appreciate. One of the first books the students read was *The Diary of Anne Frank*. Watch *Freedom Writers* to discover the impact this book, and meeting Mies Giep, has on them.

2. In *The Freedom Writers Diary*, the students read a more recent diary of a young girl in Yugoslavia who has an experience not all that different from Anne Frank's. Ask students to read *Zlata's Diary: A Child's Life in Wartime Sarajevo* by Zlata Filipovic, and note similarities and differences between her account and Anne Frank's account.

3. Ask students if they know about or to investigate other diaries written by teenagers or young adults living in a war zone or living with difficult political strife.

Unit 4: Saving Our Water (pages 66–87)

Linda Greenlaw

1. Linda Greenlaw was a character in the movie *A Perfect Storm*. Watch the movie to learn what else you can about her and about fishermen in Maine.

2. Linda Greenlaw also wrote *The Lobster Chronicles* about her life off the coast of Maine as a fisherwoman.

Global Warming

1. As a result of the movie *An Inconvenient Truth*, global warming has become a topic more people are familiar with. Ask students to investigate one of these issues in greater detail to look at how global warming is affecting it:

   • Polar bears and the polar ice cap

   • Hurricane Katrina and warmer ocean waters

2. Ask students to investigate three ways they can save energy in their lives or changes they can make to help cut down on ozone gases.

Unit 5: Exploring Space (pages 88–111)

Going to the Moon

1. HBO broadcast a series now available on DVD called *From the Earth to the Moon*. This series features dramatizations of some of the early space challenges and successes and also reveals much about the early NASA program. Watch some episodes as a class.

2. The movie *Apollo 13* starring Tom Hanks is a fascinating and harrowing in-depth look at the spacecraft that nearly was trapped in space.

3. The U.S. space shuttle program also has had successes and failures. Ask students to investigate some of these successes and failures.

4. The space station MIR is a joint operation between the United States and Russia. What is it like to live on this space station?

Unit 6: Seabiscuit and the Great Depression (pages 112–131)

Seabiscuit

1. The movie *Seabiscuit* tells the story of the horse, his trainer, his jockey, and his owner—all of whom endured tough times before achieving success through the horse. Watch the movie.

2. In the United States, three horseraces—the Kentucky Derby, the Preakness, and the Belmont Stakes—are called the Triple Crown. No horse has won all three races since 1978 when Secretariat, often considered the greatest racehorse of all time, won it. Several horses have won two of the three races; ask students to research horses that have accomplished this. Which horses have won each of these races most recently?

The Great Depression

1. There have been several movies that show how difficult the Great Depression was on Americans. One recent movie is *Cinderella Man* starring Russell Crowe. This movie also depicts the power of sports figures during this era. Compare James Braddock of *Cinderella Man* with Seabiscuit and their appeal during this tough time.

2. One of the ways President Franklin D. Roosevelt helped pull the country out of the Great Depression was by giving people work through the government-sponsored Works Progress Administration (WPA). These projects were responsible for many of the parks, dams, and highways in the country. Investigate WPA programs done in your state.

Vocabulary Mastery 2

Using and Learning
the Academic Word List

LINDA WELLS
GLADYS VALCOURT

Ann Arbor
The University of Michigan Press

ISBN-13: 978-0-472-03313-3

2012   2011   2010   2009   4   3   2   1

Acknowledgments

Many thanks to all those who have encouraged and supported me in this project. I am grateful for your unwavering energy, enthusiasm, and advice. A huge thank you especially to my editor, Kelly Sippell, for her continuing friendship and editorial guidance, and to Bob Carocari for his support and patience throughout. Many thanks also to the staff at the University of Michigan Press for their hard work, and to all the students and colleagues who have contributed to this volume in one way or another over the years. To all, my heartfelt thanks.

—Linda Wells

Grateful acknowledgment is given to the following authors, publishers, and individuals for permission to reprint their materials or previously published materials.

AWL List

Permission granted by Averil Coxhead to use the Academic Word List in the appendix and in the book's subtitle.

Unit 1

Unit-opening photo courtesy of Jupiter Unlimited.

Adapted excerpts from *Iacocca: An Autobiography* by Lee Iacocca with William Novak (New York: Bantam Doubleday Dell, 1984), 64–74; *Shameless Exploitation in Pursuit of the Common Good* by Paul Newman and A. E. Hotchner (New York: Doubleday/Random House, 2003), 3–6; *Jiffy, A Family Tradition: Mixing Business and Old-Fashioned Values* by Cynthia Furlong Reynolds (Chelsea, MI: Chelsea Milling Co., 2008), 14, 18, 30, 32, 64–65, 68.

Photos courtesy of Ford Division of Public Affairs (Detroit, MI) and Chelsea Milling Co. (Chelsea, MI).

Unit 2

Unit-opening photo courtesy of the Library of Congress.

Adapted excerpts from *Maya Lin: Architect and Artist* by Mary Malone (Springfield, NJ: Enslow Publishers, 1995), 73–81.

Photos courtesy of the Library of Congress and the Southern Poverty Law Center.

Unit 3

Unit-opening photo courtesy of Jupiter Unlimited.

Adapted excerpts from *Who Was Roberto?* by Phil Musick (New York: Bantam Doubleday Dell, 1974), 97–105; *The Story of Roberto Clemente* by Jim O'Connor (New York: Bantam Doubleday Dell Books for Young Readers, 1992), 86–90, 103–4; *A Whole New Ball Game* by Sue Macy (New York: Puffin Books/Penguin USA, Inc., 1993), 4–5, 8–10.

Photo courtesy of Jupiter Unlimited.

Unit 4

Unit-opening photo courtesy of the Library of Congress.

Adapted excerpts from *Billie Jean* by Billie Jean King with Kim Chapin (New York: Harper and Row Publishers, 1974), 177–86; *Outrageous Acts and Everyday Rebellions* by Gloria Steinem (New York: Henry Holt and Co., 1983), 139–58.

Photos courtesy of the U.S. Tennis Hall of Fame and Jupiter Unlimited.

Unit 5

Unit-opening photo courtesy of Jupiter Unlimited.

Adapted excerpts from *Colin Powell: Soldier/Statesman—Statesman/Soldier* by Howard Means (New York: Penguin Putnam, 1992), 32–37, 92–93; *Thurgood Marshall: American Revolutionary* by Juan Williams (New York: Times Books, 1998), 209–27; *Sandra Day O'Connor: How the First Woman on the Supreme Court Became Its Most Influential Justice* by Joan Biskupic (New York: HarperCollins Publishers, 2005), 174–77.

Photos courtesy of Tuskegee University Archives and the Library of Congress; illustrations from Jupiter Unlimited.

Unit 6

Unit-opening photo courtesy of Jupiter Unlimited.

Adapted excerpts from *Portrait of an Artist: A Biography of Georgia O'Keeffe* by Laurie Lisle (New York: Washington Square Press, 1986), 79–82, 352–53; *Frida: A Biography of Frida Kahlo* by Hayden Herrera (New York: Perennial, an imprint of HarperCollins Publishers, Inc., 1983), 74–75; *The Fabulous Life of Diego Rivera* by Bertram D. Wolfe (New York: Cooper Square Press, 1963/1991, 240–43.

Photos courtesy of The Georgia O'Keeffe Museum and the Library of Congress.

Every effort has been made to contact the copyright holders for permission to reprint borrowed material. We regret any oversights that may have occurred and will rectify them in future printings of this book.

Contents

To the Teacher

Teachers and students alike realize that strong vocabulary skills are necessary for academic success. Specifically, students need to know the vocabulary they will most frequently encounter in their academic studies in order to successfully complete their reading and writing assignments. The *Vocabulary Mastery* series teaches students the words they need to know to succeed in their academic work. These words come from the Academic Word List (AWL) developed by Averill Coxhead ["A New Academic Word List," *TESOL Quarterly* 34, no. 2 (2000): 213–38]. The Academic Word List resulted from Coxhead's analysis of a broad corpus of academic texts—about 3.5 million words—from 414 academic texts in 28 topic areas. Out of this corpus, Coxhead selected the 570 word families that occur most frequently in academic texts. *Vocabulary Mastery* teaches these word families.

Learning vocabulary involves more than simply recognizing a word. In order to truly know a word, students must:

- **Have multiple exposures to the word.** Nation [*Teaching and Learning Vocabulary*, Newbury House, 1990] concluded that a word needs to be encountered anywhere from five to more than 16 times before it is learned. The readings and exercises in *Vocabulary Mastery* provide students with multiple exposures to the target vocabulary. Activities that require student to do outside reading also increase their exposure to the target vocabulary.

- **Know more than the meaning, spelling, and pronunciation of a word.** Students must also learn the grammar of the word, the words it frequently occurs or collocates with, the associations a word has, the frequency with which it occurs, and its register. *Vocabulary Mastery* uses an effective interactive approach that develops both explicit and implicit word knowledge. The exercises in this book provide students with word knowledge that is explicitly taught (spelling, meaning, pronunciation, and collocation). It also provides numerous encounters with words to help students develop their own implicit, contextual knowledge (association and register) of words.

- **Be familiar with other members of a word's family.** By learning some or all of a word family, students are able to use the correct form of a word within a particular context. Every unit in *Vocabulary Mastery* contains exercises that focus on word families and derivations.

- **Understand collocations.** Knowledge of collocations makes word use more natural. Exercises teach some of the more common collocations of the target vocabulary. More important, though, these exercises raise students' awareness of collocations, which may help students notice collocations when they occur and build their own knowledge of collocation.

- **Know that one word can have different meanings used in different contexts.** Exercises show the different meanings of a target word in the appropriate contexts. Students are encouraged to use a dictionary to help them learn these different meanings.

- **Learn to focus on the words they want to learn.** The readings and exercises in *Vocabulary Mastery 2* contain 200 words from the AWL. To aid students in learning, the target vocabulary in the readings is marked in **bold.** Other AWL vocabulary items in the readings are <u>underlined</u>. Words and idioms that occur infrequently but are needed to understand the text are glossed in the margins.

The readings and vocabulary appear in an order so that skills and concepts are built upon as students progress through the book.

In addition to academic vocabulary, this text helps students develop the critical-thinking skills necessary for academic achievement. Activities in each unit require students to think about and analyze what they have read. In addition, writing assignments require students to think critically about what they have read as they learn and practice skills they will need in their academic classes. These skills include answering questions and supporting answers with concrete examples, interpreting a chart and answering questions about it, ordering information chronologically and writing paragraphs that give that information, making a schedule based on information given, analyzing and writing about a problem they select, summarizing, giving an opinion, and identifying causes and effects.

Vocabulary Mastery 2 has six units, each on a particular high-interest theme. Each of the six units is divided into

- **Vocabulary Preview 1 and 2.** These exercises help students and teachers discover how much target vocabulary is already familiar.

- **Reading Preview.** These questions are designed to activate students' prior knowledge of the topic.

- **Introduction to the Readings.** An introductory reading about the topic provides background information about the readings that follow.

- **Three short readings on a theme or topic that contain 15 target words from the Academic Word List.** At least one reading is biographical or autobiographical, and the other readings are non-fiction. The variety of readings exposes students to the target words in different writing styles and voices. In addition to the target vocabulary, all of the readings expose students to a number of other words from the AWL and recycle AWL words already learned.

- **Comprehension Check.** This series of True/False questions determines how well students understood the Introduction and Readings.

- **A list of 15 target vocabulary words from the Academic Word List.**

- **Ten vocabulary-based activities that include**

  ➤ Understanding Words
    —Word Parts: suffixes, prefixes, and roots
    —Word Relationships: synonyms, antonyms, collocations, and analogies
    —Word Families Chart: a target word and its most commonly used derivatives
    —Word Meanings: multiple meanings of a word
    —Word Forms and Derivatives

  ➤ Understanding Words in Context
    —Using Words Correctly
    —Making Inferences
    —Constructing Sentences

  ➤ Using Words in Communication
    —Reading activities that encourage research and outside reading about the topic
    —Writing activities that ask students to react, summarize, and give an opinion

  ➤ Critical-Thinking Questions
    —Questions to be used for writing assignments or class discussion

The exercises and activities in *Vocabulary Mastery 2* give students the opportunity to study academic vocabulary in two important ways. Students encounter each word as a discrete language unit and also within natural contexts as part of a whole language system.

We hope that you and your students find this textbook is a useful and enjoyable way to learn vocabulary from the Academic Word List. Good luck in your endeavors!

To The Student

Vocabulary Mastery 2 will help you learn the vocabulary words that you will need to know in order to do well in your academic studies. These words come from the Academic Word List (Coxhead 2000). This list contains 570 words that are most commonly used in academic reading. These words may be different from the words you hear and use in your everyday life, but by learning these words along with a basic 2,000-word vocabulary, you will be able to understand more than 85 percent of your academic reading assignments. Here are some suggestions for using this text. Your teacher may have others.

1. Start by finding out how much vocabulary you already know by doing the **Vocabulary Preview** exercises in each unit.

2. Go over the list of words in the **Word Study** section of the unit, and cross out the words that you already know.

3. Use your dictionary to find the meanings of words you do not know. Write these in a vocabulary notebook or make vocabulary cards. (See How to Make Vocabulary Cards on page xv for some ideas.) By the time you finish this textbook, you will have your own academic learner dictionary or set of academic vocabulary cards.

4. Read the introduction and readings in the unit. Check your dictionary for words that are not listed on your vocabulary list that you need to know to understand the reading.

5. As you read, check to see whether you understand what you are reading. Ask yourself: Did I understand what I just read? Which sentence or word is giving me a problem? Why? What or who can help me understand this? Can I ask a classmate or my teacher to help me?

6. Answer the **Comprehension Check** questions, which will show you how well you have understood the introduction and readings. The questions here are answered with True or False. If you have trouble answering these questions, you may want to reread the introduction and readings.

7. Once you feel like you understand the introduction and readings, do the activities in the **Word Study** section.

8. When you have finished all of the activities in the **Word Study** section, check your answers in the online Answer Key, if your teacher says it's okay.

9. Reread the introduction and readings to find out if they have become easier to understand.

10. Use outside materials such as books, magazine articles, videos, and films to help you learn more about the topic in each unit. Your local library and the Internet are good places to find outside material. For example, the film *A League of Their Own* might be a fun and interesting way to learn more about the All-American Girls Professional Baseball League.

Completing this textbook will help you to learn the words you need for academic success. Good luck in your studies!

How to Make Vocabulary Cards

Vocabulary cards are an easy way to study and review new vocabulary words. Make your own vocabulary cards by following these directions.

1. Use one card for each word. You can buy inexpensive index cards at most supermarkets or drugstores.

2. Write each vocabulary word on the front of a card.

3. Write the meaning or meanings of each word on the back of the card in English. You might also want to write the meaning in your native language if you are learning English.

4. Add other helpful information on the back of the card. You might want to include:
   - how the word is pronounced
   - an example sentence for the word
   - a picture that helps you remember the meaning of the word
   - other members of the word's family
   - words that collocate or often appear with that vocabulary word

5. Keep your cards in a box or put them on a ring. Practice with the cards for a few minutes every day. Look at the word on the front of the card, and see if you can remember its meaning. Check the definition on the back of the card to see if you are correct.

6. When you know a word well, move the card to the back of the box. If you don't know a word, keep it near the front where you will practice it often.

7. Review the vocabulary words frequently. This will help you remember and master these important academic vocabulary words.

Business

Vocabulary Preview

These sentences contain information from the readings. Fill in the blanks with the word that best completes each sentence.

adapt   **assembled**   **converted**   **distributed**   **research**

1. Paul Newman made the first bottles of salad dressing in an old _____ barn.

2. _____ showed that adults between the ages of 18 and 34 would buy more than half of the cars purchased in the 1960s.

3. The Ford Motor Company was able to _____ parts from the popular Ford Falcon and use them in the new Mustang.

4. Bottles of Paul Newman's salad dressing were _____ as gifts to neighbors on Christmas Eve.

5. The very first Mustang was _____ on March 9, 1964.

Preview 2

Look at the way the underlined words are used in the sentences. Match each word with its meaning or definition.

1. The Mustang was built using <u>components</u> from the Ford Falcon, rather than newly designed parts.

2. Paul and Hotchner planned to bottle and put a <u>label</u> on Paul's homemade salad dressing to give as gifts.

3. The Mustang was a basic car, but buyers could add as many <u>options</u> as they wanted or could afford.

4. Making and bottling that much salad dressing was a huge <u>project</u>.

5. Flour milling was the largest single industry in the country, and one mill had the <u>capacity</u> to produce 20,000 barrels of flour.

    _____ 1. **components**   a. possible choices

    _____ 2. **label**   b. the amount that something can hold or produce

    _____ 3. **options**   c. the parts that make up something

    _____ 4. **project**   d. a piece of paper that is glued to a bottle or box

    _____ 5. **capacity**   e. a task or job

Reading Preview: What Do You Already Know?

Circle the correct answer. If you don't know the answer, guess.

1. Lee Iacocca is

    a. the president of the General Motors car company

    b. the president of a well-known computer software business

    c. the father of the Mustang

    d. the chief executive officer of Microsoft

2. All of the following are American car manufacturers except

    a. Honda

    b. General Motors

    c. Chrysler

    d. Ford

3. Paul Newman is

    a. an actor

    b. famous for his salad dressings

    c. a race car driver

    d. all of the above

4. The company Newman's Own® is unusual because

    a. it makes only one product: salad dressing

    b. all of the company profits are donated to charities

    c. Paul Newman and A. E. Hotchner are the only employees

    d. it was the first company to make organic food products

5. The flour milling business

    a. started in Alaska

    b. created Jiffy mix

    c. did not need farmers

    d. used too much water

Introduction to the Readings

(1) America is a country driven by businesses of all kinds: big corporations, small local businesses, and entrepreneurs* with new and different ideas. Some American children even explore the business world with neighborhood lemonade stands or babysitting services. This unit introduces three very different kinds of successful business people: the automobile executive Lee Iacocca; two unlikely entrepreneurs, the actor Paul Newman and the writer A.E. Hotchner; and the creators of Jiffy Biscuit Mix.

* **entrepreneurs:** people who start businesses with an idea and make it grow.

(2) Lee Iacocca was born in Allentown, Pennsylvania, in 1924. In 1946, after graduating from Princeton University with a degree in engineering, he went to work for the Ford Corporation. At Ford, Iacocca quickly established that he was better at sales than engineering. He worked hard on development and production, and by 1960, he was a vice president in the company. In the 1960s, Iacocca became famous for his leading role in the development and marketing of the Mustang, a sports car developed by Ford that captured the heart of Americans as no other car had in many years.

(3) After being dismissed by Ford in 1978 for his unusual way of doing things, Iacocca accepted the position of chairman of the board of the Chrysler Corporation. At that time, Chrysler was facing bankruptcy. The country was living through a serious oil crisis, and no one wanted to buy any of the many big luxury cars the company had in its inventory. Iacocca asked the federal government for financial aid, and he got it. The company was guaranteed $1.5 billion in loans. The move paid off. Four years later Chrysler announced record profits of more than $2.4 billion. Since then, Iacocca has been a national celebrity. The first reading in this unit tells about another great Iacocca achievement, the development of the Mustang.

(4) Paul Newman was born on January 26, 1925, in Shaker Heights, Ohio. An interest in acting led him to the Yale School of Drama. While at Yale

he was spotted by talent agents who encouraged him to come to New York and <u>pursue</u> a professional acting career. Newman's good looks and amazing blue eyes quickly got him plenty of acting jobs. Over the course of his career, he appeared in 51 films and four Broadway plays. He won the Academy Award for Best Actor in 1987.

(5) More recently, Paul Newman was best known as the founder of Newman's Own®, a hugely successful company that produces popular food products like salad dressings and spaghetti sauce. All the profits from Newman's Own® are given to charity. As of May 2008, these donations had exceeded $220 million U.S. dollars! The second reading discusses the beginnings of Newman's Own®. In addition to acting and charity work, Newman was a passionate racecar driver since the early 1970s. He won four Sports Car Club of America National Championships and was listed in the *Guiness Book of World Records* as the oldest driver (at age 70) to win a professional race.

(6) Paul Newman's business partner, Aaron Edward Hotchner, was born in St. Louis on June 28, 1920. He is an <u>editor</u>, novelist, playwright, and biographer. Like Newman, Hotchner donates all of his profits from Newman's Own® to charity. One of these charities is the Hole in the Wall Gang Camp, which he and Newman built in Connecticut for children with cancer and other life-threatening diseases. Newman's Own® currently supports five other such camps in the United States and Europe.

(7) Today we could not imagine living without the convenience of pre-packaged, canned, or frozen food. Believe it or not, the origin of pre-packaged baking mixes dates back to 1930 and was developed by perhaps the oldest processing business, milling. Reading 3 explores the history of the milling business and the beginning of Jiffy Mix, the world's first prepared baking mix.

Reading 1: The Mustang

Excerpt adapted from *Iacocca: An Autobiography* by Lee Iacocca with William Novak
(New York: Bantam Doubleday Dell, 1984), 64–74.

(8) In the early 1960s, our public relations department began to get a lot of letters from people who wanted us to produce another Thunderbird. This was a surprise to us, because that car had not been very successful. But the mail was telling us <u>consumer</u> tastes were changing. Maybe the Thunderbird was simply ahead of its time, we said to ourselves. We were starting to get the impression that if the car were still on the market, it would be selling well.

(9) At the same time, our market **researchers** were telling us that the youthful image of the new <u>decade</u> actually existed. For one thing, the average age of the population was falling at a rapid rate. The teenagers born in the baby boom that followed World War II were becoming <u>adult</u> <u>consumers</u>. The 20- to 24-year-old group would increase by more than 50 percent in the 1960s. Moreover, young <u>adults</u> between 18 and 34 would account for at least half of the huge increase in car sales during the next ten years.

(10) There were equally interesting changes going on among older car buyers. We were now starting to see buyers move away from the <u>economy</u> cars of the late 1950s that had helped the Falcon set new records. <u>Consumers</u> were beginning to look beyond the plain and the purely <u>functional</u> to <u>consider</u> more sporty and more luxurious models.

(11) When we <u>analyzed</u> this information, we <u>concluded</u> that while the Edsel had been a car in search of a market it never found, here was a market in search of a car. Normally Detroit carmakers built a new car and then tried to identify its buyers. But we were in a position to develop a new car specifically for a hungry new market.

(12) Any car that would appeal to these young customers had to have three main **features:** great styling, strong performance, and a low price. Devel-

oping a new model with all three would not be easy. But if it could be done, we had a shot at major success.

(13) We went back to the **research** to learn more about the changing market. First, there was <u>enormous</u> growth in families, with the second car typically smaller and more sporty than the first. Second, women, who preferred small cars with easy handling, were buying a growing number of cars. Single people, too, were also among new car buyers, and they were choosing smaller and sportier models than their married friends. It was also clear that in the next few years, Americans would have more money than ever before to spend on transportation and entertainment.

(14) The more our group talked, the more <u>definite</u> our ideas became. Our car had to be sporty and beautifully styled with just a touch of nostalgia. It had to be easy to identify and unlike anything else on the market. It had to be simple to operate but still <u>capable</u> of seating four people, with enough room left for a good-sized trunk. It had to be a sports car but more than a sports car. We wanted to develop a car that you could drive to the country club on Friday night, to the shopping center on Saturday, and to church on Sunday.

(15) In sum, our intention was to appeal to several markets at once. We had to attract many different kinds of customers because the only way we could afford to make this car at a great price was to sell a ton of them. Rather than offer several different versions of the same car, we decided to develop one basic car with many **options.** That way, the customer could buy as much economy, luxury, or performance as she wanted—or could afford.

(16) But the question was: Could we afford the car? An all-new car would cost $300 to $400 million. The answer lay in using <u>available</u> **components.** That way we could save a lot of money on production costs. The car parts for the Falcon already existed, so if we could **adapt** them, we wouldn't have to start from scratch. We could build the new car with the old parts of the Falcon and save a fortune. In the end we were able to develop the new car for only $75 million.

The 1964 Ford Mustang. Photo compliments of Ford Division of Public Affairs, Detroit, MI. Reprinted with permission.

(17) On March 9, 1964, the first Mustang rolled off the **assembly** line. It was a huge <u>success.</u> During the first week it was on sale, four million people visited Ford showrooms. People liked the car much more than we had expected.

(18) It became immediately clear to me that we had to open up a second manufacturing plant. We had <u>initially</u> thought that the Mustang would sell 75,000 units during the first year. But the projections kept growing, and before the car was even out, we were planning on sales of 200,000. To build that many cars we had to talk top management into **converting** a second plant, in California, into producing more Mustangs.

(19) People were buying Mustangs in record numbers. The **options** were moving just as quickly. Our customers <u>reacted</u> to the **options** like starving people <u>react</u> to food. More than 80 percent ordered white sidewall tires, 80 percent wanted radios, 71 percent chose eight cylinder engines, and 50 percent ordered the automatic <u>transmission</u>. For a car that cost $2,368, our customers were spending an average of $1,000 each, just on **options.**

(20) I had a <u>target</u> in mind for the first year. During its first year, the Falcon had sold a record 417,174 cars, and that was the figure I wanted to beat.

We had a slogan: "417 by 4/17"—the Mustang's birthday. Late in the evening of April 16, 1965, a young Californian bought a sporty red Mustang convertible. He had just bought the 418,812th Mustang, and we finished our first year with a new record.

(21) The accountants, who had <u>predicted</u> that the **project** was headed for failure, finally admitted that there was more than one way to build a car. It was the styling that did it, which was something they hadn't counted on. But they weren't shy when it came time to count the money. In the first two years alone, the Mustang earned net profits of $1.1 billion!

Reading 2: The Beginning of Newman's Own®

Excerpt adapted from *Shameless Exploitation in Pursuit of the Common Good* by Paul Newman and A.E. Hotchner (New York: Doubleday/ Random House, 2003), 3–6.

(22) It is December 1980, a week before Christmas. We are <u>laboring</u> in the space beneath Paul's **converted** barn, an <u>area</u> that had once been a stable for farm horses. There is an array of bottles of olive oil, vinegar, mustard, spices, and so forth. There is also an empty tub and bottles of various shapes and sizes that had been somewhat sanitized* for this occasion.

> * **sanitized:** made clean
> * **batch:** an amount of something made at one time

(23) The **project** was to mix up a batch* of Paul's salad dressing in the washtub and fill all those old wine bottles using the **assembled** funnels and corks and **labels** and so on. Then, on Christmas Eve our families would go around the neighborhood singing and **distributing** these gift bottles of Paul's dressing. (Paul was very proud of his salad dressing.)

(24) That evening the basement operation seemed to go on forever. We had never tried to mix a vat of salad dressing before. Paul carefully measured amounts of olive oil and vinegar, for he had no feel yet for dealing with a quantity like this, which, he decided, <u>required</u> six boxes of black pepper. He was almost crazed as he stirred the dressing with the wooden paddle.

(25) Finally, the <u>precise</u> number of gift bottles was lined up on the dirt floor, but there was still a quantity of dressing left in the tub. That's when it occurred to Paul that we could bottle the rest, sell them to some upscale local food stores, make some money, and then go fishing. But Hotchner, a former lawyer, put on the brakes: "It's against the law! Look at this place! The bugs can't even stay alive here! If somebody dies from eating this stuff, you'll be in court with no insurance. You could wind up without your basement and everything above it. There are certain rules and <u>regulations</u> to be followed—it must be hygienic* and it must have the proper labeling."

> * **hygienic:** must meet guidelines for public health

(26) With his barn at stake, Paul agreed that they'd have to take out insurance, create a proper **label,** get a bottler, and see if it would sell. And that is how our baby, Newman's Own Salad Dressing, got started.

Reading 3: Baking Mixes in a Jiffy

Excerpt adapted from *Jiffy, A Family Tradition: Mixing Business and Old-Fashioned Values* by Cynthia Furlong Reynolds
(Chelsea, MI: Chelsea Milling Co., 2008), pp. 14, 18, 30, 32, 64–65, 88.

(27) The <u>profession</u> of grinding grains into flour, milling, is often called the oldest <u>profession</u> in the world. The claim is not far from the truth. With mills producing the food for farmers' families and their animals, the owners of the mills, millers, were often the first entrepreneurs in a community. These millers bought, sold, and traded homegrown **commodities.** Mills were usually the first commercial building in any town or village, and their production of ground meal was essential to settlers. Towns developed and flourished around them. Mills also served as informal <u>community</u> centers, bringing farmers from remote <u>locations</u> together with each other and with townspeople. Politics, prices, the weather, and local gossip were "grist for the mill" as much as the grains were.

(28) The <u>success</u> of these grain mills **relied** heavily on the local farmers. During the nineteenth century, farming was a labor-**intensive** business that

The Jiffy biscuit mix on display. Photo courtesy of Jiffy.

required all the help it could get. Farms of 120 acres or more required two or three farmhands throughout the year and every able-bodied worker who could be recruited for harvesting. *Generations* of schoolchildren worked in the nearby fields; picked, husked, and scraped ears of corn; raked hay; picked and shelled beans; and helped harvest and thresh grains. Schools would close at harvest time so that children could work in the fields, drive wagons, or help with the farm work.

(29) In 1896, in Chelsea, Michigan, a village about 60 miles from Detroit, a new mill was one of more than 700 mills in Michigan. This mill had a **capacity** of 20,000 barrels. At this time in the United States, flour milling was the nation's largest single industry. Michigan ranked tenth in the nation in flour mills, boasting an annual production of four million barrels of flour. The average price paid for a bushel of wheat was 69 cents, the average price for a barrel of flour, $3.73. Clearly, milling was a big business in a prosperous period. The old-time mill had, over a relatively short period of time, grown from a cottage industry* into big business.

(30) In 1906, owner E.K. White expanded the mill and added new equipment. Two sifting machines were installed to do the work of 32 of

* cottage industry: work that can be done at home

the old-style sifters. A steam heating machine was bought to toughen the bran of the wheat while a wheat grader would now separate the poor quality grain from the good.

(31) Business for the Chelsea Flour Mill took a new and welcome turn for the better when Mable White Holmes developed the nation's first packaged mix in 1930. The Jiffy Biscuit Mix came before its competitors by at least six months. Many believe that the muffins and other baking mixes started the entire convenience food industry.

(32) Not only was the biscuit mix a new product line, but it also solved the problem of what to do with low-grade flour. Previously, flour that was not good enough to sell on its own was used to make crackers, but now, it could be used in the biscuit mix by blending it into the self-rising biscuit flour. Problem solved.

(33) At first, it wasn't easy to **promote** the products. The public considered the idea to be too revolutionary. Women were hesitant to use the baking mixes, afraid that their reputations as bakers would suffer. Consumers did report that they liked the taste, cost, and convenience of the products and that they secretly stocked them on their pantry shelves. They also admitted, however, that they didn't want family members or neighbors to know that they were using shortcuts.

(34) Throughout the history of the company, the Chelsea Milling Company, Jiffy sales have been pretty accurate indicators of the health of the national economy—and vice versa. If the economy was slow, people looked for bargains, but if the economy was good, consumers would experiment with high-priced brands. Nevertheless, the Jiffy business survived because it offered products that made life more convenient, especially once more women joined the workforce and looked for ways to feed their families and put a meal together more quickly.

(35) Consumers today know the Jiffy name for not only biscuits, but also for cornbread muffins.

Comprehension Check

Did you understand the readings? Mark these sentences true (T) or false (F).

_____ 1. The Mustang was the most popular economy car built in the 1960s by the Ford Corporation.

_____ 2. Researchers confirmed that, in the coming decade, Americans would be able to afford more expensive cars.

_____ 3. In order to appeal to several markets at once, Iacocca decided to design several versions of the Mustang.

_____ 4. The Ford Corporation saved on making the Mustang by using car components already available.

_____ 5. The most popular option for the early Mustang was the automatic transmission.

_____ 6. Paul made a large batch of salad dressing in an old washtub.

_____ 7. A.E. Hotchner gave Paul the original recipe for the salad dressing.

_____ 8. They needed to follow government rules about hygiene and labeling if they wanted to sell the salad dressing.

_____ 9. Mills used grains from local farmers.

_____ 10. Consumers bought packaged baking mixes right away.

Word Study

Target Vocabulary

adapt	**convert**	**option**
assemble (assembly)	**distribute**	**project**
capacity	**feature**	**promote**
commodity	**intense (intensive)**	**rely**
component	**label**	**research**

Word Parts

A useful way to figure out the meaning of a word is to look at the way it is put together. Consider the parts of the following words.

	Prefix	Root	Suffix
malfunction	**mal-** meaning "bad or wrong"	**function**	
inappropriate	**in-** meaning "not"	**appropriate**	
researcher		**research**	**-er** meaning "one who"
useless		**use**	**-less** meaning "without"

Mal- (meaning "bad" or "wrong") and *in-* (meaning "not") are prefixes—that is, groups of letters that have been added to the beginning of a word to give it a new meaning. *Function, appropriate, research,* and *use* are roots—that is, they carry the basic meaning of the word. The suffixes *-er* (meaning "one who . . .") and *-less* (meaning "without") change the meaning by adding letters at the end of a word.

Exercise 1: Prefixes

The prefix *auto-* means "self, own, by oneself or by itself." Match each word on the left with its definition on the right by writing the letter of the correct definition on the line.

_____ 1. **autobiography**   a. an action done without thinking about it

_____ 2. **autograph**   b. self-governing

_____ 3. **autonomous**   c. a person's life story written by himself or herself

_____ 4. **automatic**   d. a dictator

_____ 5. **autocrat**   e. the signature of a celebrity

Exercise 2: Roots

The root *dec* means "ten." Match each word on the left with its definition on the right by writing the letter of the correct definition on the line.

_____ 1. **decade**   a. a crustacean (like a crab) with ten feet

_____ 2. **decathlon**   b. a ten-sided geometric figure

_____ 3. **decimate**   c. a period of ten years

_____ 4. **decagon**   d. an athletic contest consisting of ten events

_____ 5. **decapod**   e. one-tenth of a liter

_____ 6. **deciliter**   f. the Ten Commandments

_____ 7. **Decalogue**   g. to kill every tenth one

Exercise 3: Suffixes

When added to words as suffixes, *-ant, -er (-or),* and *-ist* often mean "one who . . .". For example, an *assistant* is someone who helps, a *teacher* is someone who teaches, and a *violinist* is someone who plays the violin. What do you call the following people?

1. someone who designs a car   a car _____

2. someone who is an expert on
   economics   an _____

3. someone who researches market
   trends   a market _____

4. someone who keeps the company
   accounts   an _____

5. someone who acts on stage or in
   films   an _____

6. someone who distributes goods   a _____

7. someone who bottles products
   like soft drinks   a _____

8. someone who writes for newspapers
   or magazines   a _____

Word Relationships

Words can be related to each other in different ways. Words can be **synonyms, antonyms,** or **compounds.** Words can also belong to the same **category.** Read these definitions.

Synonyms are words that have almost the same meaning. Synonyms for *cold* are *chilly, freezing, nippy, cool,* and *frosty.*

Antonyms are words that have opposite meanings. The words *cheap, inexpensive, reasonable,* and *economical* are antonyms for the word *expensive.*

Compounds are a combination of two or three words that have a particular meaning when they are used together as a fixed phrase. Some compounds are written as one word *(babysitter, online).* Others are written as separate words *(full time, industrial revolution).*

Words can also belong to the same **category.** For example, the words *apple, banana, orange,* and *cherry* all belong to the category *fruit.* The words *green, red, blue,* and *yellow* all belong to the category *color.*

Exercise 4: Synonyms and Antonyms

Identify each pair of words as synonyms (S) or antonyms (A).

_____ 1. assemble/disperse

_____ 2. economical/expensive

_____ 3. optional/required

_____ 4. feature/characteristic

_____ 5. component/part

_____ 6. available/accessible

_____ 7. convert/remodel

_____ 8. distribute/gather

_____ 9. project/plan

_____ 10. consumer/seller

The Grammar of Words and Word Families

Another useful strategy for learning a word is to pay attention to its grammar. What word family does it belong to? What part of speech is it? If a verb, is it regular or irregular? If a noun, is it countable or uncountable? If an adjective, is it generally followed by a preposition? Part of what is involved in learning a word is paying attention to the grammatical patterns in which the word occurs.

Derivatives or Word Families

Words can be learned as derivatives, as part of word families. Consider the word *economy*. Some common derivatives of the word are *economics, economist, economical, economically,* and *economize.* Generally, the words in the family are different parts of speech.

Noun	*economy, economics*
Noun (a person)	*economist*
Adjective	*economical*
Adverb	*economically*
Verb	*economize*

As you are learning derivatives, remember that not all words have every part of speech in their word family.

Exercise 5: Word Families

Use these words to fill in the word family chart. Follow the example given. Some words will be used more than once.

adapt	assemble	capacity	commodity
adaptability	assembled		
adaptable	assembler		
adaptation	assembly✗		
adapted			
adaptor			

component (2x)	convert	distribute	feature (2x)
	conversion	distributed	featured
	converter✗	distribution	
	convertible	distributor	

intense	label (2x)	option (2x)	project
intensely	labeler	optional	
intensify			
intensive			
intensively			

promote	rely	research (2x)	
promoter	reliable	researcher	
promotion	reliably		
	reliance		

Noun	Noun (person)	Verb	Adverb	Adjective
adaptation adaptability adaptor	—	adapt	—	adaptable adapted
assembled	assembler	assemble	—	assembly
capacity	—	—	—	—
commodity	—	—	—	—
component	—	—	—	component
conversion	—	convert	—	convertible
distribution	distributor	distribute	—	distributed
feature	—	feature	—	featured
—	—	intensify	intensely intensively	intense intensive
label	labeler	label	—	—
option	—	option	—	optional
project	—	—	—	—
promotion	promoter	promote	—	—
reliance	—	rely	reliably	reliable
research	researcher	research	—	—

Exercise 6: Word Forms

Complete each sentence with the correct form of the word.

1. Iacocca _____ some of the parts from the Falcon in order to save money on the Mustang.

     adapt   adapted   adapting   adaptable

2. The new Mustang had many popular _____. People loved its sporty styling and smaller size.

     feature   featured   featuring   features

3. You should read the _____ on packaged foods carefully if you want to avoid eating too much salt, fat, and sugar.

     label   labeled   labels   labeler

4. The _____ of homemade gifts in a small neighborhood is a social event.

     distribute   distributed   distribution   distributor

5. It was easy for Paul to _____ space in his barn to make salad dressing.

     converter   convertible   convert   conversion

6. Local farmers were successful because of the flour mills' _____ on the farmers' grain.

     reliably   rely   reliable   reliance

Understanding Words in Context

Guessing from Context

One strategy for finding out the meaning of an unknown word is to consult your dictionary. Another is to try to learn its meaning by using context clues, if they are available. There are various types of context clues.

a. *a brief definition or synonym*

Economics is *the study of the production and distribution of goods.*

To build the Mustang, he had no *option,* no *choice,* but to use available components.

b. *an example*

Luxury cars *such as the Jaguar and the BMW* are status symbols.

c. *a contrast*

There were equally interesting changes going on among older car buyers. We were now starting to see *a shift away from the economical cars* of the late 1950s that had helped the Falcon set new records. Consumers were beginning to look *beyond the plain and the purely functional* to consider *more luxurious models.*

d. *an inference*

But the question was: Could we afford the car? The answer lay in using *available components.* The *car parts for the Falcon already existed, so if we could adapt them, we wouldn't have to start from scratch.* We could build the new car with the old parts of the Falcon and save a fortune.

e. *a direct explanation*

The notion that *decimate* means to kill every tenth person may seem strange today since, at present, the word commonly means to kill a huge number of people. However, a long time ago the word was used to describe the common wartime practice of separating groups of captured soldiers at random and then killing every tenth one.

Exercise 7: Context Clues

Read the following passages. Then identify which of the context clues suggests the meaning of the underlined word or phrase: (a) a brief definition or synonym, (b) an example, (c) a contrast, (d) an inference, or (e) a direct explanation.

_____ 1. It was all the <u>options</u>—the automatic transmission, sidewall tires, and radios—that made the Mustang so popular.

_____ 2. It made no sense to build elegant, <u>luxurious</u> cars during an oil shortage.

_____ 3. Unlike the Thunderbird, which had been such a great disappointment, the Mustang was <u>flourishing</u>.

_____ 4. In car manufacturing, the <u>assembly line</u> process consists of pulling the chassis, or body of the car, through a number of stations. At each of these stations, the car gets another part. At one, it gets the engine, at another the tires, and at still another, the seats. By the end of the line, the car is generally assembled.

_____ 5. We had thought we would sell 75,000 units during the first year. But the <u>projections</u> kept growing, and before the car was even out, we were planning on sales of 200,000.

Exercise 8: Word Meanings in Context

Scan Readings 1, 2, and 3 for the words and phrases in the lists. The number of the paragraph containing the word or phrase is given in parentheses. Circle the letter of the meaning that best fits the context of the reading passage.

1. feature (12)

   a. a movie program

   b. physical beauty

   c. characteristic

2. research (13)

   a. letters from consumers

   b. data about consumers

   c. information about car sales

3. components (16)

   a. radios

   b. parts

   c. models

4. converted (22)

   a. changed

   b. abandoned

   c. emptied

5. assembled (23)

   a. put together

   b. sanitized

   c. gathered

6. relied (28)

   a. used

   b. worked

   c. depended

Using Words in Communication

Using the outline and information you learned in Reading 1, write a few paragraphs about the consumer trends in the late 1950s and early 1960s that led Ford to develop the Mustang.

Consumer Trends

    1. Changing economy

        a. The American economy is thriving.

        b. Consumers have more money to buy cars.

    2. New kind of consumers

        a. young consumers

            (1) ready to start a family

            (2) leaving the city and moving into the suburbs

            (3) needing two cars

        b. older consumers

            (1) no longer interested in economy cars

            (2) interested in sportier and more luxurious cars

        c. single women

            (1) trained during wartime for all kinds of jobs

            (2) joining the workforce

            (3) want a car that reflects their new independence

            (4) want a car with great style and performance

Exercise 10: Reading

Compare your paragraphs with those written by another student. On a separate page, note what you think needs to be corrected or changed. Share these comments with the other student.

Exercise 11: Critical Thinking

These questions will help you develop your critical-thinking skills. Critical thinking helps you evaluate information and reach good conclusions using the information that is given. Ask yourself the questions as you work on your answers: What information in the reading supports my answer? What other information do I have to support my conclusion? Where can I get more information about the topic?

1. Discuss how Paul Newman went from making his salad dressing for family and friends to the idea of selling it on a larger scale. What would he have to do differently for this new market and why? Support your answer with information from Reading 2.

2. If you were a miller, what role might your business play in the life of the community? How would you convince people to buy your new packaged baking mixes? Support your answer with information from Reading 3.

3. Businesses have to know the market. They succeed in part when they provide a product consumers want at a price they are willing to pay. Analyze why a business you know is successful in a certain market. Support your answer with ideas from the readings in this unit.

The Civil Rights Movement

Vocabulary Preview

Preview 1

These sentences contain information from the readings. Fill in the blanks with the word that best completes each sentence.

adjustments   civil   discrimination   quote   site

1. The _____ rights movement of the 1950s and 1960s helped end legal discrimination against blacks in America.

2. The Civil Rights Act of 1964 prohibits _____ based on race, color, religion, or national origin.

3. After agreeing to design the memorial, Maya Lin had to go to Montgomery and see the _____.

4. "The minute I read King's _____, I knew that the whole piece had to be about water," Lin said.

5. Workers stayed well into the night making last-minute _____ to the Civil Rights Memorial.

Preview 2

Look at the way the underlined words are used in the sentences. Match each word with its meaning or definition.

1. The Southern Poverty Law Center of Montgomery, Alabama, <u>commissioned</u> Maya Lin to design and build a memorial to the civil rights movement.

2. The <u>initial</u> controversy over the Vietnam War Memorial discouraged Maya Lin from trying to design another memorial.

3. All over the country, thousands of people had <u>demonstrated</u> in support of civil rights for African Americans.

4. Maya Lin thought a memorial <u>design</u> that used water would work well with the King's words about "justice rolling down like water."

5. It also <u>occurred</u> to Lin that water would be cooling and refreshing in the hot climate of Alabama.

_____ 1. **commissioned**   a. something that happens at the beginning

_____ 2. **initial**   b. came to mind

_____ 3. **demonstrated**   c. to ask someone to create a piece of work and pay him or her for doing it

_____ 4. **design**   d. publicly gathered or marched to support or oppose something

_____ 5. **occurred**   e. the way something is planned and made

Reading Preview: What Do You Already Know?

Circle the correct answer. If you don't know the answer, guess.

1. Maya Lin is a renowned

   a. Chinese American

   b. Japanese American

   c. Native American

   d. Mexican American

2. At age 21, Maya Lin won a national competition for designing

   a. a presidential library

   b. a war memorial

   c. a sculpture for a train station

   d. a door for a museum

3. In the United States today, "the Wall" refers to

   a. a Washington, DC war memorial

   b. a famous Civil War battlefield

   c. racial discrimination

   d. a wall-sized painting of a war scene

4. Which of the following occurred as a result of the civil rights movement?

   a. Segregation of public schools became illegal.

   b. It became easier for African Americans to vote.

   c. Discrimination against minorities in hiring, finance, and housing was prohibited.

   d. all of the above

Introduction to the Readings

(1) During the 1960s, America was a divided country. Many people, especially young men who were being drafted to fight in Vietnam, were unhappy about U.S. <u>participation</u> in the Vietnam War. The Vietnam War <u>created</u> a divide between young people and older <u>generations</u>. In addition, African Americans were still kept apart, or segregated,* from whites. In many parts of the country, black people were <u>required</u> to sit at the back of the bus and weren't served by businesses that accepted only white customers.

*segregated: separated according to race

(2) The readings in this unit explore some of the major events of the American **civil** rights movement of the 1950s and 1960s and discuss the memorial that was created to honor those who had worked to gain equal rights for African Americans. The readings introduce the creator of the Civil Rights Memorial, a young Chinese-American woman named Maya Lin.

(3) In 1981, 21-year-old Lin had become nationally known for having won a competition to **design** a war memorial. The memorial, **commissioned** by a group of war veterans, honored members of the military who had died in the Vietnam War. Like the Vietnam War itself, Maya Lin's **design** turned out to be very <u>controversial</u>. It caused much argument and disagreement among members of the military, the government, and the general public. Instead of **designing** a sculpture or memorial building, Maya had **designed** a V-shaped wall made of polished black stone on which the names of the dead and missing were to be etched in gold. Many people were offended by "the Wall." There were newspaper attacks, hearings, and even personal attacks against Maya, in particular, insulting <u>comments</u> about her Chinese-American background. Today, however, "the Wall," as the Vietnam Veterans War Memorial has come to be known, is regarded as a treasured work of art. People from all over the country come to see it, to run their fingers over the names of loved ones, to leave notes, flowers, poems, and . . . to remember.

(4) The second and third readings in this unit tell about the **design,** development, and <u>construction</u> of a second memorial <u>undertaken</u> by Lin: the **Civil Rights Memorial,** in Montgomery, Alabama.

Reading 1: Civil Rights Timeline—1954 to 1968

May 17, 1954

(5) The U.S. Supreme Court rules on the landmark case *Brown v. Board of Education of Topeka, Kansas*, and unanimously* agrees that segregation in public schools is unconstitutional, saying, "separate educational facilities are inherently unequal." It is a triumph for NAACP (National Association for the Advancement of Colored People) attorney Thurgood Marshall, who will later become the country's first African-American Supreme Court justice.

*unanimously: agreed to by everyone

August 28–31, 1955 (Mississippi)

(6) A 14-year-old African-American boy, Emmett Till, is kidnapped, beaten, and shot, and his body is dumped in a river because he supposedly whistled at a white woman. Two white men, J. W. Milam and Roy Bryant, are arrested for the murder and acquitted* by an all-white jury.

*acquitted: cleared of having committed a crime

December 1, 1955 (Montgomery, Alabama)

(7) Rosa Parks is arrested for refusing to give up her seat at the front of the "colored section" of a bus to a white passenger. Reverend Martin Luther King, Jr., leads the black <u>community</u> of Montgomery in a bus boycott.* The boycott ends after the buses are desegregated on Dec. 21, 1956.

*boycott: refusal for political reasons to buy or use a product or business

Rosa Parks in 1955 in Montgomery, Alabama.

January–February 1957

(8) Martin Luther King, Jr., and other leaders <u>establish</u> the Southern Christian Leadership <u>Conference</u> (SCLC) and begin to organize the **civil** rights movement. King insists that the **civil** rights movement be based on non-violence and **civil** disobedience, rather than on violence and hatred.

September 1957 (Little Rock, Arkansas)

(9) The governor of Arkansas, Orval Faubus, orders that nine African-American students be prevented from entering a <u>previously</u> all-white high school. President Eisenhower sends National Guard troops to protect the students and lead them into the school.

February 1, 1960 (Greensboro, North Carolina)

*sit-in: a form of protest where people sit in one place and refuse to leave until they are moved or the problem is solved

*protests: marches or other events that show disagreement

(10) Four African-American students begin a sit-in* at a segregated Woolworth's lunch counter. Although they are refused service, they are allowed to stay at the counter. The event results in many similar non-violent protests* throughout the southern part of the United States. These protests <u>eventually</u> lead to the <u>integration</u> of parks, swimming pools, theaters, libraries, and other public places.

May 4, 1961

(11) CORE (Congress of Racial Equality) and SNCC (Student Nonviolent Coordinating Committee) sponsor "Freedom Riders." These <u>volunteers</u> begin taking bus trips throughout the southern states to test new laws that <u>prohibit</u> segregation in bus and railway stations. Several of these groups are attacked by angry groups of people.

October 1, 1962

(12) James Meredith becomes the first African-American student to attend the University of Mississippi. President Kennedy sends 5,000 <u>federal</u> troops to help stop the violence that results.

April 16, 1963 (Birmingham, Alabama)

(13) Martin Luther King, Jr., is arrested and jailed during anti-segregation protests.

May 1963 (Birmingham, Alabama)

(14) During **civil** rights protests, the Commissioner of Public Safety, Eugene "Bull" Connor, uses fire hoses and police dogs on the African Americans who were **demonstrating.** These <u>images</u> are shown on television and <u>published</u> widely. People around the world begin to support the **civil** rights movement.

June 12, 1963 (Jackson, Mississippi)

(15) Medgar Evars, Mississippi's NAACP secretary, is murdered outside his home. Byron de la Beckwith is tried twice in 1964, and both trials result in hung juries. Thirty years later, Beckwith is convicted of murdering Evers.

August 28, 1963 (Washington, DC)

(16) About 200,000 people march in support of **civil** rights in Washington, DC. <u>Participants</u> gather at the Lincoln Memorial and listen as Martin Luther King, Jr., delivers his famous "I Have a Dream" speech.

September 15, 1963 (Birmingham, Alabama)

(17) Four young African-American girls attending Sunday school are killed when a bomb explodes at the Sixteenth Street Baptist Church, a popular <u>location</u> for **civil** rights meetings. Riots[*] in Birmingham lead to the deaths of two more black youths.

> ***riots**: violent behavior by a large group

January 23, 1964

(18) The 24th amendment abolishes the poll tax, which had been <u>established</u> in 11 southern states after the **Civil** War in order to make it difficult for poor African Americans to vote.

Summer 1964

(19) A network of **civil** rights groups launches an all-out effort to <u>register</u> African-American voters during what becomes known as the "freedom

*delegates: representatives

summer." It also sends delegates* to the Democratic National Convention to protest against the official all-white Mississippi group.

July 2, 1964

(20) President Johnson signs the **Civil** Rights Act of 1964. This act prohibits **discrimination** of any kind based on race, color, religion, or national origin. The law also gives the federal government the powers to **enforce** desegregation.

August 4, 1964 (Neshoba County, Mississippi)

(21) The bodies of three **civil**-rights workers—two white and one African American—are found. The three young men had been working to register African-American voters in Mississippi, and, on June 21, had gone to investigate the burning of an African-American church. The men were arrested by the police on speeding charges, jailed for several hours, and then released after dark into the hands of the Ku Klux Klan,* who murdered them.

*Klu Klux Klan: a secret society whose members think "white" people are superior

February 21, 1965 (Harlem, New York)

(22) Malcolm X, a Black Nationalist and founder of the Organization of Afro-American Unity, is shot to death.

March 7, 1965 (Selma, Alabama)

(23) African Americans begin a march to Montgomery, Alabama, in support of voting rights but are stopped by police. About 50 marchers are hospitalized after police use tear gas,* whips, and clubs against them. The incident is called "Bloody Sunday" and helps energize the effort to pass the Voting Rights Act five months later.

*tear gas: used to break up crowds

August 10, 1965

(24) Congress passes the Voting Rights Act of 1965, making it easier for southern African Americans to register to vote. Literacy tests, poll taxes, and other requirements that were used to restrict black voting become illegal.

August 11–17, 1965 (Watts, California)

(25) Race riots occur in an African-American neighborhood in Los Angeles.

September 24, 1965

(26) President Johnson issues executive order 11246, which **enforces** affirmative, or positive, action. This <u>requires</u> people working for the government to "take affirmative action" in all <u>aspects</u> of hiring and employment toward non-white people looking for work.

June 12, 1967

(27) In *Loving v. Virginia*, the U.S. Supreme Court rules that <u>prohibiting</u> interracial marriage is unconstitutional. Sixteen states are forced to <u>revise</u> their <u>constitutions</u> and laws.

July 1967

(28) Major race riots take place in Newark, New Jersey, and Detroit, Michigan.

April 4, 1968 (Memphis, Tennessee)

(29) Martin Luther King, Jr., aged 39, is shot as he stands on the balcony outside his hotel room. Escaped prisoner and known racist James Earl Ray is convicted of the crime.

April 11, 1968

(30) President Johnson signs the **Civil** Rights Act of 1968, which <u>prohibits</u> **discrimination** in housing sales, rental, and <u>financing</u>.

Reading 2: The Civil Rights Memorial— Design, Development, and Construction

Excerpt adapted from *Maya Lin: Architect and Artist* by Mary Malone (Springfield, NJ: Enslow Publishers, 1995), 73–81.

(31) After completing the Vietnam Veterans War Memorial, Maya Lin had said that she would never **design** another memorial. The **initial** <u>controversy</u> over her **design** had discouraged her. So she had gone back to her private life, doing her own kind of work and accepting some private **commissions,** which she discovered she liked. "I'm interested in the **psychology** of the customer," she said at the time.

(32) In the spring of 1988, Maya Lin was at work in her studio when she received a call from a representative of the Southern Poverty Law Center, or SPLC, of Montgomery, Alabama. The organization had been <u>founded</u> in 1971 to protect and advance the <u>legal</u> rights of poor people and <u>minorities</u>.* On the phone, the representative told her that the SPLC had decided to erect a **civil** rights memorial and wanted Maya Lin to <u>undertake</u> the <u>project</u>.

*minorities: groups that are of a different race, ethnic background, or religion from those that are in the majority

(33) Lin did not immediately accept the **commission.** She said that she would read the material the SPLC wished to send her and would <u>consider</u> the matter. She took some time to do this, and then she accepted the **commission.** The historical <u>significance</u> of the **civil** rights movement had impressed her. She was surprised that there was no such memorial already in existence. She was also concerned that she herself knew so little about the movement because she had not studied it in school. Of course, she had been a young child during the 1960s when the important marches and the <u>legal</u> decisions had taken place. She was only eight when Martin Luther King, Jr., was assassinated.* Lin said that although there were **specific** monuments to certain people connected with the **civil** rights movement, "No memorial existed that caught what the whole era was about. It had been very much a people's movement, yet many people, who had given their lives for it, had been largely forgotten."

*assassinated: to murder in a planned way, usually of someone famous

(34) After agreeing to **design** the memorial, Lin had to see the **site.** On the plane to Montgomery, she reread some of the words of Dr. King. She came across—again—what he had said in several of his speeches. "We will not be satisfied until <u>justice</u> rolls down like waters, and righteousness* like a mighty stream." "Suddenly," Lin said, "something clicked and the form took shape. The minute I hit that **quote** I knew that the whole piece had to be about water." The longer she <u>considered</u> it, the more certain she was. "I wanted to work with water, and I wanted to use the words of Dr. King because that is the clearest way to remember history."

*righteousness: moral goodness

(35) She kept thinking about the form of the memorial as she continued her journey. It **occurred** to her that in the warm climate of Alabama, the cooling effect of flowing water would be <u>appropriate</u>. When she met the members of the SPLC, she quickly drew what she had in mind. Later, at the **site** where the memorial would stand, Lin saw the possibilities—and the need for rearranging some existing <u>features</u> there. It was agreed that she would start on the **design** as soon as she returned to New York.

(36) The SPLC's plan in 1988 was to memorialize those individuals who had been killed in the marches and **demonstrations** for **civil** rights. On the memorial, their names and the names of important events in the **civil** rights struggle would be carved. The <u>research</u> of records was done by Sara Bulard, one of the directors of the SPLC and editor of the center's book about the **civil** rights movement, *Free at Last*. Fifty-three <u>significant</u> entries would be written on the memorial. When Lin saw that list, she said she realized that creating a time line was the only way to <u>highlight</u> those names and events. They would be listed in chronological order from the first—"May 1954, the Supreme Court ruling outlawing school segregation"—to the last, "4 April, 1968, Martin Luther King, Jr., assassinated." There would be room at both ends for additions if related names and events were discovered.

(37) Back in her studio, Lin started work on the <u>project</u>. The memorial she had decided to **design** would be in two parts and was scheduled to be dedicated in the fall of 1989. There would be a huge granite disk, or table, twelve feet in diameter, inscribed* with the 53 names and events. The table, with the names arranged chronologically in a circle around the edge, would look something like a sundial. Behind the large disk there would be a black granite wall, nine feet high that would be inscribed* with the **text** that had inspired Lin's **design.**

*inscribed: written or carved in words

(38) In the completed, <u>functioning</u> memorial, water flows down the wall in a gentle waterfall over those words. The table below the wall was **designed**

to be less than three feet from the ground so that children could reach it. The table, which is narrower at the bottom, from a distance appears to be floating on air. Water rising from the center of the table spreads over it, covering the time line of names and events, which is still clearly seen through the veil of water. Visitors touch the names as they walk around the table.

(39) In the fall of 1988, not long after Lin had completed the **civil** rights memorial **design,** a fire broke out in the building where she lived and worked. Fortunately, she had mailed her model to the SPLC in Montgomery. Also fortunately, most of her other works were in a gallery, so her loss was <u>minimal</u>. But, as she explained to a **journalist** from the *Washington Post* who interviewed her shortly after the fire, even what she lost was not critical. She, like many other artists, often destroyed a finished sculpture or other work if for some reason she was not satisfied with it. She would start over. The important thing was that no one had been hurt in the fire.

Reading 3: The Civil Rights Memorial— The Dedication

Excerpt adapted from *Maya Lin: Architect and Artist* by Mary Malone
(Springfield, NJ: Enslow Publishers, 1995), 73–81.

(40) The **Civil** Rights Memorial was dedicated on time, although it had been complicated and difficult to <u>construct</u>. Ken Upchurch, who supervised the construction, said when he first studied the **specifications** of the **design,** that it was a "contractor's* nightmare." The day before the memorial was to be revealed, everyone wondered if the water was going to work as well as it was supposed to. Last-minute **adjustments** took the workers well into the night. Then, when the memorial was finally, hopefully, ready, people held their breath as the water was turned on. A cheer went up when the water began its slow movement down the wall and across the table.

*contractor: someone under contract, usually for some type of building or repair

Civil Rights Memorial outside the Southern Poverty Law Center. Photo by Penny Weaver.
Reprinted with permission.

(41) Besides being visited by families, friends, and relatives of those whose names are there, the memorial attracts people from all over the world. Tourists stop in Montgomery to see it. As Maya Lin had hoped, the memorial has become an educational experience. Schoolchildren come and learn. Maya Lin, who wanted it to be simple, said of the Civil Rights Memorial, "A child can understand it. You don't need to read an art book to understand it." One little girl said, "It makes you want to touch the names with your fingers and talk about what happened." Like the Vietnam Wall, where visitors weep as they touch the names of the dead and the missing, this memorial, too, evokes tears from the many people who visit it.

(42) Maya Lin was impressed, as she said, with the powerful effect that "words joined with water would generate." She was "surprised and moved when people started to cry."

(43) Lin received unqualified praise for her part in this memorial. Unlike the Vietnam Veterans War Memorial, this one was happily free from <u>controversy</u>. One writer <u>commented</u>, "She has once again created an architectural masterpiece." Lin herself said, "I've been incredibly fortunate to have been given the opportunity to work on not just one but both memorials."

(44) Morris Dees, <u>founder</u> of the SPLC, said about the memorial Lin had created for the center, "You can't put it anywhere else than in Montgomery, where everything happened, and you can't get anyone better than Maya Lin to do it."

⟳ Comprehension Check

Did you understand the readings? Mark these sentences true (T) or false (F).

_____ 1. The United States had a time of peace and prosperity in the 1960s.

_____ 2. At age 21, Maya Lin won a competition for designing the Vietnam Veterans War Memorial.

_____ 3. Lin's design for the Vietnam Veterans War Memorial met with unqualified praise.

_____ 4. The Vietnam Veterans War Memorial is a wall made of polished black stone.

_____ 5. The SPLC was founded in 1971 to protect and advance the rights of veterans of the Vietnam War.

_____ 6. In 1954, the U.S. Supreme Court ruled that segregated public schools are unconstitutional, or illegal.

_____ 7. Dr. Martin Luther King, Jr., based the civil rights movement around the principles of non-violence and civil disobedience.

_____ 8. In 1988, Maya Lin was commissioned to design a civil rights memorial.

_____ 9. Lin accepted the commission immediately because she had always been impressed by what she had learned in school about the movement.

_____ 10. Lin's design of the civil rights memorial was based on a quote from a speech delivered by Dr. Martin Luther King, Jr.

_____ 11. Lin didn't expect people to cry when they saw the civil rights memorial.

Word Study

Target Words

adjust (adjustments)	journal (journalist)
civil	occur
commission	psychology
demonstrate (demonstration)	quote
design	site
discriminate (discrimination)	specific (specification)
enforce	text
initial	

Word Parts

Exercise 1: Roots

Words are made up of different parts. The **root** or **stem** is the part of the word that carries the main idea or basic meaning. The root *psych-* or *psycho-*, meaning "breath, life, or soul," is the root or stem for words such as *psychology, psychiatrist, psychic, psychedelic,* and *psychoanalysis.* Study these sentences. Circle the letter of the phrase that best completes the statement or answers the question.

1. My aunt loves to go to a fortune-teller to have her palm read. She believes that fortune-tellers are *psychic.* A person who is *psychic*

   a. is very wealthy

   b. sees or understands things outside the physical world

   c. is mentally ill

2. *Psycho-* means "breath, life, or soul," and *–ology* means "the study of (something)." What does the word *psychology* mean?

   a. the study of human organizations

   b. the study of religion

   c. the study of the mind and behavior

3. A *psychiatrist* is a doctor who specializes in

   a. treating mental illness

   b. treating pregnant women

   c. treating cancer

4. The *psychedelic* art of the 1960s and 1970s was sometimes associated with the use of illegal drugs. Psychedelic art

   a. is a traditional form of art

   b. often has distorted or bizarre images and bright colors

   c. is exhibited in natural outdoor settings

5. *Psychoanalysis* is used to help people with mental and emotional problems. Psychoanalysis involves

   a. examining the client's physical body

   b. examining the client's home and workplace

   c. examining the client's thoughts, emotions, and behaviors

Word Relationships

Exercise 2: Synonyms

Four of the words in each series have similar meanings. Cross out the word that has a different meaning.

1. adjust	adapt	fit	specify	accommodate
2. demonstrate	show	occupy	protest	prove
3. enforce	make	compel	urge	prohibit
4. initial	largest	first	beginning	primary
5. site	location	building	scene	area
6. specific	exact	distinct	general	precise

Analogies

Analogies are comparisons between two sets of words. Analogies consist of four words, three of which are always given. The analogy is completed by adding a fourth word to complete the connection.

Example:

A waiter is to a restaurant as a teller is to a bank.

waiter : restaurant :: teller : _____

A doctor is to the body as a dentist is to teeth.

doctor : body :: dentist : _____

The Bible is to Christians as the Koran is to Muslims.

Bible : Christians :: Koran : _____

Exercise 3: Analogies

Use one of the target vocabulary words from Units 1 and 2 to complete each analogy. Change the word form by adding a word ending if necessary.

1. movie : film :: book : _____

2. study of groups : sociology :: study of the mind : _____

3. function : functional :: option : _____

4. collect : gather :: disperse : _____

5. economy : economist :: research: _____

6. end : last :: beginning : _____

7. stay : remain :: change : _____

8. general : vague :: particular: _____

The Grammar of Words and Word Families

Exercise 4: Word Families

Use these words to fill in the word family chart. Follow the example given. Some words will be used more than once.

adjust	civil	commission (2x)	demonstrate
adjustable	civilian		demonstrable
adjusted	civilly		demonstrably
adjuster			demonstration
adjustment			demonstrator

design (2x)	discriminate	enforce	initial
designer	discriminating	enforceable	initially
	discrimination	enforcer	
		enforcement	

journal	occur	psychology	quote (2x)
journalism	occurrence	psychological	quotable
journalist		psychologically	quotation
		psychologist	

site (2x)	specific	text	
	specifically	textual	
	specification	textually	
	specify		

Noun	Noun (person)	Verb	Adverb	Adjective
adjustment	adjuster	adjust	——	adjustable adjusted
——		——		civil
	——	commission	——	——
		demonstrate		
		design	——	——
	——	discriminate	——	
		enforce	——	
——	——	——		initial
journal		——	——	——
	——	occur	——	——
psychology		——		
quote	——		——	
site	——		——	——
	——			specific
text	——	——		

Phrasal Verbs

Phrasal verbs consist of a verb and a preposition (for example, *account for*) or a verb and an adverb (for example, *paid off).* Keep in mind that a phrasal verb often has a different meaning than its parts. *Paid* means "gave someone money" and *off* means "away." *Paid off*, as in *the move paid off*, however, means "worked out well" or "was a good idea."

Exercise 5: Phrasal Verbs

Look at how each verb is used in the reading (the number in parentheses indicates the paragraph where the verb appears). Match the verb on the left with its meaning on the right by writing the letter of the correct definition on the line.

_____ 1. **keep apart** (1)   a. found on

_____ 2. **turn out** (3)   b. begin suddenly

_____ 3. **give up** (7)   c. separate

_____ 4. **base on** (8)   d. result in, prove to be

_____ 5. **break out** (39)   e. do again from the beginning

_____ 6. **start over** (39)   f. start the flow of

_____ 7. **turn on** (40)   g. abandon, leave

Exercise 6: Word Forms

Complete each sentence with the correct form of the word.

1. As interest rates rise, many consumers are no longer able to pay off their _____ rate loans.

   adjustable   adjust   adjusted   adjustment

2. The salesperson began _____ the features of the tiny cell phone.

   demonstration   demonstrator   demonstrating   demonstrate

3. Law _____ is a top priority in our community. We have a strong police force.

   enforce   enforcing   enforceable   enforcement

4. Many travel writers keep a _____ of their experiences.

   journalism   journalist   journal   journals

5. To work properly, the fountain had to be made to strict _____.

   specific   specified   specify   specifications

6. Maya Lin often uses quotes or some other type of _____ in her designs.

   texting   text   textual   textually

Understanding Words in Context

Collocations

Collocations are words that often go together. Consider, for example, common collocations with *consumer,* one of the targeted vocabulary words in Unit 1: *consumer credit, consumer goods,* and *consumer spending.*

Exercise 7: Collocations

Match the adjectives with the nouns they often appear with. Write the combinations on the lines provided. Can you think of any other words that collocate with them? Add them.

Example: *legal aid, legal age, legal holiday*

Nouns

tests	evaluation	age	issues
income	aid	holiday	rights
wage	problems	speed	union

Adjectives

1. legal

_____

_____

2. psychological

_____

_____

3. civil

_____

_____

4. adjusted

_____

_____

Exercise 8: Collocations

This paragraph from Reading 2 is about the civil rights movement. Underline the five collocations that refer to the civil rights movement. Some collocations may be repeated.

Lin did not immediately accept the commission. She said that she would read the material the SPLC wished to send her and would consider the matter. She took some time to do this, and then she accepted the commission. The historical significance of the civil rights movement had impressed her. She was surprised that there was no such memorial already in existence. She was also concerned that she herself knew so little about the movement because she had not studied it in school. Of course, she was a very young child during the 1960s when the important marches and the legal decisions had taken place. She was only eight when Martin Luther King, Jr., was assassinated. Lin said that although there were specific monuments to certain people connected with the civil rights movement, "No memorial existed that caught what the whole era was about. It had been very much a people's movement—yet many people, who had given their lives for it, had been largely forgotten."

Using Words in Communication

Exercise 9: Reading

Read about one of the works created by Maya Lin. Use the suggestions to help you find material on this subject. You can research information in the library or on the Internet. Be sure to only use credible sites for your research.

Suggestions:

1. Vietnam War Memorial—Washington, DC
2. Civil Rights Memorial—Montgomery, Alabama
3. Juniata Peace Chapel—Huntingdon, Pennsylvania
4. Women's Table—Yale University, New Haven, Connecticut
5. Eclipsed Time—Penn Station, New York City, New York

Exercise 10: Writing

Write one or two paragraphs about the work by Maya Lin that you read about in Exercise 9. Use the questions as a guide when writing your paragraphs. Be sure to answer all the questions.

1. What is it?

2. What is its purpose?

3. Where is it located?

4. What does it look like?

5. Who commissioned it?

6. What else do you know about it?

Exercise 11: Critical Thinking

These questions will help you develop your critical-thinking skills. Critical thinking helps you understand and evaluate information and reach good conclusions using the information that is given. Ask yourself the questions as you work on your answers: What information in the reading supports my answer? What other information do I have to support my conclusion? Where can I get more information about the topic?

1. The timeline at the beginning of the unit lists many important events and people connected to the civil rights movement. In your opinion, which event or person was the most important to the movement? Explain why you think so.

2. Compare the design of "the Wall" with the design of the Civil Rights Memorial in Montgomery, Alabama. How are they alike and different in their forms and in the way visitors react to them? Use information from the Introduction to the Readings and Reading 2 in your answer.

3. If you were asked to design a new memorial to the civil rights movement, what would it look like? Why would you choose this design? Explain in detail.

Baseball

3

 # Vocabulary Preview

These sentences contain information from the readings. Fill in the blanks with the word that best completes each sentence.

approached   drafted   experts   minor   selected

1. The players were _____ on the basis of their batting, running, catching, and pitching skills.

2. By the beginning of 1943, only nine out of 26 _____ league teams had enough players left to form a team.

3. During World War II, many major league players were men who were either too old or too young to be _____ into military service.

4. One by one, all the Latin players on the team _____ Clemente and hugged him.

5. Most baseball _____ think that Clemente played the game better than any other player at that time.

Preview 2

Look at the way the underlined words are used in the sentences. Match each word with its meaning or definition.

1. Roberto was hurt by some of the unkind <u>comments</u> people made about him.

2. New rules and changes <u>indicated</u> that the All-American Girls Professional Baseball League was going to play a game more like men's baseball than women's softball.

3. The All-American Girls Professional Baseball League played an exhausting <u>schedule</u>: one game every day and two on Sundays.

4. The World <u>Series</u> is a post-season, best-of-seven games between champions of the National League and the American League.

5. Roberto was confused by the way Americans <u>supplemented</u> their speech with hand gestures and movements.

_____ 1. **comments**　　　a. sequence

_____ 2. **indicated**　　　b. added to

_____ 3. **schedule**　　　c. showed

_____ 4. **series**　　　d. a list of events and the times they will occur

_____ 5. **supplemented**　　　e. something said that expresses an opinion

🌀 Reading Preview: What Do You Already Know?

Circle the correct answer. If you don't know the answer, guess.

1. Roberto Clemente was born in

  a. Cuba

  b. Puerto Rico

  c. the Dominican Republic

  d. Mexico

2. Clemente was a famous

  a. baseball player

  b. basketball player

  c. tennis player

  d. golfer

3. For most of his professional career, Clemente played for

  a. the Pittsburgh Pirates

  b. the New York Yankees

  c. the Baltimore Orioles

  d. the Philadelphia Phillies

4. The All-American Girls Professional Baseball League

  a. had team uniforms that were red, white, and blue

  b. used volunteer players

  c. was formed during World War II

  d. competed against men's minor league teams

5. Phillip K. Wrigley

  a. was worried about what the war was doing to baseball in America

  b. owned the Chicago Cubs

  c. started the All-American Girls Professional Baseball League

  d. all of the above

Introduction to the Readings

(1) Many people <u>consider</u> baseball to be a <u>uniquely</u> American sport. Fans and players all over the world love it, but it has its roots in America. Currently, professional baseball <u>focuses</u> on men who hit the ball hard and pitchers imported from foreign countries.

(2) The first two readings are about the great Puerto Rican baseball player, Roberto Clemente: his early difficult years in the <u>major</u> leagues, and later, when he was already recognized as a true champion. Clemente was the winner of four batting titles. In right field he performed in a way unlike anything seen in the game before. He ran to catch balls behind second base, grabbed home run balls just before they cleared the walls of the baseball park, and threw out runners at all bases. He had one of the most powerful throwing arms in the game. He was the master player, the Great One of Pittsburgh.

(3) But there was another side to Roberto Clemente. He never forgot where he came from, and he worked hard to help others. He had great pride in himself, in his homeland, and in his race. Nowhere was Roberto Clemente's humanity more <u>evident</u> than in the manner of his death. In 1972, after hitting his 3,000[th] hit, a rare feat, Clemente returned to Puerto Rico for the Christmas holidays. While he was there, he heard about a deadly earthquake that had struck the Central American country of Nicaragua. The earthquake had destroyed the capital city and had killed more than 7,000 people. Clemente went into action. With the same dedication and <u>energy</u> he applied to baseball, Clemente dedicated himself to the task of raising money and gathering food and clothing for the people of Nicaragua.

(4) On New Year's Eve, Clemente boarded a plane filled with food, clothing, and <u>medicine</u> for the people of Nicaragua. Unfortunately, soon after taking off, the plane developed engine trouble and fell into the Atlantic Ocean. Although a long search was <u>conducted</u>, no <u>survivors</u> were ever found. Baseball had lost one of its heroes. To honor him, the Baseball Writers Association of

America voted him into baseball's Hall of Fame. He was the first Hispanic to be honored in this way.

(5) The third reading is about the All-American Girls <u>Professional</u> Baseball League, which was <u>established</u> during World War II to keep baseball alive in the United States, while American men were fighting the war. These young women were exceptional athletes who traveled around the country playing <u>professional</u> baseball. The 1992 movie *A League of Their Own* was inspired by the Rockford (Illinois) Peaches <u>team</u> and the All-American Girls <u>Professional</u> Baseball League.

Reading 1: A Rookie's* Frustration

*rookie: an athlete who is in his or her first year in a league

Excerpt adapted from *Who Was Roberto?* by Phil Musick (New York: Bantam Doubleday Dell, 1974), 97–105, and from *The Story of Roberto Clemente* by Jim O'Connor (New York: Bantam Doubleday Dell Books for Young Readers, 1992), 86–90, 103–4.

(6) In the 1950s Roberto Clemente arrived in Pittsburgh to play baseball for the Pittsburgh Pirates. He was very young, just <u>emerging</u> from a boy to an **adult.** Many things surprised Clemente about Pittsburgh. Above all, he was confused by people with a different language and a strange way of speaking. They spoke English instead of Spanish, and they **supplemented** their way of speaking with a lot of hand gestures and jerks of the head.

(7) Pittsburgh was <u>different</u> from Puerto Rico. Where could a homesick 20-year-old buy fried bananas? Or listen to the music of the *coqui,* a tiny frog that sings more sweetly than any songbird? Or hear a comforting *Como esta usted?* Why did strangers laugh when you tried to speak their language? And why didn't the sun ever shine?

(8) "I couldn't speak English," Clemente said. "Not to speak the language . . . this is a terrible problem. Not to speak the language meant you were <u>different</u>." To not be white meant you were <u>different</u>. Not to know that bananas were sliced on cereal instead of fried meant you were <u>different</u>. Being <u>different</u> was not easy. "Some people act as though they think I lived in a jungle," Clemente said.

(9) Clemente <u>found</u> very few friends in the Pirate clubhouse. He could be seen by himself signing autographs for fans, hours after home games. "I was lonely . . . I had nothing else to do," he said. He was also unhappy about the cool weather, and, for the first time, he was faced with an unexpected enemy: prejudice.*

*prejudice: unfair bias against someone or something based on opinion not facts
*withdrawn: quiet, not communicative

(10) "I know Roberto was hurt deeply by some of the unkind **comments** he heard during his first years here," said one of his <u>teammates</u>. "He was withdrawn* partly because of the language. He'd only been away from Puerto Rico one other time. Everything was new and confusing to him."

(11) Nothing confused Clemente more than newspaper reporters. They often <u>quoted</u> his ungrammatical speech: "I no play so gut yet . . . . Me like hot weather . . . . I no run fast cold weather." Why would reporters want to make fun of his English when he was trying so hard to learn it? Roberto wondered.

Reading 2: A True Superstar

Excerpt adapted from *The Story of Roberto Clemente* by Jim O'Connor (New York: Bantam Doubleday Dell Books for Young Readers, 1992), 86–90, 103–4.

(12) On July 24, 1970, more than 43,000 fans packed into Three Rivers Stadium, the new home of the Pittsburgh Pirates. They came to celebrate a very special event: Roberto Clemente Night.

(13) In June, the Pirates had played their last game at Forbes Field. Walking off the field for the last time had been difficult for Roberto. He had played in Forbes Field for 15 seasons. It had been like a second home to him. Now there was a new stadium, a new home for the <u>team</u>, and Roberto was being honored for his remarkable **contribution** to the Pirates, who were winning a lot of games.

(14) The crowd cheered when Roberto walked onto the field at Three Rivers Stadium that July evening. As he looked around, Roberto saw many familiar faces. He also saw hundreds of Puerto Ricans wearing *pavas*, the straw hats that the workers wore in the sugar cane fields. Many of them had come

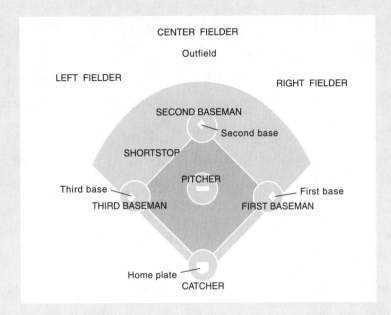

CENTER FIELDER

Outfield

LEFT FIELDER

RIGHT FIELDER

SECOND BASEMAN

Second base

SHORTSTOP

PITCHER

Third base

First base

THIRD BASEMAN

FIRST BASEMAN

Home plate

CATCHER

from Puerto Rico to Pittsburgh just to attend the game. Everyone was there for the same reason—to honor Clemente.

(15) To begin Roberto Clemente Night, all the Latin players in the Pirates <u>team</u> lined up in front of Roberto. One by one they **approached** him, placed a hand on his shoulder, and gave him the *abrazo*, a ceremonial embrace. Roberto was very touched by this gesture. Then all the awards and gifts were presented to Roberto. Among other things, he was given a paper signed by more than 300,000 people in Puerto Rico. Roberto was also told that thousands of dollars had been collected and given in his name to his favorite charity, the Pittsburgh Children's Hospital.

(16) After the ceremony, Roberto ran out to right field. During his years with the Pirates, he had played in a World **Series** and nine All-Star Games. He had been awarded the Most Valuable Player title, four batting titles (given to the player with the highest batting average), and ten Gold Gloves.*

*Gold Gloves: an award given in baseball to players who are outstanding at catching and fielding the baseballs and make the fewest mistakes (errors)

(17) After the game Roberto told the reporters what had been going through his mind during the ceremony: "In a moment like this, you can see a lot of years in a few minutes . . . I don't know if I cried, but I am not ashamed to cry. We are a sentimental people. I don't have the words to

say how I feel when I step out onto that field and know that so many are behind me and know that I represent my island and all of Latin America."

(18) Today, visitors to the Baseball Hall of Fame (in Cooperstown, New York) can see the bronze plaque* that lists many of the **statistics** that qualified Clemente for the Hall of Fame. But there is a lot about Clemente that is not on the plaque. The plaque does not say that Roberto Clemente played right field with a combination of grace and power that many baseball **experts** agree have never been equaled. It does not say Roberto still inspires young ballplayers everywhere. The plaque does not say that Roberto lost his life helping people he hardly knew. It does not say that Roberto showed the people of his country, his friends, and his fans how to be proud to be Puerto Rican. The plaque gives the reasons why Roberto Clemente is in the Hall of Fame. But it does not give many of the other reasons why Clemente still lives in the hearts of many baseball fans, especially in the hearts of Puerto Ricans.

*plaque: metal or stone plate with writing on it in memory of a person or event

Reading 3: The All-American Girls Professional Baseball League

Excerpt adapted from *A Whole New Ball Game* by Sue Macy (New York: Puffin Books/Penguin USA, Inc., 1993), 4–5, 8–10.

*Phillip K. Wrigley: president of the W. Wrigley Jr. Company and owner of the Chicago Cubs baseball team.

(19) In the fall of 1942, Phillip K. Wrigley* was worried about the effect that the war was having on baseball. The major leagues had lost more than half their players to the military, replacing them with men who were too old to be **drafted** and boys who were too young. The **minor** leagues were even harder hit. By the start of the 1943 season, more than 3,000 **minor** league players had joined the service or taken jobs in the war **sector.** Only nine of the nation's 26 minor leagues had enough men left to play ball. Wrigley **assigned** a group from the Chicago Cubs to explore the *possibility* of developing a professional baseball league with women players.

(20) While Wrigley worked out the business details of the league, his baseball scouts searched the United States and Canada for top women ball players.

Women baseball players in the 1930s.

Although the four planned <u>teams</u> had room for only 64 players, hundreds of women showed up for the <u>initial</u> tryouts. In May 1943, 280 of them were invited to Wrigley Field in Chicago for the final **selection** <u>process</u>.

(21) In Chicago, league officials made the players take a **series** of tests. Players had to play their position, run, slide, and hit. Those who were **selected** were in for a <u>challenging</u> summer. <u>Teams</u> in the league would play every day and twice on Sundays. These longtime softball players had to play by new rules: Softball <u>teams</u> usually had ten players, but Wrigley's <u>teams</u> used nine; base runners were allowed to lead off and steal bases.* These were some of many changes that made the game faster and more like baseball. As an **indication** of changes still to come, Wrigley renamed the league the All-American Girls <u>Professional</u> Baseball League.

> ***lead off and steal bases**: before a base-ball player takes another base (or steals it) while another batter is at the plate, he moves farther from first base

(22) Despite the new rules and the challenging **schedule,** women jumped at the chance to join the league. It was a chance to get paid for something most of them would have done for free. The women were paid relatively well because playing ball was their only job during the summer months. Wrigley wanted his players to <u>focus</u> all of their <u>energies</u> on the league. Wrigley looked for women who were skilled, strong, and attractive. He wanted women who could play like men, but he never wanted the fans to forget that they were women.

⊙ Comprehension Check

Did you understand the readings? Mark these sentences true (T) or false (F).

_____ 1. The Pirates are a baseball club based in Pittsburgh, Pennsylvania.

_____ 2. When Clemente first started to play for the Pirates, he was very homesick for his homeland, Nicaragua.

_____ 3. Clemente played right field for the Pirates.

_____ 4. Clemente is the first Hispanic to be inducted into baseball's Hall of Fame.

_____ 5. Roberto Clemente Night was held in Forbes Field, the baseball park where Clemente had played ball for 15 years.

_____ 6. Clemente tried to help the victims of an earthquake in Nicaragua by collecting food, clothing, and medicine for them.

_____ 7. Clemente died when terrorists bombed the airplane he was flying to Nicaragua.

_____ 8. The All-American Girls Professional Baseball League initially recruited players from America and Canada.

_____ 9. The League started with only six teams.

_____ 10. Women in the League had to be great ball players, but it didn't matter what they looked like.

✺ Word Study

Target Vocabulary

adult	draft	sector
approach	expert	select (selection)
assign	indicate (indication)	series
comment	minor	statistic
contribute (contribution)	schedule	supplement

Word Parts

Exercise 1: Roots

The root -leg-, which comes from the Latin *legalis* meaning "law," is the stem for these words:

legal   illegal   legislate   legislature   legislator   illegitimate

Complete each sentence with the correct words.

1. The _____ is the group of people in a country with the power to make and pass laws.

2. An _____ act is one that is not allowed by the laws of the country.

3. The person who makes and passes laws is called a _____.

4. _____ business activities are not permitted by law.

5. The office of _____ aid will help people who do not have the money to pay for a lawyer.

6. To _____ is to pass a new law.

Exercise 2: Prefixes

A. The prefixes *in-* and *un-* mean "not." The prefix *mis-* means "incorrect" or "bad." To which of the following words can you add *in-*? Which words can take *un-*? Which ones can take *mis-*? Write the newly formed words in the correct lists. Add word endings if necessary.

appropriate	discriminate	quote
available	emotion	schedule
civil	label	voluntary

in-	*mis-*	*un-*
_____	_____	_____
_____	_____	_____
_____	_____	_____
_____	_____	_____

B. Use the newly formed words in Part A to complete these sentences. Add word endings if necessary.

1. Dr. Sanders is going on vacation, so he will be _____ for the rest of the week.

2. The topic was _____ to the occasion. How can you be talking about funerals at a wedding?

3. You _____ Laertes. He didn't say, "Get thee to a nunnery." Hamlet did.

4. Everyone was surprised that Miriam cried so much at her father's remarriage. She's generally so _____!

5. The wind was so cold that I started to shiver _____.

6. This jar is _____. It's not molasses; it's maple syrup.

Word Relationships

Exercise 3: Synonyms

Four of the words in each series have similar meanings. Cross out the word that has a different meaning.

1. adult	mature	young	grown-up	ripe
2. hero	champion	victor	loser	conqueror
3. contribute	take	assist	donate	give
4. fall	drop	move	sink	tumble
5. sector	area	region	section	site
6. statistics	data	multiplication	charts	graphs

The Grammar of Words and Word Families

Exercise 4: Word Families

Use these words to fill in the word family chart. Follow the example given. Some words will be used more than once.

adult (2x)	approach (2x)	assign	comment (2x)
adulthood	approachable	assignment	commentary
	approaching		commentator

contribute	draft (2x)	expect	indicate
contribution		expectant	indication
contributor		expectation	indicative
contributory		expecting	indicator

minor (2x)	schedule (2x)	sector	select (2x)
minority			selection

series	statistic	supplement (2x)	
	statistical	supplementary	
	statistically		
	statistician		

Noun	Noun (person)	Verb	Adverb	Adjective
adulthood	adult	—	—	adult
approach	—	approach	—	approaching approachable
	—	assign	—	—
comment	commentator	comment	—	—
contribution	contributor	contribute	—	contributory
draft	—	draft	—	—
expectation	—	expect	—	expecting expectant
indication	—	indicate	—	indicative indicator
minority	minor	—	—	minor
schedule	—	schedual	—	—
sector	—	—	—	—
selection	—	select	—	select
series	—	—	—	—
statistic	statistician	—	statisticaly	statistical
supplament	—	supplement	—	supplamentary

Transitive and Intransitive Verbs

Transitive verbs are verbs that take a direct object. *Withdraw* means "to pull something back," "to move," or "to remove." It is a transitive verb, so it takes an object. For example:

> The cat *withdrew* its *claws*.

> I plan to *withdraw* my *name* from the list of candidates.

> He *withdrew money* from the bank.

> After we argued, I *withdrew* my *friendship*.

Withdraw means "to retreat," "to retire," or "to go away from a place." It is intransitive, so it does not take an object. When used intransitively, *withdraw* is often followed by a preposition, usually either *to* or *from*. For example:

> Mrs. Holmes *withdrew from* the room.

> Laura *withdrew to* the study.

> Mr. Allen *withdrew from* the race.

Exercise 5: Transitive and Intransitive Verbs

Write *C* when *withdraw* is used in the sentence correctly and *NC* when it is used incorrectly.

_____ 1. David was thinking of withdrawing his support from the party.

_____ 2. John withdrew his office to take the phone call in private.

_____ 3. I want to withdraw the discussion because I don't have all the facts.

_____ 4. Yesterday, I withdrew some money from the bank machine.

_____ 5. She withdrew his sailboat from the race.

_____ 6. After dinner, Jennifer withdrew the bed because she was very tired.

Understanding Words in Context

Exercise 6: Word Meanings in Context

Reread the passages from the readings. Then complete the sentences or answer the questions by circling the letter of the correct choice.

1. In the 1950s Roberto Clemente arrived in Pittsburgh to play baseball for the Pittsburgh Pirates. He was very young, just emerging from a boy to an adult.

   Emerging in this case means

   a. coming out of

   b. becoming visible

   c. disappearing

2. Many things surprised Clemente about Pittsburgh. Above all, he was confused by people with a different language and a strange way of speaking. They spoke English instead of Spanish, and they supplemented their way of speaking with a lot of hand gestures and jerks of the head.

   Supplemented their way of speaking means the people of Pittsburgh

   a. used their hands and heads a lot when they spoke

   b. were very stiff and rigid

   c. became very emotional

3. After the ceremony, Roberto ran out to right field. During his years with the Pirates, he had played in a World Series and nine All-Star Games. He had been awarded the Most Valuable Player title, four batting titles, and ten Gold Gloves.

   This paragraph is about

   a. Clemente's feelings about baseball

   b. Clemente's reaction to being honored by the Pirates

   c. Clemente's accomplishments

4. Today, visitors to the Baseball Hall of Fame (in Cooperstown, New York) can see the bronze plaque that lists many of the statistics that qualified Clemente for the Hall of Fame. But there is a lot about Clemente that is not on the plaque. The plaque does not say that Roberto Clemente played right field with a combination of grace and power that many baseball experts agree have never been equaled. It does not say Roberto still inspires young ballplayers everywhere. The plaque does not say that Roberto lost his life helping people he hardly knew. It does not say that Roberto showed the people of his country, his friends, and his fans how to be proud to be Puerto Rican. The plaque gives the reasons why Roberto Clemente is in the Hall of Fame. But it does not give many of the other reasons why Clemente still lives in the hearts of many baseball fans, especially in the hearts of Puerto Ricans.

Choose a title for this paragraph.

a. What the Plaque Does Not Tell Us about Clemente

b. The Statistics that Entitled Clemente to Be in the Hall of Fame

c. How Clemente Died

Exercise 7: Guessing from Context

1. Can you find the meanings of the following Spanish words in the readings? Write the meanings.

    a. *coqui* _____

    b. *abrazo* _____

    c. *pava* _____

2. How were you able to figure out the meanings of these words?

    _____

3. What is one good clue, then, for determining the meaning of a word in a particular context?

    Context clue: _____

Exercise 8: Collocations

Some common collocations for the vocabulary words in this unit are listed.

final selection   supplementary materials

expert opinion   World Series

minor league   vital statistics

Answer the questions by circling the letter of the correct choice.

1. What did players have to do in order to make the *final selection* into the All-American Girls Professional Baseball League?

   a. They had to play their position, run, slide, and hit, and do it all well.

   b. They had to be beautiful.

   c. They had to be single and live at home.

2. What was many people's *expert opinion* about Roberto Clemente?

   a. He did not speak English well.

   b. He played with more grace and power than any other player.

   c. He had a lot of Puerto Rican fans.

3. There are major leagues and *minor leagues* in many professional sports. What is the difference between a minor league and a major league?

   a. minor league players are not professionals

   b. minor league teams are more competitive

   c. minor league teams are not ranked as highly as major league teams

4. If a person buys *supplementary materials* for a textbook, what might he or she buy?

   a. a glossary

   b. a table of contents

   c. cassettes, CDs, or DVDs

5. What is the *World Series*?

   a. a competition between baseball teams from all over the world

   b. the annual championship of U.S. and Canadian major league baseball

   c. a competition between the top major league team and the top minor league team

6. Which of the following can someone get at the Bureau of *Vital Statistics*?

   a. a birth certificate

   b. a driver's license

   c. a voter registration card

Using Words in Communication

Exercise 9: Reading a Table

Study the statistics of Clemente's performance in two World Series.

Year	Club	AB	H	2B	3B	HR	RBI	BA
1960	Pittsburgh Pirates	29	9	0	0	0	3	.310
1971	Pittsburgh Pirates	29	12	2	1	2	4	.414

AB = times at bat   H = single base hits   2B = two base hits
3B = three base hits   HR = home runs   RBI = runs batted in
BA = batting average: the number of hits divided by the number of times at bat

Answer the questions by reading the table. Answer in complete sentences.

1. When did Clemente play in the World Series?

   _____

2. What ball club did he play for?

   _____

3. How many times was he at bat (AB) in 1960? In 1971?

   _____

4. Compare the number of home runs (HR) he hit in 1960 with the number in 1971.

   _____

5. Compare his batting average (BA) in 1960 with the one in 1971.

   _____

Exercise 10: Writing

Work with two or three other students to make a list of the emotions Clemente probably experienced when

      a. he first played baseball for the Pirates.

      b. he heard about the earthquake in Nicaragua.

      c. he was honored at Three Rivers Stadium during Roberto Clemente Night.

Write a short paragraph describing Clemente's emotions during one of these occasions.

_____

_____

_____

_____

_____

_____

_____

_____

_____

_____

Exercise 11: Critical Thinking

These questions will help you develop your critical-thinking skills. Critical thinking helps you evaluate information and reach good conclusions from the information that is given. Ask yourself the questions as you work on your answers: What information in the reading supports my answer? What other information do I have to support my conclusion? Where can I get more information about the topic?

A. Reread Reading 3: The All-American Girls Professional Baseball League, and answer these questions.

1. What are some of the reasons Mr. Wrigley started the All-American Girls Professional Baseball League? Support your answer with information from the text.

   _____

   _____

   _____

   _____

2. How was the baseball that the All-American Girls Professional Baseball League played different from a typical women's softball game? Support your answer with information from the reading.

   _____

   _____

   _____

   _____

B. Evaluate one of the changes to the game of baseball that you read about in this unit—including non-white players or creating a women's professional league. How did the change affect the game? How do you think it changed the way fans enjoyed the game? Does the change still influence the game of baseball today? If so, how?

The Women's Movement

🌀 **Vocabulary Preview**

Preview 1

These sentences contain information from the readings. Fill in the blanks with the word that best completes each sentence.

alternative   concentrate   injury   mental   transformation

1. No one wondered about my mother's _____. To relatives, this new Ruth was simply a sad event.

2. She could rarely _____ long enough to read a book.

3. Billie Jean's _____ strategy was to play a base-line game.

4. The explanation of _____ illness made it seem like Ruth's depression was her fault.

5. At the rules meeting before the match, the players decided to have a special ten-minute _____ time-out.

Preview 2

Look at the way the underlined words are used in the sentences. Match each word with its meaning or definition.

1. The way that she made him run around the tennis court and kept him from getting control made him feel less <u>secure</u>.

2. She worked at a newspaper as the Sunday <u>editor</u>.

3. The family <u>assumed</u> that mental illness was just part of her personality.

4. She worked with my father at an <u>isolated</u> vacation spot out in the country.

5. The match was difficult both <u>mentally</u> and physically.

_____ 1. **secure**   a. believed that something is true, sometimes wrongly

_____ 2. **editor**   b. in or with the mind

_____ 3. **assumed**   c. someone who examines and corrects a piece of writing

_____ 4. **isolated**   d. safe

_____ 5. **mentally**   e. kept apart or separate

🌀 Reading Preview: What Do You Already Know?

Circle the correct answer. If you don't know the answer, guess.

1. Billie Jean King is

   a. a famous Olympic gymnast

   b. a popular television sports reporter

   c. the daughter of Martin Luther King, Jr.

   d. one of the greatest female tennis players ever

2. Which of these sports tournaments did Billie Jean King NOT win?

   a. Wimbledon

   b. the American Open

   c. the World Series

   d. the Australian Open

3. The tennis match between Billie Jean King and Bobby Riggs became a symbol of

   a. the women's movement

   b. the civil rights movement

   c. the gay pride movement

   d. the anti-war movement

4. Gloria Steinem

   a. attended Harvard University

   b. started *Ms. Magazine* in 1972

   c. was president of Smith College

   d. developed new drugs to treat mental illness

5. Gloria Steinem is best known

    a. for her work on women's issues and human rights

    b. for her work with the mentally ill

    c. for her work on the environment

    d. for her work in education

6. In America in the 1940s and 1950s,

    a. mental illness was generally ignored

    b. there were no treatments for mental illness

    c. mentally ill people were often put into hospitals or given drugs

    d. mental illness was very common

7. Women in America in the 1940s and 1950s

    a. were expected to marry and have children

    b. were expected to have careers of their own

    c. usually kept working after they married and had children

    d. got divorced if they were not happy in their marriages

Introduction to the Readings

(1) This unit introduces two famous women who were widely known for their roles in the feminist, or women's rights, movement of the 1960s and 1970s. The first two readings are by Billie Jean King, who was born in Long Beach, California, in 1943. As a young girl, Billie Jean was a natural athlete who showed exceptional talent in softball. Her parents, however, encouraged her to play tennis, and she quickly became a gifted player. At the age of 18, Billie Jean beat the world's best woman tennis player, Margaret Court Smith, at Wimbledon.* During her career King went on to win Wimbledon, the French Open, the Australian Open, and the U.S. Open (the biggest tennis tournaments in the world) many times, in both singles and doubles competition.

*Wimbledon: a tournament played in England on a grass surface

(2) In addition to her excellence as an athlete, Billie Jean King is known for her dedicated work to improve the treatment, and pay, of women in sports, for being the first woman athlete to earn $100,000 in a single year, and for <u>establishing</u> the first successful women's <u>professional</u> tennis tour. Billie Jean's most <u>publicized</u> victory may have been when she defeated Bobby Riggs in the "Battle of the Sexes" <u>exhibition</u> match in 1973. Riggs had been the top tennis player in the world, and he came out of retirement to play the match. This "man versus woman" tennis match quickly became a <u>symbol</u> of the women's movement and helped to popularize the women's movement among ordinary American women. In the first two readings here, King tells about preparing for and playing that famous match.

(3) The last reading is by Gloria Steinem. Steinem is one of the most influential woman writers, **editors,** and political activists of our time. Born in 1934, Gloria Steinem began writing shortly after graduating from Smith College in 1956. The following year she traveled to India and worked with followers of Mahatma Gandhi. The trip to India influenced Steinem greatly and was the beginning of her work as a non-violent political activist. Steinem is

probably best known as an **editor** of the feminist *Ms. Magazine*, an international magazine <u>devoted</u> to women's issues, which she <u>founded</u> in 1972. Steinem also works worldwide for other causes related to inequality and women's rights. In the excerpt, Steinem writes about her **mentally** ill mother, Ruth, and their life together.

Reading 1: Preparing for the Match

Excerpt adapted from *Billie Jean* by Billie Jean King with Kim Chapin
(New York: Harper and Row Publishers, 1974), 177–86.

(4) I'd begun preparing seriously for my match against Bobby Riggs the day after I lost the match to Chris Evert.* I got into the routine that I always try to use when I'm playing tennis at night. I forced myself to stay up late and sleep until ten or eleven in the morning. I did this so that during the match, which would take place in the evening, my body would be at its high point. I did a lot of weightlifting for my legs and knees, and it really helped. My legs were so strong the night of the match that I couldn't believe it. I took good care of myself and got a lot of rest. And I prepared **mentally** for the match.

*Chris Evert: at the time, the best women's tennis player

(5) Pete Collins, the <u>resident professional</u> tennis <u>instructor</u> at Hilton Head (South Carolina), played twice a day with me for about an hour each time. We mainly just rallied* a lot, and I tried to **concentrate** on each shot, each swing of the racket, to get a good rhythm going. Sometimes we just hit to see how long

*rallied: hit back and forth without errors

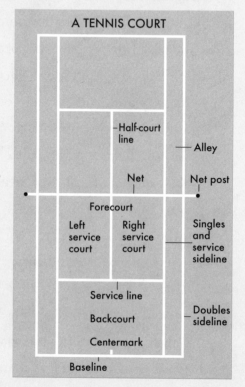

A TENNIS COURT

Half-court line
Alley
Net
Net post
Forecourt
Left service court
Right service court
Singles and service sideline
Service line
Doubles sideline
Backcourt
Centermark
Baseline

we could keep the ball in play, and I got very patient inside. When I get that way, I can play from the base-line all day if I have to.

(6) That was going to be my **alternative strategy**—the base-line game. I wanted to be able to mix it up—go in some, stay back a little. What I wanted to do at the start was to win some points because I thought that would break Bobby down faster <u>psychologically</u>. I also practiced a lot of volleying. I felt sure that Bobby didn't realize how quick I was or how good a volley I had. He knew, of course, I had a good volley—for a girl. But I thought my volley was strong compared to anyone, man or woman, and I was counting on him under<u>estimating</u> me in that respect.

(7) I practiced <u>shifting</u> my serve, going from a hard, flat serve to a slice serve to a topspin serve to a twist. This is not easy to do because it takes real <u>accuracy</u> and **precision.** During the match I planned to keep changing my serve around and serve the ball into his body a lot. I felt that was going to be important: to serve into him and then go wide—to make him go exceptionally wide—to always keep him off balance, because he's the type of player who <u>relies</u> on his own balance to keep the rally under control.

(8) Finally, I worked on keeping my shots to his backhand side—his weak side—and then hitting very sharply to his forehand. Again, the idea was to confuse him, run him around the court, keep him from getting control, make him feel less **secure.**

Reading 2: The Match

Excerpt adapted from *Billie Jean* by Billie Jean King with Kim Chapin
(New York: Harper and Row Publishers, 1974), 177–86.

(9) The show began. Bobby was wheeled out onto the court in a ridiculous rickshaw,* and I was carried out onto the court in one of those throne-like litters.* Then Bobby presented me with a huge

*rickshaw: small cart pulled or carried by a person
*litter: a frame of cloth for carrying someone

lollipop—about the size of a tennis racket—and I also gave him a gift: a little "male chauvinist"* piglet brought in for the occasion.

*male chauvinist: a term first used in the 1970s for a man who did not think women were equal to men

*heavyweight title: refers to the champion in boxing

(10) When we walked out on to the court to warm up, I couldn't believe the crowd. It was really like a circus, or a baseball game, or maybe even a heavyweight title* fight. Balloons, bands, noise—everything. People were shouting, "Right on, Billie Jean," or "Go, Bobby," from the moment we entered and well into the match. I loved it. Just the way a tennis crowd ought to be everywhere.

(11) But once the match started, everything was very serious—nothing except tennis. At the rules meeting the day before, when we'd decided on things like the special ten-minute **injury** time out, I'd **emphasized** that I didn't want there to be any doubts at all about the match. It had to be on the level, and it was.

(12) Just before the match began I told myself, "Okay, this is it. Take each point by itself and don't rush things." I served first and won the first game. I couldn't believe how slow Bobby was. I thought he was faking it. He had to be. At the change after the first game I asked my coach if Bobby was putting me on. Dennis assured me I was seeing the real thing, but I think Riggs did coast the first three or four games, trying to figure me out and at the same time not give away all of his wonderful secrets.

Billie Jean King in action in the 1970s.

(13) I was kind of shocked because I thought he would be a lot better than he was. He didn't have a big serve, and the spins on his shots weren't that great either. And I was absolutely right about him not realizing how quick I was at the net or how well I could volley. I **concentrated** hard on winning that first set, and when I did, I knew he was in big trouble. That meant he would have to play at least four tough sets to win the match, probably more competitive tennis than he'd played in years. I felt I was in pretty good shape and that things were going my way.

(14) About halfway through the second set, I knew that the match was mine if I could just keep up the pace. But I didn't let up because I'd gotten into trouble too many times before thinking I had a match won before it was over. Everything that I thought would work before the match did work. I played conservatively those last two sets, and at the end I was playing with complete confidence.

(15) At the end of the match, I threw my racket in the air, and just when I looked down, I saw him finish his jump over the net. He came over to congratulate me, and then he was really nice. He said, "You're too good," and that was it. Ten weeks of getting psyched up for one night of tennis and then, boom, it was all over.

(16) The match was tough, **mentally** and physically. I've played better matches, but under the **circumstances** I played as well as I possibly could, and so, I think, did Bobby. As far as the importance of the match, it proved just two things. First, that a woman can beat a man. Second, that tennis can be a big-time sport.

Reading 3: "Ruth's Song (Because She Could Not Sing It)"

Excerpt adapted from *Outrageous Acts and Everyday Rebellions* by Gloria Steinem (New York: Henry Holt and Co., 1983), 139–58.

(17) Happy, or unhappy, families are all mysterious. The question is: Why are some mysteries more important than others?

(18) For many years I couldn't <u>imagine</u> my mother, Ruth, any way other than the way she was when I was born. She was someone to be worried about and cared for; someone who lay in bed with her eyes closed and lips moving in **response** to voices only she could hear. She was a woman to whom I brought endless amounts of toast and coffee, sandwiches and pie, in a child's version of what meals should be. She was a loving, **intelligent**, and terrorized woman who tried hard to clean our house whenever she <u>emerged</u> from her private world but who rarely finished a <u>task</u>. In many ways our roles were <u>reversed</u>: I was the mother and she was the child.

(19) I suppose I must have known that years before I was born, my mother had been different. She had been an <u>energetic</u>, adventurous young woman who struggled out of a working class family and into college and who had a career. She loved her job and continued it even after she was married and had my older sister to care for. The family must have watched this <u>energetic</u> woman, who loved books and fun, turn into someone who was afraid to be alone.

(20) Yet I don't remember my family wondering about the mystery of my mother's **transformation**. Outside events were never suggested as reason enough for her problems. Giving up her own career was never seen as a cause for her <u>depression</u>. Even the explanation of **mental** illness made it seem like it was all my mother's fault. She had suffered her first "nervous breakdown" before I was born, when my sister was about five. This breakdown followed years of trying to take care of a baby, be the wife of a kind, but <u>financially</u>

irresponsible man, and still keep her job as a reporter and newspaper **editor.** After many months in a **mental** hospital, she was pronounced "cured." That is, she was able to take care of my sister again and to move away from the city. She left the job she loved and worked with my father at an **isolated** vacation spot out in the country in Michigan.

(21) But she was never again completely without the times of <u>depression</u>, anxiety, and <u>visions</u> into some other world that <u>eventually</u> turned her into the "non-person" I remember. And she was never again without a bottle of tranquilizers* that the doctor gave her. To me it always seemed an embarrassing but necessary evil. It made her speech difficult to under-stand, and she became <u>physically</u> awkward. But without the <u>medicine</u> she would not sleep for days, even a week at a time. Then her tired eyes would begin to see only a private world where wars and angry voices threatened the people she loved. It is no wonder that no relative ever <u>challenged</u> the doctor who gave my mother this <u>medicine</u>. No one asked if some of my mother's suf-fering and the <u>visions</u> she saw might be due to the drugs. No one even <u>consulted</u> another doctor about its use. The <u>medicine</u> helped us as much as it helped her.

*tranquilizers: pills that calm or relax

(22) But why was she never taken back to that first hospital? Or taken to other doctors for help? Partly, it was her own fear of returning to that pain. Partly, it was too little money and the family's **assumption** that **mental** illness was just a part of her personality. Looking back on it, perhaps the biggest rea-son my mother was cared for but not helped for twenty years was the simplest: My mother's <u>functioning</u> was not that necessary to the world. She was like the women alcoholics who drink in their kitchens while male executives who drink get expensive care. She was like the homemakers who are calmed with drugs while male patients get help and personal attention instead. My mother was not an important worker.

(23) My father kept our household going until I was eight or so and my sister went away to college. Then I replaced my father. I did not blame him for

leaving us once I was old enough to bring meals and answer my mother's questions. That's why our lives, my mother's from 46 to 53 and my own from 10 to 17, were spent alone together. Most of those years we lived in a house in Toledo, Ohio. We lived off the small amount of money that my mother got from renting out her share of the land in Michigan.

A photo taken at the
1848 Woman's Rights Convention in Seneca Falls, NY.

(24) Later, when I was finishing high school, my father took my mother with him to California for a year. Suddenly I was far away from her, in Washington, living with my sister. Then I could stop to think about the sadness of my mother's life. I realized that as a child my sister had known a very <u>different</u> person who lived inside our mother, an earlier Ruth.

(25) This Ruth was a person I met for the first time when my mother was in a **mental** hospital near Baltimore, after my sister had had the courage to get her the help she needed. At first, this Ruth was the same frightened woman I had lived with all those years. But gradually she began to talk about her past life and to share her memories. I began to meet a Ruth I had never known.

. . . a tall, <u>energetic</u>, red-haired high school girl who loved basketball and reading. A girl who tried to drive her uncle's car when it was the first car in the neighborhood.

. . . a good student at Oberlin College, whose <u>traditions</u> she loved. A student who was good at mathematics and poetry. A daughter who had to return to Toledo, live with her family, and go to a local university when her mother—who had lived cheaply and saved, worked, and made her daughters' clothes in order to have money to send them to college—ran out of money.

. . . a daughter who became a part-time bookkeeper in a shop, going to classes, and listening to her mother's <u>lectures</u>. She was also a young woman who was rebellious enough to fall in love with my father, a funny and charming young man who was unacceptably Jewish.

(26) I know from family stories that my mother had married my father twice. They married once, secretly, and once a year later in a <u>public</u> ceremony, which some members of both families had refused to attend because it was a "mixed marriage." And I also know that my mother had gone on to earn a teaching certificate and had taught college mathematics for a year. After graduating from the university, she wrote a newspaper column. Soon after that she got a job as a reporter for one of Toledo's big daily papers—<u>eventually</u> she earned the respected job of Sunday **editor.**

(27) It was a strange experience to look into those brown eyes I had seen so often and realize suddenly how much they were like my own. For the first time I realized that she really was my mother. I began to think about the <u>stresses</u> that might have led up to her first nervous breakdown: leaving my sister at home with our grandmother; trying to keep a job she loved but that my father asked her to leave; wanting to go to New York to <u>pursue</u> her own dream of writing but punishing herself for even thinking about it. She was <u>convinced</u> that divorce was impossible. A husband could not be left for a career. A daughter could not be deprived of her father.

(28) At the hospital, and later, when my mother told me stories of her past, I used to say, "But why didn't you leave? Why didn't you take the job in New York?" She would say that it didn't matter, she was lucky to have my

sister and me. Sometimes she would add, "If I'd left, you never would have been born." I always thought but never had the courage to say: *But you might have been born instead.*

(29) I'd like to tell you that this story has a happy ending. The best I can do is an ending that is happier than its beginning. After many months in that Baltimore hospital, my mother lived on her own in a small apartment near my sister. When she felt the old terrors coming back, she returned to the hospital at her own request. She was <u>approaching</u> 60 by the time she <u>emerged</u> from the hospital, and in fact, she never returned to it again. She had some independent life and many friends. She worked part-time in a shop. She went away with me on vacation every year and took one trip to Europe with relatives. She went to women's club meetings. She found a multi-racial church that she loved and attended most Sundays. She took meditation classes and enjoyed many books. Once out of the hospital for good she continued to show flashes of a different woman inside. This other woman had a dry kind of humor, a sense of adventure, and a love of learning. She died just before her 82nd birthday.

(30) The world missed a <u>unique</u> person named Ruth. Though she dreamed of living in New York and traveling in Europe, she became a woman who was afraid to take the bus across town. Though she drove the first car in her neighborhood, she married a man who wouldn't let her drive at all. I can only guess what she might have become. There were clues in her moments of spirit and humor.

(31) I miss her. But perhaps I miss her no more since her death than I did during her life. Dying seems less sad than having lived too little. But at least we're now asking questions about all the Ruths in all our family mysteries. If her song inspires that, I think she would be the first to say: It was worth the singing.

◎ Comprehension Check

Did you understand the readings? Mark these sentences true (T) or false (F).

_____ 1. Billie Jean always got up late and went to bed late, even when she wasn't preparing for a match.

_____ 2. Billie Jean wanted to break Bobby psychologically by winning volleys at the beginning of the match.

_____ 3. Bobby had a strong backhand, but his forehand was weak.

_____ 4. Billie Jean ate a lot of candy before the match because she was nervous.

_____ 5. Billie Jean was surprised that Bobby played so slowly. She thought he was pretending.

_____ 6. The match was important because it proved that men and women were equal.

_____ 7. When Gloria Steinem was a child she took care of her mother, Ruth.

_____ 8. Ruth was from a wealthy, upper-class family.

_____ 9. Relatives thought that Ruth's mental illness was her own fault and that she could get better if she tried to.

_____ 10. Ruth needed to take tranquilizers to sleep, but the medicine had some bad side-effects.

_____ 11. Ruth had been a normal, active young woman until she had a nervous breakdown.

_____ 12. Gloria thought that her mother's mental illness was a result of the social and family stresses that many women experience.

Word Study

Target Vocabulary

alternative	**emphasis (emphasize)**	**precise (precision)**
assume (assumption)	**injure (injury)**	**respond (response)**
circumstance	**intelligence (intelligent)**	**secure**
concentrate	**isolate**	**strategy**
edit (editor)	**mental (mentally)**	**transform (transformation)**

Word Parts

The prefix *trans-* comes from the Latin *trans* and means "across," "beyond," "through," or "so as to change." It is used to form many English words. Each of the following words is a combination of *trans-* and other word parts of Latin origin.

Word	Prefix	Root
transfer	**trans-** +	**ferre** "to carry"
translate	**trans-** +	**latus** "to change from"
transport	**trans-** +	**portare** "to carry"
transform	**trans-** +	**formare** "to form"
transmit	**trans-** +	**mitiere** "to send"

Exercise 1: Prefixes

Complete each sentence with the correct word. Add word endings if necessary.

transfer   **translate**   **transport**   **transform**   **transmit**

1. The United Nations employs highly skilled interpreters and _____ to ensure clear communication between delegates from different countries.

2. Trucks have replaced trains as the most efficient way of _____ goods across the country.

3. Televisions and radios both pick up signals that are _____ from one point to another.

4. In frogs the _____ from tadpole to adult frog takes place in several weeks.

5. More than 100 employees were _____ from the main office out to smaller branch offices.

Exercise 2: Suffixes

The suffixes -*ous* and -*ive* are added to words to form adjectives. The suffix -*ous* means "full of [something]" or "having [something]." For example, the word *famous* (from *fame)* means "having much fame." The suffix -*ive* means "that which performs the indicated action." For example, the word *exclusive* (from *exclude*) means "that which limits or excludes." Remember, some words change spelling before adding a suffix. Check your dictionary if necessary.

A. Add either -*ous* or -*ive* to each of these words to form the words that are defined. Write each new word on the line next to its definition.

alternate   **injury**   **conserve**   **analogy**   **define**   **nerve**

_____ 1. moderate or cautious; something that tends to maintain existing conditions

_____ 2. appearing to be easily excited or irritated; acting worried or frightened

_____ 3. harmful or hurtful; something that causes injury

_____ 4. something that is related to another thing or like it in a certain way

_____ 5. an option; a different choice

_____ 6. defines or specifies precisely; a perfect example of something

B. Use one of the new words to complete each sentence.

1. A person who is extremely _____ may feel cold, perspire, turn pale, and tremble.

2. _____ medicine, which uses therapies like herbal medicine, massage, and acupuncture, can be just as effective as western medicine for some illnesses.

3. "Bread" is _____ to "food," as "tea" is related to "beverage."

4. The Republican Party has a _____ policy on welfare spending. The Democratic Party tends to be more liberal on this issue.

5. *The Old Man and the Sea* is considered by many to be Ernest Hemingway's _____ work.

6. Despite denial by tobacco companies, scientific research has shown that cigarette smoking is _____ to health.

Word Relationships

Exercise 3: Synonyms

Three of the words or phrases in each series have similar meanings. Cross out the word or phrase that has a different meaning.

1. emphasize	ignore	stress	make prominent
2. isolate	segregate	include	separate
3. precision	accuracy	exactness	carelessness
4. respond	react	answer	disregard
5. secure	dangerous	safe	guaranteed
6. strategy	plan	trick	method

Analogies

Remember that an **analogy** shows how two things are related in some way. Look at these examples.

1. cat : kitten :: dog : puppy

   Dog is related to *puppy* in the same way that *cat* is related to *kitten*. The first word in each pair is the adult animal; the second word is the young animal.

2. kitten : puppy :: cat : dog

   Kitten and *puppy* are both a type of young animal. *Cat* and *dog* are the adult types of these animals.

As the examples show, some sets of words may form more than one analogy.

Exercise 4: Analogies

Make an analogy from each group of four words, and write it on the line. Remember that more than one analogy may be possible. Then describe the relationship that exists in your analogy.

1. brain   body   strength   intelligence

_____

relationship: _____

2. nervous   relaxed   tense   calm

_____

relationship: _____

3. doctor   mental   physical   psychologist

_____

relationship: _____

4. write   editor   edit   author

_____

relationship: _____

5. alternative   mandatory   given   choice

_____

relationship: _____

6. concentrate weaken   strengthen   dilute

_____

relationship: _____

The Grammar of Words and Word Families

Exercise 5: Word Families

Use these words to fill in the word family chart. Follow the example given. Some words will be used more than once.

<u>alternative</u> (2x)	<u>assume</u>	<u>circumstance</u>	<u>concentrate</u>
alternate	assumption	circumstantial	concentrated
alternatively			concentration
<u>edit</u>	<u>emphasis</u>	<u>injure</u>	<u>intelligence</u>
edited	emphasize	injurious	intelligent
edition	emphatic	injury	intelligently
editor	emphatically		
editorial (2x)			
<u>isolate</u>	<u>mental</u>	<u>precise</u>	<u>respond</u>
isolated	mentality	precisely	response
isolation	mentally	precision	responsive
<u>secure</u> (2x)	<u>strategy</u>	<u>transform</u>	
securely	strategic	transformation	
security	strategically		
	strategist		

Noun	Noun (person)	Verb	Adverb	Adjective
alternative	—	alternate	alternatively	alternative
assumption	—	assume	—	—
circumstance	—	—	—	circumstantial
consentration	—	concentrate	—	consentrated
editorial edition	editor	edit	—	edited/editorial
emphasis	—	emphasize	emphatically	emphatic
injury	—	injure	—	injurious
intelligence	—	—	intelligently	intelligent
isolation	—	isolate	—	isolated
mentality	—	—	mentally	mental
precision	—	—	precisely	precise
response	—	respond	—	responsive
security	—	secure	securely	secure
strategy	strategist	—	strategically	strategic
transformation	—	transform	—	—

Understanding Words in Context
Multiple Meanings of a Word

Sometimes a word can have more than one meaning. The word *shift*, which occurs in Paragraph 7 of Reading 1, has several meanings. Read the definitions for the word *shift* given here.

a. *shift* v: 1. to change place, position, or direction; 2. to change gears

b. *shift* n: 1. a loose-fitting or semi-fitted dress; 2. a shirt

c. *shift* n: a scheduled period of work or other duty

Exercise 6: Multiple Meanings of *shift*

Look at the way the word *shift* is used in the sentences. Write the letter of the meaning that best fits *shift* in each sentence. Why did you choose that meaning? Write your reason on the line.

_____ 1. While driving, be sure to push in the clutch before attempting to <u>shift</u> gears.

Reason: _____

_____ 2. Many factory workers prefer to work either the day or evening <u>shift</u>, even though the night shift pays higher wages.

Reason: _____

_____ 3. Billie Jean <u>shifted</u> her weight from side to side as she waited for Bobby to serve.

Reason: _____

_____ 4. The weather was very hot so the girl wore a light <u>shift</u> and sandals.

Reason: _____

_____ 5. If you <u>shift</u> the books around, you can probably fit a couple more in the box.

Reason: _____

Exercise 7: Associations

Which topic is each of these words associated with? Write the words under the appropriate topic. Some words may fit more than one topic. Add one more word to each list.

alcohol	consult	depressed	drug
evolve	finance	income	mental
nervous	reverse	transform	economy

Health	*Money*	*Emotions*	*Change*
_____	_____	_____	_____
_____	_____	_____	_____
_____	_____	_____	_____
_____	_____	_____	_____

Exercise 8: Word Meanings in Context

Reread the passages from Reading 3. Then complete the sentences or answer the questions by circling the letter of the correct choice.

1. I began to think about the stresses that might have led up to my mother's first nervous breakdown: leaving my sister at home with our grandmother; trying to keep a job she loved but that my father asked her to leave; wanting to go to New York to pursue her own dream of writing but punishing herself for even thinking about it. She was convinced that divorce was impossible. A husband could not be left for a career.

Which of these is NOT given as a reason for Ruth's nervous breakdown?

a. trying to keep a job that her husband wanted her to leave

b. getting a divorce

c. giving up her dream of going to New York to write

2. At the hospital, and later, when Ruth told me stories of her past, I used to say, "But why didn't you leave? Why didn't you take the job in New York?" She would say that it didn't matter, she was lucky to have my sister and me. Sometimes she would add, "If I'd left, you never would have been born." I always thought but never had the courage to say: *But you might have been born instead.*

Gloria thinks that her mother

a. was lucky to have had two daughters

b. didn't really want to work in New York

c. should have taken the job in New York

3. Perhaps the biggest reason my mother was cared for but not helped for twenty years was the simplest: my mother's functioning was not that necessary to the world. She was like the women alcoholics who drink in their kitchens while male executives who drink get expensive care. She was like the homemakers who are calmed with drugs while male patients get help and personal attention instead. My mother was not an important worker.

Maybe the biggest reason Gloria's mother was not helped was because

a. her mother did not do any work that was considered important

b. her mother drank

c. her mother was not an executive

4. She was also a young woman who was rebellious enough to fall in love with my father, a funny and charming young man who was unacceptably Jewish. I know from family stories that my mother had married my father twice. They married once, secretly, and once a year later in a public ceremony, which some members of both families had refused to attend because it was a "mixed marriage."

Why didn't some family members attend the second wedding?

a. Family members had attended the first wedding.

b. The families didn't approve of a Jewish man marrying a non-Jewish woman.

c. Family members were not invited to the second wedding.

Exercise 9: Constructing Sentences

Use each set of words to write a question. Use all the words given. No additional words are needed.

1. was / at / Billie Jean's / she / routine / night? / when / played / What / tennis

   _____

2. alternative / was / strategy? / Billie Jean's / What

   _____

3. are / and / precision / needed / tennis? / Why / in / accuracy

   _____

4. hour / Billie Jean? / was / the / Why / before / for / match / so / the / stressful

   _____

5. ten-minute / Who / injury / the / out? / emphasized / time

   _____

6. physically / Do / harder / think / the / was / or / match / mentally? / you

   _____

Using Words in Communication

Read the timeline about the women's rights movement. Then answer the questions.

1850: First National Women's Rights Convention is held in Worcester, Massachusetts.

1893: Colorado is the first state to give women the right to vote.

1920: 19th Amendment to the Constitution gives all women the right to vote.

1961: Eleanor Roosevelt becomes the chair of the President's Commission on the Status of Women.

1966: The National Organization of Women is founded.

1972: *Ms. Magazine* is first published.

1996: All-male Virginia Military Institute must admit women to continue to receive public funding.

1. What state first allowed women to vote? _____

2. What does the 19th Amendment establish? _____

3. When was *Ms. Magazine* first published? _____

4. Where was the first National Women's Rights Convention held? _____

5. Who was chair of the President's Commission on the Status of Women?
   _____

6. When did the Virginia Military Institute have to admit women? _____

7. What organization was founded in 1966? _____

Exercise 11: Writing

Choose one event on the timeline in Exercise 10, and write two or three paragraphs of explanation about it. You can research information in the library or on the Internet. Be sure to use only credible sites for your research. Share your paragraphs with a small group.

Exercise 12: Critical Thinking

These questions will help you develop your critical-thinking skills. Critical thinking helps you evaluate information and reach good conclusions from the information that is given. Ask yourself the questions as you work on your answers: What information in the reading supports my answer? What other information do I have to support my conclusion? Where can I get more information about the topic?

1. a. Refer back to Reading 1, and list all the things that Billie Jean did to prepare for the match with Bobby Riggs.

   b. Look at your list. Which things did Billie Jean do to prepare herself for the match? Underline them. These are the "self" items. Which things were part of Billie Jean's game strategy to beat Bobby? Circle them. These are the "game" items.

   c. Choose the three most important items for "self" and for "game." Be prepared to explain why you chose those items.

2. How did the attitude of Ruth's family affect the way she was treated during her illness? How do you think she might have been treated if she had been a man?

3. What do you think still needs to be done to achieve equal rights for women? How do you think this change might happen?

Serving One's Country

Vocabulary Preview

Preview 1

These sentences contain information from the readings. Fill in the blanks with the word that best completes each sentence.

aware**justify****theoretical****diversity****guarantees**

1. Justice Marshall said that the difficulty black children experienced from segregation was not _____ but real.

2. Justice O'Connor wanted the school board to be able to first _____ its actions of discrimination.

3. Colin Powell is _____ that life in the segregated Army was very difficult for African-American soldiers.

4. The Fourteenth Amendment _____ all persons equal protection under the law.

5. Sandra Day O'Connor felt that states should be allowed to promote racial _____ in public schools.

Preview 2

Look at the way the underlined words are used in the sentences. Match each word with its meaning or definition.

1. Some people who were teaching the men new aviation skills believed in the men's <u>ultimate</u> failure.

2. The Tuskegee airmen became one of World War II's most respected fighter groups <u>despite</u> segregation and discrimination in the Army.

3. Bussing students to a school outside of their own neighborhood was one method of trying to make schools more racially <u>integrated</u>.

4. It was easy to <u>predict</u> how each justice would vote based on their positions in previous cases.

5. Chief Justice Warren Burger was against the school board's <u>policy</u> that laid off white teachers and protected the jobs of African-American teachers.

_____ 1. **ultimate**   a. to say that something will happen

_____ 2. **despite**   b. blended together

_____ 3. **integrated**   c. in spite of

_____ 4. **predict**   d. an idea that a decision is based on

_____ 5. **policy**   e. what happens at the end; final

Reading Preview: What Do You Already Know?

Circle the correct answer. If you don't know the answer, guess.

1. Colin Powell is

    a. an Asian American

    b. an African American

    c. a Native American

    d. a Mexican American

2. He has worked most of his professional life in

    a. government

    b. education

    c. the military

    d. business

3. Thurgood Marshall

    a. was a newspaper reporter

    b. believed that segregation in schools was wrong

    c. was a sociologist who studied race

    d. did research for the Supreme Court

4. Sandra Day O'Connor is

    a. the First Lady

    b. the first woman to become a United States senator

    c. the first woman to be appointed to the Supreme Court

    d. the first woman to become President

5. Sandra Day O'Connor

   a. grew up on a ranch in Arizona

   b. was a justice on the Supreme Court from 1981 to 2006

   c. became known for her ability to gain support from her fellow justices

   d. all of the above

6. Affirmative action is intended to

   a. limit access to education and employment

   b. help minorities have access to education and employment

   c. integrate schools

   d. segregate the workplace

Introduction to the Readings

(1) This unit introduces you to three Americans, Colin Powell, Thurgood Marshall, and Sandra Day O'Connor, who have spent their lives serving their country. They all represent the American Dream—the <u>idea</u> that anyone, including poor African-American boys or a girl raised on a cattle ranch—can go on to do great things in their lives. All it takes is hard work and determination.

(2) Colin Powell was born in Harlem to <u>immigrant</u> parents. He overcame the rough life of the streets to become a four-star general, national <u>security</u> advisor, chairman of the Joint Chiefs of Staff,* and Secretary of State.

> ***Joint Chiefs of Staff:** the top military leaders who report to the President of the United States

(3) The first reading is from Howard Means's *Colin Powell: Soldier/Statesman—Statesman/Soldier*. The excerpt is part of a powerful speech Powell gave at the national <u>convention</u> of the Tuskegee Airmen, the famous African-American fighter pilots of World War II.

(4) Thurgood Marshall graduated first in his class from Howard University in 1933 and then went to work for the National Association for the Advancement of Colored People (NAACP). In 1940, he became the chief of the <u>legal</u> staff, and in this <u>capacity</u> he argued 32 cases before the U.S. Supreme Court, 29 of which he won. Among those cases was the "case of the century," *Brown v. Board of Education of Topeka* (1954), in which racial segregation in American public schools was declared unconstitutional. Until that time, African-American children had been <u>required</u> to attend separate schools. In 1967, Thurgood Marshall was named Justice to the Supreme Court, an office he held until his retirement in 1991.

(5) Sandra Day O'Connor grew up on a cattle ranch in southeastern Arizona. Life on the Lazy-B was hard. The ranch didn't have electricity or running water until Sandra was seven. With the nearest neighbors 25 miles away, and no brothers or sisters until she was eight, Sandra <u>participated</u> in most ranch activities. She could drive a car when she was seven and was able to ride and shoot well by the time she was eight.

(6) From this rural childhood, O'Connor went on to become a lawyer, <u>assistant</u> state attorney general, and Republican senator of Arizona. O'Connor <u>eventually</u> became the Arizona state senate <u>majority</u> leader, a first for women in the United States. In 1979, O'Connor was nominated to the Arizona Court of Appeals. Two years later, President Reagan nominated her as the first woman to the Supreme Court. Feminists wanted to see a woman on the Supreme Court, and Reagan had made a campaign promise to appoint one. As the first woman on the Supreme Court, Sandra Day O'Connor seemed to <u>approach</u> each case <u>individually</u> and work within the system to find practical solutions. Although conservative at first, O'Connor's opinions became more moderate over time. This moderation and her ability to gain support from fellow Justices gave O'Connor greater influence on the Court. She retired from the court in January 2006.

*affirmative action: employment policies that encourage women and minorities to apply for jobs

(7) Reading 3 describes the case of *Wygant v. Jackson Board of Education.* O'Connor's vote decided the case, and she later wrote a separate opinion that gave her reasons for supporting affirmative action.*

Reading 1: At Tuskegee

Exerpt adapted from *Colin Powell: Soldier/Statesman—Statesman/Soldier* by Howard Means (New York: Penguin Putnam, 1992), 32–37, 92–93.

(8) That Colin Powell is very **aware** [conscious] of the segregated past of the Army that has been his home for more than 30 years, that he feels a debt to the black men and women who served in those armed forces, was never more <u>evident</u> than in August of 1991 when he addressed the 20th annual national <u>convention</u> of the Tuskegee Airmen in Detroit.

(9) "At Tuskegee, surrounded by some of the most vicious racism in America, the best and the brightest of their time set their <u>individual</u> and collective minds to what, even in retrospect, seemed an incredibly impossible

*Tuskegee Airmen. Photo compliments of Tuskegee University Archives.
Reprinted with permission.*

task," Powell told the surviving airmen and their guests. "The men—and women—at Tuskegee didn't just need to master aviation and military skills and the support of their husbands in time of war. They had to do it while much of the power of the United States Army tried to stop the entire enterprise. While the civilians who surrounded them wasted no opportunity to express their hatred. While some of the very people who were teaching them their new aviation skills believed without question in their **ultimate** failure. And while the general feelings of the people in America were at best those of neglect and at worst violent disagreement with the whole idea.

(10) "But these were not ordinary men and women at Tuskegee," Powell went on. "If there is one thing about the history of the Tuskegee Airmen that is as unmistakable as the outline of a P-51, it is the fact that *these were not ordinary people* [Powell's emphasis]. They were *extraordinary* men and women.

*Jackie Robinson: the first African-American base-ball player in the Major Leagues
*brooked: tolerated
*resilience: ability to restore one's strength

Like Jackie Robinson,* they stood above the crowd. They brooked* no opposition to their goals, accepted no shortcuts, and took comfort in the fact that they were paving the way to the future. Courage. Character. Determination. Drive. Devotion to duty. Love of America **despite** ~~regardless of~~ her imperfections. These are the things that made up their character, that gave it strength, that gave it resilience,* and pointed the way to the future.

(11) "It is on this road to the future, paved with the sacrifice and blood of African-American patriots—especially the Tuskegee Airmen—it was on this road that I traveled to become the first African-American chairman of the Joint Chiefs of Staff. I never forget for a day, or for an hour, or for a minute, that I climbed to my position on the backs of the courageous African-American men and women who went before me."

Reading 2: Arguing before the Supreme Court

Excerpt adapted from *Thurgood Marshall: American Revolutionary* by Juan Williams (New York: Times Books, 1998), pp. 209–27.

(12) On December 9, 1952, a line of more than 200 people stretched beyond the cold white marble steps leading to the Supreme Court. Many of the people had been there overnight, hoping to get a seat to hear the celebrated case, *Brown v. Board of Education of Topeka.* Every seat in the courtroom was filled, and the anxious crowd just about leaped to attention.

(13) The crowd was hushed as Bob Carter rose to make the first presentation for *Brown* for the NAACP. He did not hesitate. He said black students in Topeka, Kansas, who attended segregated schools, even equally good facilities, were being denied equal education opportunity. "The Constitution does not stop with the fact that you have equal educational facilities, but it covers the whole educational process," Carter said.

(14) The real <u>drama</u> began as Thurgood Marshall, also for the NAACP, stood to make his oral presentation. The newspaper the *Afro-American* reported that "all of the Supreme Court justices came to attention" when Marshall stood to speak. Even without microphones his voice boomed throughout the crowded room and its high ceiling.

(15) "We are saying that there is a <u>denial</u> of equal protection under the law," Marshall told the packed courtroom. Inferior schools and <u>resources</u> were not the <u>issue</u>; it was segregation itself. Racial separation hurt the "development of the personalities of [African-American] children" and "deprived them of equal **status** [position] in the school <u>community</u> . . . destroying their self-respect." He <u>concluded</u> that the "humiliation" black children went through was not "**theoretical** [hypothetical] <u>injury</u>" but "actual <u>injury</u>."

(16) Marshall pointed out that not a single lawyer from any of the states with segregated schools had argued against any of his sociological <u>evidence</u> of the damage done to black children. And because there was nothing to argue against the point, he said the states had an obligation to **integrate** [blend] their schools. All black parents wanted, Marshall said, was for state segregation laws to be ruled unconstitutional.

(17) After the case was argued, the Supreme Court took it under <u>consideration</u> for a <u>period</u> of more than two years. Marshall was beginning

to think that the court was trying to delay things when he received a phone call in Mobile, Alabama, in May of 1954, telling him he might want to be at the Supreme Court on May 17. Marshall took the next train to Washington.

(18) At 12:52 PM Chief Justice Earl Warren, with all of the associate justices in attendance, started reading the Court's decision. As Warren began to read, Marshall was not certain which way he was going. Warren said, "In approaching this problem we cannot turn the clock back to 1868 when the [Fourteenth] **Amendment** was adopted or even to 1895 when *Plessy v. Ferguson* was written. We must consider public education in the light of its [current role] in American life."

(19) Marshall, seated in the lawyers' section, focused a glare at Justice Stanley Reed. Marshall thought Reed, who was from Kentucky, was the most likely leader of a group of votes to keep school segregation in place. Marshall heard that Reed had prepared a dissent,* with the help of a privately hired law clerk. He wanted to watch Reed's face as a clue to what was going to happen. Reed only stared back at him, wide-eyed.

***dissent:** in judicial terms, the written statement against a decision

(20) While Marshall and Reed were staring each other down, Warren continued: "In these days, it is doubtful that any child may reasonably be expected to succeed in life if he is **denied** the opportunity of an education . . . a right which must be made available to all on equal terms . . . To separate black children from others of a similar age and qualifications solely because of their race generated a feeling of inferiority as to their **status** in the community."

(21) Then in dramatic style Warren made a historic pronouncement: "We conclude that in the field of public education the doctrine* of 'separate but equal' has no place. Separate educational facilities are inherently unequal." Marshall recalled that when he heard those words, "I was so happy I was numb."

***doctrine:** statement of beliefs that guide behavior

(22) "When Warren read the opinion," Marshall recalled, "Reed looked me right straight in the face the whole time because he wanted to see what happened when I realized that he didn't write the dissent and I was looking right at him. I'm sure Reed laughed at that."

(23) In fact, one of Reed's clerks had done <u>research</u> on arguments to support a possible dissent. Reed, however, decided to vote with the <u>majority</u>. The ruling was unanimous. "Earl Warren," said E. Barrett Prettyman, Jr., a clerk to Justice Jackson, another possible dissenter, "worked very hard, to his <u>credit</u>, to *persuade* **convince** people and particularly the last one or two holdouts that it would not be in the interest of the Court or any country to have divergent views on this vital subject."

(24) The *Afro-American's* next <u>edition</u> read: SEGREGATION ILLEGAL NOW. The story <u>quoted</u> Marshall as saying: "It's the greatest story we have ever had . . . the thing that is gratifying to me is that it was unanimous and on our side."

Reading 3: Affirmative Action

Excerpt adapted from *Sandra Day O'Connor: How the First Woman on the Supreme Court Became Its Most Influential Justice* by Joan Biskupic (New York: HarperCollins Publishers, 2005), 174–77.

(25) In the early 1980s, white teachers in Jackson, Michigan, had been laid off to protect the jobs of African-American teachers with less time on the job. The whites had been let go and the African Americans protected under an agreement that <u>required</u> the school district not to lower the <u>overall</u> <u>percentage</u> of <u>minority</u> teachers.

(26) Wendy Wygant and other laid-off [white] teachers said that they had been discriminated against because of their race, in violation of the Fourteenth Amendment's guarantee of equal protection under the law. But lower federal courts ruled that the agreement was an acceptable way to make up for past discrimination and ensure role models for minority schoolchildren.

(27) On Friday, November 8, 1985, the Supreme Court justices prepared to vote on the closely watched appeal brought by the white teachers. O'Connor and the other justices gathered in the room adjacent to Chief Justice Warren Burger's office for their regular session. The justices' opinions and votes on *Wygant v. Jackson Board of Education* were **predictable,** based on their positions in earlier cases. Burger spoke against the school board's affirmative action **policy.** Byron White voted with Burger, as did Lewis Powell, who had seen **integration** battles as the president of the Richmond School Board. William Rehnquist, always opposed to special government treatment of African-Americans at the expense of whites, joined them.

(28) Brennan voted for the decision to lay off whites to keep black teachers who had less time on the job, as did Thurgood Marshall, who said, "discrimination is worse today than before." Harry Blackmun also voted to uphold the lower court's ruling. John Paul Stevens did the same.

(29) So, the vote was tied 4 to 4 when the case came around to O'Connor. She wanted neither to affirm nor reject the school **policy.** She thought the best alternative was to refer the case back to a lower court for a hearing. Justice O'Connor wanted the school board to be given a chance to **justify** its actions based on past discrimination in the district.

(30) A month later, she wrote to Justice Powell, "I am not really at rest on this, but I am inclined to think there is a legitimate state interest in promoting racial **diversity** in public schools." She also said a school board that believed it had engaged in past race discrimination should be able to take steps to ensure that African Americans were hired and stayed on the job.

(31) This worried Justice Powell. He could not go as far as O'Connor wanted and still keep the votes of Burger, White, and Rehnquist. Over the next few weeks, Powell and O'Connor inched toward a compromise. **Ultimately**, O'Connor ended up agreeing with enough of Powell's opinion to cancel the layoff of the white teachers. But she wrote a separate opinion describing her reasons for when government could use affirmative action. She believed that public employers could use affirmative action to correct past discrimination as long as it does not "unnecessarily trammel* rights" of "innocent individuals."

*trammel: prevent

(32) The *New York Times* reported, "at least five Justices [referring to O'Connor and the four liberals] . . . rejected the . . . broad position that the Constitution bans governments from using any racial preferences in employment that, at the expense of innocent whites, benefit members of minority groups. O'Connor's receptiveness to affirmative action was noticed."

◎ **Comprehension Check**

Did you understand the readings? Mark these sentences true (T) or false (F).

_____ 1. Colin Powell immigrated to the United States at an early age.

_____ 2. He was born in Harlem.

_____ 3. The Tuskegee Airmen were a unit of African-American fighter pilots who distinguished themselves during Desert Storm.

_____ 4. The case that ended segregation in American public schools was *Brown v. Board of Education of Topeka.*

_____ 5. It took the Supreme Court seven years to rule on *Brown v. Board of Education.*

_____ 6. The Supreme Court vote on desegregation was unanimous.

_____ 7. Sandra Day O'Connor became the first female state senate majority leader.

_____ 8. President Reagan refused to appoint a woman to the Supreme Court.

_____ 9. Justices Burger, White, Powell, and Rehnquist were opposed to special government treatment of African Americans at the expense of whites.

_____ 10. Sandra Day O'Connor feels that affirmative action policies can be used in some situations.

Word Study

Target Vocabulary

amend (Amendment)	diverse (diversity)	policy
aware	federal	predict (predictable)
convince	guarantee	status
deny	integrate (integration)	theory (theoretical)
despite	justify	ultimate (ultimately)

Word Parts

Exercise 1: Prefixes

The prefix *con-*, as in *convene,* means "totally," "together," or "with." Complete each sentence with the correct word.

consensus	convened	contact	contract
confrontation	congregation	convince	consulted

1. The _____ between the rioters and the police was horrible! Several people were seriously hurt.

2. The rental _____ said that the tenant was responsible for paying all utilities, as well as $950 rent, every month.

3. The meeting was _____ in the conference room; her office couldn't handle ten people.

4. St. Mark's church has a very busy _____; the members are always having one activity after another.

5. The _____ was that the athlete did not deserve an Olympic medal.

6. She could not _____ her parents to let her study in France; they wanted her to stay home.

7. You can't _____ him until this evening; he'll be in New York until seven.

8. A psychologist was _____ to see what could be done about the boy's depression.

Exercise 2: Word Parts and Word Meanings

A. Think about the word *unpredictable*.

1. What is its root? _____

2. What does its root mean? _____

3. What is its prefix? _____

4. What does the prefix mean? _____

5. What is its suffix? _____

6. What does it mean? _____

7. What are some synonyms for *unpredictable*? _____

8. What are some antonyms of *unpredictable*? _____

9. If the weather is *unpredictable,* it is _____

B. Think about the word *disintegrate.* For Number 7, finish the sentence.

1. What is its root? _____

2. What does its root mean? _____

3. What is its prefix? _____

4. What does the prefix mean? _____

5. What are some synonyms for *disintegrate*? _____

6. What are some antonyms of *disintegrate?* _____

7. A substance that *disintegrates* in water _____

Word Relationships

Exercise 3: Synonyms

Four of the words in each series have similar meanings. Cross out the word that has a different meaning.

1. team	squad	crew	person	platoon
2. aware	alert	conscious	informed	ignorant
3. diverse	varied	different	alike	mixed
4. ultimate	final	essential	maximum	inferior
5. amend	worsen	fix	improve	correct
6. predictable	dependable	changeable	expected	anticipated
7. eloquent	expressive	unclear	fluent	articulate
8. justify	explain	question	rationalize	validate

The Grammar of Words and Word Families

Use these words to fill in the word family chart. Follow the example given. Some words will be used more than once.

amend	aware	convince	deny
amendment	awareness	convincing	denial
		convincingly	

despite	diverse	federal	guarantee (2x)
(preposition)	diversification	federally	guaranteed
	diversified		guarantor
	diversify		
	diversity		

integrate	justify	policy	predict
integrated	justifiable		predictability
integration	justifiably		predictable
	justification		predictably
	justified		prediction

status	theory	ultimate	
	theoretical	ultimately	
	theoretically	ultimatum	
	theoretician		
	theorize		

Noun	Noun (person)	Verb	Adverb	Adjective
amendment	—	amend	—	—
awareness	—	—	—	aware
—	—	convince	convincingly	convincing
denial	—	deny	—	—
diversification diversity	—	diversify	—	diverse diversified
—	—	—	federally	federal
guarantee	guarantor	guarantee	—	guaranteed
integration	—	integrate	—	integrated
justification	—	justify	justifiably	justified justifiable
policy	—	—	—	—
predictability prediction	—	predict	predictably	predictable
status	—	—	—	—
theory	theoretician	theorize	theoretically	theoretical
ultimatum	—	—	ultimately	ultimate

Exercise 5: Word Forms

Complete each sentence with the correct form of the word.

1. The parts were expertly _____ by the operator.

   assembled   assembly   assembler   assembling

2. The group was _____, three men and four women from six different countries.

   diverse   diversity   diversify   diversified

3. The warranty _____ that the auto dealer will do all repairs for three years for free.

   guarantee   guaranteed   guarantees   guarantor

4. There was absolutely no _____ for his violent actions.

   justify   justified   justification   justifies

5. In 1954, it was not _____ that the Supreme Court would rule in favor of desegregation in schools.

   prediction   predictable   predictability   predict

6. The teacher asked the class to _____ about why some lakes in northern Canada do not stay frozen as long as they used to.

   theoretician   theoretical   theorize   theory

◎ **Understanding Words in Context**

Exercise 6: Collocations

Match the four words with their common collocations. Write the combinations on the lines.

speaker	**speech**	**policy**	**trip**
operations	**appeal**	**gesture**	**survival**
law	**government**	**court**	**reality**

1. eloquent

_____

_____

2. ultimate

_____

_____

3. federal

_____

_____

4. military

_____

_____

Reread the passages from the readings. Then complete the sentences or answer the questions by circling the letter of the correct choice.

1. "After the case was argued, the Supreme Court took it under consideration for a period of more than two years. Marshall was beginning to think that the court was using delaying tactics when he received a phone call in Mobile, Alabama, in May of 1954, telling him he might want to be at the Supreme Court on May 17. Marshall took the next train to Washington."

   Marshall probably expected that

   a. the court might not wait for him to arrive

   b. the court would rule on the issue of school integration

   c. the court would present delaying tactics

2. "Marshall, seated in the lawyers' section, focused a glare at Justice Stanley Reed. Marshall thought Reed, who was from Kentucky, was the most likely leader of a bloc of votes to keep school segregation in place. Marshall heard that Reed had prepared a dissent, with the help of a privately hired law clerk."

   How did Marshall look at Reed?

   a. with anger

   b. with respect

   c. with trust

3. "[Justice O'Connor] wanted neither to affirm nor reject the school policy. She thought the best alternative was to refer the case back to a lower court for a hearing. Justice O'Connor wanted the school board to be given a chance to justify its actions based on past discrimination in the district."

   What did O'Connor want the school board to be able to do?

   a. get a new policy

   b. go to a lower court

   c. explain what it had done

4. "If there is one thing about the history of the Tuskegee Airmen that is as unmistakable as the silhouette of a P-51, it is the fact that *these were not ordinary people* [Powell's emphasis]. They were *extraordinary* men and women. Like Jackie Robinson, they stood above the crowd. They brooked no opposition to their goals, accepted no shortcuts, and took solace in the fact that they were paving the way to the future. Courage. Character. Determination. Drive. Devotion to duty. Love of America despite her imperfections."

At Tuskegee, the airmen felt

a. that they would have to compromise to achieve their goals

b. that their country was full of imperfections

c. that, eventually, they would make their dreams come true

5. "It is on this road to the future, paved with the sacrifice and blood of black patriots—especially the Tuskegee airmen—it was on this road that I traveled to become the first black chairman of the Joint Chiefs of Staff. I never forget for a day, or for an hour, or for a minute, that I climbed to my position on the backs of the courageous African-American men and women who went before me."

Powell gave credit for his success

a. to the black men and women who had preceded him

b. to his school

c. to the Army

Using Words in Communication

Use the words given to complete this reading selection.

aware	devoted	relied
challenge	eloquent	task
dedicated	military	ultimately

Plato's Ideal Society

Preeminent among the Greeks of the fifth century BCE was Plato, the Athenian philosopher who is best remembered today for *The Republic*, the dialogue in which he presents an _____ vision of the ideal society. *The Republic* is primarily _____ to Plato's notion that only the wise should rule. Plato was against the idea that men should rule just because they had proven to be powerful _____ leaders. All one had to do, Plato pointed out, was to look at what Pericles, a renowned general and statesman of Athens, had done for his people. True, he had _____ much of his energy to the beautification of Athens, but he had also plunged his beloved city-state into a disastrous war that had _____ led to its downfall.

The _____ facing every man, Plato argued, was to search for eternal wisdom. Only those who dedicated many years of their lives to considering eternal questions such as, What is truth? What is honor? What is justice? ultimately arrived at wisdom and were then qualified to become philosopher-kings.

Many people are not _____ of the fact that Plato was one of our first feminists. Unlike almost every other well-known thinker of his time, Plato held that women could become as wise as men and thus could also be _____ upon to provide wise guardianship.

But what about the rest of the people; what was their role to be in Plato's ideal society? Well, those who were spirited, courageous, and interested in honor and glory were to become the protectors and defenders of the state. The rest, the common people, were to be laborers whose _____ it would be to employ whatever special gift or ability they had for the benefit of the state.

And what if some of these common people refused to conform to what the state dictated for them? Well, said Plato, they would have to be taught the value of working for the common good.

Exercise 9: Writing for Different Discourse Communities

Think about writing in different situations and for different audiences. Do you write a letter to a friend using the same style and vocabulary as when you write a letter to a business associate? Generally, no. A letter to a friend is often very informal, uses conversational language, and does not need to follow special rules about form. On the other hand, a business letter is more formal, uses vocabulary related to business, and does follow rules about form. A friend and a business associate are members of two different *discourse communities*. A discourse community is a group of people who share specific interests, goals, vocabulary, writing styles, and ways of sharing information or giving one another feedback. Another example of a discourse community would be your professors and teachers. Can you think of different discourse communities within your university or college? Write them here.

_____ _____ _____

In order to be successful in your studies you will need to learn and follow different *conventions*, or set ways of doing things, when writing for different discourse communities in your college or university.

It is also important to realize that writing conventions are different from culture to culture, even for the same discourse community. The standard format of a Japanese business letter is very different from the standard format of an American business letter. Likewise, the conventions of academic writing in the United States are probably quite different from those followed in other countries.

Practice writing for two different discourse communities by producing two letters. First, reread Reading 3.

a. Write a letter of three to five paragraphs to the editor of the *Washington Post* supporting or protesting the Supreme Court decision against affirmative action in *Wygant v. Jackson Board of Education*. Be sure to give clear reasons for either supporting or disagreeing with the decision.

b. Write an informal letter to a friend with your comments and reactions to the Supreme Court decision in *Wygant v. Jackson Board of Education*.

Exercise 10: Critical Thinking

Review the Introduction to the Readings in this unit and the readings to answer the questions. Support your answers with information from these readings.

1. What is the American dream? Why are Colin Powell, Thurgood Marshall, and Sandra Day O'Connor considered the embodiment of the American dream?

2. In *Wygant v. Jackson Board of Education,* what were the reasons given to not support affirmative action in this case? When did Sandra Day O'Connor believe that affirmative action was appropriate?

3. Not everyone can be a military general or a Supreme Court justice. How do you think ordinary American citizens can serve their country? Explain your ideas.

Women in Art

6

◎ Vocabulary Preview

These sentences contain information from the readings. Fill in the blanks with the word that best completes each sentence.

abstract   confined   instruction   revealed   visualized

1. Georgia sometimes _____ abstract shapes during her frequent headaches.

2. Frida spent a year in the hospital, _____ to bed after a terrible accident.

3. Some of Frida's paintings were quite realistic, but many were rather _____.

4. Unlike Georgia O'Keeffe, Frida Kahlo was self-taught. She never received any art _____.

5. Georgia thought that her paintings _____ a feminine or female feeling.

Preview 2

Look at the way the underlined words are used in the sentences. Match each word with its meaning or definition.

1. After her accident, Frida was in <u>constant</u> pain. She never had a day without it.

2. Despite the pain, Frida had a <u>positive</u> attitude about life.

3. Georgia O'Keeffe was <u>reluctant</u> to talk about her work; she would rather let her paintings speak for themselves.

4. Artists like O'Keeffe and Kahlo explored the endless <u>variations</u> of color in their paintings.

5. Frida <u>displayed</u> a talent for practical jokes. She loved to play tricks on people in authority.

_____ 1. **constant**   a. unwilling

_____ 2. **positive**   b. shown or exhibited

_____ 3. **reluctant**   c. changes or differences

_____ 4. **variations**   d. never ending

_____ 5. **displayed**   e. hopeful, confident

Reading Preview: What Do You Already Know?

Circle the correct answer. If you don't know the answer, guess.

1. Georgia O'Keeffe was

   a. a famous fashion designer

   b. an art critic

   c. a 20th century painter

   d. the first professional woman photographer

2. Georgia O'Keeffe is well known for

   a. her use of unusual black and white fabrics

   b. the use of brilliant colors in her paintings

   c. her black and white photographs

   d. her reviews of famous art exhibits

3. Georgia O'Keeffe died

   a. very young

   b. an unknown artist

   c. after a long illness

   d. nearly blind at the age of 98

4. Frida Kahlo

   a. was born in Mexico City in 1907

   b. painted many self-portraits because she was confined to bed

   c. was married to the famous artist Diego Rivera

   d. all of the above

5. Frida's life changed when she was eighteen because

   a. she married Diego Rivera

   b. she joined the Communist Party

   c. she was in a serious auto accident

   d. she traveled to the United States

6. Frida's paintings are

   a. personal and sometimes strange

   b. all in black and white

   c. painted on glass

   d. enormous

Introduction to the Readings

(1) Georgia O'Keeffe is considered the most important American woman painter of the twentieth century. She was born in 1887 and died in 1986, painting for most of her 98 years. O'Keeffe's art was original in its style and subject matter. Her brilliantly colored paintings of bold, sensuous flowers and sun-bleached animal bones are still admired today.

(2) In Reading 1, O'Keeffe recalls her "breakthrough" into her own unique and feminine style of artistic expression. Reading 2 explains how O'Keeffe used color and her art as a way to <u>communicate</u> the ideas she wanted to express.

(3) Reading 3 introduces Mexico's most famous woman artist, Frida Kahlo. She was born in 1907 in Coyoacan, a suburb of Mexico City. She died in the same house at the age of 47. She was a <u>contemporary</u> of Georgia O'Keeffe, and the two artists met more than once at art galleries in New York.

(4) Frida's childhood was fairly ordinary, except for a case of polio at age six. To help her body heal after the polio, Frida's parents encouraged her to participate in all kinds of sports. She became a very athletic, "tomboy-ish" girl. During high school Frida also met her future husband, the famous Mexican painter, Diego Rivera. Rivera had been hired to paint a mural (art on walls) in the school's auditorium.

(5) Frida married the famous muralist Diego Rivera in 1929. In addition to art, the couple shared strong political beliefs. Like many other artists and intellectuals of the time, they were both Communists. Diego's huge murals often <u>promoted</u> <u>revolution</u> and Communism.

(6) Frida's personal life was as colorful and dramatic as her native dresses. Although she and Diego loved one another deeply, the couple lived apart much of the time they were married. In 1939, Frida and Diego divorced, but they remarried a year later and remained very close until Frida's death in 1954. The exact cause of Frida's death is unknown, but she was ill

with pneumonia shortly before her death. She, like Georgia O'Keeffe, lives on in her **distinctive** art.

Reading 1: An Important Decision

Excerpt adapted from *Portrait of an Artist: A Biography of Georgia O'Keeffe* by Laurie Lisle (New York: Washington Square Press, 1986), 79–82.

(7) Georgia recalled the breakthrough she had experienced in her art. At that time art still represented the freedom of expression that it had when she was a teenager.

I grew up pretty much as everybody else grows up. One day seven years ago I found myself saying: I can't live where I want to, I can't go where I want to, I can't even say what I want to. School and things that painters have taught me even keep me from painting as I want to. I decided that I was a very stupid fool not to at least paint as I wanted to and say what I wanted to when I painted. That seemed to be the only thing I could do that didn't concern anybody but myself. My painting was nobody's business but my own.

(8) Georgia put all her old artwork away in order to clear her mind completely of the influence of others. She also put away her watercolor paints, not wanting to have to think about colors. She decided to work only in black and white until she exhausted all their possibilities. At the age of 27 she started all over again, in the simplest way: drawing with charcoal. "It was like learning to walk again," she remembered.

(9) Every night she spread rough student sketch paper on her bedroom floor and sat on the floor. She worked, rubbing the paper with charcoal, until her body ached and the charcoal fell apart in her fingers. Sometimes she wondered whether the **abstract** shapes that she saw in her mind meant that she was crazy. (This was a reasonable <u>idea</u> because both <u>creativity</u> and insanity

have been <u>linked</u> to the ability to see reality <u>differently</u>.) Those weeks were a high point in Georgia's life that she would always try to recreate. "I was alone and free, working into my own unknown, with no one to satisfy but myself," she recalled.

(10) Later, people who looked at those **abstract** drawings saw violent, explosive emotions, driven by feminine <u>energy</u>. This <u>energy</u> seemed to threaten to tear the artist apart. Sharp edges pushed against soft forms. Moving shapes jumped up like flames reaching for oxygen. One of the drawings showed volcano-like shapes erupting with fire and steam, which Georgia had **visualized** during one of her then frequent headaches.

(11) Georgia clearly knew that she was **revealing** a female feeling. "The thing expresses in a way what I wanted it to, but it also seems rather feminine. It is essentially a woman's feeling. It satisfies me in a way," she told a friend. However, a few years later, when some art critics began to criticize it, Georgia **rejected** their <u>comments</u>.

Reading 2: Thinking in Colors

Excerpt adapted from *Portrait of an Artist: A Biography of Georgia O'Keeffe* by Laurie Lisle (New York: Washington Square Press, 1986), 352–53.

(12) Georgia thought in color the way other people think in words. She joked that she hoped to give up reading and writing with the help of the telephone, tape recorder, and radio. Despite the fact that Georgia had an expressive and **distinctive** writing <u>style</u>, she said that words were often false, meaningless, and limited. On the other hand, color was something she could trust. It was a world in which new **variations** could still be <u>found</u>.

(13) Georgia thought that her color vocabulary—of colors ranging from shiny blacks to airy white—was superior to the English language. Because of this she often refused to talk about her work and was **reluctant** to try to describe it in words. "I see no reason for painting anything that can be put

Jimson Weed (1932) by Georgia O'Keeffe.
Oil on canvas. 48 × 40 inches. Copyright
The Georgia O'Keeffe Museum. Reprinted with permission.

into any other form just as well," she once said. She explained that she would rather paint her feeling about something than talk about it. She used to tell frustrated interviewers that she didn't like to think in words. Words were too stiff and unbending.

(14) Once when someone asked Georgia why she painted skulls, she said that she was unable to explain it in words and would have to paint a picture to explain it. "Probably I would do a picture with another skull in it and then where would we be?" she asked with a little smile. Sometimes her sense of humor left her entirely. "The meaning is there on the canvas," she said angrily to an art critic. "If you don't get it, that's too bad. I have nothing more to say than what I painted."

(15) Georgia's natural way of <u>communicating</u> was to place lines, shapes, **symbols,** and colors together so they spoke eloquently and smoothly. Her genius lay in her ability to <u>create</u> an artistic "language" that translated her <u>intense</u> feelings. When Georgia explored the vibrations of the color blue, for <u>instance,</u> she could awaken feelings in viewers with her cobalt blue tones. She could lead their <u>imaginations</u> into "almost unknown relationships with life," as Blanche Martin said in 1926. It was clear that O'Keeffe's skillful use of shapes and **symbols,** which was **constantly** enriched by her fertile <u>imagination</u>, could affect the viewer's senses on a gut or emotional level. This was the reason Georgia disliked it when her **symbols** were explained, because this lessened a painting's emotional **impact.**

Reading 3: Frida Kahlo

Excerpts adapted from *Frida: A Biography of Frida Kahlo* by Hayden Herrera, (Perennial, an imprint of HarperCollins Publishers Inc. 1983), 74–75, and *The Fabulous Life of Diego Rivera* by Bertram D. Wolfe (Cooper Square Press, an imprint of the Rowman and Littlefield Publishing Group 1963/1991), 240–43.

(16) A photo of her [Frida] at the time of her entrance into the school **reveals** an almost boyish beauty, bright eyes, long-lashed under thick black eyebrows meeting above her nose, full lips, black hair cut short, an undefinable nationality due to a mixture of German-Jewish and Mexican bloods. Her favorite companions were newsboys in the great city plazas from whom she <u>acquired</u> a lot of street wisdom. She climbed trees, stole fruit, just missed jail on one occasion for stealing a bicycle to take a "joy ride," **displayed** great <u>creativity</u> in thinking of pranks to bother policemen, professors, and others with <u>authority</u>.

(17) Sometime after finishing her schooling, Frida was in a terrible auto accident. Her spine was <u>injured</u>, the pelvic bone fractured in three places, a foot and leg badly damaged. Surgeons who looked at the X-ray photos of the fractured pelvis found it difficult to believe that they could belong to the living

and lively girl before them. For a whole year after the accident, they did not know whether her bones would mend <u>sufficiently</u> for her ever to walk again. The girl was strapped to a board, encased in a plaster cast. In her boredom she called for paints, brushes, and an easel stand within reach of her arms, which alone were free. She had never painted, nor received any special **instruction,** but she had an <u>imagination</u> and a sense of form and color. Her brushwork, from the beginning, was light and sensitive. As she was strapped to the board, not only were her hands free, but her fantasy also; out of the difficult situation she became a painter.

(18) In her paintings Frida wanted to make painful feelings known. "I paint myself because I am so often alone," Frida said, "because I am the subject I know best." The **confinement** as an invalid made Frida see herself as a private world. Even when she painted fruit or flowers, it was with a **vision** seen through the lens of herself. "I look like many people and many things," Frida said, and in her paintings, many things look like her. "From that time [of the accident]," she explained, "my obsession was to begin again, painting things just as I saw them with my own eyes and nothing more. . . . Thus as the accident changed my path, many things kept me from fulfilling the desires which everyone considers <u>normal</u>, and to me nothing seemed more <u>normal</u> than to paint what had not been fulfilled."

(19) Painting was part of Frida Kahlo's battle for life. It was also very much a part of her self-<u>creation</u>: In her art, as in her life, a <u>dramatic</u> self-

presentation was a means to control her world. As she <u>recovered</u>, relapsed, <u>recovered</u> again, she reinvented herself. She <u>created</u> a person who could be mobile and make trouble in her <u>imagination</u> rather than with her legs. A friend of Frida's, Lola Alvarez Bravo, explains, "The struggle of the two Fridas was in her always, the struggle between one dead Frida and one Frida that was alive." After the accident came a rebirth: "Her love of nature was renewed, the same as for animals, colors, and fruits, anything beautiful and **positive** around her. The public Frida was happy and strong. Wanting to surround herself with people, she <u>emphasized</u> qualities she already possessed—liveliness, generosity, and <u>intelligence</u>. Gradually, she became a famous personality." Aurora Reyes remembers, "She always acted happy; she gave her heart."

Comprehension Check

Did you understand the readings? Mark these sentences true (T) or false (F).

_____ 1. Georgia O'Keeffe was frustrated by her early artistic education because it did not allow her to paint the way she wanted to.

_____ 2. At 27, Georgia taught herself to draw again using only black and white.

_____ 3. Art critics claimed that Georgia's artwork showed strong emotion in a feminine way.

_____ 4. Georgia's work was largely unknown during her lifetime.

_____ 5. Georgia enjoyed explaining her art to people.

_____ 6. Frida Kahlo was born in 1910.

_____ 7. As a girl, Frida was very active and loved to play tricks on people.

_____ 8. The doctors were confident that Frida would walk normally again.

_____ 9. Frida started drawing during the time she was confined to bed.

_____ 10. Frida and Diego had a long, peaceful, and happy marriage.

_____ 11. Painting helped Frida survive and invent a new self after her accident.

Word Study

Target Vocabulary

abstract	impact	reveal
confine (confinement)	instruct (instruction)	symbol
constant (constantly)	positive	vary (variation)
display	reject	vision
distinct (distinctive)	reluctance (reluctant)	visual (visualize)

Word Parts

Exercise 1: Suffixes

When the suffix *–ize* is added to a word, a verb is formed. These verbs describe processes by which things or people are changed into a particular state or condition. For example, if *–ize* is added to the word *priority,* the new word *prioritize* is formed. *Prioritize* means "to list in order of priority or importance."

Look at the way the underlined words are used in the sentences. Then match each word with the correct definition.

1. The bank had to <u>authorize</u> his loan before he could buy a new car.

2. I need to <u>finalize</u> my holiday travel plans as soon as possible.

3. We can all <u>economize</u> on gas if we take the bus or ride the subway.

4. The cow skull in the painting does not <u>symbolize</u> death. It's just a cow skull.

5. The hospital began to <u>mobilize</u> emergency teams immediately after the earthquake.

6. Assembly line production <u>revolutionized</u> the auto industry.

_____ 1. **authorize**   a. to do more cheaply

_____ 2. **finalize**   b. to greatly change the way something is done

_____ 3. **economize**   c. to give official permission

_____ 4. **symbolize**   d. to prepare for action

_____ 5. **mobilize**   e. to complete the arrangements for something

_____ 6. **revolutionize**   f. to represent or stand for something

Exercise 2: Prefixes

The prefixes _in-_ (or _im-_) and _un-_ mean "not." Add the correct prefix meaning _not_ to each word, and write the new word on the line. Write a short definition of the new word. (Use your dictionary if you need to.)

1. <u>aware</u> _____

   definition: _____

2. <u>critical</u> _____

   definition: _____

3. <u>constant</u> _____

   definition: _____

4. <u>fertile</u> _____

   definition: _____

5. <u>reliable</u> _____

   definition: _____

6. <u>sufficient</u> _____

   definition: _____

7. <u>distinct</u> _____

   definition: _____

Word Relationships

Exercise 3: Synonyms

Three of the words in each series have similar meanings. Cross out the word that has a different meaning.

1. fertile	rich	sterile	productive
2. intellect	reason	thought	emotion
3. reveal	tell	uncover	hide
4. superior	better	equal	greater
5. confined	limited	allowed	imprisoned
6. impact	influence	effect	actions
7. reject	accept	dismiss	unacceptable
8. positive	good	certain	negative

The Grammar of Words and Word Families

Use these words to fill in the word family chart. Follow the example given. Some words will be used more than once.

abstract (3x)	confine	constant	display (2x)
abstraction	confined	constantly	
	confinement	constancy	
	confines		

distinct	impact	instruct	positive
distinction		instruction	positively
distinctive		instructive	
distinctively		instructor	
distinctly			

reject (2x)	reluctance	reveal	symbol
rejection	reluctant	revealing	symbolic
	reluctantly	revelation	symbolically
			symbolism
			symbolize

vary	vision	visual	
variability	visionary (2x)	visualize	
variable		visualization	
variation		visually	

Noun	Noun (person)	Verb	Adverb	Adjective
abstract abstraction	—	abstract	—	abstract
confine confinement	—	confine	—	confined
constancy	—	—	constantly	constant
display	—	display	—	—
distinction distinctive	—	—	distinctively distinctly	distinct
impact	—	—	—	—
instruction	instructor	instruct	—	instructive
—	—	—	positively	positive
rejection reject	—	reject	—	—
reluctance	—	—	reluctantly	reluctant
revealation	—	reveal	—	revealing
symbol symbolism	—	symbolize	symbolically	symbolic
variation	—	vary	—	variable variability
vision	visionary	—	—	visionary
visualization	—	visualize	visually	visual

Understanding Words in Context

Exercise 5: Words in Context

Complete each sentence with one of the words. Change the word form by adding –s, -ed, –ing, or –ize if necessary.

impact	reject	reluctant	symbol	vision	visual

1. The color red often _____ passion or anger.

2. He was _____ to call so late at night.

3. The chemistry students wore goggles in the lab to protect their _____.

4. When the car hit the wall, the _____ released the airbags.

5. She _____ the idea that global warming is a natural occurrence.

6. Just close your eyes, and try to _____ what the room will look like when it's furnished.

Exercise 6: Collocations

Write these phrases next to the verbs they collocate with. Then write two more words that are commonly used with each verb.

a policy	**a product**	**a secret**	**a picture**
a plan	**an idea**	**a view**	**the meaning**
an essay	**a building**	**an outline**	**the ending**

1. sketch _____

_____

2. reveal _____

_____

3. criticize _____

_____

4. design _____

_____

Using Words in Communication

Exercise 7: Constructing Sentences

Use each set of words to write a sentence. Use all the words given. No additional words are needed. Add punctuation.

1. acquired / after / paintings / death / abstract / The / her / museum / many / Georgia's/ of

   _____

2. go / The / confined / glad / all / to / day / children / outside / after / were / being / inside

   _____

3. until / vision / Georgia's / nearly / blind / worsening / was / she / began

   _____

4. formal / never / Frida / instruction / any / received / art

   _____

5. thought / her / displayed / feeling / Georgia / that / paintings / feminine / a

   _____

6. personal / her / paintings / Frida / in / revealed / feelings / very

   _____

Exercise 8: Read, Outline, and Describe

A. Read the text that describes the process Georgia O'Keeffe followed when she painted a picture. Then, outline the process that Georgia used to paint an abstract painting.

B. Describe the paintings. Be sure to include all important information.

(1) Georgia's painting methods developed early. Although she was not the type of artist who goes into the studio each day to paint, she did prepare for the moment when she would feel ready to begin. She stretched canvases and prepared them with a white undercoat.

(2) She learned to wait during the weeks or months it took for a design to form in her mind. "I know what I'm going to do before I begin, and if there's nothing in my head, I do nothing," she explained. Her ideas came in various ways. "I have the kind of mind that sees these shapes—many come from realistic or natural bases, but others are just beautiful shapes that I visualize in my mind."

(3) By the time Georgia began to paint a canvas, it was basically a matter of putting down the elements already in her head. Generally, she made a preparatory sketch and then mixed her paints and placed them on her palette.* She painted rapidly, pausing only to eat, and usually she was finished with a small canvas by the time the daylight faded.

*palette: a range of colors typical of an artist's style

(4) Since she had been a girl, Georgia had done paintings in a series. As she worked, she simplified the image so that it lost its resemblance to the original object. "Nothing is less real than realism. Details are confusing. It is only by selection, by elimination and by emphasis, that the real meaning of things is revealed." The last picture in a series was often just her concept of the subject's core. O'Keeffe said, "It can be nothing but abstract, but it is my reason for painting, I suppose."

Exercise 9: Critical Thinking

Review the readings in this unit to answer the questions. Support your answers with information from the readings.

1. Explain in detail what Georgia O'Keeffe's view was of her paintings.

2. What did painting mean to Frida Kahlo? How was it important in her life?

3. Explain what kind of art you like to view. Tell what you see in the art, what it means to you, and why you like it.

Appendix 1
Academic Word List

This list, compiled by Coxhead (2000), contains 570 word familes that are important for students to know to read texts and do well in academic settings. Words explicitly studied in this text as target words are set in **bold** and marked by the number of the unit in which they appear. Words that are not studied explicitly but occur in the text are set in ordinary type and marked by the number of the unit in which they appear. Words studied as target words in *Vocabulary Mastery 1* are shown with an asterisk.

abandon
abstract Unit 6
academy
access
accommodate*
accompany
accumulate*
accurate Units 1, 4
achieve Units 1, 5
acknowledge
acquire* Unit 6
adapt Unit 1
adequate
adjacent
adjust Unit 2
administrate
adult Units 1, **3**
advocate
affect
aggregate
aid Unit 1
albeit
allocate
alter
alternative Units **4**, 5
ambiguous
amend Unit 5

analogy
analyse (analyze) Unit 1
annual
anticipate
apparent
append
appreciate
approach Units **3**, 4, 5
appropriate* Unit 2
approximate
arbitrary
area Unit 3
aspect Unit 2
assemble Unit 1
assess
assign Unit 3
assist Unit 5
assume Unit 4
assure
attach
attain
attitude
attribute
author
authority* Unit 6
automate*
available Units 1, 5

aware Unit 5
behalf
benefit* Unit 5
bias
bond
brief*
bulk
capable* Unit 1
capacity Units **1**, 5
category
cease
challenge* Units 3, 4
channel
chapter
chart
chemical*
circumstance Unit 4
cite
civil Unit 2
clarify
classic
clause
code
coherent
coincide
collapse
colleague

commence
comment Units 2, **3**, 6
commission Unit 2
commit
commodity Unit 1
communicate* Unit 6
community Units 1, 2, 5
compatible
compensate
compile
complement
complex
component Unit 1
compound
comprehensive
comprise
compute
conceive
concentrate Unit 4
concept*
conclude Units 1, 5
concurrent
conduct Unit 3
confer Unit 2
confine Unit 6
confirm
conflict*
conform
consent
consequent
considerable Units 1, 2, 3, 5
consist
constant Unit 6
constitute Unit 2
constrain
construct* Unit 2
consult Unit 4
consume* Unit 1

contact*
contemporary Unit 6
context*
contract*
contradict
contrary
contrast
contribute Unit 3
controversy* Unit 2
convene Unit 5
converse
convert Unit 1
convince Units 4, **5**
cooperate
coordinate*
core
corporate
correspond
couple
create* Units 2, 6
credit Unit 5
criteria
crucial
culture
currency
cycle
data*
debate
decade* Unit 1
decline
deduce
define*
definite Unit 1
demonstrate Unit 2
denote
deny Unit 5
depress* Unit 4
derive

design Unit 2
despite Unit 5
detect
deviate
device
devote Units 4, 5
differentiate Units 3, 4, 6
dimension
diminish
discrete
discriminate Units **2**, 5
displace
display Unit 6
dispose
distinct Unit 6
distort
distribute Unit 1
diverse Unit 5
document*
domain
domestic
dominate*
draft Unit 3
drama Units 5, 6
duration
dynamic
economy* Unit 1
edit Units 1, **4**, 5
element*
eliminate
emerge* Units 4, 6
emphasis Units **4**, 5, 6
empirical
enable
encounter
energy* Units 2, 3, 4, 6
enforce Unit 2
enhance

enormous Unit 1
ensure Unit 5
entity
environment*
equate
equip* Units 1, 5
equivalent
erode
error
establish* Units 1, 2, 3, 4
estate
estimate* Unit 4
ethic
ethnic
evaluate
eventual Units 2, 4, 5
evident* Units 3, 5
evolve*
exceed
exclude*
exhibit Unit 4
expand
expert Unit 3
explicit
exploit
export
expose
external
extract
facilitate Unit 5
factor*
feature Unit 1
federal Units 2, **5**
fee
file
final*
finance* Units 2, 4
finite

flexible
fluctuate
focus Units 3, 5
format
formula
forthcoming
foundation
found Units 2, 3, 4, 6
framework
function* Units 1, 2, 4
fund
fundamental
furthermore
gender
generate* Units 2, 5
generation Unit 2
globe*
goal* Unit 5
grade
grant
guarantee Units 1, **5**
guideline
hence
hierarchy
highlight Unit 2
hypothesis
identical
identify*
ideology Units 5, 6
ignorance
illustrate
image* Units 2, 4, 6
immigrate Unit 5
impact Unit 6
implement*
implicate
implicit
imply

impose
incentive
incidence Unit 2
incline Unit 5
income*
incorporate
index
indicate Unit 3
individual* Unit 5
induce
inevitable
infer
infrastructure
inherent Unit 5
inhibit
initial Units 1, **2**, 3
initiate
injure Units **4**, 5, 6
innovate
input
insert
insight
inspect
instance Unit 6
institute
instruct Units 4, **6**
integral
integrate Units 2, **5**
integrity
intelligence Unit **4**, 6
intense Units **1**, 6
interact
intermediate
internal
interpret
interval
intervene
intrinsic

invest*
investigate Unit 2
invoke
involve
isolate Unit 4
issue* Unit 5
item
job
journal Unit 2
justify Units 2, **5**
label Unit 1
labor* Unit 1
layer
lecture Unit 4
legal* Units 2, 5
legislate
levy
liberal Unit 5
licence (license)
likewise
link Unit 6
locate* Units 1, 2
logic
maintain
major Units 3, 5
manipulate
manual
margin*
mature
maximise (maximize)
mechanism
media
mediate
medical Units 3, 4
medium
mental Unit 4
method
migrate

military* Units 3, 5
minimal Unit 2
minimise (minimize)
minimum
ministry
minor Units 2, **3**, 5
mode
modify
monitor*
motive
mutual
negate
network
neutral
nevertheless
nonetheless
norm
normal* Unit 6
notion
notwithstanding
nuclear*
objective*
obtain*
obvious
occupy*
occur Unit 2
odd
offset
ongoing
option Unit 1
orient
outcome
output
overall Unit 5
overlap
overseas
panel
paradigm

paragraph
parallel
parameter
participate* Units 2, 5
partner
passive*
perceive
percent* Unit 5
period Unit 5
persist
perspective
phase
phenomenon
philosophy
physical* Unit 4
plus
policy Unit 5
portion
pose
positive Unit 6
potential
practitioner
precede
precise Units 1, **4**
predict Units 1, **5**
predominant
preliminary
presume
previous Units 1, 2
primary
prime
principal
principle
prior
priority
proceed
process* Units 3, 5
professional* Units 1, 3, 4

prohibit* Unit 2
project Units **1**, 2
promote Units **1**, 5, 6
proportion
prospect
protocol
psychology Units **2**, 4
publication Unit 4
publish Unit 2
purchase*
pursue* Units 1, 4
qualitative Unit 1
quote Units **2**, 5
radical
random
range
ratio
rational
react Unit 1
recover* Unit 6
refine
regime
region
register* Unit 2
regulate* Unit 1
reinforce
reject Units 5, **6**
relax
release Unit 2
relevant
reluctance Unit 6
rely Units **1**, 4
remove
require Units 1, 2, 5
research Units **1**, 2, 5
reside Unit 4
resolve
resource* Unit 5

respond Unit 4
restore
restrain
restrict* Unit 2
retain
reveal Unit 6
revenue
reverse* Unit 4
revise
revolution Unit 6
rigid
role Unit 5
route
scenario
schedule Unit 3
scheme
scope
section Unit 5
sector Unit 3
secure Units **4**, 5
seek
select Unit 3
sequence
series Unit 3
sex
shift Unit 4
significant* Unit 2
similar Unit 5
simulate*
site Unit 2
so-called
sole Unit 5
somewhat
source*
specific Unit 2
specify
sphere
stable

statistic Unit 3
status Unit 5
straightforward
strategy Unit 4
stress Unit 4
structure
style Unit 6
submit
subordinate
subsequent
subsidy
substitute
successor Unit 1
sufficient* Unit 6
sum
summary
supplement Unit 3
survey
survive* Units 1, 3, 5
suspend
sustain*
symbol Units 4, **6**
tape
target Unit 1
task* Unit 5
team Unit 3
technique
technology*
temporary
tense
terminate
text Unit 2
theme
theory Unit 5
thereby
thesis
topic
trace

tradition Unit 4
transfer
transform Unit 4
transit
transmit Unit 1
transport
trend
trigger
ultimate Unit 5
undergo
underlie

undertake Unit 2
uniform
unify
unique* Units 3, 4
utilize
valid
vary Unit 6
vehicle
version
via
violate Unit 5

virtual
visible
vision Units 4, **6**
visual Unit 6
volume*
voluntary Unit 2
welfare*
whereas
whereby
widespread

Appendix 2
Expansion Activities

Unit 1: Business (pages xiv–25)

The Mustang/Car Manufacturing

1. The Mustang has had an interesting history in American culture. Ask students to research the various Mustang models over the years. Which parts of the design are the same? Does Ford market this car to the same audience that it did in 1964?

2. Ask students to research other car models from the 1960s. Ask them what they notice about models being released today?

Paul Newman

1. Paul Newman was initially best-known as a film actor; he won an Oscar for his role in *The Color of Money*. Later in life, he started Newman's Own® and wanted all the money from the company to go to charity. Ask students to research the various brands of Newman's Own®—or try them out in class (like the popcorn!)—and the different charities the money from Newman's Own® supports.

Jiffy Mixes

1. The original idea behind Jiffy Mixes was that they were simple and fast. Try making one of the famous biscuit or muffin mixes.

2. The word *jiffy* has an interesting etymology. Ask students to research it using *www.dictionary.com* or other similar sources. How many different phrases can students come up with using the word *jiffy*?

Unit 2: The Civil Rights Movement (pages 26–51)

Civil Rights Timeline

1. The timeline on pages 31–35 lists some of the most famous events from 1954–1968, but not all of them. What others can students find? Other significant events happened after 1968. Ask students to list and research them.

2. PBS has several wonderful documentaries on different aspects of the civil rights movement. Watch one as a class, or assign different ones to students. A few examples are: *American Experience: Citizen King; This Far by Faith: 1946–1966; American Experience: Eyes on the Prize.*

3. On November 4, 2008, Barack Obama, an African American, made history by being elected President of the United States. Many historians believe that race is still the Achilles' heel of U.S. history. Ask students to find and read Barack Obama's speech on race (the text is available on various sites, as is the video). Now that Obama has been elected President, does it mean that race is no longer an issue in the United States? Ask students to explain.

Maya Lin

1. PBS also has several documentaries about the building of the Civil Rights and Vietnam Veterans Memorials and Maya Lin: *Maya Lin's Vietnam Veterans Memorial; Maya Lin: A Clear Strong Vision.*

2. Ask students to research the making of the Vietnam Veterans Memorial and the impact of the memorial for Vietnam veterans and their families.

3. Ask students to research other memorial designers and other work by Maya Lin.

4. A memorial for Martin Luther King, Jr., has been commissioned. Ask students to research the controversy surrounding the memorial and the selection of its artist; see *www.mlkmemorial.org.*

Unit 3: Baseball (pages 52–75)

Roberto Clemente

1. Depending on the time of year that you teach this unit and the city you teach in, talk about the major league baseball teams your students know and that people in your community follow. Follow the team's progress during the course of the term using newspapers or the Internet. Plan an outing to a game. If you have access to a minor league team, those games can be more fun (and certainly less expensive) than attending major league games.

2. Today, in contrast to when Roberto Clemente was playing, players from Central and South America (and Cuba and Dominican Republic) dominate the rosters of major league baseball. Ask students to research when this happened and to explain why they think it happened.

The All-American Girls Professional Baseball League

1. Watch the film *A League of Their Own*, which documents well the life of the women baseball players and life in America during World War II. Should women be allowed to play in today's major leagues?

Unit 4: The Women's Movement (pages 76–105)

Billie Jean King

1. The made-for-TV film *When Billie Played Bobby* (available on DVD) accurately portrays the build-up to the match and the match itself. It also attempts to show the influence of this event on young American girls and on American society.

2. Billie Jean King was responsible for many changes in the way women athletes were treated in the United States. Ask students to investigate the "rights" she advocated on behalf of.

Gloria Steinem

1. Gloria Steinem is best known as one of the women who started the feminist magazine called *Ms.* in 1972. Ask students to research the magazine's interesting history regarding subscriptions and advertising.

2. Gloria Steinem is also associated with NOW, the National Organization of Women. Ask students to research the history of this organization.

3. The photo on page 88 features several famous feminists. Ask students to research the suffragettes and other women in American history who fought for women's right to vote and for equality.

Feminism

1. PBS has a documentary, made by Ken Burns, called *Elizabeth Cady Stanton and Susan B. Anthony* that depicts the lives of these two important women.

2. In 2008, Hillary Clinton, a senator from New York and former First Lady, narrowly lost her bid to become the Democratic nominee for President. Her campaign was historic in many regards. However, it was the Republican party that put a woman on the ticket (Sarah Palin, Governor of Alaska). Ask students to research how a candidate's gender may help or hurt a woman seeking a position previously only held by men. Some people believe that people will more readily accept a man, no matter his race, for a powerful and high-ranking position than a woman. Ask students if they think that the 2008 Presidential election proved this point.

Unit 5: Serving One's Country (pages 106–33)

Colin Powell

1. Colin Powell was the first African-American Secretary of State of the United States. Ask students to research the role of the Secretary of State as part of the Cabinet and the kinds of things Powell did when he had that position.

Thurgood Marshall

1. Thurgood Marshall was nominated for the U.S. Supreme Court in 1967. As a lawyer, he represented and won more cases before the Supreme Court than any American. During his time as a lawyer and justice, he consistently supported causes like the rights of immigrants, limited government intrusion in cases involving illegal search and seizure, double jeopardy, and right-to-privacy cases. Ask students to research one of the other cases Marshall defended as an attorney or where he wrote the majority opinion.

2. PBS has several documentaries that feature Marshall, either in regard to the *Brown vs. Board of Education* case or his time on the Supreme Court.

Sandra Day O'Connor

1. PBS has an excellent 4-DVD set called *The Supreme Court* that reveals not only the history but in-depth profiles of many of the justices, including Marshall and O'Connor.

2. Sandra Day O'Connor was the swing vote on many important court cases in the 1990s and until her retirement in 2006. Ask students to investigate one of the cases where she wrote the majority opinion or where she was the swing vote.

Unit 6: Women in Art (pages 134–56)

Georgia O'Keeffe

1. This textbook includes a reproduction of *Jimson Weed*, but O'Keeffe had many famous pieces of artwork. Ask students to find other O'Keeffe works and research her thought process as she created them.

Frida Kahlo

1. The film *Frida* depicts the life of Frida Kahlo (as played by Salma Hayek), including her injury as a child and her marriage to Diego Rivera (played by Alfred Molina).